Agents of Power

ANNENBERG/LONGMAN COMMUNICATION BOOKS
George Gerbner and Marsha Siefert, Editors
The Annenberg School of Communications
University of Pennsylvania, Philadelphia

J. Herbert Altschull
Indiana University

AGENTS OF POWER

The Role of the News Media in Human Affairs

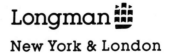

Longman
New York & London

*This book is lovingly
dedicated to D and to J,
for their faith in me as
journalist, scholar, and man*

Agents of Power
The Role of the News Media in Human Affairs

Longman Inc., 1560 Broadway, New York, N.Y. 10036
Associated companies, branches, and representatives
throughout the world.

Developmental Editor: Gordon T.R. Anderson
Editorial and Design Supervisor: Harriet Sigerman
Production Supervisor: Ferne Y. Kawahara
Manufacturing Supervisor: Marion Hess

Library of Congress Cataloging in Publication Data
Altschull, J. Herbert.
  Agents of Power
  (Annenberg/Longman communication books)
  Bibliography: p.
  Includes index.
  1. Journalism — Social aspects. 2. Press — United
States. I. Title. II. Series.
PN4731.A388   1984   302.2'34   83-14906
ISBN 0-582-28417-1
ISBN 0-582-28418-X (pbk.)

Manufactured in the United States of America
Printing: 9 8 7 6 5 4 3 2   Year: 92 91 90 89 88 87 86 85 84

Contents

Preface

This book has been an ongoing project for more than thirty years. Not that I have been working on it directly all that time. But I have been building up experiences and memories. And I have drawn heavily on those experiences and memories, as well as on documentary research, direct observation, and interviews I have conducted in various parts of the world.

I entered the world of journalism while still in high school and became a practicing reporter at the age of eighteen. Before I withdrew from the world of active journalism to become a teacher and researcher—not without some soul-searching at first, however—I had pursued "news" in many places, including Washington and Western Europe, and had worked for a variety of "news media," including newspapers, news agencies, radio, television, and magazines. Although I later added to my store of information and analytical capacity in my graduate studies in political science and history, still it was those years as a "professional" journalist that taught me the most about the reality of the news media. One personal experience was perhaps most instructive of all.

The time was 1957 and I was working as chief correspondent for The Associated Press in the West German capital of Bonn. The Christian Democratic Union of Konrad Adenauer had just been returned to power in an election in which for the first (and still only) time in German history a single political party won an absolute majority of the seats in Parliament, the Bundestag. I had duly reported the election results to morning papers on the night of September 15, and on the next morning stopped by the table of several leaders of the CDU as they were drinking coffee in the Bundestag restaurant. I still had to prepare a follow-up story for the next day's afternoon papers and was looking for quotes.

I found these deputies in a surprisingly sober and thoughtful mood. They were not as pleased with the results as I had expected. Of course they were delighted that their party had won the election, but they were worried about the extent of the victory. Not that they were fearful of Adenauer's leadership; it was the principle that concerned them. Not many years earlier, the German people had willingly followed a demagogue, Adolf Hitler, wherever he led them. It now seemed to those pensive CDU deputies that the German people had not yet learned their lesson; perhaps they were still too eager to follow a leader unthinkingly.

Delighted with this turn of events, I returned to my office and composed a story for the afternoon papers. The CDU, I reported in my lead, had won an election victory so sweeping that it had them worried. No one else, I knew, would have that story.

A half hour later, a message arrived over the direct teletype wire that linked the Bonn bureau with the central AP control point in New York, asking me, in effect: "Who are the sources for the story?" The message implied that the people on the "desk" in New York were feeling a lack of confidence in me, as if I had made up those sources. In any case, there was concern about the accuracy of the information. In New York, the leadership of the AP was made up of men who had once worked in Germany, chief among them the general manager of the AP, Wes Gallagher, who will figure in another way in these pages.

I dutifully replied, providing the names of my sources, one of whom was Ludwig Erhard, then the minister of economics and later Adenauer's successor as chancellor, as good a source as anyone in the country. Still, the next message from New York asked me to revise the lead, dropping the reference to the CDU deputies' concerns to the third paragraph and putting the "news" at the top of the story. This I did reluctantly.

But the back-and-forth communicating did not end there. The next message, a lengthy one, commented that what the American public was most interested in was how the election fit into the Cold War struggle between the United States and the Soviet Union. My story ought, I was told, to emphasize that the Adenauer victory was a "defeat" for the Communists, who had actively campaigned against the CDU in favor of the SPD, the Social Democratic opposition.

No, I told the "desk" in a return message, that was an incorrect assessment. The Soviet Union actually wanted Adenauer to win; the Russians were more comfortable dealing with bona fide conservatives, whom they could attack as imperialist warmongers. To deal with an SPD leadership, especially at that time, was embarrassing for the Soviet Union, because both the Communist Party in the Soviet Union and the SPD in West Germany traced their lineage back to Marx, and differences between them had to be painstakingly (and usually inadequately) justified. The campaign against Adenauer, I told New York, was designed not to defeat Adenauer but to gain votes for him from anticommunist Germans.

The dialogue then came to an end. Power resided at the other end of the wire, and I was instructed to follow orders and write a story declaring the Adenauer victory a defeat for the Communists. I had two choices: to follow orders or turn in my resignation. My wife and children would likely not favor any romantic heroism, so I swallowed my pride, and convictions, and wrote what I was asked to write. Left to me only was the consolation of requesting that the story be dispatched without a byline. "Keep my name off it," I declared with a touch of bravado.

The story illustrates the nature of news in international settings. It is inevitably reported as *Us* versus *Them*, as the Good Guys versus the Bad Guys. The essence of "news" is conflict, and it is difficult for the individual journalist to paint in the shadings of gray or even to point out where Us and Them agree and share the same goals and values. The notion that news has a kind of independent character or that stories tell themselves is simply wrong, just as it is incorrect to think that reporters and editors somehow stand apart from the political, economic, social, and cultural system that has shaped them. Conflict between Us and Them is driven into the belief system of journalists as thoroughly as it is into that of their fellow citizens. It is part of their ideology. To imagine that journalists are a breed apart, somehow able to be "objective" about the world around them in ways that others cannot is to believe in a logical absurdity.

Some journalists—more than one might expect—manage, through the exercise of logical and analytical skills, to free themselves of their ideological straitjackets and go beyond the conflictual norms that dominate their culture. Behind the writing of this book is a desire to honor those journalists. Despite my essentially critical stance toward the news media in the pages to come, it is not my intention to condemn journalism or the institution of the press. That institution has been part of my entire adult life. As practitioner, academic, and critic, I have carried on a lifelong love affair with the press, and the criticism contained here should be viewed in that light.

While the conflictual image is easiest to recognize in an international setting, it exists everywhere in news "stories." Indeed, the very designation story describes a narrative with conflicting forces. Thus, what follows deals with news in all its settings. News is a troublesome term; so indeed is news media. In this book, the term news media is used interchangeably with press. In discussing television and radio journalism, I focus almost exclusively on the news functions of broadcasting rather than on entertainment programming. Therefore, in this context, broadcast news is similar to newspaper news.

The book is divided into four sections. Part I provides the historical background that is essential to understand what follows. The scholar of journalism history will notice, of course, that the interpretations of historical developments are sometimes at variance with traditional points of view. These shifts in interpretation support my view that traditional journalism history is faulty in its adherence to the folklore of progressive, Great Man views that cannot provide adequate explanations of the direction of the history of journalism. In addition, the historical account in Part I underscores the relationship between U.S. press history and the origins and growth of journalism in Western Europe, from where the U.S. system sprang. Part II examines in detail the three press models on which the classification system in Part IV is based. Part III explores three fundamental areas that play a significant role in this classification scheme. Issues involved in discussions of social responsibility, which often obscure understanding, are examined in Chapter 8. Chapter 9 presents a detailed history and analysis of the controversies surrounding the proposed new world information order at UNESCO and elsewhere. Chapter 10 seeks to clarify the relationships between the news media and their financiers in all parts of the world.

In the bibliography that appears at the end of this book, I have acknowledged my debt to a number of Indiana University graduate students, whose research and analysis have invariably helped to teach me, even as I have sought to teach them. I would like to single out for special mention Olatunji Dare, Tim Gallimore, Hemant Shah, and Gonzalo Soruco, all of whom assisted with specific research for the book. Several colleagues and students at Indiana University provided helpful commentary on portions of the book, including Owen Johnson, David Nord, Christine Ogan, Judy Ruch, Carol Stevens, and Craig Tenney. I would also like to express my thanks to Mary Miller and Judy East for their excellent work in providing sketches, charts, and designs. I am grateful for the typing skills and the patient editorial assistance of Kathleen Ristow Harriman and Inez Woodley. I owe thanks also to Diana Johnstone for steering me in the right direction many years ago. And to my colleague George Juergens I owe a special measure of gratitude, not only for his thoughtful comments on the manuscript but also for his friendly guidance.

J. Herbert Altschull

PART 1

The Rialto Bridge, Venice.

One

The Origins of the Press: Early Agency Relationships

THE FIRST JOURNALISTS

It is only human to view the past through the eyes of the present. After all, they are the only eyes we have. The most dedicated of historians have similar problems, and the history of history is shot through with illustrations of the fallacy of anachronism. Certainly, our view of the origins of the press is subject to this fallacy. We are likely to conceive of the earliest press as a device designed to provide "news" to the "public." But to do so is to apply modern meanings for these verbal symbols to a historical setting in which the words, if they existed at all, referred to something quite different.

If, as the Scottish historian-philosopher David Hume suggested, "our ideas are copy'd from our impressions," then our ideas about the press are derived from what we see, hear, and experience. Perhaps the most important word in that sentence is "we," for the modern press, which began in Belgium in 1605, has developed in different ways in different parts of the world. If the reference is to an American, his impressions are likely to be based on his experiences with his hometown newspaper and his television stations and the weekly newsmagazines. But if the "we" is a Czech, his impressions will be based on what he has read in *Rude Pravo* or seen on his own television stations — and, of course, in both situations on what he has been taught in school and has discussed across the breakfast

3

table or at the corner tavern. The pattern can be repeated to cover everyone on earth. One might be tempted to except the intelligentsia from this formulation, but Hume would not. In fact, he went so far as to maintain, "To explain the ultimate causes of our mental actions is impossible." Hume's observation may, of course, be challenged (although we find it perfectly acceptable), but it is difficult to dispute the physiological reality that we see only through our own eyes and think only with our own brains — and that we train those eyes and brains in our own special environment.

Let us examine how a press developed. What needs did it come to satisfy? What, in fact, is meant by "news"? Certainly, there could be no reading "public" before the arrival of widespread literacy, be it for "news" or any other form of written matter. How indeed did a press originate?

Movable type did not appear in the Western world until the middle of the fifteenth century. Before that time, the ability to read and write was confined to the great merchants and to the first two estates, the nobility and the clergy; primarily indeed to the clergy, for a merchant class was slow in developing, and the nobility was devoted to warfare and statecraft rather than to the gentler arts. It was the invention of the printing press more than any other event that shattered the medieval world and gave rise to modernism; the growth of a reading public led inevitably to the spread of ideas, ideas that contributed to the philosophical and technological innovations that ultimately destroyed the power of the clergy and the nobility and led, also to new forms of political, economic, social, cultural, and religious systems. The press was never separate from these developments, always a part of them. To forget this simple truth is to fail to understand the history of the press.

When did journalism originate? Certainly, journalism did not spring full-blown from Gutenberg's machine in the fifteenth century. In fact, intelligence about what was taking place at the seats of power dates back to the earliest days of recorded history. Shakespeare's accounts of ancient Rome in the days of Coriolanus and Caesar are filled with tales of messengers delivering written intelligence. Indeed, the "correspondent" was an important figure in Rome. It is not insignificant that the earliest news media in the Western world were devoted to supplying information about the economy of the Roman Empire.

Marshall McLuhan said of the process of communication that the media are the message. More importantly, the media may be said to be the economy. Try to imagine the American economy without the media. For while political information may or may not be of utility to the "public," commercial information — intelligence about goods — is indispensable to that public, since it is within the media in their various forms that the individual learns what goods are for sale in the commercial marketplace (and indeed in the marketplace of ideas).

It was as a factor in the distribution of goods that the news media emerged as instruments of communication. Their role has always been different from that of transportation, the other major instrument of communications in the world of commerce. The press has resembled the letter, rather than the coach or the railroad. In Roman days, news traveled by foot, in the form of letters. The Roman elite who resided in the provinces dispatched one or more personal correspondents to the capital for the purpose of preparing and sending back written reports of the events of the day, especially about the commercial and political transactions that affected life in the provinces. More often than not, these correspondents were intelligent slaves, who rather early on learned that they could pick up extra money on the side by sending their letters to additional provincial residents. The money earned through these journalistic exploits was sometimes used to buy their freedom.

The Romans in the provinces needed information to carry out their commercial as well as their political activities. The journalists who supplied that information, often culling it from the *diurna* — or news sheets — posted on the walls of the forum, were personal slaves; later, many came to look on themselves as wage slaves, that is to say, captives of the market. Indeed, today's journalists work for what might be called "news factories," financed not by owners or even by employers but rather by commercial interests the journalists never meet and whose existence they often do not recognize. We will return to this topic later.

Harold Lasswell identified "surveillance of the environment" as one of three communication activities that must be conducted by any society (the others involve information gathering and transmitting). Information is not a matter of societal responsibility or desire but a matter of *need*, Lasswell pointed out, as if a society were a biological organism that needs must survey the environment in order to guarantee its survival as a species. Now, substitute for the abstraction society a concrete portrait of the individuals in that society in a position of power over their environment, and it can be seen that those individuals cannot continue to assert their power unless they are able to keep an eye and ear on the world they inhabit. The significance of Lasswell's insight is difficult to overstate; it places the abstraction "press responsibility" in its proper position, that is to say, subordinate to the need for survival. In other words, "press responsibility" represents a layer of intellectual cosmetics used to coat over the raw power needs of those in a position to control their environment. The environmental surveillance, in Lasswell's taxonomy, is to be made in order to disclose "threats and opportunities affecting the value position of the community and the component parts within it." As has often been said, information is power — or, better perhaps, control over information is necessary for the gaining and maintenance of power. It is obviously necessary for the powerful to know about the threats and opportunities that affect their value position; it is equally necessary that the channels of information be used to ward off the threats and to safeguard the opportunities affecting those in positions of power — *in other words, as agencies of social control.*

Thus, the provincial entrepreneurs of the Roman Empire saw the utility of dispatching correspondents to Rome — to do their surveying for them, to be their eyes and ears and indeed their pens — for their life savings and their power bases were directly involved. Surveillance of this nature has continued in one form or another ever since. The societal structure that existed following the fall of the Roman Empire was far less complex than that of the empire, and the journalistic system of the following millennium was a more haphazard one than that of the empire. Even the arrival of the printing press did not give the journalistic system modern form; indeed, it was not until the rise of a mass market in the nineteenth century that a modern press — or mass media, to give it another name — came into being. All through that period, however, it retained its importance as an agency of social control, in the hands of the powerful, surveying the environment for threats and opportunities.

It was the arrival of the printing press, however, that made possible for the first time a reading "public." It was no longer necessary for written material to be copied laboriously by hand, and no longer could the clergy — who had been occupied in this copying process for a thousand years — claim a monopoly on written information. As a direct result of the loss of the monopoly, the Church was now destined to lose much of its power. With the printing press, information became available to a greater number of people, but it should not be imagined that information had not been flowing in limited circles during the fifteen centuries that intervened between the fall of Julius Caesar in Rome and the triumph of Gutenberg in Mainz. Information was already established as an instrument for the maintenance of power and for social control. Three early agency relationships can be identified. In that millennium and a half the press served as an instrument — or agent — of three different classes of the powerful. The flow of information in each of the three cases served as an early warning about potential threats and as a kind of tip sheet about potential opportunities.

The pre-printing press served *first* as an agency of communications among princes and statesmen and, as towns and medieval guilds developed, among the political leaderships of the towns. Information had flowed between rulers even before the rise of Rome, but the agents of communications then were messengers and heralds who reported directly to the rulers and then broadcast carefully selected "news" in public announcements from the towers of buildings. The masses received no other "news."

The *second* group among which information circulated was the clergy in their roles as spiritual leaders and also as educators. In more than a few instances, the monks and bishops briefed illiterate statesmen on the contents of the received intelligence and thus were able to make use of their monopoly in reading skills to influence political decisions, as well as to color the information disseminated in their schools. For centuries the clergy also maintained control over the education in universities; indeed, all the great European universities were organized by the Roman Church until the Reformation. As education spread, of course, direct control became more difficult.

With the growth of towns and commerce, opportunities arose for the acquisition of great wealth. There developed then a *third* group for which information was a device both for social control and the acquisition of power: the merchants and financiers. By the sixteenth century, the House of Fugger had its own news agency in full operation, a kind of Renaissance Associated Press. Throughout the previous two centuries, the news-gathering systems of the great financial houses had been expanding. It is not surprising then that the earliest news center was Venice, the capital of the world of commerce. It was essential for the merchants of Venice to know the location of their vessels and the value of the jewels and spices they carried. The word *gazeta*, which was used in Italy as the name for the early, irregularly published information sheets, derived, not surprisingly, from the name of a small Venetian coin. The association of press with the world of commerce was as natural as the flow of rain from heaven.

These "information sheets," a direct translation of the Italian *fogli d'avvisi*, by which they were known, were being compiled even before the invention of printing. The Council of Venice ordered the collection of information and the dispatch of "news" to ambassadors, consuls, ship captains, and merchants, from whom information was also sought. As time passed, duplicates of these dispatches were made available inside Venice to merchants, who then made use of the information in their own business dealings. Occasionally, the merchants relayed the *fogli d'avvisi* to friends and business acquaintances abroad in the form of newsletters. The spread of the newsletter phenomenon in the sixteenth, seventeenth, and eighteenth centuries was remarkable, in the American colonies as well as across Europe. With the spread of newsletters came wider dissemination of information to the masses and the incorporation of political information.

Like their fellows in ancient Rome, enterprising Venetians discovered the potential profit to be made in the exchange of news, in the gathering and dissemination of information. By the middle of the sixteenth century, a veritable guild of *scrittori d'avvisi* — or "news writers" — had developed in Venice, selling their information sheets on the Rialto bridge across the Grand Canal to anyone possessing ducats enough to be able to purchase news about the arrival and departure of ships, the dangers of the pirates and highwaymen, trade news, and, most threatening of all to established authority, news of political events. In Rome, scribes became known as *novellanti* — "feature writers" — and *gazettani* — "newsmen" or "journalists." Two popes went so far as to ban the writing of *avvisi* on pain of branding or sentence to the galleys. But, as with later journalists, the threats were ineffective. The business of news gathering and dissemination continued to expand, moving across the continent of Europe and across the seas. It was only among the elite that the newsletters circulated; it would not be until the nineteenth century that modern journalism with its mass circulations would make its appearance.

Still, the confluence of the Protestant Reformation and the growth of the business of printing doomed the medieval social order and tumbled the great principalities, as well as the immense power of the Roman Church. One can offer the plausible argument that it was only the ready availability of the printing press that made possible easy and speedy transmission by the Protestant leadership of information about the excesses of the Roman Church to the rising "public," or at least to the intelligentsia among that public, who then were able to make use of their own persuasive powers to move the masses to support for their causes. Indeed, although the percentage of those among the public who could read or write remained small, their influence in spreading information was great; there developed an even greater desire among the masses as well as the intelligentsia for direct information, rather than information filtered through the Church. *But information about what?*

THE SELF-RIGHTING PRINCIPLE

It is a commonplace in the contemporary world to hold that there is a great need for information among the public, indeed, that there is a "thirst for news." And who can dispute the fact that men and women are interested in hearing about what is going on, that in all parts of the world people read their newspapers, listen to their radios, and tune in their television sets? Yet this fact does not constitute evidence that the world public has ever had an active interest in accurate information about public affairs. The argument that it is the appropriate role of the press to provide accurate information about public affairs because such is the desire of the public cannot be sustained by mere evidence of a need for and/or interest in information. The key question remains: Information about what? It is relevant to inquire whether the information needed or desired relates to complex public issues, to life-threatening situations, to humorous occurrences, or to mere gossip.

Human beings have always needed and desired information about life-threatening situations. Long before Gutenberg's press, communications in the American West, the African savannas, the forests of Central Europe, and the deserts of the Middle East passed along through primitive channels that provided information about the impending arrival of hostile armies or stampeding animals or thunderstorms. Such information constituted news of genuine significance to all who received it; indeed, in the traditional world such "news" often was crucial for survival. In a social setting where daily survival is a challenge, interest in the external world is necessarily limited. It was only after commercial transactions had moved out of the neighborhood that an audience was created for news about external events. Unsurprisingly, the earliest intelligence from distant places was commercial. The "thirst for news" was experienced first by the nobility, the clergy, and the tradesmen. The function of the media of communications before the rise of printing was to provide information of utility to the politically and economically powerful.

The final centuries of the Middle Ages were marked by the slow, painful growth of a middle class, a middle class that began to challenge the dukes and the royal houses for what it perceived to be its fair share of power. Frustrated after a serious challenge in Flanders in the fourteenth century, tradesmen, artisans, and political rebels turned to the printed page to fuel the revolutionary fires that flamed after the Reformation. The flames boiled up into a conflagration with the startling advances in technology and the companion rise in the rate of literacy. As more people were able to read, they began to clamor for more information. The first "newspapers" followed. In the early years of the seventeenth century, periodicals appeared almost simultaneously from one end of Europe to the other. It would be an error, however, to assume that these periodicals were available to the masses or that there was a ground swell of interest in public issues. The growth of the press kept pace with the explosion of ideas that accompanied the collapse of the old medieval order, but it would not be for centuries that those ideas would interest the masses, if indeed such has ever been the case.

During the seventeenth and eighteenth centuries, as a popular press emerged throughout Europe and the New World, the periodicals appeared to be serving four functions, in many situations overlapping one another. In all cases, the periodicals were agencies of social control, powerful forces surveying their environment for threats and opportunities. The clergy, long accustomed to written communications, found in the new popular journals, now appearing in weekly editions, an avenue for the spread of religious doctrine. Shipping and other commercial operators saw the utility of the press as a means of providing speedy information about the market. The entrenched political forces, as well as the rising challengers of political orthodoxy, also turned to the printed page as an instrument to disseminate their forms of political persuasion. And gradually the press came to be recognized as a potential tool to educate the people. It can be said that the clergy, the commercial interests, and the political forces all sought to use the press for purposes of education, which to them meant to propagandize target audiences. For the first time it became significant to the powerful to use information to win over the masses.

For purposes of analysis, we can classify the early printed press in Europe and the American colonies as agencies for the publication of information about: (1) religious doctrine, (2) commercial matters, (3) political persuasion, and (4) popular education. In all four cases the press was seen as carrying out the role of an agent or of an instrument, designed to accomplish specific objectives.

In no way were the periodicals of the seventeenth and eighteenth centuries newspapers in the modern sense. The earliest publications that can properly be identified as newspapers appeared only in the second third of the nineteenth century, originating, appropriately enough, in the city of New York. The origin of the word "newspaper" is lost in the mists of time; the word evidently had its origin in the *diurna*, which, of course, is the etymological ancestor of "journal," and the word "journalist" seems to have made its first appearance in seventeenth-century England as a synonym for "writer" or "mercurist." The reference to the messenger of the gods of Greece indicates the function of the journalist as the agent of his employers, commissioned to transmit messages.

Historians have frequently dated the world's first "newspaper" in the year 1605 in Antwerp; the first to appear in England is usually identified as *The Weekly News*, printed in 1622 by one Nathaniel Butter. His "news" publication, as well as similar sheets in Germany, Sweden, Italy, and elsewhere, differed from the other pamphlets and broadsheets appearing at that time in that they were issued from printing presses with the appearance of regularity. They did not print "news" as we know it. News, of course, is related to the idea of something new; it is a brother of the French *nouvelles* and the German *das Neue*. One early interpretation that somehow seems to persist despite its spuriousness is that the word news derives from the four points of the compass. It is to be noted, however, that the early spelling was "newes," as set forth in a bit of doggerel in 1640:

> When doth come, if any would discuss
> The letter of the word, resolve it thus:
> Newes is conveyed by letter, word or mouth,
> And comes to us from north, east, west, or south.

The early English publications, following a pattern established in Venice, tended to call themselves "news letters," as the printers simply made use of the new technology of printing to pass information from one place to another. News pamphlets were employed by many seventeenth-century writers, the most notable in terms of influence on the ideology or folklore of the press being John Milton, whose 1644 pamphlet, *Areopagitica*, argued in ringing phrases for free expression in print. In fact, Milton's assertion of the "self-righting principle" has stood for more than three centuries as moral justification for a free press system as that system is understood in the capitalist West. We will see that in Marxist society, Milton's maxim is assigned a different interpretation and that, for different reasons, it is also classified differently in the newer countries.

The self-righting principle is set forth in unmistakable language in this oft-quoted passage from the *Areopagitica*:

> And though all the winds of doctrine were let loose to play upon the earth, so truth be in the field, we do injuriously by licensing and prohibiting to misdoubt her strength. Let her and falsehood grapple: who ever knew truth put to the worse in a free and open encounter....
>
> For who knows not that truth is strong, next to the Almighty? She needs no policies, nor stratagems, nor licensings to make her victorious; those are the shifts and the defences that error uses against her power. Give her but room and do not bind her when she sleeps....

It is from this passage that the concept of a "free marketplace of ideas" originates, although it was not until 1919 that this particular combination of words appeared, under the pen of Justice Oliver Wendell Holmes of the United States Supreme Court. But the idea that "truth" would triumph over "falsehood" in a free and open encounter is an idea that thrilled the great experimenters who followed Milton in the eighteenth century and who drafted the American Bill of Rights and Constitution, both of which gave the self-righting principle the legitimacy that comes from being codified into what, for Americans at least, is honored as sacred writ. Not only Marxists and philosophers of the developing world have spoken out against the self-righting principle. So indeed have certain iconoclastic Western thinkers, including John Stuart Mill, who cautioned: "The dictum that truth always triumphs over persecution is one of those pleasant falsehoods which men repeat after one another till they pass into commonplace, but which all experience refutes."

Although the self-righting principle originated in English thought and although it has played an important part in British philosophy, it was in the United States that the principle achieved the stature and veneration usually reserved only for revealed Truth. Jefferson and Madison preached it in the days of the American Revolution; Justices Holmes and Brandeis added to its glory from their seats on the Supreme Court; and the contemporary fraternity of practicing journalists and journalism teachers has placed after it the exclamation point, that embellished dot of finality. Yet in other parts of the world, where the American Constitution is not accepted as dogma, that principle is viewed not as the pinnacle of morality in a lofty marketplace of ideas, but rather as part of a semantic con game whose objective is the acquisition of dollars in the grubby marketplace of the exchange of goods.

It is appropriate to note the significance of two English writers whose names are all but unknown today but whose writings, according to Clinton Rossiter, were "the most popular, quotable, esteemed sources of political ideas of the colonial period" in the United States. The reference is to John Trenchard and Thomas Gordon, who, over a ten-year period dating from 1720, penned a series of essays published in London newspapers under the byline of Cato, a Roman statesman-writer of the first century before Christ celebrated for impeccable honesty and renowned as a stubborn foe of the imperial Caesar. Circulated in the American colonies under the title *Cato's Letters*, the essays of Trenchard and Gordon extolled what would later come to be known as "the free flow of information." Freedom of government and freedom of the press, they averred, prosper together or die together. Free speech, they wrote, is "the right of every man, as far as by it he does not hurt and control the right of another." The Americans who enshrined free speech and a free press in the First Amendment to the Constitution were guided by the ideas and the rhetoric of Milton and Cato.

There can be little doubt that the age of the Enlightenment inspired stirring speech and equally stirring letters in passionate praise of free expression and of unlimited circulation of information. Yet the questions remain: What kind of information? For what purpose? One searches in vain for an advocate of free speech who would use that speech to undermine the fundamentals of the society's belief system. The same Milton who expressed contempt for censorship of his ideas was to become himself a censor who would suppress ideas that to him were unacceptable. Cato proposed limits to free speech when that speech would damage the rights of another; on the subject of what those "rights" consisted of, he was silent. Might not a hostile judge hold rights to be violated when the exercise of those rights interfered with the judge's well-being? The same Jefferson who at one point elevated the press to a position more honored than that of government would come to urge prosecution of newspapers that published licentious matter.

It is clear that while free expression was glorified, little agreement — indeed, little discussion — occurred over what kind of information ought to be authorized. Nor was "free expression" closely defined. The American revolutionaries clearly sought license to say and write what they wished about the wickedness of their British masters; they were less enthusiastic about permitting similar grants to Tory sympathizers. Rebellion against Britain was indeed condoned, but nowhere was there agitation for free expression against the prevailing economic system or accepted ethical values. Indeed, Charles Beard was later to declare the Constitution to be a conservative defense of the property holdings of the Founding Fathers. Beard's analysis no doubt went too far, but one cannot deny his argument that the Founders managed to secure their own economic well-being and did nothing to encourage free expression of revolutionary *economic* doctrine. We will turn to the Founding Fathers in the next chapter and discuss the birth of the most persistent legend in the history of the press.

Those who express lofty ideals in their philosophical writings condemn themselves to personal loneliness or pecuniary embarrassment if they live in accord with their principles. But the history of the press is as marked by hypocritical horse trading as is that of any other institution. Consider for example the situation of Thomas Gordon, the impassioned coauthor of *Cato's Letters*. Like his partner, John Trenchard, Gordon was a dissatisfied Whig politician, eager to use the *London Journal* as a platform for denouncing the financial crisis in which the Tory government of Robert Walpole found itself in 1719 — and, incidentally, to overthrow Walpole. *Cato's Letters* were filled with ringing praise of a free press, but Walpole, whose surveillance was ever conscious of threats to his power, moved in and bought off the publisher of the *London Journal* in 1722. Gordon and Trenchard were fired, and for a while they continued to write *Cato's Letters* in a different newspaper, *The British Journal*. But, devotion to a free press being what it was, when Trenchard died shortly afterwards, Gordon allowed himself to be lured away by Walpole — and he began to write articles in support of the same government he had been condemning.

The price Walpole paid — and a small one it was — was to give Gordon the job of commissioner for wine licenses. As one of Gordon's less-favored colleagues pointed out bitterly, at least one political writer had managed to achieve financial security through the use of his talents.

The story of Thomas Gordon represents an unusually vivid illustration of the agency nature of the press. The journalist is not an independent figure. He writes, as did the Roman slaves at the Forum, as agent for others — others who pay his salary, determine his working conditions, and possess the power to force him to shift directions when their surveillance demonstrates that he has become a threat to their power or, as Lasswell observed, to their "value position." Exceptions to this rule arise from time to time, but the power of journalistic mavericks is inevitably limited. The American devotees of a free press may have paid little attention to the turncoat role of Gordon, but critics of Anglo-Saxon press ideology portray themselves as unsurprised at this element in the growth of an ideology endorsing a free flow of information.

Whatever the realities in the life of Cato, there can be little doubt that the writings of Gordon and Trenchard were received with enthusiasm by the American colonials eager to use the press as an instrument for rallying support in opposition to their British rulers. How ironic that Gordon could have joined Trenchard in Number 100 of *Cato's Letters* in writing:

If they [men] are not permitted...to communicate their Opinions and Improvements to one another, the World must soon be overrun with Barbarism, Superstition, Injustice, Tyranny, and the most stupid Ignorance. They will know nothing of the Nature of Government beyond a servile submission to Power....

On the continent of Europe, phrases such as those that flowed from the pen of Cato were almost unknown. In Germany and France, one does not find developing the English tradition of editors and writers struggling to win the right to criticize political authorities in print. The rulers of Prussia and France, like Walpole and the British leaders and like the royal governors of the American colonies, insisted on unequivocal support from the press for the actions of the authorities. In Prussia and France, until the heady days of the French Revolution, the journalists seem to have accepted the directives of the crown without apparent protest. Frederick the Great, after his accession to the Prussian throne in 1740, not only demanded unconditional loyalty from the Prussian journalists but went so far as to write some of the very reports in the Prussian press. Frederick launched two newspapers of his own and composed a column that appeared irregularly under the heading, "Journal of a Prussian Officer." In 1935, a Nazi newspaper would write that it had been Frederick personally who had given the newspaper nearly two centuries earlier "a definite task to perform...namely, the education of the people of Silesia to serve the Prussian state." Frederick, a man who understood the utility of myths, appears also to have been the first German ruler to recognize the potential importance of newspapers in exerting pressure on his enemies abroad and in furthering his policies at home.

In France, the Bourbon kings pursued a press policy not dissimilar to those of Walpole, Frederick the Great, and the colonial governors of the American colonies. As might have been expected, however, the passionate applause for reasonable discourse and free expression that accompanied the French Revolution brought demands for a free press. Frankly acknowledging his debt to Milton, Count Mirabeau implored the Estates General in 1789: "Let the first of your laws consecrate forever the freedom of the press. Of all freedoms, this is the most untouchable, the most unlimitable. Without it, other freedoms can never be secured." Sweeping laws guaranteeing a free press were enacted, and all across the country journals and gazettes sprang into being, applauding the triumph of the Jacobins. In 1788, the year before the Revolution, only 4 newspapers were listed as being published in Paris, but by 1790 the number had increased to 355! As seems to be the universal experience, those heady days endured but briefly. The laws that had proclaimed the freedom of the press were already being amended by August of 1791, when the Constituent Assembly enacted a law banning "voluntary slander against the probity of civil servants, or against their rectitude in carrying out their duties." Publications were censored and seized, editors flung into prison, their presses smashed. With the assertion of power by Napoleon, the presses became once again the organs of the ruling forces.

Borrowing from Frederick the Great, Napoleon converted the French press into agents of propaganda. Foreign governments and journalists abroad saw the Napoleonic press as mouthpieces of the government, failing (as is common enough) to detect comparable practices at home. Metternich's comment is justly renowned: "The French press is worth three hundred thousand men for Napoleon." So distorted were the French accounts of Napoleon's military victories that his fall would come not merely as surprising but as quite unbelievable to the French public. Indeed, throughout modern history, the domestic press has so frequently failed to discuss military disaster that rarely has a public been prepared for defeat on the battlefield.

We turn now to an examination of the most enduring and remarkable of all the elements in the folklore of the press: the First Amendment to the Constitution of the United States.

Editors at work.

Two

Birth of a Legend:
The First Amendment,
Agency for Revolution

THE DEMOCRATIC ASSUMPTION

The First Amendment has stood for two centuries stalwart and firm, glittering in the sunlit splendor of hope in a chapel of freedom rising on a distant mountain of liberty, toward which men and women and the nations they inhabit have struggled, their unfulfilled dreams swimming through their hearts and minds. To reach the top of that mountain many have died, and many more have suffered torture and imprisonment.

For Americans, however, the mountain has not been distant. It has been close at hand and not difficult to climb. It has, as it were, been a gift, a gift from the Founding Fathers, handed down from generation to generation as a part of what they saw as the American Dream. Not for all Americans, however. When the First Amendment went into force in 1791, free expression in print was not available for Indians or for blacks or for most women. Nor, to be sure, was it available for illiterates or those without the means to gain access to a printing press. It is not asked of legends, however, that they be consistent, and the mythology of the First Amendment has endured from its inception, so much so that it can be said by now to be an inseparable element in what might be called the dogma of the press. Indeed, belief in the idea of the First Amendment is as fixed as is belief in religious doctrine, so much so that in the United States, the First Amendment is extolled as a crucial ingredient of the American Way of

Life. Throughout the rest of the world, the liberty of the press codified in the First Amendment has served as an ideal to be attained. Not everywhere, however, has it been accepted that the ideal is matched by reality. In capitalist Europe, the American press is often seen as self-serving rather than noble. In the Marxist world and in the newer countries, serious doubts are expressed about the extent of "real" freedom in a press system largely financed by advertising and committed to the earning of profit for its owners. Among the disenfranchised in the United States as well, the belief is not universal. For example, when Martin Luther King preached the doctrine of "free at last," he was expressing the hope that blacks as well as whites might climb the mountain of liberty.

Let us pause to examine the position of the press within the institutional framework of the American system of democracy and direct our attention to the enshrinement of the First Amendment in American ideology. To confront the press in its American context, one must begin by noticing that it represents one of the most tangible and apparent of American institutions; perhaps the press is the most tangible and apparent of all. Indeed, the news media are everywhere. It is said that the average citizen watches television five to seven hours a day. Supermarkets and drugstores, record shops and department stores, all display newspapers, magazines, and books about persons in the news. Radios wake up millions and can be heard on street corners as well as in automobiles; some Americans walk along city streets and beaches with transistor radios clamped to their ears. The motorist cannot drive more than a few miles, even on the otherwise unencumbered interstate highway system, without encountering billboards. The list of places where an American can go to become informed about the "news" could be endless. We sometimes hear that Americans are ill informed, but if so, it is their own fault. An American need not go far to learn about the public life around him. If his radio or TV set, his newspaper or his magazine does not tell him, his friends and neighbors will.

In short, news is everywhere. Not only can it be found everywhere, but it is also everywhere respected. One must search long and hard to find an American who will say that "news" is not good for him; who would deny that it is an American's duty to be informed? The point is critical to an understanding of the role and the meaning of the news media in American life. Of course, the news media are unpopular in many American homes, or so the pollsters are informed. But the American public distinguishes between the news media and the news, or the information which is disseminated by the news media. The media themselves may be despised, but not the "news" itself.

Indeed, we can say with a large measure of certainty that *one of the primary assumptions held by the American citizen is that democracy thrives in part because of the information disseminated by the news media.*

The assumption can be summarized as follows: In a democracy, it is the people who rule. The voice of the people is heard in the voting booths. The decisions made by the people in the voting booths are based on the information made available to them. That information is provided primarily by the news media. Hence, the news media are indispensable to the survival of democracy. To carry the assumption a bit further: A democracy is a free society. In no other form of government, in fact, are citizens free. Hence, for a society to be free, the flow of information to the citizens must come from news media that are themselves free. We shall return in later chapters to a more detailed examination of the concept of "free flow of information," but for the moment it is important to recognize the significance of that concept in the basic assumption that Americans (and others in the industrialized capitalist nations) maintain about liberty and democracy.

It is but a short step from proclaiming the overwhelming importance of a free press to asserting its power. Controversies over the power of the press predated the First Amendment. Medieval churchmen and rulers, as well as the governors of all the countries of the Western world, sought to place that power at their disposal; the idea of a free people presupposed the liberty of their press to pronounce their sovereignty over that of kings and bishops. Small wonder that journalists as a class have tended to succumb to the tempting hubris that is inevitable in any proclamation of power.

Proclamations of press (or media — the words are usually interchangeable) power have become commonplace. Metternich spoke of the printed word in France as an agency in the service of Napoleon, and the propagandists of the twentieth century would develop a reliance on radio and television as agencies of social and political control, while advertisers would rely on a "media mix" to gain their ends. Power, of course, is implied in all these cases. The point to remember as we examine the folklore of the press is that the flow of information has been widely viewed over the centuries as of transcendent importance with regard to both liberty and power. Of course, there is great strength in language; words are indeed mighty instruments. The error is to proclaim the independence of the press, to fail to recognize that the news media are agencies of someone else's power. The folklore, in fact, blinds us to the reality, and if on occasion evidence is assembled to direct our attention to it, the temptation (as with all legends) is to ignore the existence of the evidence. We find ourselves in a position similar to the perhaps apocryphal position of the woman in an often-told English tale. In the story, the canon of Worcester Cathedral is informing his wife about Darwin's theory of evolution. This was her response: "Descended from the apes! Let us hope, my dear, that it is not true. But if it is, let us pray that it will not become generally known."

In the United States and elsewhere in the capitalist world, it is difficult to find a person prepared to argue in opposition to "a free press." The assumption about the centrality of the press in a democratic society is held almost universally, even though grousing about "press abuses" is also not uncommon. To be noted here, however, is that support for a free press may be more ritual than belief. Studies have shown that many among those who express themselves in support of a free press do not in fact want anything of the sort. It is more likely that what is desired is a press that presents not a portrait of the real world but rather a portrait of the world as people would like it to be. A study made public in 1960 illustrated the point definitively. In that study, residents of Ann Arbor, Michigan, and Tallahassee, Florida, two university communities in which highly educated and thoughtful individuals are liberally represented, produced the anticipated heavy support for abstract declarations in support of free speech and other democratic principles. Over 90 percent of the respondents supported the abstract declarations, but that support vanished when concrete situations were cited. For instance, only 63 percent would have authorized a person to make a speech "against churches and religion," and a mere 44 percent would have agreed to allow an admitted Communist to speak in favor of communism. The authors concluded that "consensus in a meaningful sense" does not exist with regard to cases of concrete behavior that endorses minority views — "even among those with high education."

The study's findings have been confirmed in subsequent surveys dealing with similar questions. Even so, they do not appear to have received the attention they deserve. Although it is clear that many who say they believe in the democratic assumption do not actually believe in it, the fact that they say they do is of great significance. For Americans cling to the idea, the *perception*, of the democratic assumption with ferocious tenacity. The assumption is linked, indeed, intertwined, with the search for Truth. The Cold War, embodying the power struggle between two military titans, the United States and the Soviet Union, was portrayed by Winston Churchill, that unparalleled connoisseur of words, as "the battle for men's minds," or — placed in the language of the democratic assumption — the struggle between the free play of ideas in U.S. ideology and the chained rigidity of Soviet ideology. We will turn later to the Soviet view of this "struggle."

Representatives of the American press and those who share with them a common faith in the democratic assumption often find in the phrase "a marketplace of ideas" the appropriate metaphor. The metaphor is an excellent one to describe the assumption, since it postulates an open quest for the Truth in a public arena. The origin of the metaphor is unknown, but it was given expression by the Greek philosophers (Aristotle once said: "Plato is dear to me, but truth is dearer still") and by Jesus ("Know ye the truth and the truth shall make ye free"). Indeed, Socrates and Jesus, we are told, lost their lives in defense of that very metaphor. With specific reference to modern democratic theory, the concept is most dramatically expressed in Milton's essay *Areopagitica*.

Only a churlish fellow would devote more than a sentence to noting that Milton's objections to censorship and licensing were limited to those who would place restrictions on the defenders of Cromwell and Protestantism; Milton himself served as Cromwell's censor of "the ideas of popery" when Cromwell came to power. For the might of Milton's words is evident in their bold assertion of the moral rightness of an unfettered search for Truth. The democratic assumption is rooted in Milton's self-righting principle. Thomas Jefferson gave his endorsement to that principle in his act to establish religious freedom in Virginia; in his 1779 draft, Jefferson declared "that truth is great and will prevail if left to herself, that she is the proper and sufficient antagonist to error, and has nothing to fear from conflict." It is well to note, however, that the thoughtful Jefferson did add that the self-righting principle is invalidated when truth is "by human interposition disarmed of her natural weapons."

The marketplace image was added to the self-righting principle only in the twentieth century, by the time capitalism had been firmly established in the United States. No one gave it clearer, more vivid expression than Oliver Wendell Holmes, the distinguished Supreme Court justice:

> When men have realized that time has upset many fighting faiths, they may come to believe even more than they believe the very foundations of their own conduct that the ultimate good desired is better reached by free trade in ideas — that the best test of truth is the power of thought to get itself accepted in the competition of the market, and that truth is the only ground on which their wishes can safely be carried out. That at any rate is the theory of our Constitution.

Holmes's opinion was filed in dissenting from the view of the Court majority, which ruled in *Abrams* v. *United States* (250 U.S. 616, 1919) that the conviction of five Russian nationals on charges of sedition during World War I was within constitutional limitations. Holmes argued that the conviction was unconstitutional on the ground that the free expression of ideas, even of hated ideas, was proper, thus implying the transfer into the U.S. Constitution of Milton's self-righting principle. Holmes's position subsequently emerged as that of the Court and is today part of the American dogma, of conservative as well as liberal philosophies.

THE CENTRAL TENSION

The road from Milton to Holmes is the road traveled by the American economy as the institutions of capitalism became more deeply linked with the belief system of political liberalism. That Holmes spoke correctly when he described the self-righting principle, or the marketplace metaphor, as "the theory of our Constitution" cannot be doubted. The Founding Fathers were themselves men of the Enlightenment, men who shared not only Milton's belief in the strength of Truth, but also his trust in reason to overcome the evils of falsehood. It was not immediately, however, that there developed a general idea that the rights and privileges of free expression should be extended to all.

In fact, the English Bill of Rights, the earliest of codes of the rights of man, from which the basic concepts of the American Bill of Rights sprang, endorsed free expression only for members of Parliament, not for the citizenry at large. The English Bill decreed "that election of members of parliament ought to be free; that the freedom of speech and debates of proceedings in parliament ought not to be impeached or questioned in any court or place out of parliament." The implication, of course, was that free expression, orally or in print, was a grant only to the privileged, to those who would make wise use of that right.

The American Founding Fathers went well beyond the English Bill, responding not only to the different environment in the colonies but also to the ideas generated by the philosophers of the Enlightenment: by the endorsement by Bacon, Descartes, and others of the empirical methods of scientific inquiry; by the affirmation of Locke, Montesquieu, and like thinkers of the triumph of reason among the affairs of man and of the significance of the majority in political decisions. For if right will inevitably triumph when challenged by error, that right will be shared and recognized by the same majority. Majority rule is, in fact, an extension of Milton's self-righting principle to the people. Only through free expression could the people be granted access to the Truth, or to right thinking. So it need not be considered strange that the American Founders endorsed a free press.

Indeed, the glorification of a free press in the colonies came much earlier than the Bill of Rights. In the celebrated case of John Peter Zenger in 1735, the venerable Philadelphia lawyer Andrew Hamilton argued with memorable persuasiveness that free expression by American printers of information about tyrannical acts of the mighty was not only an important goal for colonial society, but, in fact, "the best Cause. It is the Cause of Liberty." In urging the jury to free Zenger, a German immigrant printer of modest means, from charges of seditious libel in presenting information criticizing the royal governor, Hamilton concluded with words whose clamor has been heard down the ages. To free Zenger, Hamilton told the jurors,

will not only entitle you to the Love and Esteem of your Fellow-Citizens; but every Man who prefers Freedom to a Life of Slavery will bless and honour

You, as Men who have baffled the Attempt of Tyranny; and by an impartial
and uncorrupt Verdict, have laid a noble Foundation for securing to ourselves,
our Posterity, and our Neighbours, That, to which Nature and the Laws of our
Country have given us a Right — the Liberty — both of exposing and opposing
arbitrary Power (in these Parts of the World, at least) by speaking and writing
truth.

Zenger was, in fact, judged not guilty of seditious libel, the earliest
case in recorded history in which the truth of the comments written in a'
journal was accepted as a proper defense against libel. Yet the Zenger case
was an isolated event; others were to be jailed for seeking to write what
they perceived to be truth for half a century and more still to come. The
seed had been planted, however, and agitation for free expression in print
was to become part of the American experience. Indeed, the agitation has
by no means come to an end, in all parts of the world.

We are, of course, not privy to how far Hamilton would have extended his "Right...of exposing and opposing arbitrary Power...by
speaking and writing Truth." Such a right may well have been denied to
those Hamilton believed to be speaking falsehood, just as Milton sought to
censor Catholics he believed were preaching falsehood. In any case,
Hamilton's own words limited the right when applied in other "Parts of the
World." Patriotism and xenophobia were thus an element in the earliest
expressions of press freedom, as indeed they remain today. Totally free
expression has never been practiced anywhere.

The Zenger case has been the most widely discussed over the years,
but it did not mark the first occasion that free expression in print had
become a public issue in the United States. As the means to print opinions
became widespread following the development of movable type in the
Western world, man's apparently biological impulse to assert his own
opinions in the new medium became equally widespread. In Boston, a
decade and a half before Zenger's articles were printed, The *New-England
Courant* began a practice which has now become commonplace, that of
airing controversial issues in print, even when the controversy involved
people in power — one might go so far as to say *especially* when the
controversy involved the powerful. The *Courant* began publishing in 1721,
under the leadership of a group of men scornful of the mighty Calvinist
theocracy of Massachusetts. These men, including Benjamin Franklin's
older brother James, to whom Ben was then apprenticed, dared to defy
Increase and Cotton Mather and their endorsement of inoculation as a
method to ease the ravages of a smallpox epidemic. Franklin's colleagues,
John Checkley and William Douglass, lambasted the Mathers and the
inoculation scheme to such an extent that the *Courant* came under heavy
attack from the entire power structure of colonial Boston. Ultimately the
Courant was forced out of existence, but not before it had laid the

groundwork for the declared critical role of the American press in carrying out the democratic assumption. In 1721, it was almost unthinkable to attack the leaders of the church in public print, and yet when the Mathers struck back, James Franklin replied:

> As, in controversies of religion, nothing is more frequent than for divines themselves to press the same texts for opposing tenets, they cannot fairly condemn a man for dissenting from them in matters of religion; much less can any man be thought to hinder the success of the work of a minister, by opposing him in that which is not properly a minister's work.... Even errors made publick, and afterwards publickly expos'd, less endanger the constitution of church or state, than when they are (without opposition) industriously propagated in private conversation. Hence, to anathemize a printer for publishing the different opinions of men, is as injudicious as it is wicked.

The central point of a free society, Franklin was saying, was that controversy must be aired in public, that it was *essential* that the collision between truth and falsehood take place in the public print. The line from James Franklin (who, incidentally, appears not to have written anything else of memorable quality) to Oliver Wendell Holmes is a direct one, although characteristically the twentieth-century metaphor is an economic one, the marketplace, whereas that of the eighteenth century was religious, with its emphasis on virtue and wickedness. The part that James Franklin plays in history is a small one, although chroniclers of the American press tend to award him a minor niche among the statuary of press heroes, for he was condemned by the Boston power structure, briefly imprisoned, and so denied work opportunities that in effect he was exiled — to Providence, where he sought unsuccessfully to repeat his Boston efforts.

Not so for his brother Benjamin, who is accorded the position of a hero of the first rank among the statuary of the Press Hall of Fame. Indeed, the words of Ben Franklin are perhaps the most lucid of all that were spoken by American pressmen in that early legend-making period. Of course, it is appropriate to point out that Ben Franklin was much more than a writer or journalist; he was also politician, statesman, armchair philosopher, and businessman. In Boston he had learned some important rules about the world in which he lived. A journalist might, as his brother and his partners had done, write articles criticizing the holders of political, economic, and religious power, but if one were not careful, the criticism might well bring ostracism, imprisonment, debts, even bankruptcy. So Franklin determined to conduct his presses within the system, for commercial profit, engaging cautiously in criticism but not straying past the boundary beyond which such criticism became unacceptable to those in power. His endeavors permitted him to build a fortune, to enter political life, and to rise to the most revered position ever enjoyed by an American.

journalist. In fact, when Franklin is remembered today, it is rarely as a journalist, but rather as one of the most distinguished — if in fact not the most distinguished — of the Founding Fathers.

It was Ben Franklin who first asserted the commercial realities of a free press. In short, he asked questions about "the price of Truth." Although his questions were not so phrased, he was examining the fundamental dilemma of a capitalist press. The dilemma can be characterized as the "central tension" in a capitalist press system. On the one hand, there is the ideal, of which legends have been sung for more than two centuries: The model goal of the press is to provide information for the good of mankind and a free society, to serve as a beacon to illuminate wickedness and abuse of power and by so doing to hasten their end. On the other hand, there is the drive for private profit in the commercial world of the free marketplace. In the second half of the equation, truth and the exposure of the untrustworthy are assigned a position inferior to that of financial gain. There is much of religious symbolism in the first half of the equation; not so, of course, in the second. Ben Franklin did not shy away from the commercial.

In his personal statement in the first issue of his *Pennsylvania Gazette* and in his well-known "Apology for Printers," Franklin, like his brother, endorsed the journalistic ethic of presenting all sides of controversial issues so that the reader may decide for himself which is true and which is false. Franklin also observed that he might realize higher profits if he were to present sensationalized information but said he would not stoop to the lowest common denominator. His portrait of the heavy demands placed on the editor is also in keeping with the dogma that asserts the weighty burdens on the conscientious journalist. Yet Franklin the businessman went on to tell his readers that his newspaper would not be ponderous and dull but, in fact, "as agreeable and useful Entertainment as...Nature... will allow." Not only would Franklin's papers serve all sides to a dispute, he said, but they would also pay well those who expressed those views. And even though Truth is the highest calling, still Franklin avoided "printing such things as usually give offense to Church or State." Ben had no intention of going to jail, as his brother had done; thus, he would not undertake a direct assault on the authorities of Pennsylvania. There was not in Ben Franklin a fanatical devotion to great principles. To him, there were clearly limitations on the freedom of the press, and he had no intention of pursuing a challenge that might lead beyond those limits to a confrontation with civil authority.

Like Thomas Gordon, the coauthor of *Cato's Letters*, Franklin achieved public office and lived to espouse the power base which he had entered. Indeed Franklin abandoned his career as journalist — in favor of that of statesman — and his voice rang out no longer as a critic of power. No doubt Franklin believed in the virtue of the political system of which he was a part and was not moved to criticize it; yet one might also imagine that this rational, analytical man would himself have acknowledged, had he been asked, that a system embodying a fully free flow of information was no more likely to be found in the colonies than a fool who would not somehow part with his money.

THOSE SPARE FORTY-FIVE WORDS

The First Amendment to the U.S. Constitution embodies a revolutionary idea, and for more than two hundred years it has summoned to the barricades the men and women who believe that no liberty is genuine unless it contains the right to express one's opinion, however unpopular, hated, or inflammatory. No doctrine announced by the new republic has been more widely cheered around the world than the declaration of free expression. The declaration has fueled the fires of every revolutionary movement for two centuries. It is doubtful in the extreme that the drafters of those spare forty-five words could have imagined their impact, for, after all, there was nothing new in an assertion of the right of free expression. What was to be new, however, was the wide circulation of the declaration and the broad interpretation that came to be placed on the right, as well as the universal adulation that was to be heaped upon it.

The great code of the press embodied in the First Amendment declares, with deceptive simplicity, that "Congress shall make no law. . . abridging the freedom of speech, or of the press." The language was largely the work of James Madison, whose assignment in the first Congress was to analyze the dozens of proposals advanced by the states for inclusion in a Bill of Rights. In order to win approval of the Constitution of 1787, the framers found it necessary to agree to a formal Bill that would enshrine in the positive law not only the major elements of the English Bill of Rights, but also the accumulated wisdom of eighteenth-century thought. Madison's original draft followed the constitution of his own state of Virginia with reference to the press. The third article of Madison's draft of a federal Bill of Rights guaranteed religious freedom; the fourth declared:

> The people shall not be deprived or abridged of their right to speak, to write, or to publish their sentiments; and the freedom of the press, as one of the great bulwarks of liberty, shall be inviolable.

After days of debate on his draft, Madison prepared twelve amendments for submission to the states. All twelve were approved by Congress and submitted to the states. The first two, establishing a numerical formula for proportional representation in the House and denying congressmen the right to raise their salaries without an intervening election, were not ratified by the states. The third, now grouping religious liberty with guarantees of free speech and press and the right to assemble peaceably for redress of grievances, was approved and became the First Amendment. Although some later jurists were to assign this amendment preeminence over the others because it is first among the ten amendments of the Bill, what is now first was, in fact, third in Madison's original draft. Considering Madison's deep concern about the existence of "factions" among the thirteen colonies, it can be assumed that he perceived the press as a vehicle available to conflicting factions on an equal basis, so that none might emerge with dictatorial powers. In his well-known essay Number 10 among the *Federalist Papers*, Madison spoke again and again of the dangers of passionate devotion to factions. Like the writers of the English Bill of Rights and the majoritarian thinkers of the seventeenth and eighteenth centuries, Madison was wary of the potential excesses of any faction that would consist of a majority of the people. Democracies have ever been short-lived and violent, Madison wrote in *Federalist 10*, for where "a common passion or interest" was felt by the majority, nothing might check the excesses of the majority faction. The resolution, he maintained, lay in a plural society, in the existence of a multitude of factions serving as a check to unbridled power. One of the most important such factions would inevitably be the press, and the more newspapers, pamphlets, and broadsheets the better:

> Extend the sphere, and you take in a greater variety of parties and interests; you make it less probable that a majority of the whole will have a common motive to invade the rights of other citizens; or if such a common motive exists, it will be more difficult for all who feel it to discover their own strength, and to act in unison with each other.

Few Americans have been more forceful than Madison in asserting the centrality of the press in the democratic assumption. Within seven years of the adoption of the Bill of Rights, the threat of war with France induced President John Adams to secure congressional approval of the Sedition Act, which threatened journalists with prison for writing material that cast aspersions on the political leadership of the country. Well aware of the abusive language and sensationalism to which a licentious press was tempted, Madison, in responding to the Sedition Act, issued this ringing declaration of the importance of press freedom:

> Some degree of abuse is inseparable from the proper use of everything, and in no instance is this more true than in that of the press. It has accordingly been decided by the practice of the States, that it is better to leave a few of its noxious branches to their luxuriant growth, than by pruning them away, to injure the vigour of those yielding the proper fruits. And can the wisdom of this policy be doubted by any who reflect that to the press alone, chequered as

it is with abuses, the world is indebted for all the triumphs which have been gained by reason and humanity over error and repression; who reflect that to the same beneficent source the United States owes much of the lights which conducted them to the ranks of a free and independent nation, and which have improved their political system into a shape so auspicious to their happiness.

The argument advanced by Madison is crucial to what will follow in these pages as we examine the perceptions of the press and of press freedom by journalists, press critics, scholars, and private citizens. The democratic assumption holds that the press may be noxious, abusive, sensational, even inaccurate, but that its freedom is vital to the survival of American society. Its freedom has never been absolute, as it indeed was not intended by the Founding Fathers, who were themselves pragmatists, not absolutists. The goal of "objectivity" was one that did not even occur to the Founders, for there did not exist in the press of that era any publisher or editor who did not see his journal as an instrument for spreading good, or Truth, and not merely as a catalog of points of view. What was desired, not only by the American Founders but by the thinkers of the Enlightenment, was open discussion in the pages of public print. To Madison as well as to others, there apparently was nothing, at least in theory, that ought to be excluded from the pages of public print. Yet, from the very beginning, the practice did not coincide with the theory.

The same Thomas Jefferson who could write the most ringing support for a free press could also condemn journalists as a pack of liars and argue, at least once, that they ought to be thrown in prison for what they printed. In 1787, years before he took office as president of the United States, Jefferson wrote:

> The basis of our government being the opinion of the people, the very first object should be to keep that right; and were it left to me to decide whether we should have a government without newspapers, or newspapers without a government, I should not hesitate a moment to prefer the latter.

So attractive are those words to the practitioners of journalism that samplers and printed reproductions have been framed and hung in newspaper offices across the United States. But few newspaper offices note other words that Jefferson wrote years later, when he was in fact president and beleaguered by waves of vitriol in the Federalist press. It was then, in 1803, that Jefferson wrote:

> So abandoned are the tory presses that...even the least informed of the people have learnt that nothing in a newspaper is to be believed. This is a dangerous state of things, and the press ought to be restored to its credibility if possible. The restraints provided by the laws of the states are sufficient for this

if applied. And I have therefore long thought that a few prosecutions of the most prominent offenders would have a wholesome effect in restoring the integrity of the presses.

Clearly, the revolutionary message of the First Amendment was not entirely acceptable to the most celebrated of the libertarian heroes among the Founders, at least after he had attained the pinnacle of power. To President Jefferson, unlimited freedom for newspapers brought on "a dangerous state of things." The journalistic value of "objectivity," of presenting fairly the various sides of an issue so that truth might emerge victorious in a kind of Tournament of Reason — the exercise of this value needed to be restrained, Jefferson said, in the best interests of the American people. There was in the doctrine of the First Amendment, then, a serious threat to the fabric of society. In short, Jefferson was saying that the Federalist press was not serving as a proper vehicle of social control; the masses were in danger of being polluted by the lies he believed were being disseminated by the Tory newspapers.

It was a troublesome theme for Jefferson, who found his abstract endorsement of a totally free press in dangerous collision with his practical concern with developing the kind of society he considered necessary to build in the new nation. How modern the dilemma, for the problem confronting Jefferson was markedly similar to that faced two centuries later by libertarian thinkers in the new nations of Africa. Still, however impractical the revolutionary idea of the First Amendment, it had now become a powerful force in the world of practical politics. In office, nevertheless, libertarians have found the revolutionary idea unsuitable. It must be remembered that the drafters of the First Amendment were members of a social and cultural elite; they were themselves fearful of the potential excesses of democratic government, for they believed the masses to be unlettered, culturally apathetic, and intellectually incapable of steering the ship of state. Rather than envisaging the average man as a participant in power, they perceived him as a cooperating consumer prepared to turn over the direction of the state to his cultural and intellectual betters. To insure such cooperation on the part of the reading public was, in their view, the task of the press. For the press to vary from that role was to court, as Jefferson wrote, "a dangerous state of things."

Those newspapers that endorsed Jeffersonian ideas found little to quarrel with in the revolutionary declaration, for, after all, *they* were at liberty to write as they pleased and in so doing to help the reader better understand the wisdom of their joint political course. To the Tory press, on the other hand, support for Jeffersonian ideas was tantamount to destruction of the society, and the Tories pursued *their* political objectives very much under the banner of free expression. In fact, the entire press supported the revolutionary idea; where they differed was in their interpretation of what was meant by free expression. A century and a half earlier, Milton had encountered a similar dilemma; endorsing free expression for the Cromwell Protestants, he could also support censorship for the royalist Catholics, who were, in his view, expressing dangerous ideas. That particular dilemma has not yet been resolved.

Put another way, the Founding Fathers anticipated that the press would serve their political cause. The newspapers of their day spoke for and were read by the social and cultural elite: those who regularly read books and pamphlets and newspapers and who had the financial resources to pay the price, in those days about six cents a copy for the newspapers. The ideas expressed in the newspapers were, not surprisingly, the ideas of the social and cultural elite. If the publications were read by the masses, then, it was assumed the masses would be influenced by the ideas and political principles supported by the press. In this way, the press was seen as an instrument of social control, an agency for the improvement and benefit of society.

THE LAW OF JUSTICE AND LOVE

During the presidencies of Jefferson and his Virginia allies, Madison and James Monroe, the great experiment in democratic government spawned by the French Revolution ran its course, with Napoleon's brief empire followed by the restoration of the Bourbon monarchy. With an eye on the doctrine of free expression let loose in the world by the First Amendment, factions in France fought out the most bitter of their battles over the issue of freedom of the press. The sides of the struggle were similar to those faced in Milton's England and in Jefferson's America: how might the philosophical abstraction of a free press as a social good be made acceptable practically when that free press seemed to be undermining legal Authority? (It was also a question that would bedevil constitutional Germany when the Nazi press was demanding its overthrow.) Jean Baptiste de Villèle, the prime minister to whom the ailing, gout-ridden Louis XVIII delegated his power, responded by the *loi de tendance*, adopted in 1822, a measure similar to the Bad Tendency guideline proposed in Blackstone's 1769 Commentaries ("... to punish any dangerous or offensive writing ... of a pernicious tendency is necessary for the preservation of peace and good order, or government, and religion, the only solid foundations of civil liberty ...") and later to become the official position of the U.S. Supreme Court in 1917. To Villèle it was necessary, if he could not conciliate his political foes, to "silence them," as he said, by subjecting the opposition press to punishment for printing articles that sought to frustrate his legislative program or even to challenge the hereditary right of the monarch to rule. Villèle remained in power after Louis' death in 1824, when he was succeeded by his brother, the Comte d'Artois, who became Charles X, and who left most political decisions to his prime minister.

When his restrictive laws proved ineffective, drawing criticism not only from the opposition press but also from some loyalist papers and from political foes of both left and right, Villèle turned to outright bribery, a practice by no means unusual in Europe, especially in England. In fact, Louis and Charles received a better press in England than in their own country. One contemporary wrote that the correspondence of the three leading London journals was composed in the office of the French minister of police. It was during the Bourbon restoration that anti-Royalist forces had won the approval of Jefferson's old friend, the Marquis de Lafayette, to finance a society called the Friends of Freedom of the Press, which planned a coup to overthrow the king. Although the plot was uncovered and its leaders seized, Lafayette, now elderly and living in retirement, was not disturbed. Hearing of the efforts to censor the French press, Jefferson, now also in retirement at Monticello, wrote to Lafayette yet another stirring declaration in support of a free press: In keeping government honest and unoppressive, he said, "the only security of all is in a free press. The force of public opinion cannot be resisted, when permitted freely to be expressed." That letter was written in 1823; yet, a year earlier, Jefferson had written Lafayette that his opinion of the American press had sunk so low that he was content to read but one newspaper — the *Richmond Enquirer* — because none of the rest could be believed. Jefferson never was able to resolve his love-hate affair with the press, nor his dilemma in choosing between free expression and the national good.

In France, press opposition to the French invasion of Spain stirred criticism of the regime despite the existence of the *loi de tendance*. Villèle responded with an even more stringent proposal introduced in the Chamber of Deputies in December 1826 by the arch-conservative minister of justice, Count Charles Ignace de Peyronnet, who gave the measure what for the monarchy was a most unfortunate identification. Criticized for introducing a measure its foes called a plan to annihilate the press, Peyronnet responded by saying the bill was conceived as "a law of justice and love." And so it was named, with consummate Gallic irony, by its enemies, among whom were not only Stendhal, Chateaubriand, and Benjamin Constant, but also, remarkably, the French Academy, which rarely has taken a purely political position. The "Law of Justice and Love" never did, in fact, become law, and in the end it went far toward forcing Charles from office and ending the Bourbon restoration. Moreover, the introduction of the law evoked the most extensive public debate the world has ever experienced on the nature of the press and its role in the political and cultural life of society.

The debate occupied nearly the total attention of the Chamber of Deputies for a full month and dominated public life in the French capital as have few issues before or since. Seventy-eight deputies spoke in the debate, thirty-two in favor of "the Law of Justice and Love" and forty-six in opposition. The speeches occupied not only the attention of the fourteen political dailies in Paris (only two of which endorsed the law), but also that of the public at large. Every day, fascinated crowds gathered outside the Chamber to jeer the parliamentarians and to vent their collective anger against the law that would have imposed a stamp tax on all printed matter and required all political manuscripts to be cleared by government censors.

Among the speeches in opposition to the Law of Justice and Love, the most widely applauded was that of the intellectual leader of the liberals, Pierre-Paul Royer-Collard, one of the most gifted orators in French history. So celebrated in the charged political atmosphere was his speech that its printed circulation was said to have reached a million copies. Even allowing for hyperbole, Royer-Collard's words must have struck a nerve throughout the country. Writing over a hundred years later, Guillaume de Bertier de Sauvigny pronounced the address "one of the high points of political eloquence" in the nineteenth century. Speaking with grave irony, Royer-Collard proclaimed the law an effort to "correct the mistake of Providence, which at Creation had permitted man to escape intelligent and free into the universe, from which event arose all evil and error." To what must have been stormy applause in the Chamber, Royer-Collard derided the law as at last "lifting mankind to the happy innocence of the brute." It would never work, he said, for to prevent the people from speaking out through the press against tyranny and oppression would not succeed unless all industry, all agriculture, all transportation, all activity were destroyed along with the books, pamphlets, and newspapers. "If your plows do not bury all of civilization," he taunted the Royalists, "you will not overcome our efforts."

The response of Minister of Justice Peyronnet was curiously modern. The press was being blindly critical, he said, and in its negativism was tearing down all the institutions of society; it was, he said, "intolerant, engaging in persecution for its own sake." How could the government tolerate a press that when the people were content wrote of nothing but their misery and that instructed the public to disobey the law? The government, Peyronnet said, dared not permit the enemies of the state to speak and do as they pleased.

Interestingly, the words of no less a libertarian than Thomas Jefferson were invoked on the side of the censors. On Jefferson's death in 1826, not long before the start of the debate, a letter written a score of years earlier during his presidency attacking the excesses of a licentious press was introduced to support the restrictions proposed by the Law of Justice and Love. Dismayed, Lafayette wrote Madison to ask if the reported words of Jefferson were true; Madison responded sadly that so they were but that they did not represent Jefferson's true convictions. It is impossible to know how influential the citation of Jefferson was, but it could not have damaged the cause of the censors, for Jefferson was held in high esteem in France. In any case, the law was approved by the Chamber by a vote of 233 to 134.

It was, however, a Pyrrhic victory, for the public outcry was substantial, and the Chamber of Peers, to which the measure was referred upon passage in the Chamber of Deputies, allowed the draft law to expire without a vote. When the peers adjourned, the irritated Villèle issued an executive order imposing censorship on the French press. Opponents took to the streets in protest, and in the elections that followed six months later, the Royalists suffered severe losses. Villèle resigned in January 1828, and Charles himself was cast from power after two days of revolution in 1830, an event which Peyronnet had foreseen as inevitable unless the press were checked. Charles and his chief minister, Prince Jules Armand de Polignac, certainly sped the day of reckoning by piling more and more restrictions on the press, on the peasantry, and on the rising class of merchants and tradesmen. Peyronnet and Polignac were jailed; Charles was forced to abdicate and to go into exile.

Historians have assigned the press not only a key role in the overthrow of the Bourbon monarchy in 1830 but by and large have credited the press with being responsible for it. A. J. Tudesq, for example, said that the liberal press was "the principal author of the Revolution." And Daniel Rader, in the only full-fledged treatment of the period in English, *The Journalists and the July Revolution in France*, assigned to the press the primary role not only in the overthrow of the monarchy but also in directing "the reality of history." Journalists in England as well as in France proudly proclaimed their power and immodestly draped around their shoulders the mantle of defender of freedom and scourge of abusive power. At another time and in another place, the press would drape a similar mantle around its shoulders, asserting that it was the press that had cast from power President Richard Nixon, sending his chief assistants to jail and condemning him to exile.

The implication, in both explanations, described the press as an independent force that was successfully confronting the power of entrenched industrial and political forces. It cannot be doubted that the press was a significant element in the struggle for power in both the France of 1830 and the Washington of 1974, yet it was but one element in those struggles, and indeed some members of the press could in both instances be found on the side of entrenched power as well as on the revolutionary side. It is more correct to assert that the press participated in the power struggle and that the revolutionary press, financed and prodded by the merchants, the artisans, and the growing middle class, as well as by powerful allies in the courts and among parliamentarians, aided the cause of revolt. David Pinkney pointed out that by concentrating his attention on a single element in the fall of the Bourbon monarchy in 1830, Rader exaggerated the role of the press. The revolution, Pinkney noted, had "more fundamental origins," rising from Charles's alienation of deputies in the Chamber; his failure to reward deserving politicians; and, above all, his economic measures, which were threatening both merchants and peasants with repressive taxes while the cost of living mounted ever higher.

Pinkney's question is a crucial one: Was the course of French history in the last years of the Bourbon restoration "largely directed by journalists"? His answer is no. That journalists were very influential in that revolt is not to be questioned, he says, but he adds that an unqualified affirmative would oversimplify a complex pattern of influences. Indeed, he says, the revolution would have occurred without the journalists, although perhaps not in 1830. The same conclusion can be reached about the events of 1974 and the fall of Richard Nixon.

Historians, but more importantly the journalists themselves, have popularized the avowal of press power incorporated in the claim that it was the press that overthrew Charles X and Richard Nixon. It is not to be wondered at that the journalists of 1830, as well as the journalists of 1974, pronounced themselves responsible for the overthrow of wickedness and the triumph of virtue. Historians are not infrequently overwhelmed by journalistic explanations and are sometimes channeled into narrow explanations of complex events by the pressures they feel to assign "causes" to events. Sober reflection compels us to the recognition that the press, then as now, charts no independent course but serves the interests of those who own and operate it. The enemies of Charles X and of Richard Nixon were powerful in their own right, and inasmuch as both leaders had acted in sharp opposition to the revolutionary ideology of the First Amendment, they were clearly going to be opposed by the majority of the press, the journalists thus inevitably serving as willing allies of the opposing political forces.

Three years after the fall of Charles, across the Atlantic in New York City there occurred an event that in its own quiet way propelled the institution of journalism to a dominant position in the social context. That event would turn out to have a far greater impact than the drama in the Chamber of Deputies or in the streets of revolutionary Paris. It was the appearance of the first newspaper priced low enough to be within the purchasing power of virtually the entire population, the arrival of the "mass media" and the expansion of the folklore of the press to every corner of the world.

Newsboy at work.

Three

The Commercial Press, 1833–1917: Agency for Profit

THE CITY UPON A HILL

The press, as we have seen, has always been an instrument of information, although it has been less clear what kind of information was desired by the reader. Four different types of information appear to have been circulated by the early American press: information designed to (a) spread religious doctrine, (b) tell about the commercial market, (c) persuade readers for political ends, and (d) provide popular education. Although both the producers and consumers of the press believed that the purpose of the press was to provide information, it was not at all clear then (any more than it is now) what kind of information was meant. In the nineteenth century the expansion of literacy, the development of technology, and the growth of the mass market affected the expectations of both producer and consumer of news, with increasing importance assigned to the commercial and political role of the press. The early character of the press as disseminator of religious doctrine all but disappeared in the nineteenth century, at least as far as the mass press was concerned, and while people everywhere continued to speak of the press as an instrument of education, its educational role became largely associated with the distribution of commercial and political information.

Dates are useful devices for understanding historical developments, although one must resist the temptation to assign metaphysical qualities to dates. Rarely does a historical development begin at a particular time and place; nonetheless, it is convenient to fix the date of September 3, 1833, as the beginning of the mass media. That was the date on which Benjamin Day, the publisher of *The New York Sun*, achieved success with a daily newspaper priced so inexpensively it could, for all practical purposes, be purchased by anyone in the city. The price was one cent; it was the start of what came to be known as the "penny press." Day was straightforward about his intentions. The *Sun*, he told his readers, would "shine for all." Day's reasoning was flawless: the standard price for a New York daily was six cents, and only the well-to-do could afford to buy. By reducing prices, Day saw, he could attract more readers and would thus be able to increase his profits on the basis of circulation. Such reasoning came, in the twentieth century, to be recognized as deriving the benefits of the economy of scale. Day's penny press exceeded even his own expectations. His circulation soared to unimaginable heights, and soon his New York City competitors were forced to slash their prices to a penny in order to compete. Provincial newspapers followed the lead, and for the first time, price competition entered the world of the press. Technological improvements followed rapidly, reducing the costs of the printers, thus permitting increased space for information in the news columns and increased space for advertisements.

The growth of the advertising industry paralleled the growth of the newspaper industry. It was the first get-rich-quick age mankind had experienced. For that remarkable development, it was necessary that there be a remarkable confluence of facilitating factors, and only rarely in the annals of mankind had there been such a remarkable confluence.

Of the utmost importance was the Industrial Revolution itself, born in eighteenth-century Britain and quickly spreading across Europe and into the American colonies. The rapid replacement of machinery made possible not only the growth of industry but also lightning technological improvements, widespread expansion of trade, and the growth of modern transportation systems. For the first time it became possible for farmers and the urban working classes to move from place to place. The emigration of large numbers of Europeans to the United States helped expand the Atlantic coastal towns into incipient urban centers, especially New York City. With the companion rise in the rate of literacy, increasing numbers were able to read and to clamor for information. It is not to be forgotten that mass media developed simultaneously with urban centers. In fact, it is difficult to separate the two developments: without urban centers, a mass media was unlikely; and without a mass media, the development of urban centers was unlikely.

In addition, the character of the political environment underwent a significant change, accompanying the shifts in the worlds of science, industry, commerce, transportation, and the mass media. The political leadership of the American colonies and of the United States in its first half-century derived from members of the social and economic elite. The first six presidents were aristocrats from coastal Virginia and Massachusetts. Four years before Day's penny press made its appearance, the dominance of the political world by the social and cultural elite had been shattered, permanently, as it turned out. The American public had elected Andrew Jackson to the presidency and had moved the seat of political power from the landed aristocracy represented by Jefferson, Madison, and Monroe to the commercial entrepreneurs represented by Jackson, Van Buren, and their successors. The brokers had replaced the squires; the "democrats" had turned out the "gentry."

Those two words are enclosed by quotation marks to emphasize the point that the Jacksonians were no more democrats than were the Jeffersonian gentry, perhaps less so. Yet historians have been kind enough to the Jacksonians to accept their definitions and the ideology that they successfully imposed upon the public. Jackson and his lieutenants, especially the two journalists who dominated his "kitchen cabinet," had come to recognize a deceptively simple political truth: In a society that provided nearly universal male suffrage, there existed many more "common men" than "aristocrats." And, just as Day had learned an important lesson about numbers, so had Jackson. It was numbers that won elections, and since common men outnumbered aristocrats, all that was necessary to win an election was to win over the common man. So, with a minimum of modesty, Jackson ushered in what he and his agents identified variously as the Age of the Common Man and the Age of Democracy. In 1829, Jackson's Democratic party thoroughly defeated the supporters of John Quincy Adams, many of whom were remnants of the Federalist party. With the defeat of Adams — Jackson won 56 percent of the popular vote — the Federalists disappeared as a party. The Whigs who replaced them were never able to overcome the image of a Democratic party committed to the welfare of the common man. It was not until Abraham Lincoln, the most skillful politician to emerge in the United States after Jackson, that the Democrats could be defeated and the Age of the "Coonskin Democracy" could come to an end, yielding to the political appeal of a man so "common" he was born in a log cabin. By then, the Whig party had disappeared too and the Republicans were challenging the Democrats for the right to be known as the champions of democracy.

The reality is far different from the images created by the Jacksonians and the Lincolnians. Power, as before, rested with the elite, but the nature of the elite had changed. That metamorphosis was part of the confluence discussed earlier, a confluence that resulted in a massive change in ideology, an ideological shift that affected political patterns not only in the United States but around the world, in Latin America and the Orient as well as in the countries of Europe. The new ideology was the ideology of the common man, a democratic figure, to be sure, but a figure quite different from the democrat imagined by the French revolutionaries a generation earlier. The American "democrat" was not a democrat at all in the fraternal sense dreamed of by Robespierre and his compatriots. The American "democrat" was, in fact, an incipient capitalist, a man who dreamed of "rising by his own bootstraps" to a higher economic and social class, a man obsessed not with the idea of fraternity but with that of equality. The social order proclaimed by the Jacksonians was egalitarian, where every man would be the equal of every other, even his social betters. The American environment, with its happy mixture of what seemed to be unlimited land and opportunity, made the dream possible and raised in the overcrowded class-ridden society of Europe a vision, which persists in many places to this day, of "a land of unlimited opportunity." The millions of immigrants who arrived on American shores in the nineteenth century added vitality to the American ideology and markedly influenced the development of American institutions. One can argue that the writers and editors of the new mass media were the "advance men" of the American dream: they spread the message of equality and opportunity from coast to coast. Among those media barons were penniless Europeans, men such as James Gordon Bennett and Joseph Pulitzer, profound believers in the dream and chief among its publicists.

Yet the truth was far from the illusion. The Jackson presidency ushered in a serious depression in which thousands lost their jobs and in which the tragedy of urban despair and blight, to which Europeans were growing accustomed, appeared in the cities of the United States. It was the assignment of the leaders of society, in politics and press, to spread the message of optimism. And spread the message they did, and not hypocriti- cally, for they too believed in the dream of equality and bounty. Chief among those who spread that message was a Kentucky journalist who became one of Jackson's chief advisers in his "kitchen cabinet," Amos Kendall, who served as postmaster general under Jackson and his succes- sor, Martin Van Buren. It was Kendall who wrote Jackson's illustrious message vetoing the extension of the Bank of the United States; it was that message above all that cemented Jackson's reputation as the champion of the common man, for it spoke out in stirring language against the wicked- ness of bankers and other exploiters of the common man. It was not difficult for Kendall, a poor farm boy from the bleak and rocky pastures of Kentucky, to champion the common man and condemn the financially powerful. In 1831, when among other occupations he was editing the *Congressional Globe* in Washington, Kendall wrote: "Those who produce all the wealth are themselves left poor. They see principalities extending and palaces built around them, without being aware that the entire expense is a tax upon themselves." Nevertheless, in yet another chapter in the folklore of the press and its multitude of ironies, Kendall was to amass great wealth, as a partner of Samuel Morse, in exploiting the expansion of the telegraph to many parts of the country. Some have called Kendall the country's first successful public relations agent; whether or not this is a valid description, it is certainly true that Kendall was one of a long line of journalists who grew wealthy in pursuing the ideal of informing the people. And, lamentably, Kendall also was able to find justification for suppressing "news" that he believed harmful for the public. A foe of the abolitionists, Kendall succeeded during his tenure as postmaster general in seeing to it that abolitionist tracts disappeared from federal mail sacks.

Historians have differed markedly in their interpretations of the age of Jackson, but what cannot be doubted is that the Jacksonians won substantial popular support through appeal to nationalistic impulses. The militant nationalism that flowered during the age of Jackson has indeed been a key ingredient in the American experience ever since. Not surprisingly, the press was a powerful agent in the expansionist impulses that, beginning in the Jackson administrations, led to war with Mexico; the acquisition of Texas, California, and the Southwest; indirectly to the Civil War; then to the purchase of Alaska; and by the end of the century to an imperialistic war wresting Cuba and the Philippine islands from Spain. In all these ventures, the American press played a major role.

There was nothing new in the urge for expansion; it derived in large measure from one of the most persistent elements in the belief system of Americans, the conviction that Providence had bestowed upon the happy citizens of the country a special role to be played: to lead the nations of the world to the blessedness of the freedom and equality that were the inevitable products of self-determination. The idea originated in powerful form in the words of John Winthrop, the most celebrated of the early governors of the colony of Massachusetts, within a decade of the landing of the *Mayflower*. "We shall," Winthrop asserted, "be as a city upon a Hill, the eyes of all people upon us." A century and a half later, in 1782, Benjamin Franklin bestowed his weighty endorsement on the metaphor:

Establishing the liberties of America will not only make the people happy, but will have some effect in diminishing the misery of those, who in other parts of the world groan under despotism, by rendering it more circumspect, and inducing it to govern with a lighter hand.

Frederick Merk described the sense of mission as the true expression of "the national spirit." The mission, idealistic and self-denying, found itself once again given powerful support when President Lincoln called on Americans to give just honor to those who fell at Gettysburg so that "government of the people, by the people, for the people, shall not perish from the earth." In other words, if the Union were to be destroyed, popular government would vanish from the earth and the mission of

America would be frustrated, causing grief not only to Americans but to people everywhere. Under such a banner of righteousness, it was possible for Americans to war against the indigenous Indians, the Mexicans, the Spaniards, and, much later, the Vietnamese.

In spreading the Word of the Mission, the American press was not to be outdone by statesmen. Among the many manifestations of the zealous idealism of the American press in promoting holy war against Mexico was an editorial in *The New York Sun*, the originator of the penny press, on October 22, 1847. The race of Mexicans, the editorial said,

> is perfectly accustomed to being conquered, and the only new lesson we shall teach is that our victories will give liberty, safety, and prosperity to the vanquished, if they know enough to profit by the appearance of our stars. To *liberate* and *ennoble* — not to *enslave* and *debase* — is our mission.

In similar vein, *The Boston Times* on the same date maintained that the "conquest" of Mexico (it dutifully placed quotation marks about the word) had to be recognized as "a great blessing to the conquered." The editorial continued:

> It is a work worthy of a great people, of a people who are about to regenerate the world by asserting the supremacy of humanity over the accidents of birth and fortune.

The spread of American power from coast to coast and into foreign lands was carried out under the banner of "manifest destiny," a term used by John O'Donnell, a journalist and political activist who spoke in the pages of *The Democratic Digest*, to extend the geographical boundaries of the City Upon a Hill to beyond the Rio Grande. It was the duty of Americans, in Merk's phrase, "to regenerate backward peoples of the continent." The immediate goal of Manifest Destiny was to extend the scope of the mission to, as Katherine Lee Bates's patriotic hymn would have it, "from sea to shining sea." Merk argued that the success of the campaign for Manifest Destiny lay not in an overriding popular endorsement of nationalism but rather in the popular acceptance of the sense of mission. In this he may be correct, but it seems apparent that nationalism as a cause is an inevitable result of a national sense of mission. Whether the crusading zeal that is inherent in a sense of mission would be manifested in Mexico in 1846 or somewhere else a bit later is less important than that the people could be so easily persuaded to rally round the flag in transporting the blessings of liberty south of the border.

Because the press participated in — and often led — the rally round the flag, it should not be imagined that the press was the cause — or the originator — of Manifest Destiny. As in every similar situation, the press acted as agency for those who wished for the war: those, for instance, who were eager to extend the cotton-growing area of the nation into the vast, inviting area of Texas; and those for whom Texas might be yet another slave state to counter the new states clamoring for admission to the Union from the north. Indeed, a number of political figures and newspapers spoke out against war with Mexico, and Albert Gallatin, once Jefferson's secretary of treasury, would now, in 1847 at the age of eighty-five, pronounce the contemporary idea of conquest all wrong. "Your mission," he declared, "is to improve the state of the world." It was morally wrong, he said, to "abandon the lofty position which your fathers occupied, to substitute for it the political morality and heathen patriotism of the heroes and statesmen of antiquity." Yet Gallatin did not prevail, nor did such newspapers as the abolitionist *New Englander*, which decried the war as not only "wasting millions of capital which stalwart labor must pay," but for raising "a few into the rank of a purse-proud aristocracy, vulgar and odious." It was difficult for the press to resist the emotional fervor of the time. Horace Greeley, in his *New York Tribune*, gave lukewarm support to the war although he himself was opposed to it, and he contented himself with applauding the end of the fighting. Rather than leading in moments of crisis, the press finds itself drawn into the fray on the popular side, and only occasionally do editors rise to oppose the popular will.

In the increasingly hostile moods of both northern and southern states, the press played its customary role. Southern papers condemned northern ideas and practices; northern papers performed a like service with regard to southern papers. Historian Avery Craven labeled the hostile campaign waged in the pages of the press as the first cold war. Indeed, during the Reconstruction period that followed the war and lasted until 1877, northern and southern newspapers continued to endorse sectional interests, often in inflammatory terms. With the conquest of the continent assured, the people, their leaders, and their press turned their eyes beyond the shining seas, giving weight to the idea developed by Frederick Jackson Turner that "American democracy" could be explained by the influence of the frontier, of the "safety valve" that was always present as a lure for those dissatisfied citizens who may not have liked their place of residence or employment; they could always go somewhere else. It was the ubiquitous Horace Greeley who offered the famed advice, "Go west, young man." With "west" gone and the shining sea blocking further migration or challenges, "south" rose in significance; and after a decade of agitation by political leaders, supported by the successors to the penny press, the yellow press, American troops moved into Cuba to free her from Spanish rule. The same sense of mission that had served as motivation for the invasion of Mexico served now as motivation for the invasion of Cuba. This time, the press was less modest than in the Mexican venture; the publisher of *The New York Journal*, William Randolph Hearst, announced that it was he who had "furnished the war" with Spain. This absurd claim was, surprisingly, accepted as historical truth by scores of historians and, of course, by most journalists, for what could better assert the independent power of the press than the launching of a national war!

The history of the settlement of the West, as well as that of the territorial and economic expansion of white Europeans — especially punitive against Indians and blacks — was violent in the extreme. This violence was chronicled by the penny press, and especially the yellow press. In the 1890s, Hearst and his chief competitor, Joseph Pulitzer, challenged each other daily in an effort to present the most dramatically violent of acts and, in so doing, amassed vast wealth as their circulations soared. The Spanish-American War presented the most striking opportunity of all, and Hearst and Pulitzer rose to the occasion. Hearst, an amazing personality of monumental arrogance, went so far as to charter a tramp steamer off the coast of Cuba, the hold of which contained a printing press and composing room; he based himself and a staff of reporters on the steamer, often going ashore to observe battles, sometimes even to participate in the fighting. Pulitzer contented himself with sending an array of distinguished reporters, including novelist Stephen Crane, to cover the war.

The yellow designation that has come to describe not only the sensational press of the late nineteenth century but current practices as well derived from "Hogan's Alley," a comic strip published in Pulitzer's *World*, in which there appeared the "yellow kid," a small child whose dress contained a dab of yellow. Hearst and Pulitzer, and those who followed them, carried to its extreme the search for "human interest" begun by the penny press. But the formula was more original, for both the *Journal* and the *World* also waged social campaigns designed to improve the lot of the "common man." These were, in short, sensational crusades, or perhaps crusading sensationalizers. In whichever case, circulation achieved astronomical heights.

The folklore of the press is part of a larger folklore, one that was dispatched into the wide world by those with a nineteenth-century vision of human development: an unending upward path for Americans that led across turbulent streams and rocky pinnacles to a pleasant plateau where brotherhood was preached and practiced, where the American Way would be adopted as the Way of Peace and Plenty. On this plateau each man (some would add woman, but not many) would be educated and informed about events near and far, prepared to participate in democratic practices for the greatest good of the greatest number. The plateau was also envisioned as desired by the Christian God, who looked below with a special benevolence for his American children, the Chosen to lead the Others to the plateau. It was the vision of the progressive historians and their fellows among the general public. The nineteenth century was a time of almost unbounded optimism, when it was believed men (and perhaps women) might lift themselves up by their bootstraps to attain the rewards of peace, prosperity, and power. The twentieth century has recognized the deficiencies of that view and has largely abandoned the dream of the great plateau in the sky, but the folklore remains, a curious remnant rather like the dinosaur or the Neanderthal man, unable to survive or to overcome developmental deficiencies.

Whatever else the *Weltanschauung* of the nineteenth century may have been, in the United States it was unquestionably progressive, beginning with the news of the arrival of the common man in the early part of the century and gaining momentum with the startling message of Charles Darwin in 1859 that man was an evolutionary creature attaining ever higher levels of development. Social Darwinism, which achieved its most fanatical support in the United States in the last third of the century — a period Mark Twain brilliantly described as "the gilded age" — was marked by twenty-league strides of militant capitalism with its gospel of wealth. The nationalistic impulses generated by the Jacksonians and the seductive lure of Manifest Destiny matured now into a doctrine that preached that wealth was good and American wealth was best of all, and that the holy mission of American institutions, not the least among them the press, was to spread the Word, whether through verbal symbols or through the sword. Progress was the story of mankind, and the press was its prophet. Journalism historians seem to have been especially susceptible to the plateau virus; they have painted the past in brilliant colors, splashed on the canvas of history by the Franklins and the Greeleys, the Danas and the Pulitzers, the forerunners of a mighty press that by elevating the knowledge and understanding of the people would lead them to the plateau, perhaps another version of that City Upon a Hill that Winthrop had envisioned in the New World.

As non-Americans have recognized, it was a stirringly nationalistic vision; the corrupt and expiring empires of Europe were to be left behind, even ignored. The world that was to be conquered was the American continent, and the restless energy of the nineteenth century was to be collected and channeled into the quest for the plateau. This nineteenth-century vision formed the foundation of the earliest histories of American journalism, chief among them the work of Frederic Hudson, managing editor of *The New York Herald*. The leading historians of the twentieth century, Willard G. Bleyer, Frank Luther Mott, and Edwin Emery, approached the history of journalism from an identical perspective, envisioning it as a tale of the Great Men of the press, of their influence on the development of the news media, and of the vast importance of the press in the growth of a powerful America. The word "mediocentric" describes their vision. It is a false vision, but no more false than the vision of historians in other fields whose sight is restricted by the narrowness of their aims. Indeed, this progressive image dominated thought and perceptions long after it was discredited and continues to infect the American perception of history, even though it has been challenged successfully since the 1950s. No one has as yet advanced a new synthesis of what has been learned through studies of the growth of cities and ideas, the pasts of blacks, women, the working class, and other groups overlooked by the Progressive historians. Herbert Gutman referred to "sophisticated and simple-minded 'theories' of unilinear progress." And the European intellectual historian Frank Manuel observed: "Much of nineteenth-century American history has been too thoroughly enveloped in nauseating fumes of official optimism to be tolerable to a human being." Such a simplistic view of the development of the press has persisted deep into the twentieth century.

THE PENNY PRESS

There is little reason to doubt that the human spirit craves information: we all want to know. Less clear, however, is an understanding of what it is that we want to know. Information is wanted by everyone, but what kind of information? The producers of the penny press arrived at the decision that what a mass audience desired was excitement and gossip, and they provided for the institution of journalism an enduring — if questionable — definition of "news," a definition that has spread around the planet, although the definition is by no means universal.

It is instructive to examine the first issue of Ben Day's *Sun*. Its mission, Day told his readers, was to shine for all, but in its first issue, the *Sun* cast its rays lightly on light subjects: a tale of an Irish captain, a poem entitled "August Noon," a paragraph about the delights of very small objects, police-court proceedings, advertisements, and other short items. No more than a brief moment was demanded of the reader of any item; the paper made no effort at all to report political events. Its purpose, Day wrote, was "to lay before the public, at a price within the means of everyone, all the news of the day, and at the same time afford an advantageous medium for advertising." To present "all the news," as Day put it, he would devote a small volume of space to a large number of items, and most of those items were what later came to be known in the world of journalism as "human-interest stories." Clearly, the pattern of the *Sun* and the papers that appeared as competitors almost at once was one that found ready acceptance among the new readership, the workers whose social class had been virtually ignored by the older commercial press. These were the "democratic men" to whom Jackson appealed and who were now developing a sense of identity as citizens in the American democratic experiment; these were the urban proletarians, and now they were being made part of the system, insiders instead of outsiders. In short, they had been coopted into the belief that they were significant elements in the decision-making process of the social order. The penny press, an excellent instrument for social control, served a variety of purposes. For the printer, it was a source of potential wealth; for the working-class reader, it was a source of entertainment, a glimpse into the lives of both peers and leaders, an instrument to help soften the hard, boring life of the new urban centers; for the political leader, it was a potential instrument for propaganda, for swaying the reader to support for himself or opposition to his foe; and for the commercial entrepreneur, it was a device for reaching a large group of potential buyers. When Ben Day sold the *Sun* to his brother-in-law in 1838, the price was $40,000; he had launched the paper with no capital at all. Day was the first of many who would make fortunes, small and large, out of publishing newspapers. When he arrived in New York City as a twenty-year-old compositor, Day was virtually penniless. Those who quickly copied Day's formula, men such as Horace Greeley and James Gordon Bennett, also made spectacular gains. Joseph Pulitzer, who came along half a century later, made even more dramatic advances, as did Adolph Ochs, who founded *The New York Times* in 1896. However, none of the earlier publishers amassed the prestige and wealth of Pulitzer, who emigrated from Hungary to adopt and modify the formula originated by Day and his contemporaries.

The appeal to "human interest" was not an American invention. English periodicals began experimenting with inexpensive publications in the early days of the nineteenth century. Those periodicals combined popular fiction and brief news items in packets that sold for a penny; their success was built largely on short articles on the proceedings of the Bow Street police court: crime played a crucial part not only in the fiction they printed but also in their "news" items. New England papers began experimenting with "story" newspapers, and no doubt Day, a native of Connecticut, had observed these efforts before going to New York. So had the editors of other New York dailies, but their timing was not as good as Day's. Nor did they have the advantage of George Wisner, the man Day hired as his editor shortly after the *Sun* began publication. Wisner's writing was sharp and colorful; his world was the world of brevity, the vernacular of the streets, simplification, crime, gossip. Wisner was outspoken in condemning the verbosity and dullness of the older papers and publicly refused to cater to the interests of the cultural elite. Predictably, the editors of the commercial papers sneered at the *Sun* as vulgar and degraded. But soon the editors of the older papers came to accept the vulgarization and to adopt it themselves.

No paper in colonial America had stronger literary pretensions than *The New York Evening Post*, whose publisher-editor was no less a figure than the poet William Cullen Bryant. When Bryant took over the paper in 1829, the year Jackson assumed office, its news pages consisted of little but information about the arrival and departure of ships, other commercial information, and the proceedings in Congress; its intention was in no way to provide news for the masses. The man Bryant chose as his editor, the romantic poet-essayist William Leggett (whose life is fictionalized in Gore Vidal's historical novel *Burr*), soon spoke out in support of the penny press because, as he wrote, it "communicates knowledge to those who had no means of acquiring it. It calls into exercise minds that before rusted unused." Leggett, who was a bit of a social reformer, commented that the man who writes for the masses has readers whose opinions are unformed and "whose minds are ductile and open to new impressions, and whose characters he, in some measure, moulds."

That idea, that it was in their power to mold the minds and opinions of their readers, has motivated many thousands of journalists over the years. That idea has attracted into the field of journalism many thousands of young men and women with an itch to reform society, to direct and implement social change. That many among those thousands were doomed to passionate disappointment has been well recorded, and yet the idea continues to fire the minds of men and women all over the world. As Leo Rosten commented in his excellent study, *The Washington Correspondents*: "Scratch a journalist and you will find a reformer."

The masses were not yet literate; universal education would not become a staple in American society for years to come, but it emerged as a principle, preached by Horace Mann as director of education for Massachusetts as early as 1837. The ranks of the masses swelled throughout the nineteenth century as the "downtrodden masses yearning to be free" swarmed across the Atlantic from Europe to seek their fortunes in the "land of unlimited opportunity"; between 1821 and 1850, an estimated two and a half million persons emigrated to the United States, many of them unschooled in English and large numbers among them settling in the teeming urban centers, the beginning of an indigenous American proletariat. The penny press would not only help accustom them to life in their new land but also strengthen or weaken their images of the country and its people, images they in turn would pass on to their children. Among the immigrants, many sought land in the opening regions of the West, joining the parade of covered wagons that led to the creation of thousands of villages and towns. In many of those villages and towns, enterprising printers and editors founded newspapers, printing information about political and economic activities, and seeking to spread the message of union and community. It was a message that would be repeated across the land and repeated a century and more later in the new nations of Africa and Asia.

The developmental period in the United States was an age of ferment. Not only were immigrants arriving, not only were factories being built, and not only was the new politics of the "common man" being formed, but an age of romantic reform was being carried out in the spirit of democratic zeal. Dorothea Dix worked to assist criminals and the insane; Samuel Gridley Howe promoted the ideal of community, in which the handicapped, criminals, and defectives would not be walled off but would be perfected through constant contact with the community; Ralph Waldo Emerson, Henry David Thoreau, and many others dreamed of ideal communities practicing total individualism. Reformers rallied behind the cause of abolition of slavery, and Theodore Parker, the influential Unitarian minister, urged moral revolution, even if it meant political revolt. Walt Whitman dreamed his dream of the common man and of America as the champion of a world of brotherhood. The penny press picked up each of these themes and preached them across the land.

Jackson and his advisers extolled the common man and invested in him unlimited virtue; in their adulation there is a remarkable similarity to the glorification of the proletariat in the writings of Karl Marx, a contemporary of the American reformers of the mid-nineteenth century. Indeed, Marx wrote articles from abroad for Horace Greeley's *New York Tribune*. Among those praising the American common man, none was more influential than George Bancroft, a close ally of Jackson who came to be recognized as America's first historian. Bancroft assigned absolute virtue and power to the common man:

> If the sentiment of truth, justice, love, and beauty exists in everyone then it follows, as a necessary consequence, that the common judgment in taste, politics, and religion is the highest authority on earth.

The leadership of the urban radical movement rested in the hands of a group of New York City workers who came to be known as the Locofocos, because of their use of "locofoco" matches and candles at a Tammany Hall meeting in 1835; they were assimilated into the Democratic party in the administration of Jackson's successor, Martin Van Buren. Isaac Pray, the biographer of editor James Gordon Bennett of *The New York Herald*, the most successful of the penny press, made this revealing comment:

> "Loco Foco" Matches came into use with penny newspapers, and, in fact, the progress of matches and newspapers has been somewhat analogous. The improvement of one has been attended by a corresponding improvement and use of the other. . . . The cheap matches and the cheap newspapers were sold in every street. Families before this had borrowed coals of fire and newspapers of their richer neighbours. With the reduced price, each family had a pride in keeping its own match-box, and in taking its favorite daily journal.

American historians, writers, and editors may have glorified the age of the common man and the penny press; not so visitors from abroad. Charles

Dickens, for example, was horrified. When Dickens arrived in Boston in 1842, he was but one of many distinguished Europeans coming to see for themselves how the new republican experience was working; he was the most famous of the visitors and, as it turned out, the most critical. And of all the institutions that distressed Dickens, none exceeded the press. He found the press a "frightful engine which was poisoning American society." It was arrogant and full of gossip; and, while protected against government censorship, it was, in fact, playing the role of censor itself by excluding anything good from its pages. No one, Dickens said, in his widely read travelogue, can enjoy freedom of opinion or think for himself "without humble reference to a censorship by the press which, for its rampant ignorance and base dishonesty, he utterly loathes and despises in his heart." In short, Dickens attacked the credibility of the press and, in a curiously modern image, complained that it portrayed only the seamy side of life without giving credence to the good impulses in American life. It was a portrait of a sensational press that contributed more to ignorance than understanding:

> ... while that Press has its evil eye in every house, and its black hand in every appointment in the state, from a president to a postman; while, with ribald slander for its only stock in trade, it is the standard literature of an enormous class, who must find their reading in newspaper, or they will not read at all; so long must its odium be upon the country's head, and so long must the evil it works, be plainly visible in the Republic.

The reader who would pursue with interest Dickens's further reflections on the American press is directed to the novel *Martin Chuzzlewit*, which Dickens published in 1844, two years after his visit to the United States, and in which he presents one of the more entertaining — if exaggerated — views of the American press, raucous, uninhibited, gossipy, slanderous, uninformative on any but the most trivial of subjects. However hyperbolic his presentation, Dickens perceived correctly the profitable nature of the penny press, with its open appeal to the common man and his fascination with backstairs gossip.

An earlier, more analytical European observer, Alexis de Tocqueville, the French historian, had seen that the New York City newspapers (there were eleven dailies with a total circulation of 30,000 in 1832, a year before Day gave birth to the penny press) were composed of 75 percent advertising; the remaining quarter, de Tocqueville wrote, was devoted to "political intelligence or trivial anecdotes." The journalist, de Tocqueville found, occupied "a very humble position, with a scanty education and a vulgar turn of mind." In addition:

> The characteristics of the American journalist consist in an open and coarse appeal to the passions of his readers; he abandons principles to assail the

characters of individuals, to track them into private life, and disclose all their weaknesses and vices.

It was the aristocrat de Tocqueville who spoke most tellingly of the potential "tyranny of the majority," and while he applauded the principles of democracy, he expressed grave concern for the emphasis in the United States on equality rather than on freedom. In this praise of equality, the press, he observed, was an indispensable factor, especially since it seemed to be speaking with a single voice: "When many organs of the press adopt the same line of conduct, their influence in the long run becomes irresistible." The potential of propaganda is especially great when it is unopposed and when it reflects majority opinion: "Public opinion, perpetually assailed from the same side, eventually yields to the attack. In the United States, each separate journal exercises but little authority; but the power of the periodical press is second only to that of the people."

The word socialization was unfamiliar in de Tocqueville's day, but the phenomenon was not unrecognized, at least by this thoughtful visitor. He saw how a press that reflected popular values might reinforce those values and contribute to a pattern Richard Hofstadter was to identify more than a century later as the anti-intellectual impulses in American life. In the twentieth century, press theorists in Asia and Africa would apply the U.S. experience to their own societies as they sought to use the press to build nations of many diverse ethnic and religious elements.

Among the editors of the penny press were reformers and charlatans; yet each of them was motivated by a desire for profit and the power that would come with prominence. Greeley was the prototype of Horatio Alger's rags-to-riches heroes. Like Day, Greeley came from New England to New York (he was born in New Hampshire) to find his fortune. Young Horace is said to have arrived in New York in 1831 at the age of twenty, carrying over his shoulder the traditional stick and bandanna containing his entire fortune: ten dollars. He was to become the most prominent editor of his day, achieving such fame that he was nominated as Democratic party candidate for president in 1872 (defeated, of course, by Ulysses S. Grant). Greeley, a self-educated printer, earned enough in ten years as a journeyman printer to buy the *Tribune* in 1841. Unlike Day and Wisner, he promised to elevate the taste of the masses; his paper, he said, would "advance the interests of the people, and promote their Moral, Political and Social Well-being." Greeley's paper did seek out more uplifting fare than the *Sun* and Bennett's *Herald*, which emerged as the *Tribune*'s strongest competitor; still, Greeley published crime news and gossip, as well as substantial political information. A liberal Whig in his early political career, Greeley was an abolitionist and prodded President Lincoln to free the slaves. It was Greeley who introduced into journalism the concept of the interview; he himself journeyed to Salt Lake City in 1859 to submit questions to Brigham Young, the leader of the Mormon church. In those unruly days, Greeley was not only honored but also subjected to public abuse; street fights were not uncommon.

As circulation increased and more and more Americans became readers, newspapers played a larger role in the political process. The lesson that Jackson had learned and had parlayed into his political successes was adopted by those who followed him; leaders of all political groups used the papers and their editors for their own electoral purposes. The government openly used financial reward to win support. Occasionally, as was the case of *Cato*'s Gordon, high government office was held out as an enticement. More often, such direct rewards were not necessary: the editors of the papers, long before they and their papers had achieved prominence, were devoted to particular political causes. In their news columns, they flagrantly supported those causes. For example, Greeley's *Tribune* must have surprised its readers one day in June 1861, when its front-page headline provocatively proclaimed: "Forward to Richmond." That headline was not of Greeley's doing, however; although a supporter of the Union, he was careful to avoid any possibility of being named a warmonger. Not so his talented editor, Charles Dana, who ordered the headline during Greeley's temporary absence. Greeley fired Dana a month later, but Dana was not finished as an agent of the government; in fact, that was precisely what he became. He went to work for the War Department as a special agent for Secretary of War Edwin Stanton, whose job it was to spy on General Grant, of whom Stanton was suspicious. Three years after the war, Dana took over the *Sun* and struggled to lift journalism from the vulgar style promoted by Wisner to a higher level, to the position, Dana said, of "the little sister of literature." Dana's *Sun* did achieve higher standards of writing, and such distinguished practitioners as Mark Twain and Ernest Hemingway would later write for the *Sun*. Still, it was but a small voice in the wilderness, for the inelegant literary bearing of Bennett's *Herald* and of Hearst's *Journal*, which was to follow, was the bread and butter of popular journalism.

Bennett's *Herald* was the most typical and the most successful of the penny press. A Scot, Bennett came to the United States in 1819, worked as a journalist in South Carolina and New York, and then — failing to land a job with Day's *Sun* — invested $500 and launched the *Herald* in 1835. Bennett was the first to proclaim "objectivity" as his goal. "We shall," he told his readers, "endeavor to record the fact, on every public and proper subject, stripped of verbiage and coloring." Unlike Greeley and Dana, he offered no lofty or literary pretensions. "Take no shinplasters" was his motto, and he was determined to attack "all damned rogues" and "to kick all politicians and parsons to the devil." It was the *Herald* that introduced the standard practices of modern journalism; Bennett instituted the idea of "beat" reporters, sent reporters to Wall Street to provide "inside stories" about the country's financial institutions, set up copy desks, and dispatched correspondents to distant cities. A megalomaniac, Bennett announced in print his determination to make his paper the greatest "that ever appeared in the world" and one that would dominate public life. Bennett also made no pretense about his interest in profit, but he also determined to save souls. "A newspaper," he wrote, "can send more souls to heaven, and save more from hell, then all of the churches or chapels in New York." In a passage that may have seemed arrogant to his contemporaries but that expressed an attitude shared by generations of journalists yet to come, Bennett wrote:

> Books have had their day — the theatres have had their day — the temple of religion has had its day. A newspaper can be made to take the lead of all these in the great movements of human thought and human civilization.

While Bennett, Day, and Greeley spoke openly of their interest in profit, it was Adolph Ochs of *The New York Times* who gave the clearest expression to the drive for profit of the early journalistic entrepreneurs. If the others gave impetus to the sensational press, it was Ochs who spoke of the potential conservative impact of the press. The nineteenth century was a world of industrial expansion; of budding commercial empires; of fortunes made and lost in grain, railroads, shipbuilding, mining, and ranching. It was not an era for unblushing pretense of disinterest in wealth. The announcement of the origin of the species by Darwin in 1859 was followed by the rapid growth of Social Darwinism in the United States with its emphasis on the acquisition of money and power, in what Andrew Carnegie blithely defined as "the gospel of wealth." The press, that *nonpareil* instrument of social control, spread the gospel across the land, participating equally in its message and its rewards.

It was not until 1896 that Ochs acquired the *Times*, but it had entered the New York press arena in 1851, directed by another renowned journalist of that colorful age, Henry Raymond, who had himself worked as Greeley's chief assistant on the *Tribune* ten years earlier. Ochs's most important contribution to the history of the press was his return to the principle, begun centuries ago by the *scrittori* of Venice, that "news" was itself a highly salable commodity. Gay Talese made the point tellingly in *The Power and the Glory*, his entertaining history of the *Times*: "Ochs had something to sell — news — and he hoped to sell it dispassionately and with the guarantee that it was reliable and unspoiled and not deviously inspired." How did Ochs's concept differ from that of the penny-press magnates and even from that of his own predecessors at the *Times*? It did so by rejecting the penny press's blatant appeal to the working classes; he would not, Ochs insisted, publish a paper that might "soil the breakfast linen." Not for him the shouting of editorial opinions, nor the spectacular prose of Wisner or his successors among the yellow-journalism scribes already dominating the New York press scene when Ochs acquired the *Times*. Nor would his paper espouse causes, even the traditional journalistic glorification of the underdog, Jackson's common man. His paper would do no crusading at all but would "give the news, in concise and attractive form . . . impartially, without fear or favor, regardless of any party, sect, or interest involved." The ideal of objectivity, which Bennett had endorsed, however hypocritically, had another champion now, a man who saw profitability in fair presentation of what Ochs decreed as "all the news that's fit to print," a slogan that would continue to grace the pages of the *Times* deep into the twentieth century.

It is not the intention here to suggest a Great Man doctrine for the history of the American press. Day and Greeley, Bennett and Dana, Bryant and Ochs — all these men were creatures of their times, influenced by the expansion of the country, its industrialization and urbanization; they symbolized as well the growth of the press, from a modest, almost unseen institution in the days before the penny press to the ubiquitous, noisy phenomenon it had become by the turn of the century. It had fanned the passions and hatreds of Union and Confederate forces in the Civil War; it had cheered the industrial tycoons in the East and the struggling farmers of the West; it had championed the cause of free speech while sharply restraining the views of those whose ideas it abhorred. As always, it had made men wealthy.

Of all the colorful pressmen of the nineteenth century, none were noisier and more prominent than Pulitzer and Hearst, who lifted sensationalism to its apogee in the great war for circulation and profit that characterized the age of yellow journalism. In the firmament of heroes and villains, Pulitzer is usually cast as "the good guy," although, like a true tragic hero, with distinct character flaws; and Hearst clearly as the desperado in a black hat, damned for all time by the portrait in Orson Welles's *Citizen Kane*. In truth, there was much that was dissimilar in the two men, yet there were also significant points of commonality.

Hearst came from the West and wealth, the son of a mineowner-politician who was at one time a U.S. senator from California; Pulitzer was a poor Jewish immigrant from Hungary who made it to the Land of Unlimited Opportunity by enlisting in the Union army during the Civil War. Both came to New York City after learning the newspaper business in provincial centers, Pulitzer in Saint Louis and Hearst in San Francisco. By 1880, each of these cities was a flourishing journalistic center whose newspapers were already pursuing the sensational patterns soon to dominate the American press scene. Pulitzer arrived in New York in 1883; Hearst a dozen years later, when he launched the most dramatic circulation war in press history. The pursuit of great circulations was made possible by the revolutionary discovery in the late 1880s of a process for extracting web paper from wood pulp, creating a cheap, easily produced form of paper that came to be called newsprint. The circulation of Hearst's *Journal* and Pulitzer's *World* soared past a million, past a million and a half.

The yellow formula was an expansion of the penny-press formula, making profitable use as well of the new technological possibilities. Pulitzer introduced the Sunday edition, Hearst the streamer headline that occupied a quarter of the space on the front page. Cartoons and reproductions of photographs were given lavish display. The incident that gained the greatest public attention was the war with Spain over Cuba. In that war, both Hearst and Pulitzer applauded American imperialism and the triumph of the land of the common man over the forces of aristocracy; it was a democratic crusade, following the dogma pronounced by George Bancroft in the days of Andrew Jackson: "The popular voice is all powerful with us; this . . . is the voice of God." The American mission and its execution at San Juan Hill sent millions of editions rolling off the presses of the *Journal* and the *World*.

The vast circulations did not mean vast profits. The expense of extra editions — the *Journal* issued as many as forty a day — cut into profits; so did the cost of coverage of the war, and advertising revenues declined somewhat as well. But Hearst and Pulitzer were nonetheless growing increasingly wealthy, and achieving greater power and prestige. It may well be that both men desired power and prestige above wealth. Psycho-historians would find Hearst and Pulitzer splendid subjects for analysis; certainly, each was a driven man with bottomless wells of energy that sent him forth on a quest for newer challenges, newer fields to conquer. While even the apologists for Hearst can find little in their hero's personality to applaud, there is much that is attractive in Pulitzer the man. Hearst rarely failed to appeal to the emotions; his chief editorialist, Arthur McEwen, once said that, above all, his paper sought the "gee-whiz emotion," an emphasis on "love for the woman, power for the man." Pulitzer, however, frequently appealed to the mind. Historian George Juergens said that under Pulitzer the newspaper became "a high work of art," made not only to sell but also to be responsible to the public. Pulitzer himself was to apologize for his frenetic quest for circulation, but he said that it was necessary: if he were to have "any influence, to accomplish anything worthwhile, it was necessary to have a great circulation." Certainly, he saw his *World* as having great power for good:

> The *World* should be more powerful than the President. He is fettered by partisanship and politics and has only a four years' term.

While Hearst remained a yellow journalist to the end, Pulitzer abandoned the excesses of sensationalism; in the last ten years of his life (1901–11), the *World* emerged as perhaps the most highly respected newspaper in American press history, known among insiders as "the newspaperman's newspaper." The tradition continued following his death, especially during the tenure of Frank Cobb, who remained as editor until his death in 1923. The *World* survived another eight years but died in 1931, a victim, ironically enough, of the intensive competition from the newest version of the yellow press, the tabloid, as well as from the increasingly strong challenge of *The New York Times*.

In the heady days at the close of the nineteenth century and in the early years of the twentieth century, circulation of newspapers increased across the country, spurred by the mass appeal of the sensational formula. It has been estimated that at least a third of the newspapers in the country's urban centers were strongly yellow in the year 1900, with many others, even in smaller communities, relying to a lesser degree on sensational techniques. Increased circulation meant higher profits, but the major source of wealth for the new breed of publisher was advertising revenue.

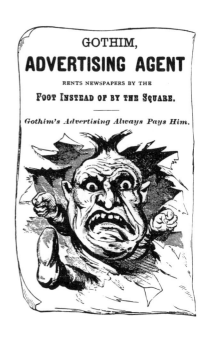

Newspaper advertisements, old style.

Four

Raking Muck and Dollars:
Of Peddling and Prying

THE RISE OF ADVERTISING

The evolution of the press from an instrument of information for the elite
to a product for consumption by a mass audience transformed its nature.
Thus, it can be said that before the rise of the penny newspapers, there was
no press in any contemporary sense of that term. This is so not only
because the shape of "news" was altered to make it more dramatic and
hence more appealing to a mass audience, but equally because the
newspaper itself was changing from a source of intelligence for those
engaged in commerce to a commodity for use by the entire market. A
commodity is an article of trade or commerce that can be transported.
Commodities are most often conceived as agricultural or mining products,
but the mass newspapers supplied information not only about agricultural
and mineral products but about all items available for purchase in the
market. We shall return to the market model in chapter six; it is sufficient
here to point out the significance of the evolutionary development — for
simultaneously with the growth of the mass media, there arose the modern
advertising industry.

It is not to be thought that advertising was a new phenomenon,
appearing only with the penny press; it is to be noted, however, that great
wealth was not possible for the publisher until he was able to solicit for
commercial notices among retailers and manufacturers. From the appear-

ance of the penny press in 1833 until the Bolshevik revolution of 1917, the press in all industrialized societies developed a similar pattern: Whatever its role as a political force or as an instrument for public education, it was expected above all to serve as an agent for the supply of information about products available for purchase by the readers, as an agent of commerce — or, more precisely, as a commodity.

Interestingly, many journalists, in the nineteenth as well as the twentieth century, spoke out, sometimes in violent terms, against debasement of the press from an educational instrument to a crass commercial enterprise. It has been rare for a journalist to recognize the anomaly of working inside a commercial enterprise and tasting of the rewards therefrom while at the same time condemning the very commercialism that is providing him or her with those rewards. In understanding the nature of the commercial press, one must be aware of the paradox inherent in an institution devoted to the lofty ideals of the First Amendment and at the same time a commodity in the marketplace. The great muckraking tradition that rose in the United States in indignant condemnation of corruption among financiers and businessmen came as the owners of the press were acquiring great wealth in marketing their commodity. This parallel development is but one of the many anomalies in the history of journalism.

From the very beginning, newspapers have been used by those with commercial interests as a source of information in surveying the environment; thus, newspapers served as sources of profit not only for the owners but also for the journalists. Roman correspondents were able to buy their freedom out of their earnings, and the *scrittori* of Venice made a decent living from their information sheets long before Ben Day and James Gordon Bennett made fortunes in the penny press. The advertising of products for general consumption, however, required first of all a consumer economy. And while the number of consumers increased steadily in Europe and the United States following the Industrial Revolution, the "great leap" in consumerism came simultaneously with the rise of the penny papers. These papers were part of the same pattern, a pattern that included the rise of the Common Man and the shift from the elite leadership of the Washingtons and Jeffersons to the Coonskin Democrats of the Jacksons and the Lincolns. The democratizing impulses inside the United States were slower to arrive in Old Europe and the newer countries of Latin America, but they appeared there as well, and more and more columns of newspapers were devoted to advertising messages.

Students of advertising tend to classify the medium in four categories: *display* (local or national messages originating from retail merchants), *classified* (commercial messages originating from individuals), *public notices* (social and/or legal announcements), and *political* advertisements. The lines of classification are not always clear, for there is a good deal of overlap; in the early years of the penny press, display advertising closely resembled what is now known as classified advertising. These display — née classified — insertions were the financial lifeblood of the publishers of the penny press, for reducing the price of their wares sixfold demanded of them either a massive increase in the number of subscribers or an alternative source of revenue — or, best of all, both. And, of course, it was both sources that provided the required capital. At the same time, public notices were crucial sources of revenue, less so for the wildly successful sensational press than for the more sedate small-town newspapers.

Advertising in one form or another has been an ingredient of printed periodicals from their earliest days. In England, the publication of a new book was announced in a paper as early as 1625; the notice stirred a flurry of criticism, however, from printers who did not consider such information to be "news." It remained for the next generation to publish the second recorded advertisement, and this one was for a commodity: coffee. *The Publick Advisor* in 1657 urged its readers to buy coffee, which it described as a kind of miracle elixir; according to the insertion, the product "helpeth the digestion, quicketh the spirits...is good against eyesores, coughs, or colds, rhumes, consumptions, head-ache, dropsie, gout," and assorted other ailments. Despite the appearance of such messages, the incidence of advertising was small throughout the seventeenth century and for the first half of the eighteenth century in England, the countries of Europe, and the American colonies. The elite readership complained frequently that such insertions took space away from the commercial and political items in which it was interested, and many publishers concurred. Moreover, early advertisements were roundly condemned on the ground they were untrue and publicized quack remedies. For more than two centuries, patent medicines remained the chief items advertised in American newspapers.

By the middle of the eighteenth century, advertising revenues were beginning to play an important role in the financing of newspapers, but subscriptions remained the largest factor until the late nineteenth century. By 1750, opposition to advertising began to wane, no doubt because it had become increasingly clear that commerce among the colonies helped assure independence and well-being. Benjamin Franklin openly endorsed the practice and regularly published two columns of ads per issue. Still, it was not until the nineteenth century that advertising began to be an element of major significance in the operation of newspapers. More than a few editors refused to solicit or even accept paid announcements, and criticism by readers remained strong.

The fact that the early press served primarily the interests of the upper classes gave rise to a special motivation for those who did publish the commercial notices: Advertisements were a way to confirm support for individual papers by the business community, just as the earlier proud pronouncements that certain newspapers were issued on the authority of government were a source of confirmation of the worth of the product. *The New York Morning Courier*, one of the leaders of the traditional press in the years just prior to the appearance of the penny press, summed up the attitude succinctly:

> ... commercial patronage is best, safest and most unstraying of any, and less affected by prejudice, whim, or petulance than any others. Merchants are ever ready to bestow their confidence and their support on those who exhibit zeal, industry and vigilance in their service and devotedness to their interests.

One cannot be certain of a causal connection between the penny press and the expansion of the advertising industry; each was a phenomenon whose time had come, and each needed the other if it were to prosper. In the decade that preceded the appearance of Ben Day's *Sun*, the pages of newspapers devoted to commercial messages increased steadily. In 1829, when *The Morning Courier* merged with *The New York Enquirer*, the new publication printed so many ads that it was able to issue four-page supplements on Saturdays and occasionally two-page inserts on other days. By 1835, the pages of the *Sun* were so filled with ads that it had room for only five columns of reading matter in a paper with a total of twenty columns. The small-town provincial press was even more overloaded with ads. The space devoted to ads in *The Pittsburgh Gazette* in 1833 consumed 74 percent of the paper; by 1860, the high mark of the advertising cornucopia, the *Gazette*'s ad content was up to 83 percent.

Prior to the 1830s, when the press was still serving primarily the interests of the upper classes, commercial notices were written for the merchants, manufacturers, gentlemen farmers, and government officials who subscribed to the papers, but now a new commercial enterprise had appeared on the scene to fill the advertising needs of the penny press: the department store, itself a product of the development consumerism. Before the department store entered the advertising lists, the space assigned to commercial notices was limited; now more space was needed to promote a larger volume of wares, and the brief classified items began to be replaced by larger display ads.

The development was mutually beneficial to advertiser and publisher. The demand for space for advertisements meant that more pages were needed to accommodate the ads and also to provide more room for the dramatic articles that filled the news pages. The press industry indulged in a binge of expansion, with almost guaranteed circulation as readers eagerly paid their pennies to receive their daily dose of sensational news items and advertising messages. Publishers no longer had to scrounge for subscribers; disappearing also was the desire for patronage benefits from government or political parties. The newspaper now represented a way to take quick advantage of the expanding capitalistic economy. We will return to the relationship between the early press and the political system, but the point to be noted is that the history of the newspaper illustrates the growing dominance of economic forces in the social and political order of the nineteenth century. Power had suddenly been vested in a new economic force: the advertiser. For it was now the advertiser who was paying the greatest share of the cost of producing newspapers, and the press itself was suddenly depending for its financial success mainly on advertising.

THE "GIGANTIC ENGINES OF PUBLICITY"

If the newspaper was a commodity, it was widely assumed to be a form of public utility, supplying the needs of the public for information about political issues and goods for sale, just as the barge and the train supplied the public need for transportation. The courts were later to rule that the newspaper is not a public utility (and hence is not automatically required to accept material submitted to it for publication). Whatever the readers may have thought, newspaper owners have never acted as if they were producing a public utility. The press has operated less in terms of what the reading public wanted of it than in terms of what the merchants who supplied the advertising revenue desired. However, it would be grossly unfair to characterize journalists as ignoring the question of public interest. Even as writers and editors were surrendering financial control of their newspapers to business managers and advertising solicitors, they were insisting on their independence as servants of the public. And disputes between journalists and business managers among the mass media have by no means subsided. In the nineteenth century, editors such as Horace Greeley roundly condemned those who would submit false ads or puffed-up messages designed to deceive the reader, and *The New York Times* came to change its course and refuse to accept patent-medicine advertising. Still, it would be difficult to imagine any editor so saintly as to fail to take advantage of the great bonanza then available, and some were naive enough, or frank enough, to express openly their devotion to the advertiser above the reader. Rejecting public outcries against the quackery of patent-medicine announcements, the *Herald*'s James Gordon Bennett gave this response in 1836 to a reader's protest about the qualities of an elixir advertised by one Dr. Brandeth:

> Send us more advertisements than Dr. Brandeth does — give us higher prices — we'll cut Dr. Brandeth dead — or at least curtail his space. Business is business — money is money ... we permit no blockhead to interfere with our business.

Business is business, Bennett said, and the order of the day was *caveat emptor* — let the buyer beware. However, the *Herald* was to modify its own position in another age; as the Civil War drew to its end in 1865, it too refused its pages to patent-medicine advertisers.

It was clear in the 1830s from comments by Bennett and others that, although they espoused the cause of the common man and were — at least in theory — performing a public service for him, the editors saw themselves not as servants to that public but rather as its teachers. There was little shying away on the part of any of the early editors from offering moral as well as political advice to readers, and at best a reluctance to acknowledge the qualifications of the reader to speak with authority equal to the journalist's. The practice of commenting with open arrogance or contempt about reader opinion has largely disappeared, but there remains a clearly implied distance between the convictions and understanding of the journalist on the one hand and those of this reader or viewer on the other. It is a state of mind that on a loftier plane has been characterized by delegates to UNESCO, the United Nations Educational, Scientific, and Cultural Organization, as a "one-way flow of communications," from the top down. Developing nations condemn the speaking down on the part of the press of the industrialized countries to their developing brothers; readers and viewers, less articulate, respond with similar hostility to a condescending attitude on the part of editors and anchormen.

Few writers in a capitalist society have spoken out against the influence of advertisers with less equivocation than Will Irwin, one of the leaders of the muckraking school of journalists in the early years of the twentieth century. In a fifteen-part series in the pages of *Collier's Magazine* in 1911, Irwin found advertisers serving the interests of powers "most dangerous to the commonweal." Irwin traced the growth of newspaper advertising and argued that the failures and the examples of outright corruption that had marked the development of the American press could be blamed not on the advertisers but on greedy newspaper publishers who had allowed their product to become commercial enterprises. The "system" of advertising, Irwin wrote, has been "the main handicap on American journalism in its search for truth." Imbued with the idealism of the folklore of the press, Irwin decried the shift of power from the editorial offices to the boardrooms and the growth of a breed of newspaper editors indistinguishable from the captains of industry, who played golf at the same country clubs and whose news values were identical to those of the directors of Standard Oil. By the twentieth century, Irwin said, it was no longer necessary for advertisers to seek to dictate content, for their allies in the executive offices of newspapers saw things in quite the same way as did the Rockefellers and the Morgans. Irwin's essays, together with *The Brass Check*, a graphic attack on the press industry by another muckraker, Upton Sinclair, exerted for a while a powerful impact on the newspaper industry in the United States, and perhaps even more significantly on the scrutiny of the American press by Marxist analysts in Europe. Irwin's portrait of the power of the advertiser is vivid:

> Slowly at first, then with increasing momentum, advertisers learned their power. Indeed, in certain quarters, the advertising solicitors helped to teach them. For the less conscientious and solidly run newspapers began offering comforts and immunities as a bonus to attract customers. Advertisers got into the way of asking for special privileges; often, in communities where the newspaper were timid and mushy, for every privilege, even to dictating policies. The extent of their demands varied with the local custom of their communities. But finally, in cities like Philadelphia and Boston, an impossible state of affairs confronted even that publisher who cared more to be an editor than a money-maker. The system had grown so set that he must make concession or fail. For if he did not, his rival would get "the business." And without "the business," he could not pay the high editorial salaries, the press bureau fees, the telegraph tolls, the heavy wages to mechanics, which first-class journalism demands. So must he cheapen product, lose circulation, and fade away.

Theorists who endorse a financial underpinning of the press through advertising argue, as Irwin noted, that the profits gained from advertising revenue have over the years led to substantial growth not only in salaries and technological devices but also in the quality of the American press, as it benefited from its well-paid experts and the opportunities for excellence created by technological progress. Others hold out for some form of public financing for the press.

With the growth of advertising revenues, whether for good or ill, the American press did become big business. By 1879, advertising revenue in the printing industry had risen to nearly $40 million dollars, and in the next decade advertising passed subscriptions and sales as the chief source of income in the industry, amounting to over 54 percent of the total. By 1919, the figure exceeded 65 percent. The Sunday edition, which Pulitzer pioneered in the 1880s, became the most lucrative resting place for commercial messages and ballooned to unimaginable dimensions. The twenty-fifth anniversary edition of Pulitzer's *World*, appearing on Sunday, May 10, 1908, boasted 200 pages, with more than 116 devoted to advertisements. The average number of pages in Sunday papers at the turn of the century was 54. Meanwhile, the per capita consumption of newsprint in the United States rose from six to sixteen pounds in the 1890s and reached twenty-five pounds by 1910. New fields of employment opened up, not only for advertising agents but also for dealers in public relations and the manufacture of images. Press agents became almost as familiar in the corridors of newspapers as the journalists themselves; all, of course, were selling something. Sociologist Alfred McClung Lee speaks of "gigantic engines of publicity," observing, mildly enough, that they "enabled newspapers to become stable business ventures, and they changed drastically the nature of editorial content."

Circulation was chosen as the advertiser's unit of measurement. The greater the circulation of the newspaper, the more eager was the advertiser to announce his wares in that publication; higher rates could be demanded when more readers were guaranteed to receive the messages. It was apparent to the managers of the press that their news columns had to present material of the widest possible public appeal if high circulations were to be maintained and large numbers of advertisers attracted. Demand for weighty articles all but disappeared, although the *World*, the *Times*, and the *Tribune* sought to direct a significant portion of their appeal to an elite audience. On the whole, however, the press that expanded and grew wealthy in the great surge of advertising and vast circulations concentrated its efforts on the formula originated in the days of the penny newspapers: heavy emphasis on "human-interest stories," on crime and romance, on gossip and entertainment. The increasing use of photographs and changes in format to render the product more "readable" led to a packaging of information not unlike that in display cases in department stores, with local news occupying a separate package — or aisle — from state, national, and international news, while "sports" news was distinct from "business" or from "women's" news. Speed became crucial. Relationships were blurred and information came in discrete dosages designed more to please the reader than to induce him to think. A popular "how-to" book that appeared in 1901 illustrates the formula:

> As an aid to securing advertising, the paper should make the most of every opportunity to demonstrate its progressiveness, be the first to bulletin news and the first to print it, and always endeavor to convey the impression that it is growing continuously and rapidly.

Progressiveness, the byword of the liberal community, was to be manifested by speed, by changes in format, and by convincing the reader the paper was doing "new" things in technology and design. Moreover, Hearst maintained that it was the business of the newspaper to give the reader the warm feeling that the content of the paper was designed to meet his wishes, that it was, in fact, "his" paper. The first step in this direction, according to Hearst, was "to stop being conventional in the editorial columns." To do what had always been done, to be traditional, was *bad business*. Although yellow journalism has acquired a negative connotation, many of its qualities continue to be seen as virtuous. Newspapers and broadcasting stations have by no means ceased to measure quality on the basis of speed, of innovation, and of circulation — or ratings.

Many editors, then as now, campaigned strenuously to limit the influence of commercial forces. They found themselves struggling against puffery, the inflating of claims about the qualities of merchandise, as well as against outright lies and clever manipulation of journalists on the part of press agents, who provided free trips, free tickets, and free products in return for articles about their merchandise. Many editors railed against such practices in speeches, in leading articles, and sometimes in the pages of trade publications, the first of which, *The Journalist: A Magazine for All Who Read and Write*, appeared in 1884. In an 1887 issue, poet Eugene Field parodied the practice of newspapermen accepting free tickets from railroads in exchange for favorable articles by reporting an imaginary schedule of advertising rates:

> For the setting forth of virtues (actual or alleged) of presidents, general managers, or directors, $2 per line for the first insertion, and $1 for each subsequent insertion. . . . For complimentary notices of the wives and children of railroad officials, we demand $1.50 per line. . . . We are prepared to supply a fine line of heptameter puffs, also a limited number of sonnets and triolets, in exchange for 1,000 mile tickets. Epic poems, containing descriptions of scenery, dining cars, etc., will be published at special rates.

The inventiveness of pioneer press agents was boundless. With no limitations on their imaginations, they created the concept of "shopping notes," which were free, often quite well-written articles about items for sale, distributed to newspapers to use as filler copy or sometimes even as front-page articles. So advanced did puffery become that advertising agents succeeded in sneaking notices past editors even when they were on the lookout for hidden messages. The extravagance of the advertising industry ultimately came under attack by the U.S. government, and in the heyday of the Progressive movement, the government responded. The Federal Postage Act of 1912 required that all paid insertions sent through the mail be labeled as advertisements in the pages of the newspapers. At first, the American Newspaper Publishers Association, a trade group established in 1887 largely in an effort to police advertising agencies, condemned the law as interference with press freedom. But later, the organization ceased its opposition and accepted as legal the authority of the federal government to impose certain restrictions on advertising practices. The merits and demerits of government regulation of advertising practices has been a subject of intense interest to publishers down to the present.

Many journalists continued to follow their star, to pursue the ideals inherent in the democratic assumption, to resist the seductive blandishments of press agents and promoters, and to maintain a press free of the excesses of sensationalism. Years of struggle against the wild claims of patent-medicine manufacturers finally brought an end to the advertising of the mysterious elixirs in the press; the most effective instrument in this campaign was a series of muckraking articles in *Collier's* by Samuel

Hopkins Adams in 1905 and 1906. *The New York Times* in 1910 published what it called an *Index Expurgatorius* identifying advertisers purged for making false claims and warning the public about additional offenders. Others followed the lead, and in 1914 *The New York Tribune* not only rejected patent-medicine advertisements but proudly boasted it would protect its readers "absolutely against loss or dissatisfaction through the purchase of any wares advertised in its columns." The heyday of quackery and blatantly false advertising had come to an end, but subtler forms of puffery persisted. Not only misleading advertising came under attack by serious editors. Horace Greeley, for example, had urged his fellow editors and publishers as early as 1850 voluntarily to reject special pleading, however lucrative, and to strive for what he called "the public good." Adolph Ochs of *The New York Times* pledged to publish only news and advertisements that were "fit to print." Pulitzer demanded honesty and accuracy. Muckrakers such as Will Irwin, Upton Sinclair, and Lincoln Steffens penned hundreds of articles storming against misuse of the press for personal profit, and the widely respected William Allen White, editor of the *Emporia Gazette*, wrote tirelessly of the need for the American press to seek truth wherever it lay at whatever cost. The editor of that Kansas weekly occupies a special place in press history as a symbol of integrity. In 1905, when the Standard Oil Company was offering heavy bribes for articles favorable to its campaign against restrictive legislation in Kansas, White refused to publish the tables and calculations that the oil company sent to all state editors, inviting them to publish the material "at their own figure." The muckraking magazine *McClure's* wrote that the offer meant as much as $1,000 to Kansas papers whose total annual profits might be no more than $2,500. According to the article, White's paper refused "the fruit," but "there were more which looked and ate." To those who later came to pronounce the doctrine of "social responsibility" for the press, White was perhaps the chief figure in the Hall of Press Heroes.

However heroic White and others less celebrated but equally staunch in their moral integrity may have been, it is evident that as the nineteenth century advanced and was succeeded by the twentieth, a substantial distance could be detected between the kind of press that was conjured up in the visionary days at the birth of the country and that which appeared following the rise of the penny press. The purpose here is not to disparage advertising as an evil force, but rather to demonstrate the weaknesses in the folklore of the press as a fearless seeker of truth that tramples on those who would lead it into temptation.

THE NEWS MANAGERS

Not only commercial interests tempted editors and publishers with financial rewards; so did political forces. From the beginning of the American republic, those in power used the expectation of financial gain to seduce the press into helping sustain their personal and political appetites. The press often did not demand lengthy wooing. In this, the powerful and the press were following a tradition long familiar in Europe. The value of a supportive press in nineteenth-century America was underscored by Martin Van Buren, a New York political leader who later became president of the United States. In a letter to a political ally in 1823, Van Buren observed that without a paper on their side, "we may hang our harps on the willows." But, he added, "with it, the party can survive a thousand such convulsions as those which agitate and probably alarm most of those around you."

The use of the press for political ends was extensively practiced. Attention has been directed to the techniques employed by European and American leaders to promote public backing for their policies. In the United States, law has established the framework for press apologias for those who hold office; it is obvious that the power of incumbents to use the press for political gain is vastly superior to that of those who are out of office. Incumbents are able to make use not only of indirect inducements, but also of the legal machinery itself.

In 1789, even as the Jacobins were taking to the streets in Paris, legislation was adopted in the first U.S. Congress giving the federal government laws that would provide a form of financial control over the press for nearly a century. The act that created the Department of State in September 1789 assigned to the secretary of state the duty to select newspapers to publish the laws and resolutions enacted by Congress. That obligation endured until 1875, through expansion of the country from coast to coast; through the War of 1812, the Mexican War, and the Civil War. Jefferson, the first secretary of state, chose five papers from five states for this form of political patronage, but the demand for these federal subsidies was too great to be limited to but a few papers. In 1799, Congress amended the law to obligate the secretary to choose at least one newspaper in every state and as many as three if one did not seem adequate. The race was on, especially after Madison, as Jefferson's secretary of state, adopted openly a system of rewards for those papers that supported the Jeffersonian program.

Indeed, *all* papers were indebted to the federal government financially. Whether these monetary benefits were provided in order to insure a docile, supportive press, or whether they were offered because the press was considered a public service, the inescapable effect was a press establishment in debt to the government; financial survival might very well depend on government largesse. The most significant subsidy provided to the press was in terms of postal rates. Between 1792 and 1845, rates assigned for letters ranged from six cents to twenty-five cents depending on the distance, but the maximum for a newspaper, whatever the distance, was a penny and a half. Even more beneficial to the newspaper was the provision of a fixed rate for papers, however much the product weighed. The rate for letters rose sharply as their weight increased. The same 1792 act that fixed postal rates also authorized newspaper publishers to send their papers free of charge to other publishers. Whenever a newspaper challenged the government, it was, its publisher knew, courting fiscal suicide. Fear of financial loss did not, however, always deter editors and publishers from attacking the government, but the practice of seeking favor was far more common, especially in the scramble to win contracts as official printers of government documents.

The appearance of the Government Printing Office in 1860 signaled the end of formal government patronage of the newspaper industry, although vestiges of the practice survived for another fifteen years. The end of the patronage system came after millions of dollars in windfall profits had been received by printers. Corruption and scandal were widespread, and wild disorder marked congressional debate on the issue.

In the administration of Franklin Pierce (1853–1857), the cost of government printing came to nearly $4 million, a figure higher than that of the total for the previous forty-four years. The bitter battles over the extension of slavery had played a part in the increase, but so too had the pressures to use the press to build a public opinion favorable to Pierce's policies. The charges and countercharges did not subside in the ensuing administration of James Buchanan (1857–1861), the last before the Civil War, and a Senate committee in 1860 concluded unanimously that the patronage system of public printing was "the worst that could have been adopted. And from its very nature inviting not only a profuse expenditure, but corrupting in its tendencies." By authorizing the General Printing Office in June of that year, Congress ended its dependence on newspapers and private contractors for its printing needs.

A great many newspapers had grown strong financially under the old system of subsidies for printing. In a number of instances, notably in the Jackson administration, journalists were rewarded with high office; Amos Kendall was perhaps foremost among the Jacksonian journalists, but Francis Blair, another Kentucky journalist, also achieved great prominence under Jackson and Van Buren as the publisher of the official White House organ, *The Congressional Globe*. In the ensuing century and a half, many hundreds of journalists moved from their newspapers to government positions. But the most effective instrument of presidential influence was neither the direct subsidy nor the promise of office. It was the practice begun by President Jackson of "management" of the news. It was not until well into the twentieth century that the concept of "news management" came to be recognized, but it had long been widespread.

News management refers to the practice, typically employing some form of duplicity, of seeing to it that what is printed is what the news manager wants printed. For example, if a president desired, as Jackson did, to have newspapers report his veto of the extension of the Second Bank in 1836 as an action taken on behalf of the "common man," the lower classes, in opposition to the vested interests of rapacious bankers, then it was the task of the president and his press agents to make sure that this was how the veto message was reported. It would have been far more difficult for Jackson to "sell" his veto to the public if it were reported in the press as motivated by a desire to crush the power of Nicholas Biddle, the president of the bank, who was not only a formidable political foe but also a leader of the urbane eastern aristocracy that represented the chief opposition to Jackson's "democratic revolution." In short, news management is a form of skillful press agentry; it can be — and is — practiced quite as deftly by resourceful politicians as it is by accomplished public relations specialists.

Put another way, news management is a form of social control. The president, or the advertiser, or the circus promoter, or whoever it is who is seeking to manage the news is attempting to evoke in print an image of reality that is of benefit to him. The president may want to win public endorsement of a policy; the advertiser may want to sell a product; the circus promoter may want to convince readers to pay their way into the big tent — in whichever case, the news manager is seeking to manipulate the press into serving his ends. In such situations, the press as an institution is serving as an instrument for the gaining of certain ends, sometimes public, sometimes private. The same opportunity for manipulation is available to others less powerful than presidents, advertisers, or circus promoters, but it is far more difficult for them to use the press to achieve their private ends than it is for presidents, advertisers, or circus promoters, who have special claims on the attention of journalists by virtue of their position or their wealth.

THE LONELY JOURNALIST

According to the folklore of the press, the news media, by exposing graft and corruption, may change the direction of public policy. Not only that; the press, by pointing out wickedness in high places, also can cause the wicked to be brought to grief so that the forces of good may prevail. An illustration of this belief is the enforced resignation of President Nixon as the result of articles about the break-in at the Watergate; or the end of the war in Vietnam. The belief is remarkably widespread; it is associated with the "watchdog" role of the press — that is, the theory that the press keeps a watchful eye on government or on other mighty institutions so as to remedy abuses of power. Yet, if the press is not an independent institution, it is not of itself capable of remedying abuses of power. It can participate in the remedy but cannot be the causal agent. The folklore is of advantage not only to journalists, whose status is thereby elevated, but also to those who may make use of the press for their own political objectives — the powerful, for example. Those who believed Nixon to be wicked and sought to overthrow him were able to make clever use of the mythology and to manipulate the press into doing their work for them. This is not to say that journalists are without power; in fact, more than a few journalists have achieved prominence and power through their writings, and have sought to exercise that power in the political arena. However, only when the goals of journalists coincide with the goals of the society they inhabit can the journalist achieve his ends. All of Hearst's efforts to promote war with Spain would have been wasted were not the Congress, the president, and the general public ready to fight.

No time frame was more important in the flowering of the legend of press power than the Age of the Muckrakers. It is impossible to assign a precise date for the appearance of the muckrakers, but their arrival accompanied a widespread reaction against the dogma of Twain's Gilded Age, when Social Darwinism adapted the message of natural selection and applied it to the social order, linking itself to the Protestant work ethic; the fittest survived in a competitive setting, which Andrew Carnegie proclaimed was "best for the world," welcoming, as he said, "the concentration of business, industrial and commercial, in the hands of a few." The poor were condemned as unfit, and the railroads, the shipbuilders, the bankers, and the steel and oil companies waxed ever more powerful. Government was unable to confine them, nor indeed did the laissez-faire governmental philosophy permit such confinement. Natural selection demanded no governmental interference; for the government to seek to direct or control the growth of industrial giants was, it was held, not only poor politics but also immoral, since natural selection was part of God's plan; and as John Fiske, the influential American philosopher, put it: "The slow process of mutation in time was part of 'the orderly manifestations of a Divine Power.' "

Surprisingly, many among the poor and the intellectual community embraced the message of Social Darwinism, its accompanying laissez-faire economics, and, perhaps most significantly of all, its glorification of rugged individualism, a glorification that was accompanied by an outpouring of books, plays, and newspaper articles elevating the exploits of the heroic loner, captured especially in the image of the laconic western hero who took his own fate in his hands at high noon. The muckraking journalist was to cast himself in the same mold as the marshal at Dodge City.

The image of the lonely battler struggling against immense odds was given lasting expression by one of the most prominent of the muckraking writers, Ray Stannard Baker. One of his magazine articles was entitled "The Lone Fighter." It appeared in the December 1903 issue of *McClure's* magazine; it related the tales of a union member who reformed his union by winning it away from control by the bosses and of a politician who remained honest under heavy pressure. "It has rather an odd sound, a hero in politics," Baker wrote, "but I want to tell of just such a hero." In a sentence Baker summed up not only the belief system of the muckrakers but the essence of the watchdog imagery: "If this republic is saved, it must be saved by *individual effort.*" His ultimate hero was the lonely journalist fighting against insuperable odds, identical to the lonely sheriff fighting against the mob of outlaws or the lonely politician battling against the mighty machine.

Baker also dabbled in poetry. In verse, he painted his image in sharp lines, especially in a poem he called "The Lone Rider":

> Lone rider on the gray cayuse—
> Gray shadow in an empty land—
> And overhead the burning sky,
>   And underneath, the sand.
>
> Look sharp to the spur, my bronc, my bronc,
> Look sharp to the spur, I say,
> For long lies the trail, the canteens fail.
>   And we ride for our lives this day.

The political hero of the muckrakers was Theodore Roosevelt; no American appeared to be a more vivid incarnation of the lone fighter or the lone rider than Roosevelt, who fought big game on the African plains, the wicked Spanish at San Juan Hill, and the mighty corporations in Washington, D.C. It was TR who supplied the enduring name of muckrakers to the crusading magazine journalists who wrote in the final decade of the nineteenth century and the first of the twentieth.

If muckraking is defined as using the press to battle entrenched power, it was not a new phenomenon. The practice is cited many times in these pages, occurring in Europe as well as in the United States. Where the crusading failed to coincide with prevailing belief, it was unsuccessful, for the powerful were able to muffle the opposition press through intimidation, persuasion, bribery, or incarceration. The opposition press in all cases was part of a social movement directed by individuals who were enemies of those in power; the establishment press, on the other hand, was directed by individuals determined to remain in power. Where the opposition was able to overturn the establishment, the "watchdog" press was applauded as a cause of the overthrow, often by itself, as in the Watergate example or in the case of the American Revolution. In the muckraking era, the watchdog press was part of a large social movement, one that embraced the Progressives and the Populists; the time frame was one of reform, similar in tone to the time frame in the years prior to the Civil War. And in this case, as in the former, the reform movement perished with the outbreak of war.

Among the nineteenth-century political leaders who recognized the utility of a favorable press was Otto von Bismarck, the chief architect of modern Germany. Press freedom, as exemplified in the First Amendment, achieved vast popularity in all the countries of Europe, even though many among them were under the tight control of strong monarchs. Earlier, we saw how in France the issue of press freedom generated political upheaval. In the revolutionary decade of the 1840s in both France and Prussia, free expression was one of the most passionately sought revolutionary demands. The reformist intellectuals who drafted a Prussian constitution at Frankfurt-am-Main in 1848 adopted a proposal that is one of the clearest and most unequivocal ever drawn on press freedom:

> Every German has the right to express his opinions freely in word, handwriting, print, photographs and the graphic arts. The freedom of the press shall under no circumstances and in no way be limited, suspended or prohibited....

Unfortunately for Germans as well as much of the rest of the world, the Frankfurt draft never became German policy, but it did enable opposition newspapers to spring up all over the country in the middle of the nineteenth century, including the *Neue Rheinische Zeitung*, established in Cologne in 1848 by Karl Marx. The opposition newspapers sought unceasingly to play the role of watchdog and to call attention in public print to the authoritarian excesses of the Prussian rulers. When Bismarck was elevated to power as chancellor of Prussia in 1862, he began one of history's most successful efforts to manipulate the press. One year after he was named chancellor, he induced the king to deny the press the right to criticize the government. The English-born wife of the crown prince, Victoria, in proper English fashion characterized Bismarck's views of the press as "medieval," especially after he ordered troops to arrest the editor of a newspaper in a part of Prussia that was then under Austrian suzerainty. At that time, Prussia was building up for war against Austria, and Bismarck was not prepared to tolerate dissident views in the press.

Victory in the Austrian war enabled Bismarck to proclaim the modern German state, with Wilhelm I now assuming the title of emperor. Under the empire, Bismarck's usage of the press shifted directions: no longer would he throw dissidents into prison; no longer would he engage in acts of physical repression. Now he would adopt the more modern tactic of "news management." And as a news manager, Bismarck knew few peers. In this campaign he was assisted by a substantial volume of money at his sole disposal, a source of money that was labeled by the liberal press as *Reptilien-Fonds*, or "reptile fund." Bismarck used the money to bribe the press to propagandize for his policies and for other political objectives; a number of journalists grew wealthy thanks to the reptile fund. Bismarck did not hesitate to use what historian Erich Eyck called his "press dogs" to gain his political ends, some internal, some external. In 1875, despite the fact that he was not in favor of war with France, Bismarck induced journalists to suggest that preventive war was imminent, in articles which agitated Europe. In 1884, he turned his journalists loose on Britain as part of a successful campaign to induce Gladstone to agree to German colonization in Southwest Africa. Bismarck was a master at guiding the German public, although he was careful, especially in his later career, not to veer too far in his public utterances from what he considered the prevailing public opinion. It was under Bismarck that the German press became a factor in power politics, as it had already become in the United States. Bismarck was the first German political leader to be faced with an opposition that appealed to the people over the head of the government. In Bismarck's view, the press was a necessary evil, and he sought, with considerable success, to subvert it to his own ends. *Realpolitik* was his creed. It is interesting to note that Bismarck's policy of suppression and bribery came under attack not only from libertarians but from Nazi ideologues as well. The Nazi writer Hans Muenster held that while Bismarck was correct in seeking to sweep aside liberal journalists, he used the wrong methods, since they were "negative." The National Socialists, Muenster wrote, adopted a "positive" approach, that of substituting "a modern people's press in the service of the state." Simply to condemn or repress, in the Nazi view, was inadequate; what was needed was a new system altogether.

The "reptile" phrase stuck. Journalist-philosopher Walter Lippmann was to apply it to U.S. press policies half a century later. The occasion was the threat on the part of the Coolidge administration in 1926 to intervene in Mexico, which seemed on the verge of nationalizing the oil and mineral holdings of U.S. companies. Lippmann, then chief of the editorial page of *The New York World*, had been speaking out against intervention; so had other journalists. An angered President Coolidge demanded that reporters submit all stories about Mexico for approval, and an equally angry Lippmann condemned any attempt on the part of the government to edit newspapers:

> There is a name for the kind of press Mr. Coolidge seems to desire. It is called a reptile press. This is a press which takes its inspiration from government officials and from great business interests. It prints what those in power wish to have printed. It suppresses what they wish to have suppressed.

It is the duty of the watchdog press to oppose such a policy, and, on this occasion at least, Lippmann found himself a steadfast adherent of the watchdog doctrine, forgetting that a few years earlier he had without critical examination printed what his earlier political heroes had wished to have printed. The pattern of behavior is one that has ensnared journalists throughout history. They have stood ready to take their inspiration from government officials and great business interests when they were expertly manipulated, but they have spoken out vigorously in opposition to those policies when the manipulative practices were less skillful or when those practices ran counter to the folklore of the press. In this sphere, contradictions abound.

The most celebrated case of press watchdoggery before the rise of the muckrakers came in 1870 when *The New York Times*, a sedate newspaper even in the years prior to its acquisition by Adolph Ochs, waged a spirited campaign against the corrupt regime of New York's famed political boss, William Marcy Tweed. Tradition has it that it was the editorial assault by the *Times* that destroyed Tweed's rule and sent him to prison. *The Times* campaign raised to public attention in highly dramatic fashion the details of Boss Tweed's rascality. All through the month of September 1870, the *Times* hammered away at Tweed and his allies, on occasion devoting almost its entire front page to its attacks. On the editorial page, the newspaper attacked not only Tweed and his allies but also Catholics, the Irish, and the poor. Tweed, long accustomed to his own reptile press, to which he provided many thousands of dollars in bribes, hit back by attempting to buy a controlling interest in the *Times*, as well as by offers of bribes and the withholding of advertising revenues owed by the city. His efforts were unsuccessful; moreover, he was helped little by the cartoon portraits of him in *Harper's Weekly* by celebrated caricaturist Thomas Nast, who portrayed Tweed as the monstrous Tiger of Tammany. The Tammany men were defeated in the election of 1871 (except for the boss himself, who won reelection to the state senate). The *Times* did not hesitate to applaud itself and to provide additional ammunition for the folklore of the press:

> For years past the TIMES has been exposing the demoralizing schemes of self-interested politicians, and its recent warfare on the Tammany Democrats has been received with universal approval.... The victory we have won is priceless, not only from what it gives us now, but because it will revive every man's faith in the ultimate triumph of truth and justice — because it will teach scheming politicians that the voice of the people is supreme.

The *Times* left little doubt that it and the press as a whole were expressing the "voice of the people," at least those newspapers that had not been prostituted by the Tweed ring. Tweed himself was ultimately jailed for his part in the misappropriation of public funds, but evidence uncovered later has cast some doubt on both the virtue of *The New York Times* and on the assertion that it was the *Times* alone that got Tweed. For example, although rumors about the wheelings and dealings of the Tammany machine had been circulating for a long time, it was not until after the death of one James Taylor that the *Times* launched its campaign. Taylor, a director of the *Times*, had been a business partner of Tweed, and at his death the city owed the *Times* $13,000 in back advertising bills. Moreover, it appeared that much of the specific evidence that the *Times* was able to print was provided by Samuel J. Tilden, himself a member of Tammany Hall, and a man who aspired not only to the governorship of New York but to the presidency of the United States as well. Tweed, however, endorsed the incumbent governor, John T. Hoffman, and not Tilden. Not long after Tweed's opposition to Tilden became clear, a certain George O'Brien, a Tilden man, handed over the documentary evidence on Tweed to the *Times*. It was Tilden then who helped to organize a mass rally against corruption, who testified before investigative committees, who became governor of New York, and who lost the presidency by a single electoral vote to Rutherford B. Hayes in 1876. On investigation, it seems clear that although the *Times* was an instrument in the downfall of Tweed, in its campaign it was serving as an agent of Tilden and his associates.

THE AGE OF THE MUCKRAKERS

The press campaign against the Tweed ring may have been the last undertaken by the *Times*; under Ochs and his successors, the *Times* spoke out against exposés and sensationalism. As such, it stood largely alone during the days of the yellow press and of the muckrakers. The muckrakers were, in fact, the magazine and book equivalent of the yellow press, although their chief practitioners — Ray Stannard Baker, Will Irwin, Lincoln Steffens, Ida Tarbell, Upton Sinclair, Jack London, Theodore Dreiser, Frank Norris — were outstanding writers and skillful investigators. They operated in an age that was reacting against the gospel of Social Darwinism and its laissez-faire economics in the name of what came to be known as Progressivism. The apparent target of the Progressives was Big Business, which was free to exploit its workers, its public, and even its government in its quest for profits. The great corporations thrived without restraints: no income tax, no labor contracts, no government regulations. Some among the critics of Big Business were Socialists, followers of the ideas of their spiritual leader, Karl Marx, as were their ideological comrades throughout Europe. Most, however, were reformers, bred in the more pragmatic American model, seeking not revolution but curative legislation. Although both revolutionaries and reformers could be found among the muckraking journalists, the revolutionaries attracted only a small following in the conservative American society. Chief among their specific goals was the regulation of government monopolies; they were solidly in the camp of the reform wing of the Republican party, whose hero was Theodore Roosevelt, famed to this day as a buster of trusts and as the father of Bull Moose Progressivism. Astute politician that he was, TR succeeded in harmonizing and arranging the muckraking sonata.

There was much that was similar in the formulas adopted by the magazine muckrakers and the yellow press. Pulitzer and Hearst were themselves reformers, everywhere promoting the cause of the common man or, placed in Marxist terms, the proletariat, the working classes. Hearst, for example, was solidly prolabor in the pages of his newspapers and was able to rely on labor support in his campaigns for political office. Although both the yellow press and the muckrakers lauded the common man, they were also hero-worshipers, demanding an American Napoleon to lead the fight against the giant monopolies and the corrupt politicians they saw as smoothing the way for the excesses of Big Business, much as, half a century earlier, Thomas Carlyle and English reformers had looked for deliverance through omnipotent leaders. The popularity of supermen, Harold Lasswell wrote, is often "due to the dislocation of older economic institutions and the rise of threatening collective ideologies." In a perceptive examination of attitudes in the England of the 1860s, Lasswell wrote:

> The new business enterpriser felt the intoxicating vanity of the self-made man, and the decayed landlords felt the necessity of individualistic protests against the age of cities and machines.

The atmosphere in the United States of the 1890s was remarkably similar. The excessive freedom enjoyed by the captains of industry and banking in the United States was indeed collapsing, and collective ideologies were on the tongue of many seeking to hasten that collapse. It was also an age when personal fame beckoned, when the writer of exposés could achieve not only wealth but also glory. Small wonder that Roosevelt invoked the image of the Pilgrim's Progress in his renowned declaration about the muckrakers.

It was not until 1906 that Roosevelt applied the term muckraker to the crusading journalists, and by that time the movement was already on the decline. Its most spectacular period came in the preceding four years, in a period marked by the appearance of perhaps the most remarkable magazine issue in publishing history, the January 1903 issue of *McClure's*, a periodical that had been providing exposés and critiques of laissez-faire excesses for a decade. S.S. McClure, an ambitious young man who had a clear eye on both political and publishing developments, launched his magazine in 1893 in the spirit of Ben Day: by cutting prices. With magazines selling at twenty-five to thirty-five cents a copy, McClure went on the market with a fifteen-cent periodical. Hearst's *Cosmopolitan* met the challenge by dropping its price to twelve and a half cents, and *Munsey's*, another renowned muckraking sheet, went down to a dime. The same war for circulation that marked competition between Hearst and

Pulitzer hit the magazine industry, and magazine readership soared. *McClure's* circulation leaped from 120,000 in August 1895 to 307,000 in 1900 and to nearly half a million by 1907, before the decline set in. Similar gains were registered by other magazines.

In the famed January 1903 issue of *McClure's*, readers eager to hear about scandal, heartlessness, and graft in high places were treated to the second article in Lincoln Steffens's enduring account of municipal corruption, "The Shame of the Cities," this one about Minneapolis. Even more titillating to the public was the open attack on John D. Rockefeller in Ida Tarbell's "The History of the Standard Oil Company: The Oil War of 1872." It was Ida Tarbell who coined a phrase to dramatize the motive of the muckrakers; she was speaking out, she said, in "righteous indignation." The third of the three outstanding features of that issue was Ray Stannard Baker's "The Right to Work," an attack on the inhumanity of the coal-mining industry in the great miners' strike and a stirring argument for unionization. McClure left little room for the public to miss the point of his issue. In an editorial, he declared his magazine to be the organ of the common man in his struggle against the forces of evil:

> Capitalists, workingmen, politicians, citizens — all breaking the law or letting it be broken. Who is there left to uphold it? . . . there is no one left — none but all of us.

McClure's plays a substantial role in the folklore of the press as the perfect model of a crusading magazine, devoted to careful documentation of its charges. It too was guilty of many excesses, but less so than its chief competitors, *Cosmopolitan* and *Munsey's*, whose crusading arms flailed out in all directions, and whose publishers, like McClure, grew wealthy. The iconoclastic William Allen White called attention to the profit-making of muckrakers on the death of publisher Frank Munsey in 1925:

> Frank Munsey contributed to the journalism of his day the talent of a meat packer, the morals of a money changer and the manners of an undertaker. He and his kind have succeeded in transforming a once-noble profession into an 8 day security. May he rest in trust.

Not all the muckrakers grew rich, however. The socialist agitator Upton Sinclair was one who didn't. In *The Brass Check*, an unabashed attack on the press industry itself, Sinclair snarled at the advertising and public relations industries, demanded public ownership of the means of newspaper production, and called for news agencies to be designated as public utilities under public control. *The Brass Check* and other Sinclair writings contain interpretations that foreshadowed those of Lenin in his analysis of the role of the press.

Few among the muckrakers were prepared to travel Sinclair's path. Their more modest goal was government regulation, especially of railroad rates and of industries directly affecting public health and safety. Roosevelt, who advanced from vice-president to president on the death of William McKinley in 1901, won wide support among the press as a trust buster, as the man who would use the powers of government for the first time to see to it that avaricious industrial lords were forced by a benevolent government to work in the common interest for the benefit of all citizens. His primary target was the railroads, and he labored untiringly to induce Congress to give him the legislation needed to control the railroads and subject their rates to government regulation; those same railroads which for years had enjoyed a favorable press, the result no doubt of the largesse offered to journalists and their families, largesse that was parodied by Eugene Field and others. Roosevelt's vehicle in Congress was a bill introduced in December 1905 by Representative William P. Hepburn of Iowa that not only regulated rail rates but also extended federal jurisdiction to cover storage and terminal facilities, sleeping cars, express companies, and pipelines. The bill also forced the railroads to surrender their interests in steamship lines and coal companies, and, in an action of more than passing interest to journalists, abolished free passes except for railroad employees, the clergy, and some charitable workers. The Hepburn Act was among the most powerful instruments in the destruction of untrammeled laissez-faire economics in the United States; the muckrakers have traditionally been given a large share of the credit for its passage, particularly because of a series of articles by Baker in *McClure's* and *Collier's* endorsing the president's trust-busting efforts and exposing railroad malpractices.

In truth, the press campaign by Baker and others was orchestrated by President Roosevelt, a practice he had begun a score of years earlier when, as police commissioner of New York City, he had sought out journalists and made personal friends of them as a device to put his name and his ideas before the public and those in political power. Baker sent proofs of his first article, completed before Roosevelt ordered a special session of Congress to promote the Hepburn Act, to the White House for Roosevelt's evaluation. In a widely publicized response, Roosevelt wrote Baker that he had not one criticism to make; indeed, he said, all image-making aside, "you have given me two or three thoughts for my own message." When the Hepburn Act was approved by Congress on May 18, 1906, Roosevelt made no effort to derogate Baker's articles. And yet, a month earlier, while the Hepburn Act was still being debated, Roosevelt had made his celebrated public attack on the reformers. It was in that attack that Roosevelt applied the title of muckrakers to the crusading journalists. The term was first used in an off-the-record speech to a society of journalists — the Gridiron Club — but Roosevelt developed his idea further in a speech on April 14 at the cornerstone-laying of the first office building for members of the House of Representatives. Roosevelt turned to the image in Bunyan's *Pilgrim's Progress* of the "Man with the Muckrake," who can "look no way but downward," who refuses to see anything good, but who "fixes his eye with solemn intentness only on that which is vile and debasing." In TR's imagery, it was essential to scrape up the filth on the floor with the muckrake, but it was equally important to recognize the good in life.

But the man who never does anything else, who never thinks or speaks or writes save of his feats with the muckrake, speedily becomes not a help to society, not an incitement to good, but one of the most potent sources of evil.

Roosevelt thus established himself as one in an unbroken line of presidents who delighted in a press that served his interests but despised a press that worked on behalf of his enemies. The experience of Theodore Roosevelt was similar to that of Thomas Jefferson. And, like Jefferson before him, Roosevelt sought to assure those among the press whose views he shared that his attack on the muckrakers was not meant for them. He said so in a private message to Baker and in another that he sent to Lincoln Steffens. It was the Hearst press, the writers of blatant sensationalism, that he had in mind, he told Steffens. And clearly he also had in mind those who were publicly condemning the institutions of capitalism; in his speech on muckrakers, Roosevelt chastised especially "the wild preachers of unrest and discontent, the wild agitators against the entire social order," for these, he said, "were the most dangerous opponents of real reform." In other words, a press in the service of Rooseveltian reform was a good press, but one that did not go far enough or went too far was not to be trusted. Rarely has there been a clearer expression of the agency role of the press in a capitalist society. Yet in his private correspondence, TR went even beyond his muckrake speech. A decade later, in 1915, he wrote the American novelist Winston Churchill that even "the more honest muckrakers," Baker and Steffens, had rarely written statements of fact that Roosevelt could trust.

The irony is delicious, for the muckrakers were not at all men and women who saw only the base and wicked, who were motivated to sort out the dirty linen for its own sake; their goals were romantically lofty. As Baker said in his memoirs: "We 'muckraked' not because we hated our world but because we loved it. We were not hopeless, we were not cynical, we were not bitter." The lone rider they envisaged, a man much like Theodore Roosevelt, had betrayed their trust.

In the later years of the nineteenth century and the early years of the twentieth, the press in the United States and, to a somewhat lesser degree throughout the industrialized world, had waxed powerful and profitable: thanks to increasing revenues from advertising, publishers had raked in the dollars; and thanks to the advancing circulations that accompanied yellow newspapers and muckraking magazines, they had raked in more dollars. The press and the journalists who wrote for it, many now achieving a high level of personal fame, were playing a more and more significant role in the political process, not generally cognizant, however, of how significant that role was. It remained for the dramatic events of the pivotal year of 1917 to bring a larger awareness of that significance and to generate the ideological division that has dominated discussions of the press ever since, in all parts of the world.

PART 2

Lenin as communicator. (*The Bettmann Archive, Inc.*)

Five

The Ideological Press:
The Planned Economy

THE PRESS PHILOSOPHY OF KARL MARX

The year 1917 was a pivotal one in the history of mankind; it marked the beginning of a tidal shift in the seat of power, away from Western Europe, which had dominated the Western world, indeed the entire planet, since the days of the Roman Empire. The shift was both westward and eastward, fulfilling a prophecy of Alexis de Tocqueville nearly a century earlier. All other nations, de Tocqueville wrote, "seem to have reached their natural limits," but the United States to the west and Russia to the east "are proceeding with ease and celerity along a path to which no limit can be perceived." According to de Tocqueville, American strength was based on freedom and Russian on servitude: "Their starting point is different and their courses are not the same; yet each of them seems marked out by the will of Heaven to sway the destinies of half the globe."

In April of 1917, the United States declared war on Germany, ending its preoccupation with its own frontiers and, as the saying went, "entering Europe." Despite a brief attempt to retreat into an isolationist posture during the 1920s, the United States was in Europe to stay and steadily increased its military and economic strength until it was able to assume a dominant role on both sides of the Atlantic. Surprisingly, and despite its insular cultural development, it was also to take over a leading role in the arts and letters, including the sphere of the press.

Six months after the United States entered World War I, a second —
even more significant — event occurred, far to the east in what is now
Leningrad: the Bolshevik Revolution, which was to propel the Soviet
Union into a position as dominant as that of the United States, not only in
terms of military and economic strength but also in the arts and letters, as
there began a struggle in which the U.S. politico-economic system was
matched against that of the Soviet Union. The role assigned to the press in
Soviet ideology was quite different from that assigned to the press in the
American model, which by 1917 had become so popular that it was viewed
as a global model of an ideal press. The folklore of the First Amendment
had, by the start of the First World War, spread across the Western world.

Not, of course, that the free-press model was widely practiced
anywhere, but it had been firmly established as the ideal. In Western
Europe, even under legal guarantees of press freedom, newspapers were
often pressured, manipulated, and sometimes forced to practice deception
in the interests of *Realpolitik*. Similar practices have been illustrated in the
United States. In much of Africa and Asia, an indigenous press was slow in
developing and tended to follow the models provided by colonial rulers. In
China, perhaps because of the complexity of the written languages,
newspapers for a reading public were not to appear until the twentieth
century. In Latin America, the early press was patterned almost entirely on
that of the United States, and the first significant newspapers were
established by American printers. Of all the countries outside the United
States, the press in Great Britain was subjected to the fewest official
controls, and the British press system was more influential than that of the
United States in the development of press patterns on the continent. The
British press, as the model for the American press, was published under
legal guarantees almost as extensive as those of the United States. Until
the Bolshevik Revolution, the ideal press system was seen, almost universally, as that of the Anglo-Saxon model, born in Britain but developed and
enshrined in the United States.

The political opposition tended to condemn the majoritarian press in
Britain, the United States, and on the continent of Europe for accepting
the role of reptiles; on the other hand, it was equally clear that the
opposition itself would have preferred a supportive press that would have
then been identified by *its* opponents as reptilian. The ideal type was
identical everywhere: a free press conjured up in the spirit of the First
Amendment, a fearless seeker of the Truth, however formidable the
obstacles cast in the path of the seekers.

The struggle over press rights was inherent in the fall of Charles X of
France in 1830. In the decades that followed, under the monarchy of Louis
Philippe, the issue of press rights never subsided completely, and a
revolutionary press was an integral element in the activities of modern
Jacobins in the uprising of February 1848 that toppled Louis Philippe and

paved the way for the Second Empire, this too to collapse in 1871 when France at last became an enduring republic. Those years, between 1830 and 1848, were years of *Sturm und Drang*, turbulence and ferment. In the United States, it was during that period that the penny press rose, to herald the appearance on the stage of history of the Common Man and to help the cause of Jacksonian democracy. In Britain, a popularized press was indulging itself in articles about the Bow Street Runners and, in the spirit of Charles Dickens, finding much to write about the English Common Man, his problems and his pleasures. In Prussia, challenges to the entrenched power of the military and the landed aristocracy were leading to the revolutionary assembly in Frankfurt-am-Main.

In a sketch of the growth of journalism published by the International Organization of Journalists, Vladimir Hudec, dean of the faculty of journalism at Charles University in Prague, characterized the appearance of a new theme in the history of journalism thusly:

> During the bourgeois democratic revolution in Germany, in 1848–1849, Karl Marx and Friedrich Engels founded and edited in Cologne the "Neue Rheinische Zeitung" — which was actually the beginning of the history of Marxist journalism. This paper was a tribune for proletarian policy in the bourgeois democratic revolution, promoting this policy in the spirit of the famous "Manifesto of the Communist Party," also published in 1848.
>
> It was for the first time that the spontaneously developing proletarian movement gradually shifted from "utopia to science," and this was fully reflected also in journalism.

That "Marxist journalism" began with Karl Marx is a cardinal principle of the press in the Soviet belief system, and yet this too is folklore, an item that is politically useful in the Soviet Union just as the folklore of an adversary press is politically useful in the United States. In truth, Marx is as difficult to pin down philosophically as is Thomas Jefferson, who can be found on all sides of the issue of press freedom at different periods of his life. Marx may have been more than merely playful when he said, "*Je ne suis pas un Marxiste.*"

The idea of the press as an instrument of propaganda is an old idea, long part of the intellectual mainstream when Marx was born in 1818. We have seen how central a position the press took in the capitalist system, both in the circulation of attitudes and beliefs and in the provision of information about the availability of goods in the marketplace. In the socialist system, which evolved in the nineteenth century and which was to be codified by Vladimir Ilyich Lenin and the Bolsheviks in the twentieth, the position of the press was equally central. It is fascinating to note that the key men and women who participated in the evolution of socialism were all journalists: Marx and Engels, Lenin, Rosa Luxemburg, Trotsky, even Stalin.

Unquestionably, however, the dominant figure in the evolution of socialist thought was Marx, for it was he who was the chief theorist of a set of ideas that challenged the dominant capitalist ideology and converted the world (and its presses) into a system of conflict so perilous as to threaten the continued existence of humankind. This characterization of Marx and socialist ideology is in no way meant to assign blame. Socialist theory holds that the peril is the inevitable consequence of historical factors, that threatened capitalism will inexorably launch warfare to preserve its position of power against the challenge of the rising class of workers. For their part, adherents of capitalism assign the blame to the Socialists for recklessly risking war in order to achieve world domination. Analysis of the rights and wrongs of the planned economy and capitalism is not within the scope of this study; it is sufficient to point out the danger that lies in the conflict model preached by the theology of both socialists and capitalists.

As with many theories, that of Marx is incomplete. He was more the scholarly analyst than the fiery revolutionary. His most thorough work was his study of history and the sociological, philosophical, and economic elements that went into the development of the capitalist world he inhabited. It remained for Lenin to adapt — and to modify — Marxist ideas into a revolutionary social and political system. Still, even though Marx is incomplete, many clues can be found in his writings that cast light on the revolutionary social and political system that survives under his name. It is the very fact that Marx *is* incomplete that has made it possible for so many different interpretations to emerge about his writings and about his ideas. Marxism is by no means a monolithic philosophy; to many it is not a philosophy at all but a description of objective reality. In the classification system developed in this book and to be discussed in detail later, the socialist movement of the symphony of the press is one with many variations; another book might well be written that would merely examine the variations. The dominant melody is, however, the philosophy (or, perhaps better, the ideology) of the press that is communicated at the center of the system, the school of journalism at the Moscow State University. Let us examine now how that philosophy has developed.

The first job that Marx held after completing his university studies in Berlin was as a contributing writer for a newspaper begun in Cologne in 1842 by Moses Hess, a devotee of the radical socialist ideas then popular in France. Within ten months of the founding of the paper, the *Rheinische Zeitung*, Hess elevated Marx to the position of editor-in-chief. Hess had the deepest admiration for his young protégé, who had already won a reputation as a scholar and writer. Hess once described Marx in these words:

He combines the deepest philosophical seriousness with the most biting wit. Imagine Rousseau, Voltaire, Holbach, Lessing, Heine and Hegel fused into one person — I say fused, not thrown together in a heap — and you have Dr. Marx.

Under Marx's iron leadership — he was never a man to shun assertiveness — the *Rheinische Zeitung* opened a full-scale attack on Prussian rule (the king of Prussia at that time ruled the commercial and industrial Rhineland as well as the territory of the landed gentry, the Junkers, of the east). Marx attacked not only the Prussian leadership but also the landowning class in general, and the paper's circulation grew rapidly. For a time the Prussian authorities treated the paper with restraint, even though the tough Prussian censorship rules provided the authorities with almost limitless opportunities to suppress it. The Rhineland territories had only recently been annexed by Prussia, and the authorities were reluctant to stir public opposition by censoring the paper. Still, Marx drew the ire of the political censors by attacking the government's failure to improve the living conditions of the vine-growing peasantry and its imposition of heavy penalties on the poor who stole decayed timber in the forests for fuel. Marx, whose way with words has rarely been equaled among political writers, managed for a time to outwit the censors and to publish double-meaning material that appeared on the surface to be properly attentive to the interests of the Prussian crown but that disseminated its democratic messages to those who could read between the lines. Some of the outwitted censors were publicly reprimanded and replaced by stricter officials. But apparently Marx went too far when he publicly called on the Prussian rulers to go to war against the oppressive Russian regime of Czar Nicholas I. A copy of one of Marx's articles was brought to the attention of Nicholas, who sent a note to the king of Prussia complaining about the inefficiency of his censors. The *Rheinische Zeitung* was promptly suppressed in April 1843, and Marx was out of a job. But he had learned well the skills of political journalism.

Perhaps the most remarkable article that Marx wrote during that period was composed not for the *Rheinische Zeitung*, but for yet another political journal, launched by fellow journalist Arnold Ruge in Paris. The publication, called the *Deutsch-Französische Jahrbücher*, was to be published in Paris, but it was shut down by the French censors before the first edition could appear. Ruge went to Switzerland and published Marx's article on censorship in a journal he called the *Anekdota*, in February 1843. It was the first and last issue of *Anekdota*. In November of the same year, Marx left Prussian territory for Paris, then the center of radical activity. The writings of Proudhon and Saint-Simon were discussed by night in flats and cafés, with the police ever on the guard for revolutionary behavior. It was in the years between 1843 and 1845 that Marx became radicalized, shifting from the libertarian humanism of his early years to the fiery revolutionary rhetoric that led to his reputation as "the red terrorist doctor." Despite this shift, Marx was never to repudiate the ideas about the press that he set forth in his article for Ruge's journal.

Marx's article, titled "Comments on the Latest Prussian Censorship Instruction," was based on the Royal Cabinet Order of December 24, 1841, which was ostensibly designed to lift some of the more repressive censorship rules that had been handed down twenty-two years earlier by Frederick William III (it was his successor, Frederick William IV, who issued the new censorship "Instruction" and who was later to smash the liberal uprising of 1848–1849). As Marx pointed out in his closely reasoned article, the modification in censorship was more apparent than real and came to be used as a device to stifle philosophical dissent, whereas the earlier rule had been directed against the expression of religious differences. Of even greater concern to Marx was the introduction in the 1841 Instruction of a rule similar to what was later to become a part of U.S. press law, the Bad Tendency test. Writings that criticize administrators and laws or propose improvements were to be free of censorship, the Instruction said, "so long as their form is decent and their tendency is well-intentioned." Good intentions were to be measured in terms of being free of spite or malice. Censors were directed to pay close attention to the form and tone of the language used and to prohibit "publication of writings if their tendency is harmful because of passion, violence, and presumptuousness."

Responding with righteous wrath, Marx declared: "According to this statement the writer is subject to *the most horrible terrorism, to jurisdiction based on suspicion. Tendentious* laws, without objective norms, are laws of terrorism." Such rules, Marx wrote, imposed penalties on citizens not for their action but for their thoughts; they denied the citizen his existence:

> I may turn and twist myself as much as possible — the evidence is not important. My existence is suspect; my innermost being, my individuality, is considered to be *evil*, and I am *punished* for that. The law does not penalize me for wrongs I commit but for wrongs I do not commit.

An ethical state, Marx said, leveling his heaviest artillery on the Prussian authorities, may not claim for itself exclusive possession of reason and morality. To drive home a point that was even more distasteful to the Prussian ruler, Marx declared that the Instruction

> aims to protect religion, but it violates the most universal of all religions: the sacredness and inviolability of subjective conviction. It replaces God as the judge of the heart with the censor.

The Bad Tendency test concerned itself not only with content but also with tone, and the censors were directed to combat a tendency on the part of the newspapers to play "on the curiosity of their readers by printing gossip, insinuations, and meaningless reports taken from foreign newspapers and written by malevolent and poorly informed correspondents." In other words, Marx commented, the censors were to decide what made for good journalism and what were the proper qualifications for editors. Marx, whose capacity for invective and acid sarcasm is legendary, turned his pen on the censors themselves (whose intellectual gifts were limited). Under the Instruction, the censors were made to pass judgment on the "scientific qualifications" for editors. But where, Marx asked, did these "universal geniuses" acquire the scientific qualifications to make such judgments? He asked, further:

> Why don't these encyclopedic minds come out as writers? If these officials, overwhelming in number and so powerful by knowledge and genius, would rise all of a sudden and by sheer weight crush those wretched writers who are active in one genre of writing only, and even there without officially tested qualifications, the confusion in the press could be terminated better than can be done by censorship. Why are these skilled men so silent when they could act like Roman geese saving the Capitol by their cackle? They must be men of great reserve. The scientific public does not know them, but the government does.

The basic premise of Marx's essay was that free inquiry is good and that censorship — in whatever form — is not only wicked but counterproductive. The purpose of journalism, he said, was the search for truth, and the entire society would be the better for the search. In language drawn from Aristotle and echoed by democrats and libertarians for two millennia, Marx wrote:

> All purposes of journalistic activity are subsumed under the one general concept of "truth." Even if we disregard the *subjective* side, namely that one and the same object appears differently in different individuals and expresses its various aspects in as many various intellects, shouldn't *the character of the object* have some influence, even the slightest, on the inquiry? Not only the result but also the route belongs to the truth. The pursuit of truth must also be true; the true inquiry is the developed truth, whose scattered parts are assembled in the result.

It was while editing and writing articles for the *Rheinische Zeitung* that Marx became intrigued by socialism and communism; in fact, he launched his study of communism only after his paper was accused of "flirting with communism." Not so, he wrote in a formal reply, adding that he himself did not know enough about the doctrines of Fourier and Proudhon "to hazard an independent judgment" of communism. His concern at the time he was writing the paper — and throughout his life — was with specific issues; his general conclusions and laws grew out of his analysis of existing matters, what he identified as "objective factors." One of those objective factors was the wretched life of the vine-growing peasants in the Moselle Valley, where he had been born, in the frontier city of Trier. The censorship laws were directed against the *Rheinische Zeitung* for its attacks on government disinterest in the plight of the Moselle peasants. It was his examination of the state of the Moselle peasants that led to Marx's lifelong fascination with the economic factors in oppression. To assist in countering the oppression, in Marx's view, a free press was indispensable. Many of his articles in the *Rheinische Zeitung* concentrated on this theme. In response to the censors who were repeatedly assailing him for the Moselle articles, Marx identified both external and internal limitations on a free press. The external limitations were easy to see; they were official censorship, prior or ex post facto restraints. Internal limitations, he wrote, were more complex and philosophically more serious.

Internal limitations on the press were historical and intangible; they involved the political and cultural atmosphere inhabited by the press. Where journalists despaired of their power and influence, where they believed that whatever they wrote would make no difference and that dissident reports would lead to punishment, they lost their courage and contented themselves with simply reporting "the news," that is to say, the correct facts as interpreted by the authorities. The next step in such an environment was the public's loss of interest in participating in public affairs. With this loss came the disappearance of "the creative force for a free and open press, as well as the condition of popular acceptance of a free and open press, the atmosphere without which the press is hopelessly sick." In other words, for there to be a free press, there had to be public desire for a free press, and that desire was killed by internal limitations on the press. The oppressed public would sink into apathy, acceptance of its wretched state, where there was no free and open discussion — and without the support of the people, such free and open discussion was impossible. Marx clearly saw his paper not only as seeking "the truth" about the plight of the Moselle peasants, but also as attempting to lift the public out of its apathy to demand social change. The press, in his view, ought never to be a mere reporter of "the news." From this conviction emerged the central theme in the socialist analysis of the press.

"OUR BUSINESS IS TO CHANGE THE WORLD"

To Marx, in his fully developed analysis of capitalism, the press was a central element of the superstructure, the *Überbau*, which the ruling classes erected as their literary, political, and ideological mechanism for maintaining power. Although the word superstructure is always used to translate *Überbau*, it can be somewhat misleading as one attempts to achieve clear understanding of Marx's meaning. The *structure* of a society, in particular that of a capitalist society, Marx held, derives from material production, that is, the producing of goods; those who own the means of producing the goods constitute the ruling class. These are the capitalists, and they maintain their power by owning the means of production of not only material goods but also of "intellectual goods." Thus, they control not only the farms and the factories, but also the governments, churches, schools, and presses. These institutions — governments, churches, schools, and presses — are the chief components of the *Überbau*, the mechanisms established for the purpose of enabling the ruling class to maintain its power. In English, the word superstructure suggests something that is built on top of something else; it is not included in the foundation and hence is additional, not necessarily a part *of* the building. To Marx, the *Überbau* is not something built on top of the social order; it is, in fact, a critical part of that social order. Its job, its function, is to facilitate the maintenance of power by the ruling class, to enable the capitalists to exploit the workers, the proletariat. Without the *Überbau*, the capitalist structure would collapse, of its own internal weaknesses — or, as Marx put it, of its contradictions.

It can be seen then that in Marx's fully developed analysis of capitalist society, the press is crucial for the ruling class's capacity to maintain power. After his arrival in France, Marx wrote nothing further of significance about the press directly, but his view of the press and of its centrality was implicit in all his work.

He did not ever entirely abandon his career as a journalist. For ten years he and his friend and associate, Friedrich Engels, wrote articles for Horace Greeley's *New York Tribune* from London, an activity that not only provided American readers with insightful articles about world political affairs but that helped Marx, now on the edge of poverty in London, to provide for himself and his family in their English exile. It was Charles Dana, then managing editor of the *Tribune*, who offered the position to Marx. Dana had met Marx while on a trip to Cologne and had been thoroughly impressed; he misread Marx as being a utopian Socialist in the vein of Fourier or Robert Owen, the English industrialist who founded a commune in New Harmony, Indiana. But few Americans were knowledgeable about the intricacies of European socialism. Marx and Engels wrote 487 articles for the *Tribune* from 1852 to 1862, for the sum of one pound (about five dollars) an article. Marx remained on the *Tribune* payroll until Dana's dismissal during the Civil War. His articles, all written in English, were largely composed of analyses of European political events; they were, on the whole, free of the invective so common in Marx's philosophical and sociological writings. His reports were among the best examples of interpretive journalism of the age.

The press, then, was an indispensable weapon in the arsenal of the capitalists. In 1846, Marx and Engels argued that the class that controlled the means of production controlled not only the manufacture of material goods but also "the means of mental production." As for the working class, those who were exploited by the ruling class, they were condemned in the capitalist system to a life of alienation, a state of incompleteness or dehumanization. Socialism would restore to the alienated proletariat not only their economic well-being and a share of political power but, even more importantly, freedom and fulfillment. Working-class men and women would have their "existence" returned to them. And in that process of restoration, the press was to play a decisive role.

Few aspects of Marx's thinking are as hotly debated today as the quality and significance of the concept of "alienation," or *Entfremdung*. In fact, the way Marx is interpreted will depend substantially on the interpretation of the concept of alienation. To some, Marx's thinking on the subject of alienation is religious, if not mystical; to others, it is economic; and to still others, it is political. It is suggested here that there is some validity in all three interpretations. Since the concept is so important in understanding the socialist press model, it is worth exploring in some detail.

The fullest examination of alienation is in Marx's early writings, especially in *Economic and Philosophical Manuscripts*, written in 1844. At that time Marx was twenty-six years old, not yet embarked on his career as journalist and revolutionary; he was still very much under the influence of Hegel, from whom Marx borrowed his fundamental analytical tool, the dialectical method of analysis. The dialectic preached conflict: history was a chronicle of struggle between opposing forces, between thesis and antithesis. The resultant synthesis itself formed the next thesis in the eternal round of conflicts that for Hegel would ultimately conclude with the realization of the Idea, a mystical concept that may well have been, in Hegel's mind, the realization of the Prussian state. For Marx, as he stood Hegel "on his feet," the ultimate was to be the realization of communism, in which the *Überbau* would no longer be necessary, since all classes would be equal, and there would no longer be a ruling class to require the existence of governments and instruments of persuasion and exploitation. All these would "wither away." In the state of communism, alienation would no longer exist either, and the self-realization of Man would become complete.

Some would accuse Marx of presenting a utopian view of humankind and its institutions, and there is some truth in this accusation. Yet Marx saw his analysis as scientific, and over and over he expressed contempt for "utopian socialism" or "crude socialism." To Marx, communism was the solution to what he called the "riddle of history," and its arrival could be objectively predicted through the application of the theory of scientific materialism. As man approached communism, he would cease to be alienated, as he was in the capitalist world. The concept of *Entfremdung* was another that Marx had borrowed from Hegel, and in his later career, when he no longer used the humanistic language he had employed in *Economic and Philosophical Manuscripts* or in his writings for the press, Marx clung to the idea that alienation would end with communism.

Whatever else Marx may have meant by alienation, it clearly had a pyschological reality for him. He looked about him, in Prussia, in France, in England, and he saw factory workers barely surviving in long hours on the job, in unhealthy and degrading conditions. The capitalists, who owned the factories and the machinery in them, owned the workers as well. The workers, in that situation, were "alienated" — estranged not merely from worldly goods but also from their life force, from their potential. Workers were commodities to be used by capitalist employers for their own gain. The very language of the workers was not their own; the words were those of the capitalists. The workers were not even masters of their consciousness. For to Marx, consciousness — awareness of self — came only through the use of language. If you couldn't talk about something, or write about it, then you could not be aware of yourself. In that case, in a certain sense you did not even exist. The words themselves and the meanings assigned to them were part of the *Überbau*, whose task it was to keep the lower classes in their place, to keep men unaware of their existence as human beings. Those who were denied the awareness of self were obviously alienated. This state would change, Marx theorized; the collapse of capitalism would signal the beginning of the end of man's alienation.

Many Marxists, chief among them Lenin, would argue that Marx's early writings are to be ignored, maintaining that as he matured, he dismissed the romanticism of much of his early, humanistic writing. And Marx himself appears to have given some weight to this reasoning. In his famous preface to *The Critique of Political Economy*, written fifteen years after his *Economic and Philosophical Manuscripts*, Marx said that he and Engels were prepared "to settle accounts with our former philosophical conscience." This phrase was enough to persuade Lenin (and many others) that nothing Marx had written prior to 1859 was to be taken as "Marxist." Yet it is doubtful Marx meant to suggest any such thing in his preface. What Marx was doing was rejecting his *philosophical conscience*; in other words, he was no longer even dealing in philosophy. For everything that went under the name of "philosophy," he was saying, was *bourgeois* philosophy. The language of philosophy was the language of the ruling class and had to be replaced by what Marx called "scientific socialism." Karl Korsch, one of the most astute analysts of Marx's thought, says that from 1859 on, Marx turned to philosophical topics only in order either to illustrate his own analysis or to attack his enemies in the socialist camp. The aim of Marxist socialism remained, as before, to free man from his alienation. Erich Fromm, who sees Marx as a messianic visionary, says that to Marx the contradiction in capitalist production that would ultimately be

its downfall was that man was alienated, the slave of things and circumstances, a powerless appendage in a world that seemed beyond his power
to combat. The values of that world — "gain, work, thrift, and sobriety" —
failed to lead to any *moral* values, such as a good conscience or virtue. In
the socialist revolution, alienated man would rise against his oppressors;
he would have nothing to lose, as Marx and Engels wrote in the
Communist Manifesto of 1848, but his chains.

In this world, the capitalist world of alienated man, the press was
assigned an important task in the *Überbau*, together with governments,
schools, and churches. It was to conceal from man the true nature of the
world he inhabited; it was to make him content with his lot as a member of
the exploited proletariat. Religion was, Marx said, "the opiate of the
masses." States were established by the ruling class in order to perpetuate
its power; governments were tools in the hands of the capitalists. It is
doubtful that Marx was assigning to the press a function as dominant as
those of government, school, and church, since in the middle of the
nineteenth century, newspapers were not widely read by peasants and
factory workers. The modern concept of the "two-step flow" is, however,
consistent with Marx's analysis. Newspapers would certainly influence the
ideology of the intelligentsia, civil servants, shopkeepers, and tradesmen
— and these in turn would pass along to the underclass the "truths" they
had read in the papers. Marx did not speak of propaganda; it remained for
Lenin a half-century later, when newspaper readership had expanded
enormously, to accord the press its central position in Marx's *Überbau*. But
even in the mid-nineteenth century, Marx envisioned the press, directed
and buffeted by official censors, as a significant agency of social control. It
was, however, also a target for subversion, and throughout his life, Marx
sought to use the printed page as a device to challenge his capitalist foes.
Journalists, in Marx's view, were themselves members of the proletariat,
but like civil servants, teachers, and priests they were compensated for
their function in the *Überbau* by being lifted from the lower strata of the
social order, the *Lumpenproletariat*, and permitted entry to the lofty
coteries of the ruling class; they were allies of the bourgeoisie in the
maintenance of its power, most importantly through deceiving the people
into failure to recognize their state of alienation.

Such a portrait of the press is diametrically opposite to the press image
in the capitalist lands themselves, where the press was viewed as a
watchdog; as a force arrayed *against* those in power; or as an instrument of
education, information, and enlightenment. In the last of his *Eleven Theses
on Feuerbach*, Marx dealt indirectly with one of the most sacred of the
canons of journalism in a capitalist society: objectivity. "Philosophers,"
Marx wrote — referring not only to those who called themselves philosophers but to historians and all those who communicated in words about
the beliefs of their society — "philosophers have previously offered

various interpretations of the world. Our business is to change it."

All interpretations, Marx was saying, are partisan, offered on behalf of one point of view or another. The historians of the past, he said, including among them the journalists who have been identified appropriately as the first historians, have examined only the surface of things. When they referred to "objective" reality, they were supplying the theoretical weapons the ruling class needed to maintain power. In *The German Ideology*, Marx called this kind of objectivity "reactionary," since whenever one objectifies reality, he is defending it. The press, in short, was serving as a decisive instrument of social control: By practicing a code of objectivity, it was denying the possibility of change. It is only in actions, Marx held, that a human being or a society expresses true beliefs. For words to be true, they must be interchangeable with action; if not, the word is a lie. It is, in short, ideology, not truth.

To overthrow capitalism, to restore man to his true identity, to make words and actions identical, the press was then, in Marx's analysis, to carry out the most important assignment of all. And Marx himself undertook to carry out that assignment. It was to thwart the efforts of the capitalists to deceive the workers and instead make the workers aware of the true character of their exploited, alienated existence. The job of the journalist (and of all other members of the revolutionary vanguard — or "advance section") was to make known to the proletariat that it was enslaved, a human commodity, that it was alienated, and that it was being systematically deprived of its true existence. Put in Marx's phrasing, the job was to transform false consciousness into true consciousness. It was to reveal to man his real and his true human needs. The mechanism was the pen, not the sword. The revolutionary Lenin would later modify Marx by placing greater emphasis on the sword, but Marx himself was foremost an intellectual and teacher, and the instrument of education was for him the word. To overcome the *Überbau*, Marx held, man must be made aware; he must come to recognize how easily he can be deceived by mere words, by the ideology of capitalism.

The *Überbau*, according to Robert Kilroy-Silk, is the secret weapon in the class struggle, "the fountain of false consciousness." The state, standing for the power of the dominant class, is in business primarily to maintain the status quo and the existing power base. Marx himself wrote: "The state is the executive committee of the bourgeoisie." The press, for its part, worked hand in hand with the state to keep the waters flowing from the fountain. Before the class of proletarians could overthrow their exploiters, it was necessary that they be made aware of the existence of their class. Marx's "advance section," composed of working-class intellectuals and journalists, was assigned the task of developing class consciousness and ultimately revolutionary consciousness. Novelist Arthur Koestler, who believed that the modern Soviet state betrayed the earlier idealism of

Marxism, challenged the idea of the *Überbau* as being vague and capable of many conflicting interpretations. "Marxist society," Koestler wrote in *The Yogi and the Commissar*, "has a basement — production — and an attic — intellectual production; only the stairs and lifts are missing." In Marx's view, the press, before it could join in or lead the "advance section," must come to recognize its own true nature; its goal must be no longer to interpret, to present an objective view of "both sides," but to work instead for change. Of course, Marx did not use phraseology of this sort; the value system of objectivity had not yet been identified, and no one spoke of presenting "both sides" of an issue in seeking objectivity. Still, he was addressing the precise point in his analysis.

Consciousness itself, Marx said, existed only through communication. Before there could be communication, society was necessary. Men experienced themselves through their interaction with other men, and the primary means of their interaction was language. Those who controlled the language controlled society and could bring mankind to slavery or to freedom. The creators of words were the state, the schools, the churches — their transmitter was the journalist. He who controlled the press controlled the ideology and the social order.

It can be seen then that the press was central in both the capitalist and socialist theories. The melodies that make up the symphony of the press in both market and planned economies are by no means totally opposed to one another. In fact, one sometimes needs a carefully tuned ear to recognize the differences. Each melody is one of turbulence, of conflict directed not only internally, against domestic discord and challenges to harmony, but also externally, against one another. The struggle has often been portrayed as a battle or war, sometimes unto death.

LENIN'S THREE ROLES FOR THE PRESS

Marxist theory was transformed by Lenin, who found it necessary to rechannel many of Marx's concepts to make them fit social conditions in Russia. Marx was convinced that before a "feudal" society such as that in Russia could even aspire to a socialist revolution, it had to pass first through the capitalist stage of development. It was in Lenin's interest to portray Marx as a dedicated revolutionary, and yet Marx himself was uncertain on the subject. In fact, he was always more at home in the cloistered corridors of a library than at the barricades. It was in the British Museum that Marx did his acting.

While Marx wrote little about the press directly, especially in his later years, Lenin's literary output on the press was prolific, and he was more decisive in developing a socialist theory of the press than his mentor. In the Soviet Union and in states with planned economies everywhere, official ideology is identified as Marxism-Leninism, and its analysis of the role of the press is carefully codified.

When Marx died in 1883, Lenin was thirteen years old. Twice exiled to Siberia for revolutionary activities against the czarist regime, Lenin turned to the press as his principal instrument for stirring up support for revolution, much as the colonial rebels in the United States had done in the eighteenth century.

In the conflictual political model that has dominated the twentieth-century world — a world that has often seemed bipolar, in ideology if not in practice — the image of the other side has been clean and monolithic. In one image, virtue and capitalism are destined to triumph; in the other, virtue and communism are equally destined to emerge from the struggle victorious. The most agitated chords of the melodies of the press on both sides have been dedicated to portraits of the wickedness of the other side. In truth, neither model has been clean or monolithic. There is not one model of capitalism and one only, and there is not one model of communism and one only. The variations are extensive, perhaps limitless.

There was not, for instance, a clear line from Marx to Lenin, nor is there today agreement on the "correct road to socialism." Lenin was reacting against interpretations of Marx that had led in the final years of the nineteenth century to a reformist adaptation of socialism, in which mass political movements led by trade unions were seeking to assume political power by using the traditional electoral processes developed under capitalism. To Lenin the revolutionary, this approach was futile and doomed to failure. He scorned mass political movements and turned instead to a plan wherein a small cadre of leaders, patterned to some degree on Marx's "advance section," would direct the workers under the tightly controlled machinery of the Communist party. The Bolshevik doctrine ultimately prevailed in Russia, but that victory was not without bitter internal struggle. While it has triumphed in the Soviet Union, it has by no means been adopted by socialist movements everywhere. In fact, the struggle goes on today in much of the developing world, as well as in the countries of Western Europe. In his *Philosophical Notebooks*, Lenin asserted: "After half a century, not a single Marxist had understood Marx!"

For Lenin, equally at home as a writer and an orator, the role of the press was vital if his Bolshevik party was to defeat its internal Marxist opposition and if the capitalists were to be overcome. In this program, Lenin was following Marx's insistence on the necessity of raising the level of class consciousness. But Lenin went beyond anything that Marx had suggested and developed a full-blown theory of the role of the press. Operating underground inside Russia, Lenin was among the founders of the Bolshevik newspaper *Iskra*, or *The Spark*. And in a 1901 article in the fourth issue of *Iskra* headlined "Where to Begin," Lenin wrote a paragraph that has become as much sacred dogma in the Soviet Union as the First Amendment has become in the United States:

> The role of a newspaper...is not limited solely to the dissemination of ideas, to political education, and to the enlistment of political allies. A newspaper is not only a collective propagandist and a collective agitator; it is also a collective organizer. In this last respect it may be likened to the scaffolding around a building under construction, which marks the contours of the structure, and facilitates communication between the builders, enabling them to distribute the work and to view the common results achieved by their organized labor. With the aid of the newspaper, and through it, a permanent organization will naturally take shape that will engage, not only in local activities, but in regular general work, and will train its members to follow political events carefully, appraise their significance and their effect on the various strata of the population, and develop effective means for the revolutionary party to influence those events.

Lenin identified three roles for the newspaper: collective propagandist, collective agitator, and collective organizer. The training of socialist journalists, at the Moscow State University School of Journalism and at all journalism schools and institutes throughout the socialist world, includes instruction in propaganda, agitation, and organization. It is made manifestly clear that each of these is a vital role to be performed in the interests of truth and human liberty. To the capitalist eye, the terms seem inconsistent with truth and liberty, a further illustration of the political character of language.

Lenin described the press as part of the superstructure and expressed the belief that newspapers and the journalists who write for them play key roles in training those who will lead the society in developing ways to influence the course of events; in other words, to educate not only the working classes into class consciousness but also to educate the leaders themselves. If Jefferson might have preferred newspapers to government, Lenin, at least in 1901, sounded as if he might have preferred newspapers to the Communist party! Neither man, of course, believed what he said, but each man was an activist, sometimes swept away by his own emotional nature into making exaggerated declarations. Nonetheless, it can be seen that Jefferson and Lenin were convinced believers in the potential power of the press, and each man believed that the end he sought was virtuous.

It was in an article published in September 1917, six weeks before the Bolshevik revolution, that Lenin presented his most thorough analysis of freedom of the press. The article has come to be cited by socialist critics in all their analyses of the capitalist press. At the time, Russia was under the rule of the provisional government of Alexander Kerensky, and the leading Russian newspapers were under capitalist control. Lenin's *Pravda*, or *Truth*, was struggling for circulation, hampered by a lack of funds.

Those newspapers with the greatest circulation were filled with advertising, much as were the leading newspapers of Europe. To Lenin, this situation did not demonstrate freedom but rather exploitation. "Freedom of the press" in bourgeois society, Lenin wrote, "means freedom for the *rich*, systematically, unremittingly, daily, in millions of copies, to deceive, corrupt and fool the exploited and oppressed mass of the people, the poor." Clearly and concisely, Lenin made his point:

> The capitalists...call "freedom of the press" a situation in which censorship has been abolished and all parties freely publish all kinds of papers. In reality it is not freedom of the press, but freedom for the rich, for the bourgeoisie, to deceive the oppressed and exploited mass of the people.

Not only was this "myth" accepted by the capitalists, Lenin wrote angrily, but also by his rivals in the socialist movement, the Social Revolutionaries and Mensheviks, who, he said, followed the definition of the capitalists "either from stupidity or from inertia." The capitalist model of a free press, Lenin asserted, was not only counterrevolutionary but in fact "yellow." The power of the bourgeois Russian press was being maintained by advertising inserted by the wealthy capitalists, who were thus able to control the content of the papers. What was needed was a prohibition of private advertisement and a subsidy by the government that would pay for advertising in all papers, including *Pravda*. Only when "the opinions of *all* citizens may be freely published" can there be genuine freedom of the press:

> The issue is not "freedom of the press" but the exploiters' sacrosanct ownership of the printing press and stocks of newsprint they have seized! Just why should we workers and peasants recognize that sacred right? How is that "right" to publish false information better than the "right" to own serfs?

If printing presses and newsprint were made available to all political movements, then there might be genuine press freedom, Lenin said, asserting that under Bolshevik rule, such distribution "could be effected easily enough." Such a move, he said,

> ... would be state aid to the people's enlightenment, and not to their stultification and deception; it would be real freedom of the press *for all*, and not for the rich. It would be a break with that accursed, slavish past which compels us to suffer the usurpation by the rich of the great cause of informing and teaching the peasants.

In power, however, Lenin elected not to make printing presses and newsprint available to holders of all opinions. In fact, the Bolsheviks established the same kind of monopoly Lenin had been decrying. His justification was that his party was not oppressing or exploiting anyone but was, in fact, representing the interests of the poor and oppressed. Of course, in Lenin's view, the monopolistic practices of the Bolsheviks were virtuous, and there is little evidence that Lenin was afflicted with doubt. No more so, it may be added, than are those who believe virtue lies in the use of private advertisements and a free press based on the First Amendment. The critical point is that each side of the conflict between capitalist and socialist ideologues is convinced of the virtue of its own belief system. And each side asserts that its models and practices are being carried out in the interests of the people, that each is practicing the doctrine of social responsibility. In the Soviet Union, great stress is placed on the value and significance of letters to the editor, which occupy many columns in every Soviet publication. It is the responsibility of the newspaper, as "collective agitator," to respond to the letter writers and thus to provide a distinct social service. TASS, the Soviet news agency, lists as its primary duty provision to the people of information that is "topical" and "truthful" but also "socially meaningful," that is to say, information that is useful and not irrelevant.

The capitalist press and the Marxist press each claims that it carries out its duties in an ethical manner. To Hudec, the Czech journalism educator, a journalist may adopt one of two attitudes in order to influence public opinion: He may identify himself as a protagonist for a particular set of ideas and try to convince his reader to adopt those ideas; or he may act as a "professional" and be prepared to advocate ideas for money whatever his own judgment about those ideas. In the first case, he is being objective; in the second he is being objectivist, or making a pretense of being fair and balanced while in reality serving as a paid propagandist for his employers. It is in the first case, where the journalist "finds his place among those forces which are the bearers of progressive ideas, that he becomes an active force in the conscious efforts to carry out historical transformations benefiting society." Hudec and the journalism teachers in Eastern Europe are following in a direct line from the fundamental ideas of Marx and Lenin, although these ideas have been modified by historical developments.

Let us examine the three goals that Lenin proclaimed for a free press. The goals were not original with Lenin; he himself credited them to the German socialist leader Wilhelm Liebknecht. *"Studieren, propagandieren, organisieren,"* Liebknecht demanded of a press organ that would serve socialist revolutionaries — "Learn, propagandize, organize." Looked at carefully, a remarkable similarity can be detected between the goal models of such disparate figures as Horace Greeley and V. I. Lenin.

Studieren — to learn — is closely associated with the verb "to inform." *Propagandieren* — to propagandize — is closely associated with the verb "to teach." The concept of *organisieren* — to organize — is a bit more complex and can be set aside for a moment. The remaining two roles, information and education, appear to have been accepted worldwide. Everyone speaks of information and education as among the roles of the press. Sometimes, in fact, those two roles are telescoped into one. The question arises as to whether one can clearly differentiate between information and education. In the United States, the difference is murky: one man's information is another man's education. Perhaps the distinction can be seen in the often-heard advice to put "the news on the news page and editorials on the editorial page." Thus, news would be information and editorials would be education. Perhaps not; the difference is obscure. French press theoreticians, on the other hand, distinguish clearly between the two, in this case adhering closely to Lenin's model. The word "collective" ought not to pose a large problem if defined as that which is assembled or accumulated into a whole. By adding "collective" to Liebknecht's definition, Lenin characterized the newspaper as providing information and education not to individuals as single units but to them as part of a whole, as a "collection of individuals." American journalists similarly see their audiences as collective, as groups of individuals.

At the Moscow State University School of Journalism, as at the other twenty-two journalism schools in the Soviet Union, the Leninist role model for the journalist is carefully taught, and collective agitation is defined as "presenting information on everyday events." This definition is from Yassen Zassurskiy, dean of the Moscow school, where at any one time 2,500 students are enrolled.

As for the basic question, "Information for what?" Zassurskiy holds that the information must provide for the objective needs of the reader. "Any information or commentary contributes to behavior and actions," he says. The first role is simply to supply information; the behavior and actions are generated under the third role, that of "collective organizer." Zassurskiy maintains that the capitalist model insists not only on supplying information about events but also about what is for sale in the market — advertisements. Readers are lured into buying newspapers for news but are in fact given information about what they don't need: unnecessary products and useless gossip. Soviet theoreticians see two different types of information: primary and secondary. The primary deals with information that meets needs; the secondary deals with unnecessary material: advertisements, gossip, entertainment. Both types fall into the category of collective agitation. To Hudec, the information role properly calls for "disseminating positive experiences and criticism of everything that hinders society in its development." If the language is carefully examined, without emotionally charged political reactions, one can see much similarity in the goals in the Marxist and capitalist models. The press in each system is designed to criticize all aberrations and work for the good of society. Indeed, one can find a parallel in capitalist press analysis with the socialist primary and secondary types of information: Primary is that which the reader *needs* to know in order to carry out his democratic duties; secondary is information he *wants* out of curiosity or a desire to be entertained. Such secondary functions, Soviet journalists are taught, involve *artificial* needs as opposed to *objective* needs, which are defined as food, clothing, housing, and essentials. "There is," Zassurskiy says, "a relationship between needs and interests."

The second role, "collective propagandist," presents few problems. To Zassurskiy, it involves "explanation of the mechanics of the work of society, and of the reasons for events." In addition, it provides "timely interpretation." There is little difference between this role in the Marxist model and the persuasion role in the capitalist system: the writing of editorials, leading articles, and columns.

More complex is the role of the press as "collective organizer." To Marx and Lenin, and to all who would change the social order, the press is a vehicle for manipulating public opinion and stirring the public to action. Zassurskiy characterizes the goal as "to mold one's views and thus to modify behavior." He cites the weather report as an elementary example: Information about an impending rainstorm will cause readers to carry umbrellas. "We are talking about a direct appeal to action," he says.

Organization is the centerpiece of Marxist-Leninist society. In this situation, the press and the public become one. As Hudec put it, "A collective organizing function is characteristic for progressive journalism which develops in a broad way for the popular masses." He added:

> Reactionary journalism, defending the exploiting minority, naturally cannot have such links with the popular masses and find support in them. It works for the disorganization of progressive movements, tries to divert the exploited and oppressed people and nations from the political struggle for liberation. It carries out its function through manipulation.... Progressive publications... utilize letters of the working people, win over for cooperation outside authors, organize themselves with the popular masses political campaigns to try to achieve the stipulated objectives. Such participation of the popular masses in progressive journalistic activities is valuable not in itself; it is essential for the broad integration of their collective experience and wisdom to solve problems of social development, in the fight against vestiges of the past and reactionary elements.

THE JOURNALIST AND THE "PATH OF TRUTH"

How closely the Soviet press adheres in practice to Lenin's model is difficult to assess. Surveys of public opinion, so widespread in the Western world, have played a more limited role in the Soviet Union. But they are on the increase, and those that do exist show that the Russian citizen sees his newspaper as the most efficient and desirable of instruments available to him for influencing local organs of administration. More precisely, one survey indicated, it was the newspaper above all that could present to the authorities "requests, remarks, suggestions, and demands of the population." Certainly, the Soviet public writes letters to the editor of publications at an astonishing rate. In the letter department of *Pravda*, no fewer than forty-five staffers are needed to sift through the letters and choose which to publish. *Izvestia* claims to publish one-fourth of the letters it receives, although such a total seems unlikely.

The Soviet people are avid readers of newspapers and, increasingly, enthusiastic viewers of television. Studies of the Soviet public show it to be remarkably similar to the American public: the more highly educated the viewer, the fewer hours devoted to television watching and the greater interest in news and cultural programming; the less educated, the greater the interest in quiz shows and human-interest programs. Rural housewives are heavy daytime viewers. And, just as does the television audience in capitalist countries, the Soviet viewers say they would like to see more programming devoted to entertainment and relaxation.

It appears, on the basis of the survey information available, that the Soviet media are not carrying out their organizing function with notable success. On the whole, the newspaper and television audience in the Soviet Union seems to pay only limited attention to news about local affairs; on the other hand, the Soviet public seems to possess an almost unslakable thirst for more news about international affairs, especially about nonsocialist countries. One 1976 Soviet study shows that of all the stories available to readers to city newspapers, those that interest them the least are those about the city itself. This may be the result of the insistence by the Soviet mass media on presenting stories in didactic form, with considerable attention to what is right and what is wrong and to what form of behavior is desirable. Even the quiz shows on television present little homilies. For example, a program called "Let's Go, Girls," telecast once a month, provides an opportunity for each contestant to win a small prize. The motive of the contestants is, of course, not to get rich but to receive the opportunity to express their views on how to improve their occupations or how to reward good work. Such programs apparently are less favorably received than are the few programs that present outright entertainment, without messages. Ellen Propper Mickiewicz, who has studied the Soviet audience in some detail, says there is a "lack of fit" between what is available, on television and in the newspapers, and what is wanted.

Soviet newspapers are limited in number of pages. *Pravda*, which claims a daily circulation of eleven million readers, consists of only six pages, and it follows a rigid form. Page one regularly presents an editorial, official news from the leadership of the Communist party of the Soviet

Union, several brief news items foreign and domestic, and some material about the state of the economy. The second page supplies stories on the Communist party (*Pravda* is the official organ of the Party). Page three carries domestic news, letters to the editor, and often the results of investigative reporting. Page four carries stories continued from the first page, as well as some foreign news, usually about developments in the communist world. Foreign news stories are on page five. The back page contains a potpourri of sports, human interest, humor, radio and television schedules, practical information about medicine, and other miscellany. Few photographs are published, nor are there articles about crime, except in unusual circumstances; rarely are there stories about celebrities or film stars. Timeliness is not notably important in the Soviet press, and articles usually cover events several days old; in Eastern Europe, however, the search for topical news seems as great as in the United States. The difference may be competition, since foreign newspapers are readily available in Eastern Europe. The content of the Soviet press is so different from the regular content of capitalist newspapers that visitors from the capitalist world invariably find *Pravda* and the other Soviet newspapers dull. By contrast, Soviet visitors to the United States condemn American newspapers as sensational and lacking in material that serves the needs of the readers.

Interestingly, Russian readers tend to find their newspapers objective. The capitalist formula — presenting "both sides" of an issue — is not considered of value in the Marxist-Leninist model, since that model holds there is one objective reality and that it is therefore counterproductive to present opposing, erroneous views of reality. In the Soviet model, objectivity is associated with truth rather than fairness.

The Soviet belief system maintains that U.S. newspapers are largely owned and controlled by Jewish capitalists; many Soviet journalists seem to retain at least some semblance of this belief, even those who have visited the United States. They are often surprised at the disorder of many U.S. newspaper offices, since the offices of *Pravda* and other Soviet newspapers bear little resemblance to those of an American newspaper. The *Pravda* building consists of long corridors, with offices on either side. Editors rarely communicate with one another, aside from conferences. Investigative reporting is encouraged in the Soviet Union, and newspapers, especially local papers, devote space regularly to muckraking articles exposing cases of local corruption and inefficiency, and raising questions about why nothing is done to correct certain abuses. Attacks on alcoholism appear regularly, thoroughly documented. In this context, the Communist party in 1979 awarded the Lenin Prize to Alexander Chaikovski, the editor of the *Literary Gazette*, the most outspoken critical organ of the mass press in the Soviet Union. Still, critical articles dealing with national and international political issues are exceedingly rare. The perimeters of investigation are carefully circumscribed. Some topics are clearly taboo. Are Russian journalists content to follow the Soviet code, to work in accordance with Marxist-Leninist guidelines? On the whole, the answer seems to be yes. A leading Russian television journalist, Svetlana Staro-domskaya, suggests her own "four theories" of the responsibility of the Soviet journalist:

> First, you please yourself: that you have done the best work you know how. Second, you please your friends, the people you know, those who are in your circle. Third, you please and inform your viewers. And fourth, you please your government, your society, your political system.

When conflicts develop among those four groups? "You hope there are none," she says, "but you must try most of all to please yourself." The admonition sounds much like Polonius's advice to Laertes: "To thine own self be true...." It is a dilemma faced by journalists everywhere, in all political systems. Indeed, many Russian journalists seem more concerned with technical journalistic problems than with ideological issues.

Restraints are, of course, fewer in pluralist capitalist nations such as the United States than in the Soviet Union. One American reporter who had worked for years in the Soviet Union recalled a trip he had taken with a Soviet reporter, who condemned not only American practices but also the high cost of living and the lack of adequate housing in the Soviet Union. The American asked the Russian why he did not attack in print what he condemned orally; after many vodkas, the Russian journalist broke down in a fit of weeping, insisting all the time that he had not been trained to criticize social developments in the Soviet Union.

We have seen how the press in capitalist societies — the United States, Britain, France, and Germany, among others — have been manipulated by powerful political and economic forces. That the press in the Soviet Union and among her allies has also been manipulated by powerful political and economic forces is equally evident. Once again we are confronted with the politics of language, for clearly "manipulation" means different things to press analysts and theoreticians in socialist and capitalist societies.

Of great importance, however, is Hudec's reference to letters to the editor and "participation by the popular masses in progressive journalistic activities." It is perhaps this element of the Marxist model that has had the greatest impact on the new nations of Africa and Asia. In the capitalist world as well, the success of the press has on the whole been dependent on appeal to the popular masses. The masses in both capitalist and Marxist systems have been stirred by the press to perceive political, economic, social, and even cultural issues in a framework of conflict: us versus them.

The most widely influential examination of the socialist press model written in the capitalist world is contained in the book *Four Theories of the*

Press, a thin volume that appeared in 1956 under the authorship of three distinguished journalism scholars, Fred S. Siebert, Theodore Peterson, and Wilbur Schramm. The chapter by Schramm entitled "The Soviet Communist Theory of the Press" was drafted at a time of intense political turbulence, memorialized under the colorful term the Cold War. Many examinations of the Soviet press have appeared in the capitalist world since then, but it is Schramm's analysis that has become conventional wisdom in the United States and elsewhere.

The problem with Schramm's analysis is that it is hostile. Its approach is within the us-versus-them framework that also bedevils the Soviet analysis of the American press. There can be little doubt of the good guys and the bad guys in Schramm's analysis.

Differences will inevitably be sought out and stressed in approaching the topic from this personal point of view. Thus, Schramm is able to arrive at the preposterous distinction between the Soviet press as an "instrument" and the American press as a "service." In truth, the media of both the Soviet Union and the United States are instruments, supporting the interests of those who publish them. It is equally true that in both countries the media represent a service to those who read newspapers and magazines and tune in to radio and television. There are indeed fundamental ideological differences between the ends that are perceived for the instruments of mass communication in the Soviet Union and the United States. It is nevertheless equally true that there are fundamental similarities. The us-vs-them framework minimizes the similarities and exaggerates the differences.

The analytical flaws that arise from the process of labeling are apparent in Schramm's statement that "from our point of view, at least, the Soviet system is an authoritarian one — indeed, one of the most closely controlled systems in history." On the other hand, he refers to the structure of the press in "the Free World." It is well to point out that one of the most critical of all difficulties we face in efforts to avoid the perils of global confrontation lies in labeling and in the language of conflict.

The labels we place on behavior and on ideas contribute to misunderstandings, and to passionate disputes about meanings and substance as well. One man's terrorist is another man's freedom fighter. Political assassinations are not murders. Robbery of the rich (or the poor) is not robbery. Sociologists have pointed out that "deviant behavior" is often in the eyes of the beholder, based on the way "deviant" is defined. John Burton suggested three possible responses by persons who become frustrated or bored inside their social environment: "withdrawal, excitement on the fringes of legality and reformist or revolutionary activities within and outside the law." To the Soviet analyst, the American environment is deviant; to the American analyst, it is the Soviet environment that is deviant. At each end of the pole, the opposite social system is seen as both boring and frustrating, and hence the citizen is perceived to be alienated. At each end of the pole, the defender of the opposite social system is perceived to be either mistaken or distorted in his defense of his system.

It is not our intention to denigrate the work of Schramm and his colleagues in *Four Theories of the Press*. Their efforts to impose a classification system on the press are much to be applauded. Yet it is well also to call attention to the misunderstandings that have been generated. Many of those misunderstandings have resulted from problems in labeling; others have arisen from the oversimplification that often accompanies attempts to classify and compress reality into clearly defined molds. The warning of the great Swiss historian Jakob Burckhardt is one that bears relearning daily. Beware, said Burckhardt, the "terrible simplifiers."

As we contemplate the significance of labeling in the world of the press, it would be judicious to take heed of Burckhardt's observation about patriotism:

> Our imagined patriotism is often mere pride toward other peoples, and just for that reason, lies outside the path of truth. Even worse, it may be no more than a kind of partisanship within our own natural circle; indeed, it often consists simply in causing pain to others. History of that kind is journalism.

Let us hope that journalism is capable of something more than "that kind" of history.

Advertising on TV. (*Judith East*)

Six

The Ideological Press:
Triumph of Capitalism

THE EDUCATION OF JOURNALISTS:
MECHANISM FOR SOCIAL CONTROL

The socialist revolt against capitalist economics that captured the Western world in the nineteenth century was by no means limited to the ideas, theories, and doctrines let loose in Germany, France, and Russia; in fact, protests against the excesses of an unchecked free-enterprise system punctuated the Progressive movement in the United States. Lincoln Steffens was a socialist who would later exult in the accomplishments of Soviet Russia; his friend John Reed, another American journalist, would join the revolution and be honored by burial inside the walls of the Kremlin near the tomb of Lenin. Upton Sinclair called for rebellion against the misdeeds of the great capitalists. In the early years of the twentieth century, even Walter Lippmann identified himself as a socialist. In other words, the same seeds that flowered in the planned economy of the Soviet Union were planted in the United States, but the flowers that sprouted from the American seeds bore little resemblance to those that blossomed in the Soviet Union. And whenever similar blossoms appeared in the United States, they were cut down, as they were, for example, in the Pacific Northwest, where lumbermen preached the gospel of Marxism and were smashed by lawmen. In Hungary and Germany, Communist revolutionaries seized power, but they too were defeated in bloody counter-rebellion. The Western allies of World War I, joined by defeated Germany, dispatched troops to Russia to try to overcome the Bolshevik revolutionaries, only to have to admit defeat.

The Western allies and Germany were unsuccessful in attempting to conquer the Bolshevik revolutionaries in their own Russian territory, but they were stunningly victorious in overcoming the Marxist movements in their own countries. Vanquished abroad in the brief but convulsive turmoil that lasted until 1921, the forces of capitalism emerged triumphant at home. Marxist doctrine, as modified and applied by Lenin, became a way of life in the Soviet Union, and the Soviet press began speedily to put into practice the theories enunciated by Lenin. His successors, Stalin, Khrushchev, Brezhnev, Andropov, made no effort to modify Lenin's theories. Stalin, himself a prolific contributor to Soviet journals, proclaimed the Leninist press doctrine wherever he went. The Soviet press became the leading cheerleader for the policies and practices of the Soviet leaders and their carefully planned economy.

At the same time, the American press, without benefit of Leninist dogma, was becoming the leading cheerleader for the policies and practices of American leaders and their by now well-established economic system. What had begun as laissez faire had been modified into a system of free enterprise and, by the end of the nineteenth century, into the modern corporate industrial state. But while the economic system of capitalism had been substantially revised and pure laissez faire was no longer practiced after the Civil War, the belief system was handed down almost intact well into the twentieth century. Despite the practical end of free enterprise, the 1920s represented an Indian summer apotheosis of laissez faire, as the American public chased in convulsive pursuit after a variety of get-rich-quick schemes.

Ironically, the extinct species, laissez faire, had become a full-blown ideology, providing room within its confines for the reforms of the Progressive movement, itself ostensibly a reaction against the dogma of free enterprise. In this, the capitalist ideology as it developed in the United States differed from that of Western Europe in important detail, at least in the latter years of the nineteenth century and the early years of the twentieth. It took several decades for the press ideology that germinated in the United States to take firm root in the remainder of the industrialized capitalist world.

By the 1920s, the federal income tax was on the books in the United States and antitrust regulations were in force, yet those reforms did little to prevent anyone from aspiring to the upper brackets of American society through the stock market or real estate or almost any business venture. The good life was available for the taking. The American proletarian needed no new consciousness, no Communist party, in order to achieve the good life. Indeed, he needed no party at all; he could do it himself. What had been seen a century earlier by European immigrants as the land of unlimited opportunity had now become for native Americans as well the land of unlimited opportunity.

During this period, the path of the press in the United States changed direction. The new development was the appearance of journalism as an academic discipline in American colleges and universities. Ben Day and James Gordon Bennett would have hooted at the idea. It was not long after Pulitzer made the proposal in 1903 that journalism programs were introduced [illegible] colleges. Pulitzer contracted to endow a program at Columbia University, but disputes over details delayed the establishment of the Graduate School of Journalism at Columbia until 1912, a year after Pulitzer's death. In the meantime, two other journalism programs had begun, that at the University of Missouri in 1908 generally recognized as the first. In the same year that the Columbia school was established, the University of Wisconsin's department of journalism was created under the direction of Willard Bleyer, whose history of journalism furnished the [illegible] which has painted the image of the press that has enchanted [illegible] generations.

[illegible] the question of the appropriate role for the press in the social order, it is important to take note of the time frame in which journalism [illegible] and of the ideology that prevailed at that time. By 1920, more than [illegible] schools and departments of journalism had been founded; during the twenties, another twenty-five to thirty, from coast to coast, opened their doors to students. The primary figures in the new field were Bleyer of Wisconsin and Walter Williams, the first dean of the journalism school at the University of Missouri. The Missouri Press Association had led the campaign to establish the school, and the university obligingly selected Williams, a veteran newspaper editor, as its first dean. Williams's curriculum was dominated by practical studies — reporting, feature writing, and advertising — and the course of study was centered on practical experience gained in working for the student newspaper, *The Missourian.* Bleyer, a professor of English, followed a somewhat different path at Wisconsin. His department did not establish a student newspaper and emphasized instead a program of general education, particularly in writing and the social sciences that, as reported in a biography of the university, was viewed as "of greater usefulness in developing journalists than preoccupation with artisan training."

Disputes over which is more valuable for journalists, practical training or general knowledge, have not ceased to this day. Even so, there is little difference between the two approaches with regard to the basic ideological underpinnings of journalism. The Missouri and the Wisconsin approaches both perceive the world through the prism of capitalism and progressivism.

Students trained at the schools of journalism in the 1920s and 1930s were taught within a belief system that was perhaps as rigidly ideological in its orientation as the system taught to students at the schools of journalism in the Soviet Union. While in later years, as journalism programs expanded to almost every college and university in the United States, teachers and professors less committed to the progressive and laissez-faire dogmas appeared in American schools, their numbers have been small, and the prevailing ideology holds sway today much as it did in 1912 or 1921.

What is this press ideology? Of what does it consist? It certainly is never explicitly expressed as it is in the socialist world, where Lenin's three functions are codified into official ideology. Indeed, American practitioners and scholars often disagree about the role of the press, and here press stands for broadcasting as well as the print media. Ideologically, there is no difference among the mass media. To some, the very idea of a role for the press, or news media, is unthinkable. "Our job," journalists say often, "is to get out the news." The idea of role somehow smacks to them of government interference or of sociological jargon. Still, an ideology does exist. It is composed of four articles of faith: (1) that the press is free of outside interference, be it from the government or advertisers or even from the public; (2) that the press serves "the public's right to know"; (3) that the press seeks to learn and present the truth; and (4) that the press reports facts objectively and fairly. These canons are listed here in declarative form; they might also be construed as moral imperatives; that is to say, instead of characterizing what the press *is*, they might declare what the press *should* be. Confusion over the "is" and the "ought," over description and prescription, permeates all discussion of the press in the capitalist world. In the hope of avoiding the morass into which this confusion always threatens to plunge the analyst, we will make no effort to separate the "is" and the "ought" and will instead assume that the capitalistic press ideology encompasses both. These four articles of faith are intrinsic in all interpretations of the press in the United States, Western Europe, and other industrial states with market economies, however interpretations may vary in detail and whatever contradictions may arise over the "is" and the "ought."

Most analysts of the capitalist press have identified three — and sometimes four — expectations of the news media. They tend to agree that the media are expected to inform, to entertain, and to serve as watchdogs on the powerful. Others insist on a fourth expectation: to advertise what is available in the marketplace. In the United States, the educative role is usually not mentioned, although it is sometimes seen as part of the informative role. In France, the distinction between information and education is given explicit expression. Most importantly, the American — or capitalist — analysis of the press is rooted in what was defined in chapter

2 as the democratic assumption, that is to say, the press provides the information that enables citizens to make appropriate democratic decisions. It is this assumption that provides the philosophical foundation for the four articles of faith — as well as for the three (or four) expectations — held for the press.

The belief system, or ideology, dealing with the press is held with the same kind of dogmatic conviction as is the ideology of the press in the socialist world. Capitalist and socialist, follower of the market (or corporate) economy and the planned economy, are equally trapped in their dogma. And each dogma — or folklore — is false. Nevertheless, the dogma, or folklore, is spread not only by newspapers and broadcasting outlets themselves but also by those who train future practitioners. Some may point to the pluralism within schools and departments of journalism and to the fact that lurking in their midsts there is an occasional Marxist and more than a few opponents of principles of the free-enterprise system. There are, indeed, islands of dissent, yet few craft end up moored at these islands; the pressures to accept the folklore are irresistible, and young journalists have no difficulty finding like thinkers among their newspaper friends, among the folklore-addicted faculties, and among the public at large. It is an enticing myth, this myth of the heroic press fighting the overwhelming power of the mighty and corrupt in the interests of the grateful citizen. It is a charming fairy tale, and it is accepted in one form or another by almost everyone who has practiced the craft of journalism in the United States in the twentieth century.

Even though a fairy tale is unbelievable, there is no cause for discarding all the elements of the romance. Certainly, much good can be wrought by the press. However, it is not independent, it operates as an instrument of power. It is an agent, but it is not a secret agent as in a spy thriller. The output of the press is in the open; it is public, but its director may be in the shadows. Whatever form power takes — government, party, corporation — it may well wish to conceal its relationship with the press. When the relationship is obscure, when the press itself operates in the shadows, there is little likelihood the press will perform any important public service. It is when the agency role of the press is exposed to daylight that it can work in the interests of all.

The schools and departments of journalism have grown from modest beginnings into major institutions. Hundreds of thousands of young men and women are enrolled in these programs, available in the majority of U.S. colleges and universities, and in thousands of secondary schools as well. Children learn about newspapers and broadcasting stations from their first year in school; they are encouraged to write articles for school newspapers when they are just learning to write. And as part of their general education, they acquire information about the free press and its significance in democratic life. By the time these young men and women accept employment as journalists, they have had twelve or fourteen years of association with press folklore in their schools, and they have also been socialized by the press itself, rarely modest in its reporting about its own power, significance, and value. Not much of this barrage of material is likely to be cynical; the folklore of the press is believed as is all dogma, with little challenge, few questions. When it is challenged and questioned, ready answers are available, for in the modern industrial state, every citizen has an "opinion" about the press and is rarely reluctant to express that opinion. Many of those who condemn the practices of the press act not out of hatred for the institution, but out of love for it and a desire to "restore" the press to the honored place it occupied before it became dishonest and corrupt. Americans have a weak sense of history, and folklore finds fertile ground among those who know little of the past. In this context, Santayana was right when he said those who do not study history are condemned to repeat it.

Schools of journalism appeared as the ideas of progressivism — and even populism — were at their zenith in the United States, especially in the Midwest, where the movement for journalism schools began. The Whig interpretation of history was universal: Every day and in every way, things were getting better. While capitalism was good, certainly morally superior to the oligarchies of nineteenth-century Europe and to the communism of Soviet Russia, nevertheless, there was room for improvement and progress. And the press marched in the vanguard of the preachers of improvement and progress; the muckrakers were the heroes, and the code of the watchdog was holy writ. Thus, the students who emerged from the schools of journalism were automatically tub-thumpers for progress and watchdoggery. They also championed the financing of newspapers and magazines by advertisers and not by government; the advertisers were seen as uninterested in political issues and unlikely to seek to exercise control over content. And if advertisers ever tried to do so, they were to be spanked sharply and reminded of who ran the papers and what the mission of the press was. The ideas of Will Irwin and his colleagues were well known, but the standard was to keep the advertiser and the business manager in the boardroom, not in the newsroom. It was a standard given clear expression by no less a figure than Joseph Pulitzer, the patron saint of schools of journalism.

Within these schools, the excesses of the sensational tabloids that had sprung into prominence came under sharp attack. Serious journalists, those who would graduate from the schools, were to eschew the sensational and to practice instead the code of objectivity, which was seen as the appropriate counter to the sensational tabloids. Fallen newspapers were, in the age of Henry Ford's flivver, practicing what was called "jazz journalism." The graduates would counter the excesses of sensationalism and follow the model of Pulitzer, who promoted truth and accuracy (at least in his later years) above sensation and profit. This was also the period in which news agencies (or wire services, as they were called) were attaining greater prominence and were preaching a form of political fence-sitting in the name of objectivity.

This then was the belief system of the schools of journalism: that unlimited years of progress lay ahead for the United States and its politico-economic system, that the press played a leadership role in bringing about that glorious future, that the financial structure of the American press assured economic health and political independence for newspapers — and that this healthy future could be insured best of all by following the path of objectivity. In the early years of journalism education, the newspaper industry itself was of mixed opinion about the wisdom of such training at institutions of higher learning. Some editors liked to recruit their staffs from the journalism schools, but more were suspicious of college-trained reporters. Many editors tended to prefer those who had studied, as the saying went, "in the school of hard knocks," drawing on experience over education. The model reporter was Hildy Johnson, the hero of Ben Hecht's stage classic *The Front Page*, a figure who appeared in hundreds of motion pictures and novels, the hard-drinking, hard-loving cynic with a heart of gold, the ink-stained cousin of the range heroes of the Wild West. Book-learning was suspect to these heroes and their followers.

Still, with the passage of time, more and more publishers came around to recruiting their staffs from schools of journalism. Whatever the appeal of tradition and the resistance to book-learning, the publishers were unable to resist the economic advantages available to them in the journalism schools. These advantages were significant; by recruiting staffs from the journalism schools, publishers could eliminate the considerable cost of on-the-job training. They could — and did — demand college and university graduates who not only were skilled in writing and reportorial techniques, but who also knew how to write headlines, who understood the principles of advertising and subscription sales, and who were already socialized into the belief systems of the publishers themselves. Who could resist such a financial bonanza? Here were staffs trained for the most part at public expense, reporters who could be relied upon to accept — and indeed seek to advance — the political, social, and economic environment in which they operated. It was the best possible mechanism of social control — adherence to the familiar, cost-effective status quo, and at virtually no cost. It was the taxpayer who footed the bill for this education, since the leading schools of journalism were situated at state colleges and universities that were supported by public funding. At the private colleges and universities, the expense was borne by students or their families in the form of tuition or endowment funds. In neither case was the cost paid by the press industry. In recent years, many newspapers and broadcasting outlets have reduced their costs even further through internship programs, often without salaries for the student interns, who are compensated instead by academic credit.

Although schools of journalism in the United States are essentially training grounds in the capitalist ideology of the press, the news media are frequently subjected to critical examination in classrooms and in research projects. Students are regularly assigned to evaluate press performance, often to examine whether or not a newspaper — or especially a television news outlet — has lived up to the ideological expectations of the student or professor. This practice is not universally applauded by media officials, who argue that journalism schools ought to concentrate on training students in newswriting and editing skills. Press theorists of a conservative bent tend to follow the lead of critics such as Spiro Agnew, the former vice-president, who in 1969 stirred the wrath of the press community by attacking the leading national dailies, *The New York Times* and *The Washington Post*, and the three TV networks, arguing that the journalists who worked for those news media were members of an eastern, liberal establishment whose views did not represent those of Middle America.

In the tradition of Agnew, a group of conservative publications in 1977 set up in Washington a National Journalism Center training program for student interns "within a context of traditional values." According to conservative columnist M. Stanton Evans, director of the center, "too many journalists have been taught that capitalism is evil or that America is imperialist and that journalism should be used as a method of advancing political ideas." For some media critics in the United States, the traditional educative role of the journalism schools is not conservative or traditional enough. Dispassionate observers would be astonished to hear that. Conventions and meetings of journalism professors and graduate students devote themselves, to a remarkable extent, to programs and research within a framework of preserving and strengthening the belief system that includes devotion to the principle of objectivity and to traditional press values.

The school of journalism, with its emphasis on practical training, is an American invention; it has not established a strong foothold in other nations with market economies, although the practice may be changing. In Western Europe, little support has been evidenced for programs in journalism practice at institutions of higher learning. Faculties have resisted the idea, and publishers have not demonstrated interest in having anyone else train their staffs of writers and editors. The difference on the two sides of the Atlantic can be attributed in large measure to the difference in the political structure of the press. In the United States, where advertising revenues long represented the chief financial support of the press, political "independence" was early seen as a virtue. Advertisers are less likely to publish their notices in press vehicles that represent opposing political viewpoints; hence, political independence helps in maximizing advertising income. In Europe, the newspaper has retained a stance of political partiality to a far greater degree; on the continent of Europe, the news media have traditionally adopted open political stands, often serving as outright instruments of political parties. These organs were less interested in maximizing advertising revenue than in political persuasion. The publishers, in these cases, sought to recruit staff members whose politics they shared, rather than those who possessed the skills of writing, editing, layout design, and headline writing. These could be taught on the job. In Great Britain, as in France and Germany, publishers have long been inclined to recruit staff members from university programs in economics, politics, or even in Latin and Greek. Few European universities publish student newspapers; Oxford students are among those who have put out their own paper for years. The American influence has been greater in Latin America and the Far East than in Europe, and a number of university journalism programs have developed in South America, Taiwan, and Korea; an increasing number are appearing also in Africa and the Middle East, but in all these cases, training is more likely to stress journalism history and philosophy, theory and methodology, rather than the practical skills.

In recent years, the European press seems to have adopted not only the American journalistic mystique embodied in the First Amendment but the American press style as well, with its emphasis on short paragraphs and sentences, on sharp, conflict-ridden phrasing — and even its method of training journalists. For instance, not only are German newspapers beginning to read like American papers, but German universities and institutes are increasing their journalism course offerings, even to the point of providing training in skills. The pace of adoption of American style and training has been slower in other European countries, but there too the movement, both ideological and pedagogical, has been flowing from west to east. And party-oriented newspapers are giving way to a press ostensibly "objective" and free of partisan posturing.

OF HENRY LUCE AND COMPETITION IN THE MARKET

The triumph of capitalism in twentieth-century America was accompanied by the appearance and expansion of new forms of mass media: the all-purpose news agency, the newsmagazine, and the broadcaster. Whereas the newspaper and the general-interest magazine predated the victory of both laissez faire and progressivism, each of the newer forms of mass media arose in an environment saturated in corporate capitalism, an environment in which the ideology of the market economy had already taken root. It was also an age in which the Communist ideology of the Soviet Union was present as a rival and a challenge. If the American ideology was "good," then the Soviet ideology was "bad."

Nowhere is this ideological division more apparent than in the first of the great newsmagazines that by now have spread to all parts of the world and play a considerable part in the mass media everywhere. The first of the newsmagazines, and the model for the others that followed, was *Time*. It was the brainchild of two precocious young students at Yale University, Henry R. Luce and Briton Hadden, who invented a new phenomenon in the world of journalism, a slick weekly periodical whose pretense (and selling point) was that it would serve up in smooth, easy-to-digest form a summary of the week's news that was both cogently written and clarified for its readers what it all meant. It was an idea whose Time had come, and before the young men, each twenty-four on the magazine's day of birth in 1923, had reached the age of thirty, they had become millionaires. They understood, with intuitive shrewdness, that the American reading public was less interested in receiving "objective" news than was popularly believed, or at least that the readers eagerly desired an antidote to the dull, dry phrases that were pouring from the news-agency teletypes. It was as if they understood that a salable commodity lay between the hyped-up sensationalism of the tabloids and the pallid paragraphs of the news agencies.

Of even greater importance, these young men were clearly tuned in to the developing ideology of the capitalist press system of the twentieth century. It was Luce who was to proclaim in a remarkable pamphlet published in 1941 that the twentieth "must be to a significant degree the American Century." A man who, before the Second World War, thought that Mussolini and Hitler may themselves have been the wave of the future, Luce became a dedicated foe of fascism. He proclaimed the American Century over and above any claims to the contrary that might be made by the Germans; "the sneers, groans, catcalls, teeth-grinding, hisses and roars of the Nazi Propaganda Ministry are of small moment" in combating American hegemony, Luce said. At the end of the war, the identity of the enemy was to change, and Luce was for the remainder of his life to lead the American troops in an all-out ideological struggle against the Soviet Union and against communism everywhere.

It is perhaps not accidental that the two most powerful and outspoken anticommunists in the United States were sons of Presbyterian ministers: Luce and the author of the doctrine of "massive retaliation," John Foster Dulles, secretary of state in the Eisenhower administration. Luce and Dulles were following in the footsteps of another son of a Presbyterian minister, Woodrow Wilson, whose moralistic pretensions set the stage for the "crusades" that were to follow and to figure prominently in the kind of journalism that emerged during the "American Century." These men, Wilson, Dulles, and Luce, were moral thoroughbreds, utterly convinced of the purity of free-enterprise America; they dedicated themselves to assisting the rest of the world to partake of the same purity through the intervention of the political Holy Ghost, that is to say, the United States. Satan, who appeared to Wilson as the embodiment of Metternich and the nineteenth-century balance-of-power theorists, was transmuted by Dulles and Luce into godless communism.

The model that Luce and Hadden introduced was characterized not only by brevity and subjectivity, but also by simplicity. To *Time*, the problems of the world were not insoluble, nor even painfully difficult; all questions had answers. As one analyst put it, Luce "resisted complexity." Additionally, Luce and Hadden introduced the idea of group journalism. Articles were unsigned and were produced by a series of editors, who sharpened and polished, and who tuned their ears to the music of the hypenated adjective. Subjects of the articles were lantern-jawed, steely-eyed, high-powered. The man (or the woman) was characterized instantly and simplistically by the hyphenated adjective. It was a clean, unclut-tered, uncomplicated world that *Time* presented to its readers, and that world glorified the United States and its economic system. The target audience was Middle America, or, as Luce put it, "the gentleman from Indiana."

Hadden died in 1929, and at the age of thirty-one Luce took over sole direction of *Time* and of its children, beginning in 1930 with *Fortune* and expanding later to include *Life, Sports Illustrated*, and others. In all his publications, Luce paid homage to free enterprise and extolled the virtues and wisdom of commercial and industrial tycoons; it was Luce who adapted the Japanese word and applied it to the Babbitts of the United States. He went so far as to identify himself with the Sinclair Lewis character and to urge his readers to express pride in their quest to make money. Luce was a brilliant businessman and converted almost everything he touched into profit; small wonder that he admired the tycoon — for he was himself the greatest press tycoon of his Time.

In his self-anointed role of enemy of communism, Luce combined progressive admiration for a capitalist economy with a theological hatred of a planned economy and the atheistic element in communism in both the Soviet Union and the emerging People's Republic of China. Luce's enemies — and there were many, especially among the enthusiasts for Franklin Roosevelt's New Deal — accused him, not without reason, of being the leading member of what came to be called "the China lobby." This group of business leaders, anti-Communist writers, and intellectuals called for strong American intervention in China to prevent a Communist takeover and, after the takeover, ceaselessly attacked Roosevelt for "selling out" to communism in China. Luce was an avid admirer not only of Chiang Kai-shek but also of the leadership of South Vietnam; his was the steadiest of voices in support of American intervention in the Far East.

Luce's image of the world was narrow and parochial, one he no doubt inherited from his missionary father, a nineteenth-century jingoist in the tradition of those American patriots who supported wars in Mexico and Cuba in order to export white American virtue to the less-developed colored races in Latin America. That same patriotism and jingoism was to influence intervention in Vietnam, designed to bring American virtue to the yellow races of Asia. The *Weltanschauung* of Henry Luce fit perfectly the image of imperialism that Lenin painted in his writings and that continues to this day as a model of American ideology for the press of the Soviet Union.

The singular success of *Time* influenced the ideology of the U.S. press in important ways. Within a short time, many American newspapers were copying the language style and story structure of *Time*. An increasing volume of "analytical" stories appeared in the daily press, stories that followed the pattern of *Time* — in the moralizing manner of the crusader, with heavy infusions of anti-Communist explanations of events and with shallow analysis that implied ready answers to complex questions. No part of this ideological orientation was new; it had always represented an element in the American press. What was new was the emphasis. The economic strength of *Time* had not been lost on the press industry, and imitation was indeed sincere flattery. Moreover, the industry had observed the widespread acceptance of the *Time* formula among the public, especially the upper middle class, from whose ranks arose the politically powerful. Overlooked, perhaps, was the tone of religiosity in the pages of *Time* and now adopted by its imitators. The journalistic crusade, the all-out moral assault on devils and malefactors, would later sweep into the press's net Joseph Stalin and Richard Nixon, Bruno Richard Hauptmann and Bert Lance. *Time* influenced the tone and content of the European press as well, and newsmagazine imitators sprang into existence in France and Germany, in Belgium and Italy, across the continent and ultimately in Africa, Asia, and Latin America.

After Luce's death in 1967, the face of *Time* changed slowly. Bylines began to appear, and with them came an end to the uncritical glorification of capitalism. Writers and editors, many of whom had not shared Luce's vision, were able now to criticize the excesses of laissez faire and to move away from adulation of Chiang Kai-shek and the corrupt leadership of South Vietnam. It became almost impossible to distinguish *Time* from its chief competitor, *Newsweek*, itself now under the management of *The Washington Post*, whose left-liberal views were anathema to Luce. But even with the modifications, *Time* (and *Newsweek* as well) continued to give its readers "the answers." Some acknowledgment was now made of the complexity of public questions, and an increased volume of criticism of American leadership emerged. Still, rarely did there appear criticism of the institutions on which the economy rested; the virtue of these institutions was taken for granted. And while more balanced analysis appeared of the Soviet Union and communism, nevertheless, it was clear that these remained the enemy. Depressions and recessions, however unsettling, were to be combated only within the system, which itself remained as inviolate as ever. Not only did profits remain high for *Time, Fortune,* and *Sports Illustrated* (*Life* had succumbed to the fate of all general-circulation magazines, unable to compete successfully with television for advertising revenue), but the corporation expanded into a new arena, that of the gossip sheet — in the form of the enormously profitable *People* magazine. News was not selling as well as it had in the simpler, preatomic days of the 1920s; it was entertainment that was selling now, in the age of video.

Whereas from its earliest days the press had been a factor in the economic well-being of the United States, by the twentieth century it had become an ever more essential ingredient in the capitalist economy. Marshall McLuhan said of the process of communications that the media are the message. In one sense, it might be said that the media are the economy. Anyone interested in abstract intellectual exercises might ponder the American economic system without the media; it will be a difficult exercise.

It is in the distribution of goods — intellectual as well as material goods — that the media's position in the American system — as in all capitalist systems — is central. Advertising was an important factor in the development of the American press. In the modern capitalist state, whose locus is the marketplace, advertising is an essential element, since consumers seeking to buy goods must know something about their quality and price, and where to find them. The economic process consists of production, distribution, and consumption. In modern mass society, the news media more than any other institution facilitate the distribution of goods. In primitive societies, prospective buyers traveled short distances to the sometimes makeshift marketplaces to test and sample the wares and then, as they desired, buy them or pass along to the next stall. By word of mouth, prospective buyers learned whose products were the most reliable; sometimes the producers would send out criers to proclaim the worth of their goods, but the unavailability of easy transportation limited the distances these criers could travel. As modern society developed, as farmers moved into towns and even distant cities, as technology exploded the old social and economic order, the traditional marketplace disappeared, to be replaced by the modern mass market.

The social and political order of the United States as well as its economy is rooted in the philosophical principles of classical liberalism, in which it is virtuous to seek and to make a profit. It is good to work hard; it is good to earn a substantial income. Borrowing from John Calvin and the Puritans, the capitalist ethic holds that it is good to use your income to aid the needy and thereby to earn your just rewards — passage to heaven. Not all Americans believe in the Protestant work ethic any longer, but it is a value system that dies hard. And in the mass media, the rewards of hard work continue to be applauded along with the basic tenets of classical liberalism and capitalism, which see individuals rousing themselves from apathy when they reason their way to an activity that they perceive to be of value to themselves. Advertising fits comfortably into this system. The producer informs the prospective buyer about goods available in the marketplace, be it a store or a mail-order catalog. It is in the mutual interests of producer and buyer to fix a balanced price for the benefit of both producer and buyer, since each is following his or her own self-interested ends. If the producer fixes the price too high, the buyer will go elsewhere. So Adam Smith's invisible hand fixes a price that is best for both producer and consumer.

For the system to work, people must know where goods are available, of what quality, and at what price. Newspapers, magazines, radio, and television provide the most efficient mechanism for furnishing this kind of information. Of course, other media of advertising are available. A growing advertising device is the unsolicited catalog or letter; others include shoppers' guides, billboards, and signs. In a mass society, however, it is the mass media that provide the most efficient mechanism for producer and consumer. The media become, in fact, the marketplace. Thus, 60 to 70 percent of the daily newspaper is made up of advertisements, and television programs are interrupted every few minutes for commercial messages. If advertising were eliminated from the mass media, they would be forced out of business, or at least forced to operate on handouts from government or the great corporations.

Marxists (and some capitalist critics) maintain that the search for advertising dollars converts the media into simple instruments in the hands of producers and advertising agencies seeking to induce customers to buy what they don't need for money they don't have. It is held by a substantial body of economists that it is not advertising that brings producers and consumers together in the market, but rather the actual price of goods; to them it is the price, not the advertisement, that represents information. They may be right, but the system of advertising is so deeply entrenched in the United States and other capitalist nations that it has become a crucial element in their economies. And the mass media are crucial, for without them the masses of people would have little information about what was available in the market.

It is no accident that the word "market" turns up in the traditional picture of the media that appears in the democratic assumption of the press as a marketplace of ideas. The media are not described as a *sample* of ideas or a *source* of ideas or a *conflict* of ideas. The media are themselves markets to which news consumers go to learn what ideas and opinions are being expressed by whom under what circumstances. In the television industry, areas in which broadcasting operations compete are officially described as "markets." We do not hear of the top twenty cities in the country, but we do hear of the top twenty markets. The image of the marketplace of ideas that Mr. Justice Holmes presented in 1919 has, appropriately, replaced the self-righting principle enunciated by John Milton three centuries earlier. That same image was invoked by Edward Bernays, one of the founding fathers of the industry that has come to be known as public relations, as his rationale. "In the struggle among ideas," Bernays wrote in 1923, "the only test is the one which Justice Holmes of the Supreme Court pointed out — the power of thought to get itself accepted in the open competition of the market."

Few spokesmen for capitalism defend any longer the idea that the marketplace should be allowed to operate free of outside controls. The rise of corporations and the regulatory instruments forged by the Progressives undid laissez faire in the nineteenth century, and the New Deal experiment in "scientific capitalism" restructured Adam Smith quite as thoroughly as Lenin and others have revised Marxism. In fact, the New Deal brought with it many elements of socialism and the planned economy; interference by the federal government became a commonplace in efforts to restrain uncontrolled capital forces and to protect the weak, much as Marx himself had urged in his campaign in support of the Moselle vine growers. In West Germany following World War II, Economics Minister Ludwig Erhard coined a new expression to describe the modifications in the theory of capitalism; he spoke of "a social market economy." It was with reluctance that the press came to tolerate the modifications; in the United States, publishers responded with overt hostility to the New Deal. Despite an unfavorable press, however, Franklin D. Roosevelt was elected president four times. Publishers got the message, and abandoned their open warfare against the modified system. But the hostility remained, mostly under-cover, and voices emerged from time to time over the next half-century to call for a return to the "good old days" of free enterprise when there was, it was said, no government interference with a free press. Open antagonism developed against efforts by the government to assure fair treatment of controversial issues on television. The banner of the First Amendment was unfurled again and again in defense of the right of the publisher and station owner to run his shop free of government interference. In these quests, the mass media could count on the support of the advertising industry and the commercial and industrial world that used the services of the advertising industry.

The Great Depression of 1929 and the New Deal reforms that followed swirled strong gusts of change through the press. Not only were the 1930s a decade of trouble and pain, but also of renewed faith in the future, if only that future could be channeled in the direction of disin-terested scientific change or — put in the terms of journalism — in the direction of objective change. The Progressive respect for science became even more strongly solidified in the New Deal belief system. The genius of the New Deal lay in the call to arms in Roosevelt's inaugural address, when he warned that the only danger confronting Americans was pessimism, "fear itself." And where the New Deal never was quite able to conquer the Depression, it was wildly successful in combating fear and restoring Progressive optimism to the public. Science was now an article of faith — countering not only the ideas of Marx but also those of Darwin and Freud, who had shocked traditional values by making manifest the animal nature of humankind and the unconscious, irrational nature of much of its behavior. Man and his institutions could be understood only through the use of the scientific method, through dispassionate observation and the assembly of verifiable data. Old values were cast in doubt; fundamental assumptions now had to be confirmed. Even the old gods were suspect in a world that no longer seemed to be playing by the rules; this fact accounted for the search for heroes who would somehow find a way out and restore the sanity of an ordered world. The fascination of Americans with Mussolini, even of such enlightened editors as Luce, can be explained in this search for heroes. For many, Roosevelt was deified, elevated to the stature of a god among men — but for many others, he was the embodiment of the anti-Christ, and counter-Roosevelt heroes had to be found. Stability, above all, was what was sought.

As an agent of power, the press was buffeted by the same winds of change, searching out a role for itself that seemed to fit the altered human environment. A deeper rift than ever developed between the publishers and their top editors on the one hand and the subeditors and reporters on the other. Such a division had always existed, but the gulf grew more profound. Unionization arrived in the ranks of the press, as it did among coal miners and steelworkers.

THE SPECIAL CASE OF "OBJECTIVITY"

If the First Amendment remains the banner under which press ideology advances in the United States (and in the industrialized world), it is the code of objectivity that is its moral artillery. Dedication to the practice or the ideal of objectivity did not arrive full-blown in the 1930s; the idea of the disinterested journalist is quite old. Benjamin Franklin was not the first spokesman for journalistic objectivity, but the fact that it was endorsed by a figure so illustrious contributed to its popularity.

The word objectivity is as slippery as an eel; no matter how you seize it, it is difficult to hold on to it. Nor is the origin of the term as it applies to journalism any easier to handle. It appears to have quite different meanings to different people. We have already seen the problem that the term presents to Marxists; many among them have sought to resolve the problem by dividing it in two, by distinguishing between "to be objective" and "to objectify." In the case of objectivity, one deals in reality, with the way things really are; objectification pretends to reality while it propagates a false ideology. The distinction is useful, at least in theory. To describe a dog as a four-legged carnivorous creature with an anticipated life span of ten or twelve years is to be "objective"; describing that same dog as "man's best friend" is "objectifying." The first statement represents reality; it is scientific. The second, on the other hand, is propaganda, and hence ideological.

Absolute objectivity is impossible to achieve, a fact that has led to interminable, useless discussions. At best, it is a relative concept. Some analysts argue that it is not meant to be thought of as attainable, that rather than a reality it is a process, an attitude, a way of thinking. Michael Schudson, for example, identifies objectivity in journalism as a belief system about what kind of knowledge is reliable. Moreover, he says, it is a moral philosophy — "a declaration of what kind of thinking one should engage in, in making moral decisions." It does not, then, appear to present a problem to believe that objectivity is unattainable but that it is good and should therefore be sought anyway; it is a way of joining the "is" and the "ought."

There is certainly an aura of the lofty and the noble about the idea of objectivity, a term that achieved prominence with the introduction of the scientific method into the study of mankind and matter. To be disinterested, to be dispassionate, to avoid prejudgment, to abandon illusion, to seek painstakingly for the real and the verifiable — these were inseparable elements in the search for scientific Truth. From Bacon and Descartes to Watt and Edison, to Fermi and Einstein, the method defined and refined itself, and passed from the world of natural science to the social sciences and the humanities. The revelation by Heisenberg that scientific Truth was unattainable, that even in the most precise of measurements there exist areas of uncertainty where differences must be tolerated, stirred the community of natural scientists but made less headway among social scientists. The "sciences" of politics and economics and the newer "science of communications" seemed sometimes to proceed with disregard for Heisenberg's findings, as if correct answers could be found if only the correct measuring instruments could be discovered. Faith in technology seemed boundless, and the methods of science seemed capable of solving the riddles of politics, economics, the social order, and indeed of the press and other means of communications.

Dispassionate analysis, in which the seeker of explanations sought to free himself of bias, was the hallmark of the scientific method: the closer he could approach the stance of objectivity, the more empirical his research, the more likely it would lead to true resolutions. The aim of the social scientists was to adapt the method to their own research. Their tragic flaw was *hubris*, the presumptuous arrogance that destroyed Agamemnon and Lear. It was in this framework that the code of objectivity flowered. How could it be a false code? Its purpose was noble: the presentation of facts, or even the truth about the facts (as the Hutchins Commission urged), and moreover it squared with the goals of science itself. That it also served the interests of the capitalist system was not at first recognized, nor is it today widely acknowledged. Objectivity tended to act as a mechanism of collective organization in ways similar to the behavior Lenin demanded of the press in the Soviet Union.

In short, the code of objectivity assists power in the capitalist world to maintain social order and to fix limits to departures from ideological orthodoxy. It turns out on close examination to be anything but scientific; rather, it hallows bias, for it safeguards the system against the explosive pressures for change. So long as "both sides" are presented, neither side is glorified above the other, and the status quo remains unchallenged. Dissent is permitted, even encouraged, under the code of objectivity, but its limits are proscribed, and the counterbalancing orthodoxy is assured a voice — and not only a voice, but the most powerful of voices, since orthodoxy is represented by the powerful, whose command not only of financial resources but also of newsworthy authority assures it of dominance in the press.

As a further guarantee, the code of objectivity requires that open persuasion be limited to the editorial pages and that the news columns be free of "opinion." Since few persons read editorial pages, their influence is minimal. The American press condemned the witch hunts of Senator Joseph McCarthy on its editorial pages but presented his harangues "objectively" on the front pages. It was only when the power of the political system was directed against McCarthy, whose excesses threatened to disrupt the system, that McCarthy was vanquished. The code of objectivity then may be used to bring evil or good; it may at one time serve the ends of a McCarthy, and at another the ends of those who would destroy him. In either case, the press is an agent of power, lacking in independence. Objectivity bestows on the conductor the baton with which to conduct the symphony of the press.

Recognizing that absolute objectivity is impossible of achievement, many practitioners and students of journalism have proposed that other words be substituted. If one cannot be objective, one can certainly be fair. Or balanced. Or truthful. Yet substitute words have not resolved the muddle over definitions, for the goals of "fairness" and "balance" and "truth" incorporate the same bias as does the word "objectivity."

Gaye Tuchman has attempted to bring clarity to the muddle by suggesting that objectivity is useful to the journalist as a defense against anyone who would accuse him of slanting or distorting his output. What is involved, she says, is "strategic ritual." Tuchman writes in the spirit of a growing number of sociologists who have been studying the media as social institutions that behave in much the same manner as other occupational institutions, with their own bureaucratic structures and value systems. The pioneer in this movement was Warren Breed, who in 1955 first discussed the social pressures for conformity in the newsroom. Edward Jay Epstein confirmed similar pressures at the television networks. The evidence amassed by Breed, Tuchman, Epstein, and others is formidable. It substantiates the value that the code of objectivity holds for the mass media.

In analyzing the code, Tuchman identifies four "strategic procedures" the journalist follows in order to separate facts from feelings: (1) presenting "both sides" of a dispute, thus identifying the truth claims of the antagonists in conflictual situations; (2) presenting corroborating statements on behalf of these truth claims; (3) using direct quotations to indicate that it is the source and not the journalist who is speaking; and (4) organizing stories in such a way as to present the most "material facts" first. In addition, Tuchman points out, the journalist practicing objectivity is careful to distinguish facts from opinions by identifying interpretive material as "news analysis." From her perspective, Tuchman writes:

> It would appear that *news procedures exemplified as formal attributes* of news stories and newspapers *are actually strategies through which newsmen protect themselves from critics and lay professional claim to objectivity*, especially since their special professional knowledge is not sufficiently respected by news consumers and may indeed be the basis of critical attack.

Others offer an economic explanation for the rise of the cult of objectivity, maintaining that the idea of objectivity grew out of the economic imperatives of the news agencies. Indeed, it is often said — although the statement cannot be confirmed — that the goal of objectivity was created by The Associated Press. That this explanation was first offered by a representative of the AP raises some questions as to its validity, but nevertheless the historical account presented in 1938 by Oliver Gramling, an AP executive, in his book *AP: The Story of News* has been remarkably long-lived. Gramling cites a comment by Lawrence Gobright, an early AP writer during the Civil War. "My business," Gobright was quoted as saying, "is to communicate facts; my instructions do not allow me to make any comment upon the facts which I communicate." Gobright continued:

> My dispatches are sent to papers of all manner of politics, and the editors say they are able to make their own comments upon the facts which are sent to them. I therefore confine myself to what I consider legitimate news. I do not act as a politician belonging to any school, but try to be truthful and impartial. My dispatches are merely dry matters of fact and detail. Some special correspondents may write to suit the temper of their organs. Although I try to write without regard to men or politics, I do not always escape censure.

Kent Cooper, who served for twenty-five years as general manager of The Associated Press, preached the code of objectivity from one end of the land to the other, defining it as "true and unbiased news." Not one for understatement, Cooper proclaimed objective news as "the highest original moral concept ever developed in America and given the world." It was Cooper too who enunciated for the first time, in 1945, a doctrine he identified as "the public's right to know."

Cooper died in 1965. Six years later, a reading room named for him was dedicated at Indiana University, which he had attended, by Wes Gallagher, then the Associated Press general manager. In eulogizing Cooper, Gallagher also delivered a eulogy to the code of objectivity:

> The critics say no man can be objective. It is of course true that all men are fallible. To be otherwise would make men saints. And the world seems to be devoid of saints nowadays. But a journalist is no more fallible in his profession than a jurist or a doctor in the pursuit of theirs. He can subordinate his feelings to his profession just as the jurist must, or a doctor in treating a patient or a lawyer representing a client.
>
> It seems to me that all men and women must have a Holy Grail of some kind, something to strive for, something always just beyond our fingertips even with the best of efforts. To the journalist that Holy Grail should be objectivity. To have anything less would be demeaning and would result in the destruction of the profession.

The crucial point about objectivity, Gallagher said, was to separate thought from emotions, to distinguish facts from feelings. The objective journalist, he said, "must not let his ego overpower his conscience or good sense. He should try to shed a cold, clear light of fact and reason where fogs of prejudice and partnership envelop so many issues. He must not make concessions to the cult of irrationality that is widely prevalent today." Gallagher's critique of "irrationality" was directed at political dissidents, especially those manning the so-called underground press, who openly condemned the code of objectivity.

It is not surprising that the chief exponent of the code of objectivity has been The Associated Press. Almost from its inception, the AP has interested itself in multiplying its subscribers, that is to say, those who use its services. Technically, the AP is a cooperative owned by its members, the thousand or more newspapers that receive AP news wires. But the AP also sells its services directly to subscribers, among whom are numbered radio and television stations; magazines; governments; colleges and universities; and many newspapers, broadcasters, and wire services abroad. The United Press International, on the other hand, is a privately owned organization that does sell directly to subscribers. The output of the two services is barely distinguishable. The AP and UPI compete fiercely for subscribers; they are also in competition with foreign news agencies such as Reuters, as well as with syndicated news services operated by the most powerful American newspapers, *The New York Times*, *The Washington Post*, and *The Los Angeles Times*. In this competition, political advocacy of any sort is disadvantageous, for it is likely to limit the lists of subscribers. Foes of any political stance would not look with sympathy at joining forces with its friends. In other words, it pays to practice objectivity; political neutrality is a commercial benefit. To maximize the number of subscribers, it is necessary to avoid taking sides politically, to give equal weight to the truth claims of Democrats and Republicans, of Ralph Nader and General Motors.

The goal of objectivity in journalism has been so widely disseminated and accepted that by now it has become a part of the belief system of the capitalist world. Not only is the goal disseminated and stamped as good in schools of journalism but also in classes in history, political science, and civics. So deeply has the notion of objectivity in journalism been implanted that it has become suicidal for a news service, or indeed a newspaper, to publicly espouse subjectivity or persuasion in its news columns. Objectivity is financially valuable to the all-purpose newspaper that seeks to expand its profitability through its advertising revenue and its subscription lists. In presenting "both sides" of issues, wire services and newspapers often present ideas that are anathema to the government, to the advertisers, and to the industrial and commercial elite, but this practice is accepted, sometimes reluctantly but nevertheless accepted, as part of the code of objectivity. After all, its perimeters are circumscribed. Moreover, journalism operates, as do all institutions, under a set of conventions that dictate what is to be published. It is well known, for instance, that the unusual is chosen over the normal: It is not news when a dog bites a man, but it is news when a man bites a dog. What happens today is more newsworthy than what happened yesterday; what happens close to home is more newsworthy than what happened thousands of miles away. What is said by a prominent person, a "celebrity," is more newsworthy than what is said by an unknown. Whatever is more dramatic and conflictual is more newsworthy than the routine or cooperative. All these — the unusual, the topical, the near-at-hand, the voice of the celebrity, the conflictual — are journalistic conventions; it is they that define "news." There is no clear definition of news; the professional journalist smells it out with his nose for news. He defines it on the basis of his news judgment. Thus, even the concept of news is subjective. As David Brinkley correctly pointed out, "News is what I say it is."

The code of objectivity and the conventions of news limit dissent in the mass media largely to criticism of individuals. The fundamental institutions are beyond the frontiers of censure. In all the noisy criticism of President Nixon and his administration in the so-called Watergate affair, the press failed to bring any charges against fundamental institutions. It was the presi*dent* who was condemned, not the presi*dency*. So long as "both sides" were heard, it was the anti-Nixon crowd versus the Nixon people. The repeated use of "Watergate" to symbolize corruption contributed to misunderstanding of the situation; it also helped many Americans to hold that there was nothing different in the behavior of the Nixon administration from that of all administrations. How serious, after all, was a break-in of the offices of the Democratic National Committee in the Watergate complex in Washington? The decisive issue, however, did not center on the Watergate break-in, but rather on the debasement of power at the highest levels of the system; on attempts to establish a secret police force answerable only to the president; on the use of the Internal Revenue Service to bring ruin to political opponents; on the positioning of the president and his advisers in a state of absolute power, answerable to no one. The evil lay in the system that gave rise to the corruption, not in Richard Nixon or H. R. Haldeman. The charge was that Nixon had corrupted the institution.

Nixon recognized the nature of the criticism and sought to ride out the attacks by cloaking himself in the majesty of the presidency and by seeking to portray his critics as challenging the institution of the presidency. His defense might even have worked, if he had not been foolish enough to permit the tapes of White House conversations to be preserved. The Watergate case confirms that under the code, fundamental institutions may not be attacked. Nor may the symbols of those fundamental institutions: the flag, for example, or "democracy"; or freedom of the press or of speech or of religion; or the presidency. Enemies of the system may not be applauded, nor symbolic representation of those enemies. Atheism may not be endorsed; freedom of religion does not extend that far. Nor may any symbol of animosity to "family" be supported. Homosexuality may be tolerated, but it may not be advocated. Motherhood may not be condemned. Communism may not be defended. Nor, for that matter, is it acceptable within the perimeters of the system to attack the code of objectivity.

Moreover, the code of objectivity appears to be operative only within the geographical limits of the United States. When the United States is in collision with another nation, it is not necessary to give "both sides" to the dispute equal attention; to do so is to be unpatriotic. It is exceedingly rare to find the views of Fidel Castro given equal weight with those of his enemies, and when Castro's stance is presented, it is usually reported in such a way as to illustrate clearly the wrongheadedness of his views. The situation is similar with regard to the views of Soviet and Chinese leaders. And one would have sought long and hard to find the position of the Ayatollah Khomeini presented in a balanced fashion in the American press during (and after) the holding of the American hostages in Iran.

There are — and always have been — individual journalists who have flouted the code of objectivity and who have presented views beyond the normal perimeters of ideological expression. These have, however, been the exception and not the rule. The pluralist structure of the United States permits and indeed encourages dissident individual voices in a way that is not permitted in the Soviet Union, but these voices are drowned out effectively by the noises raised by the institutions and the loyalist defenders of the system. Robert Paul Wolff likened the territory of American politics to a plateau with steep sides rather than a pyramid. On that plateau, he says, are all the interest groups that have been recognized as legitimate: "The most important battle waged by any group in American politics is the struggle to climb onto the plateau."

According to the logic of democratic pluralism, visibility for groups depends on the willingness of the press to accord them a place on the plateau. In deciding whether or not to grant this privilege, the press is not behaving independently, however. In this activity, the press is operating under the rigid rules of its unwritten network of conventions. Let there be authoritative voices speaking for the dissident group and it will be allowed on the plateau; let its objectives be perceived as operating within the boundaries of the accepted belief system and the plateau will be open to it. But let there be no authoritative voices speaking for it and let its goals be outside those boundaries, then access to the plateau is denied. Unless, of course, the group is able to make so much noise that its existence cannot be denied. Civil-rights activists learned this lesson in the 1960s, and other dissident and outlaw groups have sought to manipulate the press into providing coverage of their activities by defying the law or behaving in a fashion so outrageous that the press cannot ignore the unusualness and conflictual nature of the behavior. Even then, the group may not be granted the comfortable cloak of legitimacy. Communists and atheists fall into the illegitimate category; so do those labeled sexual deviates. In short, any group that threatens the social order or the politico-economic system is rejected. Thus do the mass media serve as significant instruments of social control, operating as agents of the system itself. In this sense, the code of objectivity is itself a mechanism of social control.

The political left in the United States has frequently condemned the press as conservative and even reactionary. Referring to the fact that the overwhelming majority of American newspapers support the Republican party, critics have spoken of a "one-party press." Such was the comment of Adlai Stevenson when, as the Democratic candidate for president in 1952, he found the newspapers supporting his opponent, Dwight Eisenhower, by 83 percent. Yet a dozen years later, the press was endorsing the candidate of the Democratic party, Lyndon Johnson, against Republican Barry Goldwater, who was thought to be so extreme in his rightist views that he might upset the carefully constructed social market system and perhaps even induce a disruptive movement on the left. When Nixon succeeded to the White House in 1968, he seemed determined to attempt to whip the press into docility; he seemed unwilling to accept a press role as agent of the system and insisted it become a full-fledged servant of the government. Predictably, the press responded angrily, rejecting the efforts of Nixon and Vice-President Spiro Agnew to impose restraints on press behavior. In this response, the press was joined not only by liberals already predisposed to opposition to Nixon but also by many conservatives, among them Goldwater, who wished for adherence to the status quo and maintenance of power by the commercial and industrial forces that dictated the social order.

Fighting back against the Nixon campaign, the press predictably turned for support to the First Amendment. Perhaps surprisingly, it also called on the code of objectivity that had been officially embraced by the press industry as early as 1937. In a 1970 article in the *Bulletin of the American Society of Newspaper Editors*, I. William Hill, associate editor of *The Washington Evening Star*, identified his cause with the rhetoric of Lincoln's Gettysburg Address:

> Nine score and five years ago, our forefathers brought forth upon this continent the daily newspaper, conceived in objectivity and dedicated to the proposition that all men are entitled to impartial facts. Now we are engaged in a great media debate, testing whether this newspaper or any medium so conceived and so dedicated can long endure.

In the following issue of the *Bulletin*, Derick Daniels, executive editor of *The Detroit Free Press*, constructed a different interpretation of history:

> If my understanding of history is correct, it was just the opposite — that the press in America was born of advocacy and protest — that opinion and activism were the cornerstones which the Constitution is designed to protect.

Hill and Daniels are giving expression to two different ingredients in the folklore of the press: on the one hand, that its mission is to present "facts" impartially, and on the other, that it is a watchdog to guard against abuse of power. For each man, there is a magic password to open the golden gates into the promised land where the press is free of government restraint and free to serve humankind. For Hill, the password is objectivity; for Daniels, the password is watchdog — or, to use Douglass Cater's colorful phrase, "the fourth branch of government." Neither Hill nor Daniels speaks of a more fundamental role for the press — as an instrument to help preserve the social order.

THE "POWER" OF TELEVISION NEWS

In the contemporary world, the newspaper has been forced to yield primacy to its newer, gaudier cousin: broadcasting. As instruments of social control, radio and television are perhaps the most effective ever conceived. It has become a commonplace to say that most people get most of their information — or "news" — from television, and while this may not be specifically accurate — most people probably get most of their news from other people — it is correct that the broadcasting media dominate the lives of human beings more than any previous medium of communication. Small wonder that those who wield power seek to control or to regulate the broadcasting media in their territory, or that those who seek to wrest power strike first of all at the radio and television outlets. Small wonder also that advertisers pour ever-increasing resources into trumpeting their messages over the air.

Newspapers and magazines have by no means been rendered obsolete, despite declining circulations and a declining share of advertising revenue. Those newspapers that survive the fierce competition of broadcasters and their own colleagues strengthen their position both in the economy and in terms of political influence. Still, among the media, it is broadcasting that has hastened the triumph of capitalism in the United States, Japan, and Western Europe, and in many of their former client states in the less-industrialized world. Broadcasting outlets give capitalist ideologues a tool of incalculable power to promote and expand support for the prevailing belief system.

In the United States, the stronghold of capitalism, the radio and television industries developed differently from the broadcasting industries of other capitalist countries. When radio appeared early in the twentieth century, the older nations of Western Europe placed the new medium under their control. In some instances, government officials were in direct charge, handling not only financing matters but content as well. In others, notably in Great Britain, control was placed in the hands of public corporations, ultimately responsible to the government but with a substantial degree of latitude, especially in programming content. In the Soviet Union, radio financing, distribution, and programming came under ministerial direction. By contrast, in the United States, private commercial interests were permitted to develop and profit from broadcasting as they wished.

The result was one of the most lucrative financial channels to wealth ever to appear in the United States. Those who got in on the ground floor of radio and, later, television made fortunes and established a pattern of programming that was to stress attracting the maximum audiences. These audiences were then to be delivered to the advertisers, who promoted their wares on what soon came to be a national marketplace. Radio and television networks were the most visible instruments of communication and the most widely heeded. A new name was applied to the press — media, which included the broadcasting networks and stations.

The three networks that emerged victorious in the years of financial skirmishing, ABC, CBS, and NBC, not only operated programming empires but also owned a number of radio and television stations in the nation's largest, richest "markets." The profits of all owners of television franchises were substantial, but those of the network-owned stations were the greatest of all. Each of the network-owned stations regularly returned profits of more than a million dollars a year before taxes. A network affiliate in mid-sized Dayton, Ohio, sold for $40 million in 1980; one in the somewhat larger market of Sacramento, California, went for $65 million. A joke that circulated through the industry had it that television was "a license to print money." The money could be printed from the immoderate fees charged for advertising messages. A thirty-second spot during the Super Bowl in 1983 went for $400,000. The average half-minute commercial on ABC-TV at the end of 1982 cost $91,000, an increase over the previous year of 17 percent.

Operators of the publicly owned television networks in other capitalist countries could only shake their heads in wonder at the volume of money changing hands in the U.S. broadcasting business, whose profits now exceeded those of heavy industry. Elsewhere in the capitalist world, broadcasting was financed primarily by revenue from taxes, paid by the owners of the receivers. It was often argued in defense of public financing that the reliance on commercial advertisers lowered the cultural level of the product; in this sense, public ownership was viewed as in the public interest. But before the end of the 1970s, nearly all television systems in the capitalist world found themselves forced to permit some commercial advertising to supplement their income and enable them to continue their programming efforts. The television product of the United States came under steady and unrelenting attack. One chairman of the Federal Communications Commission, the agency charged with regulating television, called it "a vast wasteland." Others said it lowered the level of communication to the lowest common denominator. It became popular to blame television for almost everything, from lowered scholastic achievement by high school students to the reported increase in the crime rates. All of these assertions are exaggerated. What is not exaggerated, however, is the profitability of television, and the role the medium has come to play in the capitalist economic system and in its ideological orientation.

Not surprisingly, viewers grumble over the frequency of commercials and complain about the juvenile content of many television programs. It is doubtful, however, that viewers would choose to eliminate commercials in favor of government or direct corporate control of the medium. As media managers point out also, significant advertising revenues are necessary if they are to turn out distinguished products. Without substantial profit, it is argued, salaries would be depressed and the media could ill afford to hire the best people for the jobs; nor could the media purchase the most modern equipment, in the form of cameras and sophisticated electronic gear.

Critics of the system often acknowledge the rationale but complain that the profits are unnecessarily high, and that so much attention is paid to profits that sight is lost of genuine concern about the public interest. No one has expressed this viewpoint more poignantly than the late Edward R. Murrow, often revered as the greatest of all television journalists, especially for his tough and courageous exposé of the methods and behavior of Senator Joseph McCarthy. Speaking to the Radio-Television News Directors Association in 1958, Murrow — who was then quarreling with CBS — argued that the public interest should carry greater weight than the demand for private profits:

> There is no suggestion here that networks or individual stations should operate as philanthropies. But I can find nothing in the Bill of Rights or the Communications Act which says they must increase their profits each year, lest the Republic collapse.

Murrow's argument was not with the free-enterprise system. Nor is it the argument of most critics in capitalist society who condemn television. They are prepared to accept profit as a systemic value, but their complaint is that the search for advertising dollars pushes the broadcasting medium into filling consumers with unnecessary and unrealistic desires so that they will buy the advertised products. This view is standard opinion in the Soviet Union; American TV critics who hold this view are not usually aware that they are, in a sense, "echoing Communist rhetoric." Supporters of the system, on the other hand, see advertising as a powerful democratic force, leading to a society of abundance. From this perspective, it is the consumers who call the tune, and the advertisers and news media who follow the public, putting on the market what the consumer really wants for his own benefit. In this sense, the argument goes, the consumers are the "voters" in a democratic system, casting their ballot at the cash register as well as in the voting booth. This form of balloting materializes in the ratings system of A. C. Nielsen and others.

Under FCC regulation of the broadcasting industry, the holders of radio and television licenses are required to use those licenses "in the public interest, convenience and necessity." To receive a license to operate a radio or TV station, one must convince the FCC of intention to work in the public interest; when the license is up for renewal in five years, the owner must demonstrate that he or she has actually operated in the public interest. Only rarely has the FCC refused to renew a license, and in nearly all those cases, the refusal was ordered because of false statements in applications or other flagrant behavior. The most dramatic case of revocation was ordered not by the FCC but by a federal court — and this because WLBT-TV in Jackson, Mississippi, had operated its license in utter disregard of the interests of black viewers in its area of operations. Whether broadcasting programs cater to the lowest tastes, or whether they offer nothing but a vast wasteland to their viewers — these factors are not considered in renewal applications. The content of the programming is outside the control of the FCC. Control of their own content belongs to the owners of licenses as part of their First Amendment protection.

The free-press guarantees of the First Amendment are not extended in wholesale fashion to broadcasters. By law, the broadcasting spectrum is considered to be owned by the public; hence, no one can "own" a piece of the broadcasting spectrum. The FCC was set up originally in order to referee disputes among potential broadcasters claiming the same piece of the spectrum. Since, unlike newspaper and magazine owners, the owners of broadcasting facilities license rather than own their means of communication, they do not then receive the same free-press guarantees as do their brethren in the print media. For decades, this status of second-class citizenship has seemed to broadcasters a demon to be exorcised. In particular, broadcasters have resented the Fairness Doctrine, first enunciated in 1949, which requires that whenever broadcasters air controversial issues, they must make sure that their coverage of those issues is fair. However powerful broadcasters may have been in other areas, they have been unsuccessful in attacking the Fairness Doctrine. They are, in short, required — in ways that the print media are not required — to practice objectivity. This is so, at least to the extent that they are not permitted to make wholly one-sided presentations of controversial issues.

One interesting result of this requirement, broadcasters point out with monotonous regularity, is that they tend to avoid dealing with controversial issues at all, limiting their editorial observations for the most part to the tried and true: urging highway safety, condemning criminals, promoting clean air and clean water. Television stations do, from time to time, endorse candidates for office and attack the wicked — but, under FCC rules, they are required to give all those condemned or criticized an opportunity for fair reply, an opportunity that inevitably eats into the profits of the stations, for this programming cannot be sold. The end result, as the broadcasters say, is that the content of television programming is notably bland. Few sides are taken on political or economic issues, and when they are taken, the "other side" must be given its innings. The thrust of television is inevitably towards the middle, towards the safe, towards the profitable.

The Fairness Doctrine does have a positive requirement. Stations are obliged to seek out and air controversial issues. This requirement is rarely enforced, partly because the FCC staff (as it says) is too small to police the

requirement. More significantly, the FCC (like most regulatory government agencies) cooperates with the industry it is empowered to regulate
more than it polices it. Columnist Jack Anderson has spoken of as the FCC
as "little more than a retriever for the networks. The network executives
soothingly stroke its fur, confident that Congress will keep the watchdog
from biting."

Few can doubt the influence of the television networks on the
members of Congress, who must regularly run for reelection and whose
"image" on the screen is thought to represent one of the decisive factors in
voters' decisions. Congress could, if it wished, increase the power of the
FCC and direct it to rigorously enforce not only the Fairness Doctrine but
also the requirement that broadcasters operate in the public interest. To do
so would, however, subject those congressmen who voted to extend the
FCC grip on the industry to criticism on the air. Few congressmen can be
expected to take this risk. And by limiting the restraints on broadcasters,
congressmen can reasonably expect to receive favorable attention on
television. A kind of three-cornered manipulation mechanism is at work
here, with pressures generated by broadcasting executives, the FCC, and
Congress. The interests of the public come fourth.

Despite the growth of interest in investigative journalism, political and
economic realities contribute to timidity and lack of adventurousness on
the part of television. But there are times when broadcasters act contrary
to their economic interests, when they take on vested power and risk their
own profitability. One such situation came in 1970 when NBC elected to air
a documentary it called "Migrant," which attacked one of the network's
principal advertisers, the Coca-Cola Company. That documentary served
primarily as a vehicle to expose the wretched living conditions of migrant
workers employed in Florida citrus groves that were owned by Coca-Cola.
When the company heard about the impending program, it attempted to
have the documentary suppressed. Failing in that, it managed to induce the
network to make some minor changes. These changes were obviously
unsatisfactory to the company, for when it put together its advertising
budget for the first quarter of 1971, it included no money at all for
commercials on NBC but provided for $1 million for CBS and $1.2 million
for ABC. In the last quarter of 1970, Coca-Cola had spent $2.5 million for
spots on NBC. By going ahead with the documentary, NBC lost millions of
dollars in potential revenue. Later, however, Coca-Cola returned to NBC,
evidently deciding it needed the network despite the poor image it had
been given in the documentary. The "Migrant" story is not altogether
isolated; networks and broadcasting stations do occasionally bite the hand
that is feeding them. But the cases are few and seem not to interfere
markedly with the profitability of the broadcasting industry.

Broadcasters enjoy most but not all of the free-enterprise benefits
enjoyed by newspapers and magazines. By and large, the news programs of

the television networks and stations are protected by the provisions of the First Amendment. The model for these programs is almost identical to the model for the news activities of newspapers. The dominant ethic is the code of objectivity, the presentation of "both sides" of issues. And even more dramatically than their print journalism brethren, they present their product in the literary style of fiction. In his book *News From Nowhere*, Edward Jay Epstein reported that TV journalists at NBC operated under direct instructions to present their reports in "fictive form" — using the device familiar in fiction of rising and falling action, with events rising at the beginning, moving through a middle to a dramatic climax, and then falling towards a clearly definable end, using the traditional fictive device of suspense to maintain interest. Newspaper articles also follow the "story" pattern, but less dramatically than reports on television. So do magazine articles. Robert Park called attention to the use of this device by the *Saturday Evening Post* during its heyday:

> The ordinary man, as the *Saturday Evening Post* has discovered, thinks in concrete images, pictures and parables. He finds it difficult to read a long article unless it is dramatized, and takes the form of what newspapers call a "story." "News story" and "fiction story" are two forms of modern literature that are now so like one another that it is sometimes difficult to distinguish them.

In his study of NBC news procedures, Epstein isolates certain "basic assumptions" about news in the television industry, chief among them these three: (1) that the interest of viewers is most likely to be maintained through easily recognized images and that it is likely to wander if the images are confusing; thus, complex issues are presented in terms of human experience rather than abstract ideas; (2) that scenes of potential conflict are more interesting than placid scenes; and (3) that the attention span of the viewer is limited and can be prolonged mainly through action or subjects in motion. These, then, are additional conventions adopted by television journalists, adding to the long-established conventions of unusualness, topicality, proximity, conflict, authoritative sources, and the others practiced by print journalists.

Much is said and written about the power of the press and the influence of the press — especially the television journalists — on the course of contemporary events. The fatal assumption in this argument is that this "power" of the press is an *independent* power, that it can be and is used in adversarial fashion against governments and the politicians and statesmen who run them. It is an easy assumption to make. There is great potential for power in the press, and the American news media do *seem* to be operating independently; they do *seem* to be challenging power — as a kind of fourth branch of government. On closer investigation, however, it is apparent that belief in the exercise of press power is a formidable weapon in the hands of those who seek to use the press for their own purposes. Governments and the politically and economically powerful have been manipulating newspapers throughout history. The opportunity for manipulation of television journalists is one that has not been lost on the powerful.

Each of the four articles of faith of press independence turns out to be useful for the manipulators: that the press is free of outside interference, that it serves the public's right to know, that it seeks to learn and present the truth, and that it reports facts objectively and fairly. Not one of these articles of faith squares with reality; belief in them, however, makes the task of the manipulators easier and assists in the maintenance of the ideology that keeps them in power. This theme will be explored in chapter 8 in a discussion of the goal of "social responsibility." We turn now to an examination of a third press ideology that stands between the ideology of the planned and market economies.

Catching up on the news in Mali. (*UNESCO/Alexis N. Vorontzoff, photographer*)

Seven

The Ideological Press: The Third World and Development

THE OLD ORDER CHANGETH

The naming of things is one of the most critical aspects of human behavior. What we call something determines to a large extent what and how we think of it. Take, for example, the term Third World. Or, underdeveloped nations. Or developing nations. Whichever of these terms is the one we choose, the flavor we taste is of inferiority. It is not even second best; it is third. The image suggested by that flavor is of something of less importance than the first or the second world; it is the image of something still developing towards a status that approaches that of its betters. That which is underdeveloped is somehow of lesser quality.

But what name *can* be applied to these geographical and political units? Are they not objectively less developed than the powerful nations of the world? The answer is a clear yes; of course the level of their industrial, commercial, and political sophistication is below that of the great nations of the world. And yet by identifying them as underdeveloped or developing, we are not expressing merely a technological reality. We are also expressing a value judgment. To be identified as underdeveloped is not merely to be categorized in terms of scientific understanding or commercial savvy. It is also to be classified as inferior, as somehow or other less good, less worthy.

The categorization is so thorough, so widespread that the affected countries themselves employ the terms Third World and developing nations (they have generally rejected the term "underdeveloped" as going too far). In so doing, these countries have themselves accepted their status as inferior, even though they may publicly challenge the very idea of inferiority. Their status is similar to that of the poor in the Anglo-Saxon world during the heyday of Social Darwinism. In those days, the poor were persuaded to believe that because they had not acquired wealth they were less developed morally than those who had grown rich.

It is true that the poor nations of the world have not always surrendered meekly to the labels applied to them. One major effort to gain self-respect is apparent in their efforts to acquire the title of "nonaligned nations." This label is an improvement, since it introduces the idea of choice. No one chooses to be a member of the Third World or to be a citizen of a developing nation. But one can choose to be nonaligned, and the quality of choice introduces a degree of dignity. Still, there are difficulties with the term nonaligned. It implies that the industrialized world is divided into two camps, for convenience's sake identified as East and West, and that the nonaligned nations have refused to choose sides. The further implication is that the political struggle between East and West is being waged in large part in order to win over to one side or the other the nonaligned nations, so that in the end one side or the other will "win." In this interesting but ultimately terrifying metaphor, it is never quite clear what it means to win or to lose.

With the increasing prominence of the countries of the so-called Third World, whether as developing or nonaligned nation-states, the mass media find themselves in a crucial position in the maintenance of world peace. Indeed, if there is some frightening validity to the metaphor, the battle is being fought as much in the pages of newspapers or on the radio and television spectrum as in the plethora of weapons systems required to win.

Poor countries existed long before the collapse of the colonial world that was one result of the Second World War. One need think only of China and Ecuador, of Cuba and Liberia, of Turkey and Afghanistan. However, after Britain and France surrendered control of Asia and Africa, the term Third World came into existence, and interest intensified around the world about the role of the mass media in the newly independent states. Thus, the countries of Asia and Africa joined those of South and Central America, which had been, almost unnoticed, wrestling with identical issues for more than a century. The first of the great European colonial empires to collapse was that of Spain, which lost its control of Latin America early in the nineteenth century. The arrival of the United Nations and its increasingly global institutions focused sharply on the media, not only as a topic for scientific research but also as a potential weapon in increasing the political and economic power of the new nation-states.

We will discard Third World as the operative term, because it is ambiguous. As used in the United States — and among English-speaking nations and those that derive their ideas from them — Third World seems to be almost synonymous with "economically disadvantaged"; in the 1960s, the Third World was often identified as "underdeveloped." The term is French in origin and in its early career was a political rather than an economic phrase. *"Tiers-monde"* is a revolutionary term, dating back to 1789 for its connotation. The Third Estate in revolutionary France was the *Tiers-état*, the body of common men as distinguished from the powerful and privileged First and Second Estates, the nobility and the clergy. It was a political body determined to wrest power from Church and State. In its contemporary incarnation, it was popularized in the English translation of Frantz Fanon's *Wretched of the Earth* not long after Third World unity was first discussed at the Bandung Conference in Indonesia in 1955. Since to some Third World has a political and to others an economic implication, we will rely on the linguistically more neutral term "advancing" to describe the nation-states involved. "Advancing" as used here is by no means free of either political or sociological significance. There is no term that can achieve this happy state.

The United Nations came into existence in 1945 with a membership of fifty countries. By 1980, the membership had more than tripled. Virtually all the countries that had joined the UN were former colonies of Africa and Asia. The industrial world, those with market and planned economies alike, had seen to it that their preeminent position would not be upset within the UN, no matter how many new nation-states appeared; the principal powers had assured that no substantive action could be taken by the UN without the unanimous agreement of the five Great Powers that had survived the Second World War — the United States, the Soviet Union, Britain, France, and China. The regime of Chiang Kai-shek, the original "China" in the UN, was replaced as a member in 1971 by the People's Republic of China, which now possesses the veto right originally assigned to the Chiang government. Nearly the entire roster of the original members of the UN came from the American continent and Europe.

How shall we label these new countries? How shall we define their press systems? The affected countries identified themselves in 1964 as the Group of 77, at once an objective description of the number of countries that created a unit at the first UN Conference on Trade and Development and an attempt to avoid the values contained in such verbal symbols as Third World. Social scientists (who are always fascinated by acronyms) have sometimes adopted the letters LDC to stand for Less-Developed Countries. No designation seems entirely satisfactory, and most are somehow demeaning. The word "advancing" characterizes not only the press systems of these nation-states but also their economies. "Advancing" is a synonym of sorts for "developing," but it lacks some of the stigma associated with whatever has so far failed to develop. Anyone — individual, institution, or nation — may advance. Even the top-seeded player in a tennis tournament must advance from round to round. Any newspaper or radio station may advance; it may acquire a larger audience or it may progress in terms of its moral judgments. Of equal importance, it is clear that those who advance must not necessarily do so through win-or-lose competition, although that is possible, as in the example of the tennis player. But individuals, or nations, may also advance together. They may advance quite as nicely through cooperation as through competition. In fact, groups that find themselves discriminated against are most likely to advance through joining forces with others on the bottom in order to approach more closely to the top. So let us speak of the press of these advancing countries as the advancing press.

Of what does the ideology of an advancing press consist? Is there, in fact, such an ideology? Or are the affected nation-states so different from one another that we cannot reasonably speak of an advancing press? There is, of course, no such thing as *the* advancing press, even as there are no such things as *the* market press or *the* socialist press. Differences abound in all three ideological structures. Still, one may with confidence identify models of all three structures. In the market model, the belief system embraces the theology of the First Amendment, the code of objectivity, the idea that an independent press stands as a protection for the people against abuses of power and, above all, as the centerpiece of the democratic assumption. In the socialist model, the belief system is codified in Lenin's three roles, fortified by assertion of its own code of objectivity, and by assignment to the press of the critical function of education. The ideology of the advancing press is derived from two sources. One is *acquired* — learned from the models of the market and the socialist press; the other is *indigenous* — rooted in the history and the culture of the new nation-states. The first is frankly imitative; the second is natural.

The press *systems* in the advancing world, on the other hand, seem to be entirely acquired. In fact, the press in the contemporary sense of that word does not seem to have existed in the advancing world before the colonial conquerors arrived and imposed their own press systems. Certainly, there were no mass media in the mountains of South America or in the bush and savanna country of Africa or in the rice fields of Asia before the appearance of the Spanish, the British, and the French. The communication patterns that predated the colonial conquerors were primitive and local, devoted almost entirely to the daily needs of the people. News, as we understand the term, did not exist. Thus, all the press institutions of the advancing world are acquired institutions, learned first from the conquerors and later from the successor powers, the United States and the Soviet Union. The important messages dispatched in Africa and Asia were similar to those circulated in ancient Rome, in the ecclesiastical social order of the medieval world, and among the merchants of Venice — all were exchanged not among the people but among the elite, among the leaders of church, state, and commerce. For the ordinary people, the mechanism of communication was not the written word; it was the drum and the smoke signal and above all the spoken word, relayed in tales, in song, and in ritual chants.

Obviously, the structures of the press that developed among the scores of new nation-states differed from one another, in the same ways that their political, economic, social, and cultural structures differed. But in a very important way, these structures were also similar — in that they were without exception acquired. It could not be surprising that among the new nation-states the expressed goals were to be free, to be objective, to educate, and to serve as an arm of the public in safeguarding against the abuses of power. Each one of these goals, it is to be remembered, was a learned goal; none of them arose from the indigenous information systems or from the beliefs that naturally grew up around those systems. It is mere quibbling to overemphasize the differences among the media in the advancing world. The essential similarity lies in the fact that these media are universally derived from the industrialized nations of the world, a world that is conveniently, if inappropriately, designated as West and East. The naming of West and East itself contributes to international tension, since it cleaves the world into two hostile camps. Repetition of these names in the press rigidifies the division. So does the characterization of the advancing countries as Third World, since it divides the industrial nations into the First World — that of the capitalists — and the Second World — that of the socialists.

With the collapse of the colonial order, with the division of political, economic, and military power into two great blocs, came also what is often said to be a communications revolution. The advancing nations emerged with the computer — and, interestingly, with the "science" of communications. Of all the intellectual pursuits that have attracted the attention of scholars in the postwar world, the most striking has been the study of communications. In all corners of the world, theorists have plunged with abandon into the arena of cybernetics, data flow, and computer models. A literature that did not even exist in 1945 has grown by now into one of the most voluminous to be found anywhere. The search for answers has intrigued not only scholars but laymen as well, and the "science" of futurology appeared. Empirical studies without end have been entered into for the purpose of collecting data about the way information travels from person to person, from nation to nation, and about how to predict the future.

The linkage of the computer, the symbol of the communications revolution, and the emergence of the advancing states is a matter of grave import. One separates these two phenomena at the risk of losing any kind of understanding of the contemporary world.

A related phenomenon of considerable significance is evident in the overriding concern of the new communications scholars with the hardware of communications. This concern has sometimes divided researchers in the field of communications from those in journalism. The studies of many communications scholars have tended to pay only limited attention to newspapers and broadcasting outlets, dealing with broader areas of communications almost as if the news media did not exist, as if global communications were imaginable without news media. On the other hand, many journalism scholars, inspired by widely publicized debates in international forums, have collected mountains of data in seeking to find whether news reports around the world give balanced information about international events.

How ironical it is that although the avowed goal of communications scholars has been to build theories of communications, their research has often been so narrow that they have muddled rather than enhanced understanding. Borrowing from the truth trees of philosophers, the stimulus-response diagrams of psychologists, and the mathematical models of physicists, communications scholars have adopted as their universal symbol the arrow. Some run in straight lines; some are curved; some even bend back upon themselves. They are alleged to describe the flow of communications, from source (stimulus) to receiver (response), with elaborate cross-arrowed mechanisms to illustrate single or multiloop feedback systems. The arrows have the fortuitous characteristic of impressing fellow scholars with the rigor behind the graphic design but do lamentably little to resolve the crucial international (and domestic) peril that lies at hand.

If the arrow symbolizes the work of the communications scholars, the table of contents typifies the efforts of the journalism researchers, who have prepared and published towering piles of books, monographs, and scholarly papers recording and comparing the contents of newspapers and of the items on the evening news reports, as they assess whether or not the media have presented balanced reports about the "news" that was taking place. The fact is that a mere tabulation of content tells little about balance. And *arguendo*, even if it did, that information would be of limited utility in attacking the real problems in contemporary journalism.

While the numbers of arrows and tables of contents have been multiplying in libraries and research centers, the attention of journalists, public officials, and many researchers in the advancing world has been directed at a different question: how to harmonize the press systems those nation-states have acquired from the industrialized nations with the traditional patterns of information in their pasts. It is in the framework of this question that an ideology of the advancing world has appeared.

THE ROAD TO A FLOURISHING AFRICAN PRESS

In the countries that gained their independence from their colonial overlords in the twentieth century, the preoccupation of the leadership was inevitably with development. This was less true in the nineteenth century when the Spanish were driven out of Latin America, but even there, the liberators dreamed of modern societies. The term development did not achieve worldwide importance until the period after World War II, when scores of new nations emerged in Asia and Africa. To the leaders of these nations it seemed merely obvious that the press could provide a kind of shortcut to development. The press folklore that had gained sway over more than two centuries assured them of the power of the press to influence and to persuade. What more useful instruments could be imagined than newspapers and radio to spread the word of political freedom, of nationhood, and the opportunity to assume an honored place at the table of reputable world society? Such an assumption was inevitable, for the leaders of the new nations had themselves been schooled in the lore of the capitalist states; their ideas derived from those of Britain and France, Belgium and Holland, and the political giant that had been spawned by all of them, the United States. Belief was universal in the power of the press and its companion in education, the schools, to raise a citizenry dedicated to the principles of democracy and social justice. In this assumption, the leaders of the advancing nations were supported by the army of development researchers, who saw the press as central in the process they came to identify as nation-building. Thus, there arose the concept of a special kind of journalism that came to be known, in a number of guises, as development journalism.

It would have been asking too much of the concept for it to have emerged as a clearly defined doctrine, understandable in all its ramifications by one and all. Few such doctrines have appeared in the history of humankind, and development journalism certainly did not enjoy that distinction. In fact, it arose in so many different forms that by now it is impossible to give it a definition on which reasonable men can agree. For this reason, as well as because the idea of development carries with it an aura of inferiority, we choose to speak of the ideology of advancing journalism, a belief system woven from the cloth from which most — if not all — the costumes worn by development journalism have been fabricated. These fundamental articles of faith include belief in the press as a unifying rather than a divisive force; belief in the press as an instrument of social justice and a device for beneficial social change; and the presumption that the press is properly an instrument of two-way communication, with equal importance assigned to the writer and the reader, to the broadcaster and the listener. Sadly, the practice in much of the developing world has been far from the articles of faith. Muzzling of the press is widespread.

In the evolution of the advancing-world ideology, the theorists and the practitioners of the press borrowed extensively from the belief systems that had grown up in capitalist and socialist societies. However, they introduced modifications of major proportions, although they were not often aware how major those modifications were, partly because the ideology was slow in evolving, but more importantly because they were instantly drawn into the political, economic, and cultural conflicts that already divided the world. The threads that made up the cloth of development journalism were never free of politics. To some, especially in Asia, it was mandatory that reporters and editors in the newly independent states be themselves independent, free of political constraints; to others, particularly in Africa, it was critical for journalists to ally themselves with the political forces seeking to build unified nations of sectional, ethnic, linguistic, and tribal components. The goal was unrealistic in both cases, since the press is never independent and free of political constraints. Moreover, the press is powerless to create a unity in a void.

Kwame Nkrumah, the influential president of Ghana, gave expression to the basic African belief in an address to a group of African journalists in 1963. "The press," he said, "does not exist merely for the purpose of enriching its proprietors or entertaining its readers." He added:

> It is an integral part of the society, with which its purpose must be in consonance. It must help establish a progressive political and economic system that will free men from want and poverty.... It must reach out to the masses, educate and inspire them, work for equality and the universality of men's rights everywhere.

The journalists at the conference adopted a resolution that rejected as a relic of colonialism the idea that the press ought to be nonpolitical. It was their duty, the journalists resolved, to show that the nonpolitical attitude "is nothing more or less than imperialist politics with which our universities, civil service and other intellectual workers have been seduced away from our Revolution." Nkrumah later fell into disgrace, accused (as were so many of his colleagues) of himself subverting the principles of a revolution of freedom by building a dictatorial regime in which all liberties were suppressed, including freedom of the press. However, the ideas expressed by Nkrumah have by no means been repudiated. The concept of the press as an instrument of unity remains today a basic tenet of the ideology of the advancing press.

In Asia, where — unlike Africa — the British had established a flourishing press system constructed on the British model and embodying the ideals of the homeland press, the impetus was in favor of the kind of

nonpolitical system that Nkrumah abhorred. Indeed, the term development press, which appeared first in Asia, was established to define a press
free of political direction, where the first duty of the press was seen as
reporting news about economic development. The term achieved prominence with the creation, in 1967, of the Press Foundation of Asia, financed
jointly by Asian newspapers and the Ford Foundation. Its chief executive
said that the credibility of PFA was "based on professionalism, objectivity,
and total independence from any government or bureaucratic control and
influence," a statement that might have been made by any U.S. or British
press executive.

The term development journalism quickly came under severe criticism, attacked as a smoke screen under which dictators subjected their
press to iron controls and strict censorship. This criticism grew in large
measure out of the special case of the Philippines, in which the idea of
development journalism was first broached. By 1973, a Department of
Development Communication had been established at the University of
the Philippines at Los Baños. At Los Baños, development journalism was
revised in name and concept to "development support communications,"
in which the media were to be simply instruments of development. Plans
for development were to be created by government agencies, and the press
was to assist in the accomplishment of the announced goals. The first
chairman of the university department at Los Baños, Nora Quebral, said
her program was aimed at rescuing the public from poverty through
economic growth "that makes possible greater social equality and the
larger fulfillment of human potential." Under this system, Philippine
journalists have been denied the right to criticize their authoritarian
president, Ferdinand Marcos, his family, or his policies. Repression, in the
name of development, is a way of life in the Philippines, as it is in many
other parts of the advancing world in Asia, Africa, and Latin America.

This reality does not diminish the principles of development journalism. So, in any case, said Narinder Aggarwala, an executive in the United
Nations Development Program, who argued that it was an aberration for
development journalism to be converted into a tool for repression of the
news media. Instead, he said, development journalism properly should be
likened to the practice in the industrialized world of "investigative
journalism." The duty of a journalist reporting on development, Aggarwala wrote, is to

> critically examine, evaluate and report the relevance of a development project
> to national and local needs, the difference between a planned scheme and its
> actual implementation, and the differences between its impact on people as
> claimed by government officials, and as it actually is.

Such a definition would seem to reduce development journalism to
the status of ordinary journalism as (at least in theory) it is practiced in

both market and socialist press systems. Of particular importance, however, is the fact that, in whatever guise, development journalism always was idealistic in tone. Some might say it was utopian. But there was everywhere a warning, sometimes implied, sometimes explicit. For it to survive, it had to serve the needs of the people of the advancing world. Tom Mboya, the respected Kenyan political leader, made the point vividly in May 1962, eighteen months before Kenya achieved independence. The African press, Mboya told a gathering of journalists in Paris, had to serve the cause of nation building; moreover, since it served an informative, critical, and educational function, it had to be permitted to operate in freedom. In addition, he said, the press had to join forces with the African leaders in their nation-building efforts: "It must learn to treat Africa in her own context on the basis of her people's emotions and not in the East-West context or on the basis of foreign interests." And, he added, with prescience: "These things it must do, or face the charge of traitor." Many editors and reporters were to face that charge, and freedom of the press was to be no more evident in the advancing world than it was in the industrialized nations.

The sounding board for discussions about the behavior and the role of the press was to become concentrated inside UNESCO and various other international bodies, as well as among journalism and communications researchers in both the industrialized and the advancing world. At UNESCO, discussions concentrated at first on the idea of the flow of information and later, increasingly, on technological developments and on the relationship between journalism — the reporting of news — and other instruments of communications and the purveying of information. The schools of journalism that sprang up in the new nation-states and in the older colonial societies of Latin America placed greater stress on research and communications models than did their forerunners in the United States, where the primary emphasis remained on the training of reporters, editors, and photographers. Those who were charged with operating the newspapers and radio stations in the advancing world rushed off to the United States in ever-increasing numbers to study what came to be called "the nuts and bolts" of journalism. And they returned to their newspapers and radio stations to put into practice the techniques they had learned from the Americans, as well as those they had observed among the British and French newspapers that had long circulated in the colonies.

In the socialist world, the breakup of the colonial empires and the creation of new nation-states was viewed as fulfilling the predictions of Marx, Lenin, and other socialist theorists, who had seen the imperialist capitalist world collapsing under the weight of its internal contradictions. To Marxist analysts, the new, revolutionary societies required a press system in the image of the Leninist model. Nation building fit comfortably into the model of collective organization. Just as in the capitalist countries researchers found an exciting new subject for study, so did theorists in Marxist lands, and, indeed, Socialist theorists in capitalist nations. To them, the operative term was "cultural imperialism." Now that the capitalists had surrendered direct political control of their colonies, they were, it was said, moving into a more subtle sphere of domination. With the help of newspapers, and especially television and advertising, capitalists were seeking to subject their former colonies to a different kind of exploitation. They were attempting to blot out the native histories of the new nation-states, to destroy their cultures and their traditions, and replace them with the mechanized consumer society they had created in industrialized lands. It was a different form of exploitation of the proletariat, and its spearhead was the press and the information industry. It was not necessary for socialist analysts to impose this kind of thinking on the advancing world. The same idea had already occurred to many Africans, Asians, and Latin Americans. Nkrumah was not alone in voicing fear of inroads by Western ideologues and journalists. Similar expressions came from other leaders and the socialist thinkers in the advancing world. Few among them was more consistent and outspoken than Julius Nyerere, the president of Tanzania, whose insistence on modernization from within has exerted a powerful influence on other leaders in Africa and in other portions of the advancing world.

During a recent visit to Tanzania, this author found a depressingly poverty-ridden press system that sought to make up for its technological and financial shortcomings with enthusiasm and energy. There were only two daily newspapers in a country of 18 million, both located in the capital city of Dar-es-Salaam, and each with the most modest of circulations. The English-language *Daily News* had a circulation of 90,000, the Swahili-language *Uhuru* one of 100,000. Nevertheless, the editors of those papers saw a bright journalistic future as the literacy rate climbed. Nyerere claims to have raised the level of literacy from 15 percent to 70 percent over a twenty-year period. "Our role is to inform and to entertain," said the editor of *Uhuru*, Wilson Bukholi. "It is important for our country to develop sophisticated newspaper readers." To Bukholi, as to Nyerere, the most effective method of avoiding cultural imperialism was to generate a discriminating public that could recognize efforts to foist an alien culture on it.

While there is no official newspaper censorship in Tanzania, Nyerere has taken strong action with regard to television. In order to keep American show biz from Tanzanians, he has barred the sale of television sets on the Tanzanian mainland. On the offshore island of Zanzibar, which is a part of the United Republic of Tanzania, television has taken a gentle toehold. On the island, a modest operation called TVZ began a struggle for existence in 1973, when the Zanzibar government provided a $5 million grant. Operating on a shoestring and hampered by Nyerere's prohibition,

TVZ was on the air for three hours a day in 1980, when we visited the island. The eager young TVZ staffers saw themselves in the vanguard of education. In the same way that editors on the mainland envisioned their newspapers as instruments to expand the education of the public, so the television staffers on the island of Zanzibar saw the broadcast medium as an educational tool. The TVZ people refused to air any scenes of violence and expressed reluctance over showing any foreign imports as a threat to the fabric of their indigenous culture. Clearly, their aspirations exceeded their capabilities. Not only could few Zanzibar residents afford a television set, but power was limited, and blackouts were a daily occurrence. Moreover, as everywhere in Africa, maintenance was a major problem. Every room in the Hotel Bwawami, Zanzibar's largest, had its own television set, but the only one in the hotel that worked was the one in the bar.

While censorship of newspapers was prohibited by law, it was nevertheless clear that news was suppressed on a regular basis. As everywhere, Tanzanian newspaper editors were skillful readers of cues and clues from Nyerere and his aides as to what kind of news would be pleasing to the leadership. On a number of occasions, Nyerere chided editors for censoring information. What was needed, all those in Tanzania associated with the press believed, was a homegrown training program to upgrade the quality of journalists and perhaps to stiffen their backbones a bit. But here also reality frustrated hope. In Dar-es-Salaam, a small coterie of enthusiastic young men were trying to build a school of journalism in a rickety building donated by the Salvation Army. Nearly half the thirty-one students had not seen a typewriter before enrolling in the school. Next to raising money to operate the school, the chief ambition of the directors was to go to a school of journalism in the United States to learn better how to train their students.

From Africa and from Asia and Latin America as well, students have been flooding into journalism schools in the United States, but many others have been traveling to the Soviet Union to study Marxist-Leninist interpretations of the press. What once was referred to as "a battle for men's minds" is to some extent today being waged among journalists of the advancing world. The belief system that has become widespread through the advancing world has pleased neither U.S. nor Soviet theorists. On the one hand, it has endorsed the goals of objectivity, fairness, and balance so dear to U.S. press thinkers; but on the other hand, it has set great store by the assignment of the press as organizer of the thinking of the public, as the political instrument prized by Soviet analysts. Moreover, the press ideology of the advancing world is rooted far more passionately than is that of the United States or the Soviet Union in belief in the press as leading a fight against racism, militarism, or antagonism among nations. Where what was embraced in the press philosophies of the market and socialist systems was conflict, the operative word in the ideology of the advancing press system was cooperation.

Of course, while cooperation was the ideal pronounced in the advancing world, the practice was often directly opposite, especially on the home front. In Nigeria, the most populous country of Africa, tribal strains led to bitter and brutal civil war shortly after independence was gained in 1960. The avoidance of conflict between the great industrialized powers was one thing; such avoidance between the rival ethnic and economic groups inside the country was another. In the end, however, unification was achieved and a succession of national governments went about the business of forging a federal system that would strengthen the national identity of Nigeria and enable it to play a leading role in international society. The press was central in this effort, even though it was evident early on that the dream of nation building through the pages of newspapers and the voice of radio was a chimera. Intertribal, interracial, and interreligious strains imposed painful frustrations on the emerging press ideology of the new nation-states and bedeviled the efforts of the defenders of the ideology to convince detractors that there was anything more to their aspirations than the "children of an idle brain, begot of nothing but vain fantasy." There was, however, a lot more substance than the detractors often recognized.

The road to a flourishing press system in Nigeria, as in Tanzania and throughout the advancing world, has been rocky. Journalists and editors have had to find new pathways through those rocks, discarding along the way as best they could the colonial heritage that had taught them all they knew about the press. In Nigeria, the first newspapers were introduced by missionaries a century before independence, and the dozens of broadsheets that were born and died throughout that century inevitably followed the British model. So it was even after 1960. In the decade that preceded independence, when the Nigerian press openly agitated for an end to colonial rule, it was still following the procedures and practices of the London newspapers. Imitation may be the sincerest form of flattery, but it is also self-demeaning. To adopt the colonial model was to accept a position of cultural inferiority. But to do so was also to be realistic; there were no other models to follow.

In the years that have passed, much attention has been devoted to the phenomenon that is labeled cultural imperialism, the imposition of the cultural norms of the industrialized world on those of the advancing world. Not only the *imposition*, but the outright *acceptance* of those norms. For years, the boulevard press of London (or, as it is often said in journalistic circles in Britain, the "popular" press as opposed to the "serious" press) has included as a feature on page 3 a photograph of a beautiful, bare-breasted woman. In the 1980s, newspapers in Lagos, the capital of Nigeria, were still printing on page 3 photographs of bare-breasted, beautiful women, and most of them were white. Such is a particularly blatant form of the acceptance of an alien culture; most of that acceptance is less showy, but more significant.

Recent criticism has been directed primarily at the introduction of the advertising techniques and forms of capitalist nations, mainly those of the United States. The great transnational corporations have been using modern merchandising and advertising messages to help create a consumer society in the advancing world that would become a market for their products and their goals, aspirations, and belief systems.

Despite general acceptance of the penetration of the bearers of the consumer society, it is difficult to find any officials in Africa who publicly endorse this particular form of cultural invasion. Instead, they suffer in relative silence the introduction of alien goals and ideals in order to gain from the transnationals the benefits of trade and technology that they consider mandatory for their economic development. The irony is supreme. Government officials, who in their hearts despise the dissemination through their countries of the products and norms of their former colonial masters, not only welcome this kind of dissemination but often crack down harshly on those who protest in public. Hundreds of African editors have suffered as a result, and more than a handful have been flung into prison, tortured, or killed for their protests.

The ideal of free expression has been endorsed everywhere throughout the former colonial world, but it is more honored today in the breach than in the practice. Like Thomas Jefferson and all the American presidents who have followed him, the leaders of the new countries of Africa and Asia have preached the cause of a free and open society before taking office but have found themselves compelled to condemn a hostile press and even to move to suppress it upon taking office. If a truly independent press has not appeared in the industrialized world, it would be ludicrous to expect one to arise in the advancing world. There, as everywhere, newspapers and broadcasting outlets are agents. In the immediate postwar years — the late 1940s and early 1950s — they were mainly agents of the foes of colonial power, who wished to drive out the British and French. In the early 1960s, in the euphoria of liberation, they were agents of the newly enfranchised leadership celebrating the end of colonial rule. In the late 1960s and early 1970s, as reaction set in, the press became agents of the military leaders who took power in an attempt to preserve order. By the 1980s, the new nation-states were progressing in different directions: in some of them, as in Nigeria, the press had been included as a partner of government and the commercial and industrial interests, and was permitted a substantial degree of latitude; In fact, it regulated itself through self-censorship, a practice not unknown in the industrialized world. In most African states, the press operated under more rigid direction. Similarly, in Asia, adherence to acceptable political and economic norms was required. In some countries, among them Indonesia and the Philippines, censorship was firm and unbending; in India, for the most part, self-censorship was considered adequate, although for a time President Indira Gandhi found that practice not to her liking and reimposed firm rules of censorship.

Perhaps the most dramatic effort launched in the advancing world to promote political objectives through the press was in Sukarno's Indonesia, where the press was designated "a tool of the revolution" to help establish the system Sukarno named Guided Democracy. From 1959 through 1965, the Sukarno regime, proclaiming its own brand of socialism, issued a series of decrees aimed at creating a frankly propagandistic press utterly free of outside influences; new training institutes would be created and paper mills built inside the country. Newspapers would remain under private ownership, but their content would be "guided" by government officials. After Sukarno was deposed in the mid-1960s, new press regulations were imposed, abolishing the Sukarno-guided press structure and installing what the new leader, Suharto, called a free press system. However, this rightist system followed the same lines as the previous leftist model, and the press was ordered to suppress any information contrary to the philosophy of the Suharto regime.

Whatever the specific rules at the particular time in the advancing world, the press acquiesced in — and promoted — the norms of the political and economic leadership. In the few countries that pursued a Marxist course — for instance, Cuba, Tanzania, Ethiopia, and Vietnam — the norms involved vigorous criticism of the consumer society and the values exported by the transnationals. In the overwhelming majority of countries, however, the accepted value system was that of capitalism, and only limited criticism of this value system appeared in the pages of newspapers or on radio and television. Still, even among the majoritarian press, there often appeared defense of traditional cultural values and criticism of the importation of alien ideas. Such criticism was even more widespread in private gatherings of journalists and editors.

In Ibadan, a Nigerian city of about four million said to be the largest African city — that is, a city that grew from native origins, not built by colonists — we attended a 1980 conference of print and broadcast journalists that included professors of journalism and communications at Nigerian universities. In one way, it was like a gathering of journalism practitioners and scholars in the market or socialist world: There was broad ideological concord among the participants. Without exception, the sophisticated journalists and professors, many of them educated in England or the United States, stood firmly behind the official policy of the national radio and television network linking the nineteen state broadcasting systems; that policy aims at preserving the country's cultural traditions, no matter how primitive in modern eyes. Everywhere in Nigeria television programming featured colorfully costumed native singers and dancers chanting in local languages and dancing to the beat of ceremonial drums. There was an occasional "Starsky and Hutch," but — compared to the capitalist world, including Latin America — very little of the comedy or dramatic programming viewed in the United States. English may be the common language of Nigeria — the news programs are broadcast in English — but cultural preservation is measured in terms of African languages; in some states, efforts were intensifying to add more programs in Hausa or Yoruba or Ibo, and to concentrate on traditional African themes.

Newspapers seemed less concerned; even on television and radio, this development was not taking place rapidly enough for some. The speech that drew the heaviest applause at the Ibadan meeting dealt with this theme. Titled "Free Flow of Information in Broadcasting: Nigeria's Cornucopia or Pandora's Box," it was written by Olufolaji Ajibola Fadeyibi, a lecturer in the faculty of Social Sciences at the University of Lagos. Fadeyibi complained that Ibadan radio and television stations were presenting too many TV programs produced in Britain and the United States. He zeroed in on a British disco program with a "London Soho background; sleazy foreground and many ill-fated misled Nigerian youths wriggling and contorting to foreign (precisely American) music — in between frequent swigs at beer bottles right on camera." To knowing laughter and ringing applause, he went on to ask: "In what way does this program educate our children, reflect our cultural heritage, and promote national unity?" Fadeyibi reserved his corker for his finale:

> The conclusion is obvious. There is no need for us to perpetuate a situation as well as condemn it at the same time. If the Western nations won't talk about us, play our music and enlighten their audiences about our culture, then we have no business talking about them, playing their music and showing "Kojak." By so doing, we'll be putting an end to our cultural genocide and communication neocolonialism. To expect the Western nations to facilitate the bidirectional flow of information is to expect a river to flow backwards. Surely no flow is better than free flow.

It is to be noted that this speech and this meeting took place in what may well be the most capitalistic country in Africa. Contempt for cultural penetration by the United States, Britain, and the rest of the capitalist world is universal throughout Africa, even where the expressed ideal of the "free press" of those countries was warmly endorsed. Over and over, Thomas Jefferson was invoked as the liberty-loving political leader who extolled newspapers above government. Emulating Jefferson, Bode Oyewole, a leading radio journalist and chairman of the Ibadan chapter of the Nigerian Union of Journalists, pronounced the mission of the journalist to educate "the society of which he is an integral part. The journalist is a mass educator. His role is as important, if not more so, than the role of the classroom teacher."

There seemed to be a clear line drawn between the cultural penetration of the entertainment programs on television and the influence of the capitalist values of news production. Yet Oyewole and his fellow journalists at Ibadan, and editors and reporters all over the advancing world, did not seem to recognize how different the goals they were expressing as part of their belief system were from those in the ideological system they were themselves extolling. Few journalists in the United States would have endorsed this comment by Oyewole:

> So long as the journalist is aware of his responsibilities towards the community — principally that of helping development — so long as he realizes that his freedom has bearing on what is good for the society and as such is not freedom without limits, then the traditional mistrust will be dissolved, and government and journalism will become twin agents of socioeconomic progress.

The linkage of freedom and responsibility is a familiar theme in discussions of journalism — and will be examined in some detail in the next chapter — but in the older capitalist nations, the need for limits on freedom is rarely mentioned, and scarcely ever are journalists and government regarded as twin agents of anything, let alone socioeconomic progress. The idea of the press as an instrument of progress dates back to the earliest days of the modern news media, but progress was to be achieved through the spread of information to the citizenry. In other words, information was the business of the press; if progress occurred, that was all to the good, but the role of news was to inform, not in any way to act as an agent of social or economic change.

In fact, in Oyewole's view, the moral worth of the behavior of the press was to be judged in terms of avoidance, rather than exacerbation, of conflict. Lasting peace, he said, was the ultimate goal of humankind; that peace could be predicated upon good communications among peoples:

> Messages must be clear and precise, not ambiguous and not censored or "doctored," if we are to avoid the conflicts which give rise to misunderstanding.

Much news reporting in Nigeria is sensationalized even today, but the excesses are usually deplored by serious journalists, as is the case in the United States. The comments of Bode Oyewole are typical among journalists and press students throughout the advancing world. An examination of the press of advancing countries turns up many similar observations and hopes; Oyewole's remarks are especially well put, and we had the opportunity to hear them delivered in person. At the conclusion of the Ibadan meeting, we pointed out to one Nigerian journalist that many — perhaps most — journalists in the United States would have scoffed at Oyewole's statements as naive, would have urged instead devotion to facts, to integrity, to truth, rather than to unrealistic demands for the press to operate as an agent for socioeconomic progress. "Why," he asked, "should we be like you? What have your ethics and morality brought the world beside injustice, cruelty, and war?" It is not an easy question to deal with, although he might have spoken also of the positive contributions of the United States in terms of political freedom and social justice.

At a separate conference that took place in the city of Jos in central Nigeria, a U.S.-trained university lecturer pursued the theme of the Ibadan meeting further along its logical course. What Nigeria and all of Africa needed, said Onyero Mgbejume, was an *African* media policy, one that was not borrowed from the capitalist countries. "A nation whose media is dominated from outside is not a nation," he said, referring not only to technological but also to ideological domination. Demands for media policies of any sort tend to ring hollow in the ears of journalists and scholars in the capitalist world. A policy to them smacks of control from without, since the adoption of policies requires the drafting and approval of laws and regulations that must inevitably be enforced by government. They point to the imposition of censorship and harsh restrictions on the press throughout the advancing world by leaders of countries that have adopted press policies.

THE REVOLUTIONARY PRESS EXPERIMENT IN PERU

The press experiment undertaken by Peru in the 1960s and 1970s is unique; its story is worth examining in some detail. The experiment, much misunderstood in capitalist press circles, has — despite its failure — continued to intrigue journalists and editors from the advancing world. They see in the Peruvian plan the elements of a press policy that might contribute to greater understanding among people and nations, and help bring about a more peaceful and harmonious world. On the other hand, newspaper publishers in all parts of the Western Hemisphere condemn the Peruvian experiment as one of the most invidious attacks on press freedom in the twentieth century. The truth is more complex.

The press in Peru developed in similar fashion to the press throughout Latin America. Peru is one of a score of nation-states that ousted the Spanish in the first third of the nineteenth century after three hundred years of harsh colonial rule. Spanish conquistadores subjugated all of Latin America south of the Rio Grande in the fifteenth and sixteenth centuries, with the important exception of the largest country, Brazil, which was colonized by Portugal. These Latin conquerors represented a different breed from the English who journeyed to North America. Instead of putting down roots and building a homeland, the Spanish concerned themselves almost entirely with military conquest and expropriation of mineral wealth. Those Spanish noblemen who stayed behind in the New World did not resemble the yeoman farmers and merchants of North America; rather, they carved out great baronies and lived like grandees. The native Indians became their servants, as did the black slaves they imported from Africa. The grandees made little effort to develop a political or economic base for their servants; they did not educate them, nor did they even instruct them in the Spanish language. The feudal society resembled the social order in the Spain the conquerors had left behind; power resided only in the colonial barons and in the Catholic church. The Latin America of 1800 was little different in political and social structure from the Spain of 1500. Colonial control was total, and it endured until the nineteenth century when the wave of revolutions begun by the U.S. and French experiences swept through the hemisphere. Thus it was that in country after country the lesser soldiery, assisted by liberal elements of the Church and by the few merchants and intellectuals who inhabited the larger cities, rose up against the grandees and drove them out.

In Peru, a mountainous country that lies along the northwest coast of South America and was once the center of the Inca empire, the Spanish rulers were not expelled until 1824. The feudal structure, however, remained largely intact; the rulers who succeeded the conquistadores comported themselves in much the same way as the Spanish before them. They owned the banks, the mines, the great plantations, and they owned the newspapers as well. The pattern was largely the same throughout Latin America, although in a number of countries, Brazil and Argentina foremost among them, industrial growth weakened the feudal structure more than was the case in Peru. The relative backwardness of Peru can be attributed in part to the difficulty of building roads through the mountains. The railroad network developed in Peru in the middle years of the nineteenth century was superior to that in other sections of the continent, however, and by the later years of the century, more information was flowing from the capital of Lima into the hinterlands than from other capital cities in Latin America. Still, the rate of illiteracy was high, especially among the Quechua-speaking Indians, who made up half the population of the country and who could not, in any case, read the Spanish-language Lima papers or those few regional papers that did appear before 1900.

It is always difficult to identify the first newspaper anywhere, since definitions of newspapers rarely agree. Certainly, the sheets put out by the missionaries in the seventeenth and eighteenth centuries do not qualify. It may be that the first daily newspaper in Latin America appeared in Peru in 1790 in the form of the short-lived *El Diario de Lima*, founded by a Spaniard. It was followed a year later by the biweekly *El Mercurio*

Peruano, established by a group of liberal Peruvian intellectuals as a literary forum. It later served as an instrument for political independence. More resembling a standard newspaper was *Gazeta de Caracas*, which appeared in the capital of Venezuela on October 24, 1808. But it was not a true Latin American product, since it was published by two printers from the United States, Mathew Gallagher and James Lamb. Thus, from the very beginning, the Latin American press was influenced by the newspapers of the United States. At the outset, as with the *Gazeta de Caracas*, newspapers served as agents of the royal governors, but as revolutionary fervor increased and more publications appeared, they divided into pro-Spanish and pro-liberation instruments, much as did the U.S. press in the revolutionary years. Within a decade or two of the achievement of independence, however, the Latin American press had settled into the usually comfortable stance of the press, defender of the status quo.

Thus, the newspaper industry that arose in Peru in the nineteenth century was a mirror of the larger feudal social order. The dominant newspaper then — as it still is today — was *El Comercio*, the oldest continuously published major daily in Latin America; it was established in 1839 by the Miró Quesada family, one of the most powerful families in the country for over a century and a half. As time passed, others among the baronial families acquired newspapers. *La Prensa*, launched in 1905, became the platform for the Beltrán family; *La Crónica*, founded in 1912, passed from the Larco Herrera family to that of the Prados; *Expreso*, a morning paper begun in 1960, and its companion, the afternoon *Extra*, became the publications of the Ulloa family. Each of these families was a powerful force in Peru; their newspapers, all situated in Lima, were only divisions of their banking, commercial, and industrial empires. At the time the Peruvian press experiment was undertaken in 1968, the public — or at least those elements of the public that paid attention to such things — correctly perceived the country's press as representative of economic and political power. Pedro Beltrán, the publisher of *La Prensa*, had served as prime minister. Four presidents of the country had been members of the Prado family, owners of *La Crónica*. Mañuel Ulloa, owner of *Expreso-Extra*, had been a cabinet minister and candidate for president, as well as an associate of the Rockefeller banking house. No fewer than forty-five employees of *El Comercio* were members of the Miró Quesada family, whose staunch support of the commerce of capitalism paralleled that of the government of President Fernando Belaúnde Terry, the man who preceded and succeeded the generals who led the Peruvian press experiment.

Belaúnde Terry headed a mildly democratic government, one far more liberal than the dictatorial regimes that had dominated Peruvian life until the middle of the twentieth century. Certainly, stability in ruling regimes was as unfamiliar in Peru as it was throughout the South American continent, where palace revolutions occurred with monotonous regularity.

Bolivia experienced more than sixty revolutions in the nineteenth century. Venezuela counted fifty. By 1950, Honduras had undergone 115 changes of government in the 125 years of its existence. Anarchy, it can be said, was a way of life in Latin America, but these exchanges in rulership scarcely affected the existence of the people, and the press seemed equally unperturbed. The Miró Quesadas and the Ulloas conducted business as usual whichever politician ran the country; whoever it was, the chances were his philosophy of government was identical to theirs.

While the journalists to the north in the United States were promoting the value system of progressivism and endorsing the code of objectivity and political disinterest, their fellows in Latin America were following their own guiding star. To the Latin journalists, as well as to the Latin poets and novelists, the literary scene in the United States was chaotic and formless. They might admire U.S. technology and know-how, but they deplored what they saw as cultural poverty, the culture of Mickey Mouse and fast-food chains. Still, belief in freedom for the press was as much an element in Latin American thinking as it was in that of the United States and Europe. Journalists everywhere preach the cause of freedom and demand for themselves the rights and benefits of free expression. However, their definitions of these terms are often so different that the dispassionate observer can see little room for conjoining of thought. Georgie Anne Geyer called attention to one central difference in the viewpoints of journalists in North and South America. In the Latin world, she wrote, "truth seldom stands alone and objectivity does not exist. Everything serves a point of view." Moreover, she added:

> Every newspaper is the organ — the vehicle — for a political movement; every writer is an advocate. Clemente Marroquín Rojas, the salty Guatemalan journalist and, for a time, vice-president, commented: "The difference in our ideas of freedom of the press is that you think of it as freedom of information. We think of it as freedom of conscience — you cannot say things that would hurt the country."

The similarity between the views of Marroquín Rojas and those of Kwame Nkrumah and Tom Mboya is readily apparent. The kind of freedom that is admired throughout the advancing world differs sharply from the freedom revered in the United States and Europe. Even India's Jawaharlal Nehru, one of the most passionate defenders of liberty, rejected the critical article of faith in libertarian doctrine that holds that the right to free expression ought to be unlimited. Words alone may produce grave international situations, Nehru said, and thus, states must be "armed with the authority to deal with" dangerous language in the press. "We cannot," he said, "imperil the safety of the whole nation in the name of some fancied freedom which puts an end to all freedom." At the same time, Nehru asserted:

> I do think that basically it is dangerous to suppress thought, and the expression of thought in any way, because this may, besides suppressing a particularly good thing, produce many kinds of evil which stunt the growth of a social group.

The ultimate freedom to Nehru — and to Marroquín Rojas and the majority of the journalists of Latin American, as well as Africa and Asia — is freedom of conscience. Information is of less importance than thought and the expression of opinion. It is in this light that the press revolution in Peru must be viewed.

In a coup on October 3, 1968, General Juan Velasco Alvarado wrested power in Peru from President Belaúnde Terry. In keeping with Peruvian tradition, the coup was bloodless; what was different was that Velasco and the "band of revolutionary colonels" who joined him in the takeover were military leaders of a different stripe. Unlike the aristocratic generals who regularly seized control throughout Latin America, Velasco was an enemy of the feudal barony, and for good reason. He was the son of a street sweeper, a *cholo*, a man of mixed Indian and Spanish blood, part of a social class scorned by the feudal powers. Included among those powers were the owners of the Lima press. Velasco and his cohorts, most of them also *cholos*, had used the army as a form of upward mobility, for it was the military and the Church that offered the greatest opportunity for social advancement. The "band of revolutionary colonels" was determined not only to modernize Peru but also to shatter the country's social order. It was not entirely clear at the outset, but there was nothing pseudo-revolutionary about the Velasco takeover. Ulloa's *Expreso-Extra* saw the danger to its own position at once and spoke up in opposition; also opposed, but to a lesser degree, was Beltrán's *La Prensa*. For the first year, however, the leading Lima daily, *El Comercio*, supported the regime. In the words of Robert Pierce, "From its head offices of marble, velvet and gilt went forth editorials calling for restructuring of the government." Pierce's account, in which he gives voice to a somewhat grudging support of Velasco's aims but in which he also assails much of what Velasco attempted, is the most thorough account of the Peruvian experience by a North American. Press reports in the United States were generally antagonistic, many of them fiercely so. George Kurian, writing in 1982 in the *World Press Encyclopedia*, declared that the Peruvian press had "reached its nadir" under the rule of the generals, and that they had "virtually destroyed every vestige of press freedom." Illustrating the passion of the foes of the Peruvian experiment, Kurian maintained that the history of the press in Peru was "a case study of survival." He added: "In a bitter decade-long confrontation with an authoritative regime, it [the press] proved its essential indestructibility. Where the press is threatened, the Peruvian experience should be an encouraging lesson." Accounts far friendlier to the experiment were written in the advancing world. The most detailed was written, from the inside, by Carlos Ortega, who assisted in the development of the Peruvian plan; by Juan Gargurevich, a Peruvian who lamented the failure of the experiment; and by Raquel Salinas, a Chilean who provided a careful account of a noble but lost cause.

The history of the Peruvian adventure is indeed complex and cannot be related in detail here. The plan itself developed slowly, over a period of eight years, and came to an end with the overthrow of the Velasco regime on August 19, 1975, by General Francisco Morales Bermúdez, who had served as prime minister and had assumed increasing powers after Velasco's health declined. Velasco died two years after surrendering power. The intellectuals and theoreticians who worked for and with the Velasco regime characterized their movement as one of "revolutionary humanism," drawing, they said, equally on nondogmatic and nontotalitarian socialist thought and the heritage of liberarian thought. Moreover, they said, they were "inspired by Christian thought." Thus, they specifically rejected both capitalism and communism and all dogmatisms, "refusing violence as a system." Three "final objectives" were identified: (a) "a participatory political system grounded in the masses"; (b) "a pluralist economic system based on a priority sector of social ownership"; and (c) "a social system upheld by a combination of components and moral values stressing justice, freedom, work, participation, solidarity, creativity, integrity, and respect for human dignity." In this lofty vision, the role of the press was crucial; indeed, many of Velasco's men looked upon themselves primarily as press theorists. A few were journalists, but none was a working professional, a fact that engendered contempt among the greater share of Peru's reporters and editors, as well as among the publishers.

Velasco's men have insisted all along that they launched their revolution with a full-blown press plan in mind but that they invoked it by degrees rather than imposing it at once. Velasco's foes, on the other hand, have maintained that there was never a clear plan and that as a result measures were put into force as expedients in response to rising criticism. Whichever view is correct, it is nonetheless clear that the program did possess a rationale, a philosophical lodestone. Both the print and broadcast press would free themselves of the domination of the grandees and come under the direction of working journalists and the important interest groups among the public at large. To some degree, this program was reminiscent of syndicalism and the corporate structure popular with Mussolini and other social engineers of the 1920s. There were also marked differences, especially in the internationalist insistence on working for cooperation among nations — "for the construction of a real community of free and sovereign countries based on equality."

The initial press decree of the Velasco regime was the Statute on Freedom of the Press, issued December 30, 1969. For the next five years, new orders and decrees flowed regularly from the presidential palace in Lima. It was the first decree that provoked a war of words between the government and the entire Peruvian press, now including *El Comercio*; under that decree, freedom of expression was to be limited by law, truth, moral considerations, national security, and the honor of individuals and families. But authorities were denied the right to censor except in time of war. Moreover, the order placed severe limitations on foreign participation in press ownership and, indeed, on absentee ownership. As such, there was little to distinguish the Peruvian decree from a similar order issued in Chile by the liberal regime of Eduardo Frei, but while the Latin American press and its allies among U.S. publishers generally accepted the Chilean orders without complaint, the response across the hemisphere to the Velasco order was sharp and fierce.

As the decrees mounted, the opposition increased. So bitter were the attacks from Ulloa's *Expreso* and *Extra* that Velasco expropriated them in March 1970 and converted them into public utilities, handing over their direction to union groups sympathetic to his regime. Not surprisingly, the Ulloa newspapers then became staunch supporters of the regime. Velasco characterized *Expreso* as "a sort of bulldog that I pushed against the big dailies." The Inter-American Press Association, a group of publishers in North and South America, took up the gauntlet from its headquarters in Miami and maintained a steady drum of condemnation of the Peruvian experiment. When the Peruvian experiment culminated in 1974 with the introduction of the Inca Plan expropriating the remainder of the country's major dailies, IAPA criticism rose to a crescendo. It must have given the son of a street sweeper infinite pleasure to respond to the IAPA attack as did Velasco: "The organization of owners of newspapers in the continent should know now that today their opinion matters very little in Peru and that their members no longer give orders here."

The nationalization of the newspapers and the radio and television stations was not an end in itself, however; that came with the declaration of the news media as "social property," belonging to the people. For radio and television, as well as other elements in the telecommunications system — telephones, telexes, and the infant computer industry — control was vested in the government itself, so that programming might be slanted for "adequate humanistic, cultural, and social training to back up the educational reform and the structural changes required by the development of the country." While important changes had appeared in the daily newspapers by the time the experiment ended, little had been accomplished in broadcasting, the result, according to Velasco's men, of inadequate time to train radio and television staffers and insufficient opportunity to raise the required funds not only for training but also to develop indigenous production teams that would produce programming to rival imports from the United States and other industrialized countries. The governments of

West Germany and France provided money and training for Peruvian broadcasters, and Velasco's men maintained they were well on their way to remodeling the industry when the ax fell on them. Another, unfulfilled goal of the Peruvian reformers was to extend the broadcasting industry from Lima, where all the important radio and television facilities were located, into the countryside as part of a campaign for national integration, much like those that are so intensely desired in Africa.

Under the social property provisions of the Inca Plan, the major dailies were taken away from their owners and turned over to those sectors of the population that could be organized into coherent interest groups. These were charged with publishing newspapers to interest and inform their readers and at the same time to keep watch on the government to see that it stayed on course in its campaign for revolutionary humanism. Access to the pages of the newspapers was guaranteed to all private citizens and organizations, even those not awarded ownership, no matter what their ideological orientation. None could doubt that the intellectuals who created the Inca Plan were dreamers; their vision was of a press that was no longer to be the voice of minority interests or of foreign ownership, a press in the hands of representative groups that would themselves keep a close watch on the government to see that it carried out the aims of "revolutionary humanism" correctly and wisely.

On two crucial points, Velasco's men made fatal misjudgments. In the first place, they assumed that their new "Peruvian press," run by workers and not by the grandees, would automatically support all their goals. When the journalists failed to live up to those expectations, the planners found their skins to be thinner than they had imagined and began to issue restrictive directives. An even more serious miscalculation was the belief in the reality of the organized sectors to which they entrusted direction of the newspapers. In truth, these sectors were not organized at all; they were, at best, wishful thinking. One day they might have become coherent units, but in 1974 they were not. Moreover, Velasco's men ignored the traditions of the newspapers. *El Comercio*, whose readership was primarily urban and sophisticated, was assigned to a social sector of peasants. *La Prensa*, which catered to agricultural interests, was turned over to industrial workers. And *Ojo*, a paper with a heavy dose of sex and violence, was given over to cultural and fine-arts workers. To Pierce, these designations were made "with either malicious humor or profound stupidity." Ortega admitted the error and blamed insufficient study of the prior readership. On the other hand, Jaworski, who had been assigned to manage the new *El Comercio*, acknowledged sadly that despite "the creative audacity of the theoretical approach," its execution was simply unrealistic. And, indeed, the Peruvian experiment, at least in the capitalist world, has been written off as at best a pie-in-the-sky plan of amateur theorists who were not living in the real world. While there is certainly some truth in that assessment, it is also true that in the countries of the advancing world, the Inca Plan and all the aspects of the Peruvian experiment became subjects of intense interest and analysis. In these circles, rather than discarding the experiment, the question being asked was: "What went wrong?" Or: "Why can't it work?"

Others, among them Kurian and the IAPA, condemned the plan as little more than an attempt to solidify authoritarian power by silencing opposition in the press. Kurian summarized this view in an ironic passage:

> The crowning rationale was the time-honored definition of the press as a "public service." What could be better than that such a public service should be controlled by that most public of all institutions, the government itself? Velasco went further and claimed that freedom of expression never existed in Peru and therefore hardly needed to be taken away. Freedom of the press, he said, was only freedom for the businessmen and families that owned it.

And when the last of the Velasco-induced press regulations were lifted by the Belaúnde Terry regime in 1980, the IAPA saluted the action as "the most auspicious event for the freedom of the press in the hemisphere in the last years." Not only did Belaúnde Terry abolish the old rules, but he appointed as his prime minister Mañuel Ulloa, the owner of *Expreso* and *Extra*, the first papers expropriated by Velasco.

The four years of rule for General Morales Bermúdez were transitional years. Some of the Velasco rules were lifted, some were modified; the newspapers were returned to their former owners but were required not to revile the government or its aspirations; the press was not permitted to "follow the sensationalist, alienating, and venal line which has characterized their reporting...[or become] twisters of the truth, and instigators of disunity among Peruvians." Still, the left-leaning intellectuals who had been serving as editors of the paper under Velasco were ousted and replaced by conservative journalists. More than one hundred staffers were fired. With the repeal of the old statute of the press, the news media were directed to provide wide coverage of events, both national and international, in order to supply readers and viewers with objective information. Large newspaper enterprises were awarded tax benefits to stimulate their growth, and the shares in the newspapers that had been given to the workers under the social property plan were invalidated. Staffers were authorized to acquire shares in the enterprises, but only if they purchased them.

What could not be known by the journalists of the advancing world who had watched the experiment with interest was whether it was an aberration, a freakish interlude in the history of the press, or whether it might have been something of greater significance, an augury of what was to come, if only the experiment were more skillfully executed. To be sure, nothing worked out as the planners anticipated, and the Velasco regime found itself behaving in ways that were not altogether dissimilar from those engaged in by the grandees of the press before the takeover. Confronted with opposition and resistance by the publishers and many among their staffs, they fired dozens of staffers. Needing support for their ideas from the press and finding little there, they began issuing directives about how information was to be interpreted. They did not seize recalcitrant publishers and editors and fling them into jail — that would have been going too far — but they did exile some of them, especially those with foreign connections. Some foreign correspondents were expelled; some were taken, briefly, into custody. Rather than invoke censorship, the Velasco regime populated the papers with staffers sympathetic to its revolution, but circulation declined so sharply that the government was forced to pump in cash to keep the newspapers afloat. And, most serious of all, the public sectors to which control of the papers was handed were themselves so weak and poorly organized that they were unable to carry out the role assigned to them. Theory was frustrated, as it so often is, by practicality. The question that remained was: Was the failure inevitable?

THE REPORTER "IS NOT A WRITER...NOT A POLITICIAN"

Of the many objections raised by publishers in both North and South America to the Peruvian experiment, perhaps the most important was its frankly political coloration. Objectivity was replaced as a value by political goals. The "news" was to be presented in such a way as to educate and instruct the readers towards the specifically described ends of "revolutionary humanism." In this, Velasco's men were pursuing ends not markedly different from those espoused by Nkrumah and Nyerere, or perhaps even those promoted by Horace Greeley and Joseph Pulitzer. Those American publishers, however, lived in a different time frame, before the apolitical value system had been firmly embraced by capitalist press ideologues. And the export of that value system to the advancing world was clearly of major importance not only to the press of the industrialized countries but also to the political and economic forces that exercised power in those nations. Indeed, support for a sympathetic press ideology was a plank in the cold-war programs of both the capitalist and socialist nations for more than a generation.

In that contest, training the journalists of the advancing world has been a matter of major importance. For the British and the French, this kind of training has long been a staple of foreign policy. In this particular game, the United States and the Soviet Union are newcomers, but their economic and military might have cast them into dominant positions. Still, of all the press instruments in the industrialized world, the most powerful in the transfer of ideology has been the British Broadcasting Corporation. Over the years, the BBC has raised studied indifference to the level of art. BBC chieftains, and staffers too, have taken pride in their dispassionate treatment of the most dramatic and shocking news events; in this, they have consciously pursued the goal of public service broadcasting. Not theirs to influence the audience to one position or another, but simply to lay out for their listeners the "facts" and coolly rational explanations of the meaning of those facts.

All around the planet, the BBC has established a reputation as the most thorough and most objective of all reporters of international news, certainly among broadcasters if not among all journalists. In former British colonies of Asia and Africa, the reputation is especially exalted, since in the revolutionary days in which the colonial powers were ousted, the BBC studiously avoided any kind of overt bias in its broadcasts. Moreover, the BBC standards have been reinforced in the advancing world by training and education. With positive support from the British government, the BBC has been providing training courses for broadcast journalists from the advancing world since 1951. Within the two decades that followed, more than 500 broadcasters attended the BBC courses, half of them from Africa. In 1965, television training was added to the program, and in the first five years, 165 journalists attended television courses. These journalists then returned to their native lands prepared to reinforce the already popular BBC model. Even before the training courses were initiated in London, the BBC had been dispatching experts throughout the British Empire to assist those who were starting radio enterprises.

In the francophone colonial empire, the French conducted similar programs, bringing African broadcasters to Paris for training. The French Office of Radio Cooperation (*l'Office de Cooperation Radiophonique*) went the British one better, by taking direct charge of developing television in France's African territories and ultimately merging the new groups into the homeland French radio and television system. The French model is not unpopular in former French territories, but it has never enjoyed the immense prestige of the BBC. For one thing, it was not unknown in Africa that French broadcasting was far more tightly controlled by the government in Paris than was the BBC in London. Hence, the public service image of the BBC has never been matched by the French broadcasting system. The reputation of the BBC is high not only in Britain's former colonies but also in Western Europe, Japan, the United States, and even in the Soviet Union and China. One might say that over the years the BBC has been Britain's most valuable export, for the BBC has exported not only a particular style of broadcasting but also a set of political and cultural values that have taken root all over the world.

Despite its public service image and its appearance of disinterest, the BBC has been no more capable of objective treatment of news than has any other medium of communication. BBC journalists are themselves part of an upper-middle-class social order with the values of that socioeconomic order; they are just as likely to view the people of the advancing world as children to be led by the hand and socialized into polite society as are any other members of their class. Try as hard as they might, these journalists have been unable to convince the people of the advancing world that they do not hold them in some form of contempt. The result is confusion. For while the BBC style is profoundly respected, the content of the news programs is often denounced.

Moreover, those African and Asian broadcast journalists who have studied in the United States have been exposed to a quite different model, that of commercial broadcasting. Few American radio or television journalists pattern themselves on the men and women of the BBC. To present the news in a cool, dispassionate manner is anathema. Conventional wisdom holds that audiences will switch dials to competitor stations if the news is not presented in dramatic fashion. To many journalism students and practitioners from the advancing world, the American style seems more suitable, for it can be adapted more easily to political ends. On the other hand, the commercialization of American television dismays the journalists of the advancing world, who, following the BBC model with which they have long been familiar, concern themselves primarily with "serious" news and not gossip or frivolous information. What does fascinate and excite the students and journalists from the advancing world is the technical quality of American broadcasting (and of newspapers as well). To be able to make use of the technological innovations in their homeland would enable them, most are convinced, not only to provide more interesting broadcasts but also to bring greater stores of information to their audience and thus ultimately assist mightily in the modernization of their nation.

Technology does not come without a price. That price is the system of values that accompanies the technology. And the value system imparted in the United States is identical in all major aspects to the value system imparted in the BBC and French training courses. It is the value system of the professional. Whatever else may characterize a professional, it is certain that he or she operates within the belief system in which the profession has achieved status — meaning the status quo. Whether pursuing the traditional public service stance of the BBC or the dramatic public interest posture of the American broadcasters, the professional carries out the role of observer rather than that of participant and, with few exceptions, makes a fetish of avoiding political pronouncements or even political involvement. As Peter Golding pointed out correctly, professionalism not only props up the status quo, it also favors proficiency over ideology, and the pragmatic over the utopian. Ideology is rejected even as it is being disseminated. And the grand dreams of the utopian journalists are ridiculed even as they are being given expression in the capitalist framework that has glorified the utopian image of a free press shining as a beacon of human liberty.

Media technology and media value systems represent important ideological weapons. The Soviet Union and her East European allies, notably Czechoslovakia and East Germany, also have been seeking to export their technology and value systems. Journalists from the advancing world are often provided full financing to study at the schools of journalism in Moscow, Prague, and East Berlin. And Soviet journalism instructors regularly travel to Africa and Asia to aid — and to convert — journalists of the advancing world to their ideological orientation. In the case neither of the capitalist nations nor of the socialist nations has the effort been successful. Instead, the advancing world has established a press ideology of its own. It is far too early, however, to speak of that belief system as one of permanence. The efforts of the so-called First and Second Worlds to dominate and ultimately undo the ideology of the advancing world continue, and with increasing determination, a phenomenon we will examine more closely in chapter 10, in discussing critical questions of economics.

The puzzlement of advancing-world journalists over the contradictions between the objectivity model of the capitalist media, whose technology and skills they much admire, and the political model of the socialist media, which is more to their ideological liking, is illustrated in a booklet by Frank Barton, who directed the Africa Program of the International Press Institute in the 1960s. His trainees, Barton reported, were tormented by "the clash of loyalties between journalism and what might be called the African idea." The IPI, an international association of publishers from capitalist and advancing-world nations, endorses with ferocity the American model in which the journalist observes and reports what he sees and is told, but avoids with painstaking patience the expression of his own political views. A major training manual supplied to African journalists by the IPI makes the point graphically: "A Reporter is just that — a reporter. He is not a writer.... And most important of all, he is not a politician." Peter Golding says this torment is reflected in the guilt complex created among journalists of the advancing world by training in the creed and practice of objective reporting as preached and conducted in European and American media.

The BBC and French broadcasting (and newspaper) models have exerted a stronger influence in Asia and Africa than in Latin America, where the primary influence has inevitably been the model provided by the United States. For one thing, advertising has been of far greater significance to the mass media of Latin America than to those of Asia and Africa, or indeed to the media of Western Europe. Radio and television broadcasting, more advanced in Latin America than in Asia and Africa, is almost entirely financed by advertising, operating largely through the leading advertising agencies. It was partly to eliminate the influence of advertisers that the Velasco experiment was conducted in Peru.

To the supporters of the capitalist press system, the prevalence of advertising as a financing agent rids the mass media of the possibility of direct control by the government. Yet even where advertising pays the freight for broadcasting, governments assert control over that form of the mass media, usually indirectly, as in Western Europe and Japan and even in the United States, but sometimes directly and forcefully, as is usual in Africa and Asia and — often — in Latin America. The relationship of advertising to government control has varied in different parts of the capitalist world, but the political and economic interests of the advertisers and the governments have been sufficiently congruent that they have almost always operated in comfortable harmony. In Latin America, for instance, where palace revolutions have been common, the printing and broadcast of commercial notices have continued without interruption from one government to the next. In other words, the fact that the presentation of news is financed by commercial interests seems to have little influence on tyrannical behavior by governments.

In Peru, of course, commercial interests lost their control of the daily press under Velasco, but advertising of commercial messages continued on radio and television, even after these media were placed under direct government control. The Velasco regime did impose numerous restrictions on the freedom of action of journalists, and the lifting of those restrictions by the successor Belaúnde Terry government drew applause from the Peruvian journalists employed by the post-Velasco newspapers. "We now have complete freedom of the press," an editorial writer for *El Comercio* exulted two years after the election of Belaúnde Terry. Yet, under questioning, he acknowledged that the freedom was not in fact complete. It was permissible to make any kind of comment on foreign affairs — even Communist journalists were accorded that privilege — but it was not acceptable to discuss certain aspects of the political or economic situation in Peru itself. However, such restrictions did not disturb the editorial writer: Why should he or any of his colleagues desire to offend their readers — and *El Comercio*, after all, supported the president and his prime minister, the owner of *Expreso* and *Extra*.

Governments everywhere have restricted the freedom of action of editors and publishers when vital interests were considered threatened; often, these governments severely limited what the press was permitted to say. Sometimes the repressions have been harsh. History is full of tales of martyred journalists who have gone to their deaths defending their right to speak their minds, and governments have been toppled because of public anger over restrictive press policies. Belief in freedom of expression does seem to be deeply held everywhere. In the advancing world, however, self-restraints have been imposed by the journalists themselves, in order to insure a unified social and political order.

That tyrants have made use of this belief to manipulate the press to their own ends is well known. Acts of repression and official terror directed against the mass media by dictatorial regimes in the advancing world have solidified the contempt for the advancing press expressed throughout the capitalist world. To media analysts in the United States and Western Europe, the press aspirations in the advancing world, as for example in Peru, have been hypocritical. A developmental press has come to be equated with one in which the government exercises tight control and prevents freedom of expression, all in the name of noble ends. Journalists from the advancing world sometimes share the same view, especially when their governments engage in unexpected acts of repression. Certainly, belief in the goals of Nehru and other democratic statesmen was shaken during the censorship imposed by Indira Gandhi in 1975. Indeed, it was not in India alone that the advancing press was affected; if censorship could be imposed in the most modern press system in the advancing world, who was exempt? Even after the "emergency" censorship was lifted two years later, advancing-world press ideologues spoke of the future with caution.

Despite the censorship, many Indian journalists sneaked into their news columns words, phrases, even sentences and paragraphs that escaped the attention of the censors and that conveyed concealed meanings to knowledgeable readers. In this, they were following the practice Karl Marx employed to outwit the Prussian censors more than a century earlier. The capacity to convey hidden and double-meaning phrases seems to be one that journalists master in all parts of the world. Freedom to say what they want may be denied journalists, but, as Marx pointed out, so long as the press and the public share an interest in the communication of information, that information will emerge, in one form or another.

Such communication has been raised to an art form in Brazil, the largest and most powerful country in South America, during the scores of years it has been under dictatorial military control. Military censors have appeared in the newsrooms of Brazilian newspapers to make sure that no information unacceptable to the government could be printed. When the papers were finally locked up, ready for printing, the censors would read through the edition, accepting some articles and rejecting others. In addition to attempting to sneak in unwanted material, hostile editors sought to hit back at the censors. In the early years of censorship, editors printed their papers with columns of white space clearly indicating censored material. When the government cracked down on that practice, the editors responded by filling censored columns on the front page with recipes and advice to the lovelorn. The most original ploy used in Brazil was conceived by the humor magazine *Pasquim*, which found a way to criticize the government without appearing to do so. In condemning the

Brazilian military, it simply substituted for "Brazilian" the word "Greek."
In the takeover of Greece by right-wing military leaders in the late 1960s,
Pasquim found a suitable target for attack. It regularly published articles
charging the "Greek military government" with violations against democratic principles, human decency, and press freedom. Its readers were well
aware that Greek was a code word for Brazilian, but it took the authorities
a year or more to figure it out. The publication was ultimately suspended
and its editors thrown into prison and tortured, but they had made their
point, and to them that was reward enough.

Brazilian censorship was never carried out well. No more than ninety
censors were ever employed at one time, scarcely adequate to police the
entire press. But the penalties were severe, and, for the most part, the
editors were careful to avoid antagonizing the leaders. They played it safe,
censoring themselves. The majority of the Brazilian press did not push too
hard. Among other factors, the editors were unnerved by the erratic nature
of the censorship program; they didn't know when they would be censored
and when they would be able to get away with incautious reports. In 1977,
the government lifted the "state of siege" and replaced it with a "state of
emergency." Direct censorship was relaxed, but the restrictions were by no
means lifted. The military leaders had become more skillful; whenever
they found a publication straying, they called in the publisher for drinks
and dinner and a friendly word about subversive comments stealing into
pages. In the name of social responsibility, they said, such practices had to
stop. The publishers, powers in Brazil like their colleagues in Peru and
throughout the hemisphere, then took over the censorship role themselves.
Hostile working journalists nevertheless kept pushing. "I always go one
step past the limits," one Brazilian editor confided. "Not too far, but I am
always trying." It was a matter of how "social responsibility" was defined.
We turn now to just that question.

PART 3

The watchdog news media. (*Mary Miller*)

Eight

Social Responsibility: The Hutchins Commission and Its Aftermath

PRESS CREDIBILITY, COUNCILS, AND ACCOUNTABILITY

In the years after the Second World War, the term social responsibility appeared as a goal model for institutions in the United States and soon swept the world as a standard to seek.* In few institutions did the term gain such wide acceptance as in the press, perhaps because of the tenuous state of the press as the only secular institution in the country to be guaranteed, under the First Amendment, freedom from government interference in its private operations. The social reforms of the New Deal had severely limited the freedom of action of the business community, and the press had no reason to assume that these limitations would not be extended to the press, the First Amendment notwithstanding.

Since publishers by and large supported the Republican party, they were concerned about the electoral successes of Franklin Roosevelt and took nervous notice of the increasing criticism of the press by Democratic party leaders, by the rising trade union movement in the press industry, and by Roosevelt himself. The criticism took two forms: that the press was unfair and slanted in its political coverage; and that it was presenting gossip, trash, and trivia in its news columns rather than information useful

*For a discussion of the origin of the term social responsibility and of its philosophical significance, see Appendix.

to the public. If this criticism were to go too far, many publishers believed, it might well lead to governmental restraints. In this situation, Henry Luce of *Time* magazine decided it was prudent to develop a counter-strategy. He provided the financing for a commission of scholars to study the state of the press and come up with recommendations for improving the quality of the press in an effort to head off any government intervention.

In 1946, a year after the end of the war, the commission was formed, chaired by Robert Hutchins, the chancellor of the University of Chicago, the "boy wonder" of academe and a man with impeccable credentials among liberals. Luce was determined the commission would not be made up entirely of persons of his own political persuasion; in this connection, Hutchins was an ideal choice. Twelve others, all experts in their own fields, were named to the study group, which came to be known as the Hutchins Commission. *Time* provided a grant of $200,000, and the *Encyclopedia Britannica* an additional $15,000.

The commission's report, published a year later, not only wrote the term social responsibility into the world of the U.S. media but also came to dominate the discussions of press philosophy and ethics that followed, up to the present day. The carefully written, concise report, entitled *A Free and Responsible Press*, identified as its task to answer the question of whether the freedom of the press was in danger. It concluded it was indeed in danger, for three reasons: (1) in the modern world the press had increased in importance and visibility; (2) the few who ran the press had not provided a service adequate to the needs of society; and (3) the few had sometimes engaged in society-condemned practices which, if continued, would lead inevitably to government regulation or control. The remedy, the commission announced, was a greater assumption of responsibility by the press and action by the informed public to see to it that the press lived up to its responsibility. The commission minced few words in its condemnation of press practices:

> Too much of the regular output of the press consists of a miscellaneous succession of stories and images which have no relation to the typical lives of real people anywhere. The result is a meaninglessness, flatness, distortion, and the perpetuation of misunderstanding ...
> The press emphasizes the exceptional rather than the representative; the sensational rather than the significant. The press is preoccupied with these incidents to such an extent that the citizen is not supplied the information and discussion he needs to discharge his responsibilities to the community.

The commission painted its picture of a sensational, irresponsible press with a broad brush, condemning the concentration of press ownership in the hands of a few representatives of "big business"; and spoke of "exaggerated drives for power and profit" as leading towards monopoly, and "a common bias" of the large investors and employers. Not only did the commission recommend a five-point program on what a free press ought to provide, but it also urged the creation of councils to review the performance of the press and reproved schools of journalism for failing to set standards for the press. The commission fell short of proposing that the press councils be given enforcement powers, but it did emphasize a need for "vigorous mutual criticism" within the press itself. If the press (and the commission studied not only newspapers but radio as well) did not reform itself, the commission said, then the government would: Freedom of the press is "essential to political liberty," and that freedom is in danger unless it becomes "an accountable freedom" — accountable to "conscience and the common good."

The commission's view of the role of the press in contemporary society was clearly spelled out. In its view, the public had a right to expect of the press five basic services: (1) an accurate, comprehensive account of the day's news; (2) a forum for exchange of comment; (3) a means of projecting group opinions and attitudes to one another; (4) a method of presenting and clarifying the goals and values of the society; and (5) a way of reaching every member of the society. The public had a right not only to expect the fact to be presented in a meaningful context but also "the truth about the fact"; in other words, not merely objective reality, but objective reality clarified and explained.

If Luce expected widespread approval by the U.S. press community, he was mistaken. Wilber Forest, president of the American Society of Newspaper Editors, accused the commission of condemning the entire U.S. press because of the "dereliction of the comparative few." Moreover, he said, if the press were to lose its freedom, it would not be because of "a blanket indictment such as passed down by the Hutchins self-appointed grand jury. It will be because there is a loss of interest or faith on the part of the newspaper reader." Other editors spoke out in similar vein. So did journalism scholars. In an article in *Journalism Quarterly*, a publication of journalism educators, Robert Desmond challenged the commission for failing to conduct systematic research and especially for its harsh criticism of journalism schools. In Desmond's view, the commission had indulged "in irresponsible statements that could have the effect of setting back as much as a decade the constructive work of the schools." *The New York Times*, in a cautiously balanced commentary, complained that the commission "holds to standards of perfection in an evolving medium and is too impatient because we have not caught up yet with these standards."

Still, while the initial reaction was cool if not overtly hostile, within a decade the U.S. press community had adopted the social responsibility thesis as if it, like freedom of the press and the public's right to know, had been handed down from some journalistic Mount Sinai. The position taken by Luce's own *Fortune* magazine was to become another chink in the armor of press dogma. The commission report was scarcely off the presses when *Fortune* appeared with not only a prominently displayed lead article but also a supplement that included the full text of the commission report. The *Fortune* article expressed a few reservations (it called the report difficult reading and said that in many cases it used "exasperatingly cryptic" expressions), but on the whole, it said, the report was meaty and important. One problem that *Fortune* noted was that whereas the Commission seemed to be urging the press to lofty goals, it provided no insight on how to write in such a way as to avoid dullness:

> One could wish that philosophers could tell journalists just how to do this, but philosophers are expected to practice the love of wisdom, not mass communication. Final answers to the problems of freedom, responsibility, and effectiveness will come, perhaps, when every philosopher is a journalist and every journalist a philosopher.

The fundamental role demanded of the press by the Hutchins Commission was rooted in the democratic assumption, which holds that democracy is nurtured and furthered when an informed citizenry makes wise judgments in choosing those who will represent them in the government. To work towards this end is to be responsible. And in carrying out this role, the press must be accountable to the public, to the society that it serves. This, then, is the central theme of the Hutchins Commission report. The role it assigned to the press is similar to the role that all institutions assign to themselves. The code of the medical profession is identified in the oath of Hippocrates. Similar codes have been developed by lawyers, engineers, teachers, and representatives of other institutions. The code of social responsibility for the press was identified and publicized by the Hutchins Commission. The ideas behind that code had been in circulation for centuries, not only in the United States but throughout the world. Marx had written of the duties of the press a century earlier, and before Marx there had been Cato and Franklin, Voltaire and Milton, and many others. Indeed, when Pulitzer proposed the establishment of a school of journalism at Columbia University, he proclaimed its purpose to be to help the journalist become more responsible in gathering and reporting news; the school would "mark the distinction between real journalists and men who do a kind of newspaper work that requires neither culture nor conviction but only business training." It was not until 1956, with the publication of *Four Theories of the Press*, that the term social responsibility became a shortcut phrase to stand as a symbol for the ideal of a "democratic" press.

In their book, Schramm, Peterson, and Siebert identified the "social responsibility" doctrine as one of four theories of the relationship between the press on one hand and government or society on the other as to "concepts of what the press should be and do." In the history of humankind, they wrote, there had been no more than two, or four, basic theories of the press. They identified the basic two as "authoritarian" and "libertarian," and said that the remaining two were but developments and modifications of the first two. The authoritarian theory had been modified into the "Soviet communist" doctrine and the libertarian into the "social responsibility" concept.

The fundamental difference between the libertarian and social responsibility ideas was that in the libertarian concept, the press was totally free, altogether unfettered, whereas the social responsibility doctrine recognized the peril of unrestrained liberty. According to the Four Theorists, libertarianism demanded two duties of the press: to serve as a watchdog, "as an extralegal check on government"; and to serve as an instrument of adult education, since "the success of democracy was posited upon an intelligent and informed electorate." To carry out these duties, the press "had to be completely free from control or domination by those elements which it was to guard against." The idea of social responsibility, they wrote, developed out of recognition of the weaknesses and inconsistencies in libertarianism, mainly that it had failed to supply "rigorous standards for the day-to-day operations of the mass media — in short, a stable formula to distinguish liberty and abuse of liberty." It had served a noble purpose, nonetheless, for it had "struck off the manacles from the mind of man" and "opened up new vistas for humanity."

Clearly, they were on solid footing in examining some of the historical factors that led to the rise of the social responsibility doctrine. Faith in progress had declined, and the increasing complexity of social and political issues had muddled public understanding. The simple rural life of harmony with nature had all but vanished with the growth of cities and the appearance of the megalopolis. The alienation recognized by Hegel and Marx had become the suicidal anomie identified by Durkheim. Belief in rationality had evaporated with the expansion of psychological and psychiatric insights. Economic power was increasingly vested in distant and anonymous corporations. And the mass media had become Big Business. The newspaper and magazine were now competing for attention with comic books, motion pictures, and radio, and television had already appeared as a reality. Computers were just over the horizon.

In short, the world of faith — in God, in one's fellowman, in the future — had disintegrated and been replaced by a world dominated more by fear of the future than by confidence in it. Institutions were on the defensive. The age of the muckrakers had been one of persistent assault on all institutions. Will Irwin, Upton Sinclair, and the others had cast so much doubt on the validity of the old assumptions that it was no longer possible to perceive the press simply as the servant of the people, as their eyes and ears in alerting them to incipient tyranny. Moreover, there was increasing concentration of the ownership of the mass media. Not only did news-papers cease to multiply in number as the population increased, but the roster of owners actually decreased. Mergers and joint-stock agreements resulted in lessened competition. Cities in which newspapers with small circulations could manage to eke out a living declined; soon only the mighty were able to survive in the great cities. Newspapers owned by absentee landlords could not hope to maintain the same kind of loyal readership as might the small-town publisher whose local interests were identical to those of other local entrepreneurs. In this situation, it was only natural that the press would slip in public esteem, that it would cease to be revered as an ally of the people, and that there would arise a new word to express an overriding need of the institution of the press: credibility.

If only the newspapers and the broadcasters could retain their image as the ally of the people, then they might preserve their position in the social and economic firmament. To maintain that image, they had to be believable, that is to say, their reports had to be perceived to be not only accurate and fair but also supportive of the interests of the public at large. The press could not be considered to possess credibility if it did not practice social responsibility, if it did not cease insisting on unchecked liberty. Instead, the press must itself condemn transgressions of the institution and proclaim that it would no longer deserve its privileged freedom under the First Amendment if it did not link that freedom with responsibility to all members of the society.

It is interesting to note that the call of the Hutchins Commission was less for a poorly defined sense of responsibility than for the more demanding aim of *accountability*. Freedom, the commission wrote, was in danger unless it became accountable to "conscience and the common good." That it provided no mechanism to police and enforce its account-ability was politically astute but not notably helpful in controlling the abuses of freedom it documented. The encoding of the doctrine of social responsibility channeled the issue into the safe harbor of theoretical constructs and turned attention away from the stormy seas of practicality: how to police and enforce the doctrine.

According to the Hutchins Commission, press accountability was to be monitored and promoted by "a new and independent agency to appraise and report annually upon the performance of the press." If no such independent body were to be chosen, the commission warned, it might be the government that would take unto itself the power to appraise and perhaps even regulate press performance. From this proposal there developed the concept of the press council, an institution that would be composed of experts, from within and outside the world of journalism, that would keep an eye not only on the press but also on the government to protect against inroads on press freedom. Despite the high reputation of the Hutchins Commission members and despite agitation by many individual journalists and by professors of journalism, the kind of press council envisaged by the Hutchins group has not materialized in the United States, although a National News Council did appear in 1973 and two dozen communities and one state have created varying forms of press councils.

The press council has established a powerful beachhead in Western Europe. The British council has served as the model for similar institutions elsewhere — in West Germany, Sweden, Switzerland, Canada, Italy, India, and for the press councils established in the United States. The impetus for a press council in Britain came at the same time as the movement in the United States, fired by charges by Socialist members of Parliament that concentration of ownership and sensational news treatment had "degraded...the honorable profession of journalism." Haydn Davis, a journalist and Socialist party member of Parliament, raised this question: "Can we or can we not have real freedom of the press in a system of combines and chain newspapers?" A royal commission was created in 1946, but it was not until 1964 that an independent British council came into existence, composed of twenty members from the press and five public members, its challenge to preserve press freedom and to review the industry in order to maintain "the highest professional and commercial standards." The council was given no enforcement powers, but newspapers were required to publish its findings, on the theory that the glare of publicity would shame offenders into desisting from questionable practices. H. Phillip Levy, who has written a history of the council, holds that it was intended to be an educator, not an inquisitor, and that its appeal was to conscience and fair play: "In a free press sanctions would be an incongruity." Levy maintains the council has been so effective that it has become "feared, respected, and obeyed." That conclusion seems overstated; sensationalism is as alive as even in the narrowing English press spectrum.

The major impetus, in England as in the United States, was to improve the level of credibility of the news media. The push for councils in the United States followed the discovery of a "credibility gap." Such a gap existed, the *APME News*, official publication of the Associated Press Managing Editors Association, reported in 1969: "This is widely acknowledged both by editors and by public officials replying to a questionnaire." Katharine Graham, publisher of *The Washington Post,* echoed the assertion: "The American people do not seem at all happy with their press... The nation's publishers are acutely aware of the general indictment." In that period, the credibility of all large and visible institutions was called into question. In 1973, columnist David Broder of *The Washington Post* observed that the public had "more faith in the competence of people who run local trash collection" than it had in those who controlled television or the press, or the Supreme Court or Congress, for that matter. Insistence that the watchdog be watched emerged everywhere, especially following an open attack on the behavior of the press by President Nixon and

Vice-President Agnew. The vice-president drew widespread public applause and outraged criticism from the press for implying possible government action to restrict the "independence" of the press. Arguing that unparalleled power had been seized by a handful of television and print journalists, Agnew said the public would not long tolerate such concentration of power in the hands of television anchormen and producers:

> Is it not fair and relevant to question its concentration in the hands of a tiny and closed fraternity of privileged man, elected by no one, and enjoying a monopoly sanctioned and licensed by government?

In such an environment, it was not surprising that news councils sprang up in communities from coast to coast and that the state of Minnesota established a state-wide council, or even that the National News Council was brought into existence. Not all the mass media agreed to support the National News Council, however, on the ground that newspapers and broadcasters were better equipped to judge flaws in press behavior than any kind of quasi-official body that might seek to impose regulations on a free press. Still, many papers did agree to cooperate with the council, and more than thirty news organizations are contributing financially. The council limits its activities to examination of "national" news reporting, meaning the product of the news agencies; news magazines; television networks; and a handful of leading newspapers, such as the *Times*, the *Post*, and *The Wall Street Journal*. It operates only ex post facto, that is to say, it deals only with complaints about what has already been published; it does not consider what might have been published and was not.

Some U.S. newspapers, in order to achieve higher credibility, have adopted the ombudsman technique widely used in the Scandinavian countries, where the public lodges complaints against official actions and the ombudsman investigates for them. Two dozen newspapers, beginning with *The Louisville Courier-Journal and Times* in 1967, have followed the ombudsman technique, with varying success. A similar function is carried out by the "house critic" of *The Washington Post*, whose assignment is to guard against "creeping bias, laziness, inaccuracy, and the sins of omission." Ombudsmen and house critics have made serious efforts to represent the public in their challenges to the performance of the press, but it has been a lonely job and has rarely resulted in more than cosmetic change. The chief difficulty confronted by ombudsmen has been the hostility of their fellow workers on newspapers, who resent, as do journalists everywhere, being second-guessed about their work. A less troublesome method to attempt to boost credibility has been the programs undertaken by most newspapers and broadcasting stations to serve as fact-finders for readers who require specialized information or who wish to complain about treatment by stores and mail-order houses. Such "action-line" programs are popular with the public but involve themselves only with mistreatment and mismanagement by institutions other than the press. Social responsibility remains the unofficial doctrine of the press, but it remains today, as it was when the idea was introduced, a vaguely worded goal model whose perimeters are ill defined and in practice largely ignored.

"THE MOST POWERFUL MEN IN THE HISTORY OF THE WORLD"

Among the three reasons offered by the Hutchins Commission as to why the freedom of the press was in danger was growth of the importance of the instruments of mass communication. The press, it was argued, had become a "vital necessity" in the transaction of public business; its scope was increasing, and so was its power. The commission termed the modern press "a new phenomenon" that might "facilitate thought or thwart progress," that might, in fact, debase and vulgarize mankind and endanger peace:

> If the press is inflammatory, sensational and irresponsible, it and its freedom will go down in the universal catastrophe. On the other hand, it can help create a new world community, by giving men everywhere knowledge of the world and one another, by prompting comprehension and appreciation of the goals of a free society.

Such assertions about the power of the mass media have by now become commonplace. So extensively have these assertions been spread that it is safe to say that today most people in the world assume enormous power for the press. That assumption has become so firmly fixed in press dogma that people everywhere believe in the power of the press with the same assurance with which they revere the public's right to know. There appeared in 1972 a book entitled *Media Power*, written by Robert Stein, a man who had spent a quarter of a century as a journalist, primarily as a magazine editor. Stein wrote:

> After 200 years of fixed tradition and accepted practice, American journalists are now facing a new situation: If knowledge is power, it is no longer concentrated in the hands of the powerful.... By shaping our picture of the world on an almost minute-to-minute basis, the media now largely determine what we think, how we feel and what we do about our social and political environment.

Similar avowals of an immense press power are broadcast almost daily by journalists, politicians, media, scholars, and by the public whenever queried in opinion surveys. For example, a spokesman for the news department of a Minnesota television station remarked: "We are the most powerful men in the history of the world, and I'm happy to say that, on the whole, I think that power is being used in the best interests of everybody." The comment was made in a study surveying broadcasters' attitudes about the part played by television news in reporting the Watergate scandal. The author of the study, Marvin Barrett, saw the power of the press in equally hyperbolic terms, maintaining that the confrontation of Nixon with the press marked the first time since the medieval confrontation of the crown with the papacy that there had been "a comparable encounter of power with equal but disparate power." In twentieth century America, Barrett wrote, "the press seemed to be assuming the role of the medieval papacy."

The assumption of prodigious power on the part of the press is derived largely from the visibility of newspapers, magazines, and especially television; it is drawn also from the perception of the majority of the population that it receives its information about the world from the news media. The question, "where do you get most of your news," is a simplistic question; in fact, most of us do not know where we receive most of our news. Information, whether of "news" or of anything else, rarely arrives in our consciousness through a single channel. We read, we listen, we speak, we hear — in all these ways, we receive information, and the mechanism of reception is not often discrete. For example, information about an airplane crash may reach us first in a conversation with another person. Then we may tune in our radio, check the evening newspaper, watch the evening news program on television, and acquire additional scraps of intelligence from other persons. It is from packages that we receive our information, and what we do receive is inevitably filtered through a reception apparatus that includes what we have learned as children at home and in school, what we have read and heard earlier, indeed, from all the forces of socialization we have encountered in our lives. Thus, to assert that we receive most of our news from television or from newspapers is to assert a pattern of learning that is at the very best misleading and at the worst thoroughly erroneous. In fact, the most clearly visible "power" of the press turns out to be a misleading power. To claim, with Stein, Barrett, and the others, that the press has the power to instruct is even more questionable, since our attitudes about our perceptions and experiences have been formed long before we watch a program on television or read an article in a newspaper. Undeniably, we are informed and we are instructed by the news media, but it is a logical absurdity to assign an exclusive role, or even primacy to the news media in these processes.

At all events, the conviction that the press enjoys remarkable power is part of the belief system held not only by Americans but by people everywhere. We have seen that the conviction obtains as much in the Soviet Union and the advancing world as it does in the United States. International discussions of the press confirm the overwhelming acceptance of the conviction: We human beings simply take for granted that the power of the press to inform and instruct is vast, greater than that of any other institution. The implication then is that the responsibility of the press is to inform and instruct. As the Hutchins Commission phrased it, to the press belongs the power to "facilitate thought or thwart progress." The public, says the capitalist doctrine of social responsibility as well as the Leninist model, has every right to expect the press to exercise this role faithfully and truthfully. According to the Hutchins Commission, the people have a right to expect the press to present them not only with the facts but also with the "truth about the facts."

Such great expectations are unrealistic; they place impossible burdens on both the press and the public, and ignore the verity that the press is an instrument rather than an independent actor. They fail to recognize also the reality that the capitalist press is part of the apparatus of private profit that regulates the economy and the political system. In seeking to modify the Four Theories structure, William Hachten joins the libertarian and social responsibility ideology into what he calls the "Western concept," under which "the media have clear obligations of public service that transcend moneymaking." Moreover, he argues:

> ... in the Western concept, the media have a positive responsibility to provide reliable and essential information from around the world. By so doing, journalists help protect political liberty by providing information that a democratic society requires if it is to govern itself.

To expect capitalist media to "transcend moneymaking" is a logical absurdity, since even the most dedicated doctrinaires rarely publish newspapers or magazines in order to lose money. Much the same can be said of the "democratic assumption" argument advanced by the Hutchins Commission, the Four Theorists, Hachten, and the overwhelming percentage of journalists who respond to surveys. Walter Lippmann wrestled with this argument long ago and concluded, sadly, that the press was a "frail reed" to lean upon for carrying out the democratic assumption.

Few journalists have thought as long and hard about public questions as Lippmann, whose life spanned two world wars, the Korean and Vietnam conflicts, the Great Depression, and the presidencies of individuals as varied as Warren Harding and John Kennedy. Lippmann was one of the first analysts to subject the phenomenon of public opinion to careful examination. At first, he adopted the line of thinking of contemporary students of the press, that the power of public opinion was overwhelming and, as the Hutchins Commission was to declare a quarter of a century later, that the future of democracy rested on the delivery by the press of truthful and accurate information. The press, Lippmann wrote, was the "bible of democracy, the book out of which a people determines its conduct." Yet Lippmann was by no means certain that the press was, in fact, delivering truthful and accurate information; he had had the opportunity to study press performance at first hand while serving with Woodrow Wilson at the Versailles peace conference after the First World War. To test press performance, Lippmann and a colleague, Charles Merz, studied the articles about the Bolshevik Revolution that appeared in *The New York Times*, which enjoyed, then as now, the reputation of being the most reliable reporter of international affairs in the United States. Over a three-year period that began in 1917 with the overthrow of Czar Nicholas II, Lippmann and Merz found a pattern of misstatements and misinformation. The contribution of those articles to public knowledge at a time of crisis was, they reported, "about as useful as that of an astrologer or an alchemist." The journalists for the *Times* had relied on hearsay and their own imaginations: "The news about Russia is a case of seeing not what was, but what men wished to see." Lippmann was describing what psychologists now identify as selective perception long before the term itself had appeared.

Fascinated and disturbed by the findings, Lippmann devoted the next two years to thinking through and writing the slim book that remains his greatest legacy, *Public Opinion*. Lippmann had now decided that the democratic assumption was faulty and that it was foolhardy to expect the press, especially in complex modern society, to provide all by itself the accurate and truthful information needed for action by citizens in a democratic society. In fact, he cast considerable doubt on the fundamentals of democratic society. Philosopher John Dewey said *Public Opinion* represented "perhaps the most effective indictment of democracy as currently conceived ever penned." Lippmann must have been concerned about being perceived as indicting democracy, for the final pages of his book expressed faith that somehow, even though the assumptions were wrong, men and women of goodwill would succeed in building the good life through "intelligence, courage, and effort."

The centerpiece of Lippmann's argument was that news and truth were different from one another and that one ought not expect them to be identical. Even with the best of intentions, the journalist was the prisoner of his own stereotypes and prejudices and the victim of manipulation by propagandists seeking to direct his understanding of events. Distortion was lodged deep in the human mind; what we assumed to be facts were often merely judgments. Thus, to ask the press to bear the burden of supplying the public with truth was asking too much. "The function of news," Lippmann wrote, "is to signalize an event, the function of truth is to bring to light the hidden facts." The best the press could do was to convey clarity to events, by shining "like the beam of a searchlight that moves restlessly about, bringing one episode and then another out of the darkness into vision." Lippmann the journalist was not about to argue that the institution was useless. To signalize and clarify events was itself a worthy task. Still, he said, neither the press nor the public ought to expect that society can be governed "by episodes, incidents, and eruptions."

His quarrel with the democratic assumption was not merely with the role of the press in it, but also with the expectation that the public would actively seek out the information it needed to carry out its assigned task in the democratic society. The average man, he wrote, had neither the time nor the ability to make sense of the waves of information engulfing him. When Lippmann wrote *Public Opinion*, television had not appeared and radio was in its infancy; thus, he could write that the average citizen had little direct contact with the world, which was "out of reach, out of sight, out of mind." Yet the present ready availability of sights and sounds that bring the images and words of newsmakers into the living room has not altered Lippmann's insight about direct contact, for those images and words are as subject to the phenomenon of selective perception as the contents of newspapers and magazines. Democracy could work, Lippmann wrote, only if men escaped from the "intolerable and unworkable fiction that each of us must acquire a competent opinion about public affairs." Indeed, Lippmann need not have troubled himself on this score, for the public in the United States and in other pluralistic societies, just as the people in the Soviet Union and other socialist states and those in the advancing world, pays only limited attention to the news that bombards it. It seems to possess little more unbiased information about the outside world than did the general public of earlier ages. Economist Anthony Downs has argued that such inattention is entirely rational, since the reasoning citizen, operating on the basis of cost efficiency, attends more to matters over which he or she has direct control than to the "news" and public policy wherein the individual is, for the most part, powerless.

Lippmann's argument that news and truth are not the same thing tends to be disputed by the body of practicing journalists and by a number of journalism scholars as well. One such is Douglass Cater, who popularized the idea that the press is a fourth branch of government, watching over the executive, legislative, and judicial. The roles of news and truth, Cater writes, are not so neatly divided as Lippmann would suggest. The leaders of the news media, Cater argues, do not "wish to abdicate the task of bringing to light hidden facts, setting them into relation with each other, and making a picture of reality on which men can act." Indeed, he argues, the main thrust of the best investigative journalism has been to seek to bring to light those hidden facts. The task of journalists, Cater maintains, is "to do more digging" and "to spend less time searching for gimmicks." Cater thus attacks Lippmann's thesis by turning to the familiar role assigned to the press of serving as watchdog over the powerful. As such, he comes down squarely on the side of the doctrine of social responsibility.

It seems to be a fact that wherever journalism is practiced today, the mission of the press is perceived in terms of social responsibility. The doctrine nonetheless comes under attack from both radical and conservative camps. Raymond Williams, whose views are closer to the Marxist than to the capitalist camp, holds that no press can ever be responsible to society so long as it operates within a commercial system. While he sees a commercial system as superior to either an authoritarian or "paternal" system, he argues that nevertheless in the end the desire for sales outweighs any desire for unbiased, socially useful information. In much of the capitalist world, Williams identifies the press system as paternal, which he defines as "an authoritative system with a conscience" wherein "an unrepresentative minority" runs the media with the purpose of protecting and guiding the people. This unrepresentative minority directs the media as thoroughly and effectively as any autocrat, although the gears of control are operated by silken threads rather than iron chains. Control is subliminal. Anything can be said in a commercial system, "provided that you can afford to say it and that you can say it profitably."

Under Williams's system, governments and media representatives would jointly establish a series of councils, for the printed press, the broadcasting media, advertising, books, theater, motion pictures, and perhaps other media. The councils would police their media and establish policy to guarantee not only the production of diversified information but also access to the media for all citizens and the elimination of the possibility of concentration of media ownership in the hands of the few. In short, according to Williams, to assure any kind of genuine responsibility on the part of the media, the institutions of the communications media would have to be changed. Personal ownership must be eliminated and private property rendered obsolete. A press that is not free cannot be responsible, Williams asserts, and no press that is operated for private profit can be free: "The only alternative to control by a few irresponsible men, who treat our cultural means as simple commodities, is a public system." In a number of important aspects, Williams's views were shared by Velasco's men in Peru, but, of course, no truly public system emerged in Peru.

From a traditional laissez-faire position, John Merrill condemns the social responsibility doctrine as passionately as does Williams from the left. Merrill rejects the doctrine on two grounds: that it leads inexorably to government control, and that it relies for its moral underpinning on situational ethics. According to Merrill:

> The only way a "theory" of social responsibility could have any significance in any country is for the governmental power elite to be the definer and enforcer of this type of press. Since in any country the organization of society — its social and political structure — determines to a large extent what responsibilities the press (and the citizen) owe society, every country's press quite naturally considers itself (or might logically be considered) as being socially responsible.

To Merrill, freedom is more important than responsibility, and "any power to make the press 'responsible' or 'accountable' is the negation of liberty." Williams's councils as well as Peru's social property would be anathema to Merrill, just as would be the kinds of press councils envisioned by the Hutchins Commission, ombudsmen, or any similar force, whether a government or a private body, since ultimately the only way the recommendations of such a body could be enforced would be through government. Thus, any effort to manage the press for social ends is a denial of the freedom of the journalist as well as the autonomy of the institution. Moreover, it denies the journalist the freedom to follow the call of duty. To Merrill, ethics are personal; it is the law that is social. Merrill's ideal journalist resists all controls; he observes the law, rendering unto Caesar what is Caesar's, but morally he is his own man. Even his boss can't touch him. With Kant, Merrill rejects any imposed code of morality. Presumably, any reporter ordered to practice deception, as for instance to pose as an inmate in order to uncover the truth about prison life, would refuse, risking dismissal rather than violating his principles. Merrill's ideal figure is romantic and lonely, an incarnation of Mill's individual or a Brontë hero — or Baker's lone rider. Freedom can be preserved only if that lonely journalist is unfettered, acting on the basis of his own "reason, sensitivity, and commitment." Only thus can he be responsible — to himself, not to society. The doctrine of social responsibility threatens to eliminate individual choice and experimentation, and to make the press simply "one vast, gray, bland, monotonous, conformist spokesman." Williams would argue that it has become such already — influenced by the doctrine of social responsibility, with its call for interpretation, analysis, and investigation. Those who love the press — and these include Merrill, Williams, the Hutchins Commission, and the Four Theorists — all urge change. The institution of the press is impregnated not only with folklore but also with paradox.

THE AWA ROLE OF THE PRESS

Of all the paradoxes, none is more intriguing than the inconsistency in the principle of watchdoggery. Anyone who studies the press finds himself confronted almost at once with a belief system in which the press is viewed as an institution whose reason for existence is wrapped up in the idea that it serves the public by acting as a kind of German shepherd — whose glittering eye is eternally fixed on Wotan and his henchmen to make certain that they do not abuse their power. Such declares an article of faith in the capitalist press system, a system sometimes described as adversarial. The idea of an adversarial press conjures up an image where the press plays prosecuting attorney, charging power — usually identified as government — with violations of law or moral rectitude. In this picture, power functions as defendant, and the reading or viewing public as judge and jury. The principle of watchdoggery notwithstanding, the literature about the press is also filled with recognition that the relationship between press and power is less adversarial than symbiotic.

What a difference! What a remarkable paradox! If in fact press and power need each other, cannot exist without each other, what becomes then of the principle of watchdoggery? What becomes of the concept of prodigious independent power on the part of the press?

In recent years, the power claims advanced for the press have pursued a new path, drawing on an assertion by Bernard C. Cohen in 1963 that the press "may not be successful much of the time in telling people what to think, but it is stunningly successful in telling its readers what to think *about*." Cohen's comment was instrumental in leading to an area of research that one of its creators identified as the "agenda-setting function of the mass media." Cater went a step further by declaring that the media "have a vast power to shape government" in the very act of selecting which information to report and which to ignore: "Those words that fail to get projected might as well not have occurred." Stein injected a variation on the agenda-setting theme by arguing that the power to select gives the media "a new kind of power over us all," since it is able to select which group to make visible to the public and which to condemn to some limbo simply by inattention. Indeed, according to Stein, it is this "power" that has intensified the adversarial relationship between the press and politicians, who see the media as usurping their prerogative to themselves shape the public agenda.

The watchdog, the adversarial, and the agenda-setting functions assigned to the press converge into a quite plausible theory that can proclaim the doctrine of social responsibility as its philosophical lodestar. The centerpiece of this theory is power. If the press sets itself up against political (and economic) leadership, it is being adversarial. If as part of its adversarial behavior it maintains a steady watch on the leadership, it is being a watchdog. And if it lets the people know what is important and what is trivial, it is setting the public agenda. In all these situations, the power of the press is formidable. The press is clearly cast in the role of an independent actor — as investigator (watchdog), combatant (adversary), and planner (agenda-setter).

Such a role is the diametric opposite of the traditional press role as that of the disinterested, objective observer. The press as adversary, watchdog, agenda-setter possesses infinitely greater power than the press as a form of transmission belt, merely reflecting events for readers and viewers. In the adversary, watchdog, agenda-setting role, the press is not content merely to stand witness, to act as nonparticipant. Conversely, in the traditional, objective role, the press would not *set* the agenda; it would merely *record* the agenda.

And yet — such is the paradox — the standard of objectivity is raised by the adversaries, the watchdogs, and the agenda-setters. It is a different kind of objectivity, of course, but nevertheless it has about it the same kind of aura of Science as the simpler, traditional version.

The paradox is resolved when it is recognized that each of these tenets is spurious. For each tenet assumes what cannot be assumed: that the press is an independent actor. Once it is accepted that the press is an agent of power and not an independent force, it can be seen that the press is no more watchdog, adversary, or agenda-setter than it is a disinterested, objective observer. The relationship between the press and power is indeed symbiotic, with all that metaphor suggests. In this metaphor, the press behaves like peas or beans and power like the nitrogen-manufacturing bacteria that feed on the vegetable-bearing plants. From the bacteria the plants receive the nitrogen that enables them to grow, and from the plants the bacteria absorb the food that enables them to survive. Without each other, bacteria and plant would perish. And in the contemporary world, political (and economic) power needs the mass media, just as the media need the power of the leadership. They are not adversaries, since they need each other. They may (and indeed do) watch each other, not for the purpose of interfering with the behavior that nurtures them both but to avoid the kind of abnormal behavior that threatens the biological — or total — system in which both live. It is together that they live and/or die, and so it is together that they disseminate information, or that they set the public agenda.

There is a good deal of benefit to both power and the media in the maintenance of the folklore of the watchdog, the adversary, or the agenda-setter. This is so because any threat to the survival of the existing system comes only from outside — that is, from those who do not share power or sup at its table. The only political or economic forces that threaten the system are those that are not part of it, those that have not arrived at the plateau of legitimacy described by Wolff. These include not only revolutionary political or economic forces but also dissident elements of the press. These are the forces that might, under other circumstances, act as adversary, watchdog, or agenda-setter. Thus, it is in the mutual interests of power to confer on the press the designation as the only *legitimate* adversary, watchdog, or agenda-setter. The press, as an institution that sups at the table of power, cheerfully accepts and broadcasts its mantle of legitimacy. It bears the stamp of approval, so to speak, of the doctrine of social responsibility — by carrying out what might be termed its AWA role, that is, the role of the press as Adversary, Watchdog, and Agenda-Setter. In playing, or appearing to play, the AWA role, the press is serving as an instrument of power, just as it is when it plays the role of objective, disinterested observer.

As objective, disinterested observer, the press is essentially a transmitter of information. In its AWA role, the press is no more independent than it is as objective observer. In fact, since the vision of journalists is clouded by the folklore, they are more easily used as AWA, for all too often they are unable to see that they are being manipulated and maneuvered. Marxist, market, and advancing press systems operate in similar ways, although manipulation of the press is more open in Marxist nations and in some advancing countries. Each press model, nevertheless, officially endorses a doctrine of social responsibility — and in each of the systems, the effort is made to manage the press. It is difficult to sever the silken cords of the folklore that enmesh the press in the market system. The news reporting of U.S. election campaigns illustrates the practice.

The doctrine of social responsibility charges the press, in its AWA role, with "watching" everybody, searching always for defects and weaknesses, and bringing those defects and weaknesses to the attention of the public. The challenge for candidates seeking political office is to maneuver the press into watching what *they* want watched and into closing its eyes to what the candidates wish to remain unseen. One memorable instance given wide publicity was the "dirty tricks" campaign waged on behalf of Richard Nixon in 1972; although especially blatant, this campaign was only marginally different from efforts made on behalf of all candidates who seek to portray opponents as weak or ineffective. Much has been written also about the use of radio by Franklin Roosevelt in his "fireside chats," and of Nixon's "selling of the presidency" by the use of television in his 1968 campaign. These efforts were by no means unique; in fact, all aspirants to all offices have by now come to allot a large share of their budget to media campaigns, attempting to invoke a good "image" of themselves and a poor one of their opponents. The promotional and advertising activities of political candidates are now well known not only to the press but also to the general public. Much of the selling program is devoted to disguising the very existence of the campaign, as candidates strive to manipulate images while appearing to stand above such practices. In these attempts, perhaps the strongest ally of the media managers has been the existence of the folklore of the press that depicts the news media as adversaries, watchdogs, and agenda-setters.

The splendid book by David Paletz and Robert Entman entitled *Media Power Politics* documents the successful campaign waged on behalf of Jimmy Carter to use the folklore and the conventional definitions of news employed by the media to gain an unlikely victory in 1976. Carter's success in winning the presidency can be contrasted with the failure in 1972 of Edmund Muskie and George McGovern. Candidates Muskie and McGovern were far less adept than Carter in manipulating the press and paid for that ineptitude, in quite different ways.

Of the three, Muskie seemed most likely to achieve the Democratic party nomination, and yet he failed while McGovern and Carter succeeded. Muskie's failure can be attributed in substantial degree to the folklore that has risen around the doctrine of social responsibility, especially with its insistence on the AWA role of the press. As the campaign in 1972 began, Muskie was accorded the position of "front-runner," a designation that has gained widespread public acceptance in the ritualized metaphor of the election campaign as horse race. Candidates hate to be saddled at the start of the race with the position of front-runner, for the racetrack drama centers on the developing contest in which long shots appear out of nowhere to nose out the front-runner at the finish line. Moreover, the press is more likely to *watch* the front-runner than the long shot, and thus modest failings of the front-runner are certain to be broadcast far and wide while the unassuming long shot waxes strong in the shadows, far removed from the light of publicity. It was not surprising that the spotlight shone on Muskie as he struggled through the snowfields of New Hampshire to triumph in the Democratic party primary; his objective in that primary was a defensive one — not to lose his position as front-runner as the horses were just starting from the post. Since the Nixon strategists viewed Muskie as their most formidable foe, it is not surprising that much of the early Nixon campaign was directed at discoloring Muskie's image. The famous scene, dutifully recorded by photographers, in which Muskie was seen to weep with anger at slurs in *The Manchester Union Leader* against his wife, became his own private Waterloo. Journalists, mindful of their responsibility role, joined Muskie's opponents in raising questions about his stability, his composure under fire, and indirectly his capacity for coping with the challenges of the presidency. Three days after the weeping incident, a front-page headline in *The Washington Post* over an article by the respected writer David Broder, proclaimed: "Support for Muskie Wavers in New Hampshire."

Moreover, Muskie was a victim of the horse-race convention. His opponents sought to create the impression that he would lose his position as front-runner if he did not win with 60 or 65 percent of the vote against four or five opponents. In that scenario, it would not be enough for Muskie to win in New Hampshire; as the saying went, he had to win "big."

Muskie did win in the primary, but he gained only 46.4 percent of the votes cast. The result was interpreted not only by his opponents but also by the press as a defeat for Muskie and as a victory for McGovern, who, unexpectedly for the press, came in second with 37.1 percent of the vote. Muskie's position in the primary derby was fatally weakened, and his candidacy eroded steadily until he withdrew from the campaign. The press was an important factor in his failure — but not because the press had acted as an independent force. It had served as an agent of the Nixon campaign by providing an immoderate volume of coverage to the weeping incident, and it had served as an agent of the McGovern forces by analyzing victory as defeat in the New Hampshire primary.

Later, in that very same campaign, the press assisted in the downfall of McGovern as well. In this case, the reporting of the press served as a mechanism of social control, much as it had done in 1964 in the overwhelming defeat of Barry Goldwater. The Republican Goldwater was perceived as a radical of the right and a threat to the social order; now it was the Democrat McGovern who was perceived as a radical of the left and a threat to the social order. The centripetal force of the politico-economic system propels all individuals and ideas from the extremes to the center. It is not necessary for any person or group to instruct or direct the journalist to join this centripetal force; he or she does so automatically, as a full-fledged member of the social order.

In the early days of the campaign, McGovern held the advantage of being a fresh personality in national politics; he was in the buildup phase while the veteran Muskie was being carefully analyzed by the watchdog press. After Muskie withdrew and McGovern won the Democratic party nomination, it was his time to be subjected to careful analysis. Nixon, in the meantime, avoided the press altogether, sending out surrogate speakers and confining his appearances to televised meetings with his supporters. For the watchdogs, McGovern was the only show in town, and when Nixon, in his acceptance speech in August, singled out for attack a statement made by McGovern in Iowa in the previous January, the press watchdogs had their cue. Invoking the doctrine of social responsibility, they devoted an untold number of articles to analyzing a proposal by McGovern to provide $1,000 in benefits to every person in America. McGovern was portrayed as a wild-eyed dreamer; he was also condemned for failing to stand behind his original vice-presidential nominee, Thomas Eagleton, after the story was leaked to the press that Eagleton had undergone treatment for an emotional disorder. The honeymoon was over, and McGovern was doomed. McGovern aides howled in protest that the journalists were being unfair, that they had not understood what McGovern had in mind in the $1,000 proposal, that he was really referring to a form of negative income tax. And they argued that the Eagleton affair was blown out of all proportion.

It does not follow that McGovern — or Muskie — would have won the election in 1976 if the press had behaved differently. However, in neither the case of Muskie nor that of McGovern did the press operate independently. It was maneuvered into watching first Muskie, then McGovern, by the Nixon strategists, who understood full well the ways of the press, and it was also maneuvered by those very ways that serve the interests of the politico-economic system. Nixon in 1972, Carter in 1976, and Ronald Reagan in 1980 all used the press effectively, succeeding in projecting their "image" and tarnishing that of their opponent, and they all won.

It is by no means only with regard to elections that attention has been directed in recent years to the independent "power" of the press. The press has been credited (or charged, depending on the point of view) with bringing an end to the war in Vietnam; with undermining Nixon's presidency; with inducing social change in combating crime, in improving race relations, in defending the environment against predatory encroachment. In all these situations, as with electoral politics, close examination demonstrates that the independent power of the press has been illusory. The continuation of the war in Vietnam was not threatened until the number of casualties mounted so high that patriotic Americans began asking themselves the unusual question: For what were their husbands, sons, and friends dying? Press criticism of the conduct of the war followed — rather than led to — public disaffection — or it was simply a reflection of the same disaffection. The undoing of Nixon was accomplished not by the press but by the congressional Republicans who were outraged by the disclosures of Nixon's behavior in open court and open committee rooms. Attention to crime in the news media has changed little since the days of the penny press; it was and is the dramatic, the unusual, and the heartwarming that has been emphasized. The criminals who have been accorded the most space have been those who have violated the conventional social order, not those who have broken the law in acceptable manner, such as merchants who overcharge customers or restaurateurs who water the wine or the ketchup, or mechanics who fail to repair what they promise to fix, or journalists or academics who accept gifts or free trips from those about whom they are expected to write critically.

To be sure, there are cases in which newspaper or television reports have led to corrective action on the part of authorities. Falsely imprisoned persons have been freed as a result of news stories. Attention has been directed to corporate peccadilloes. Swindlers have been uncovered. In these situations, the press has indeed demonstrated its power, or more precisely its potential power. It is because of this potential that those who hold political and economic power in any social order are suspicious of the press and go to great lengths not only to manipulate it to their ends but to conceal from both press and public the extent of their manipulative efforts.

Within the last generation in the United States, few occurrences have been of greater significance or included higher drama than the struggle between the races. Both the friends and the foes of racial equality have condemned the press for failing to practice social responsibility in its treatment of news items about racial issues. A press that practiced the doctrine of social responsibility would have served the interests of both whites and blacks; after all, a "society" must be color-blind. Yet before 1954, when a Supreme Court ruling set the civil rights struggle in motion, the majoritarian U.S. press had by and large ignored the issue of race. A black press had existed, almost unknown, for a century and a half. White journalists had written and broadcast about racial matters, but rarely within the larger context of civil liberties. News about black citizens was confined mainly to crime reports and stories about the problems encountered by blacks — the need for welfare, unemployment benefits, and so on. The number of black journalists working for mainstream news media was minute, and racial and ethnic minorities had only the most limited access to the news columns. The presidential (Kerner) commission that investigated the causes of the racial disturbances of the 1960s concluded: "The media report and write from the standpoint of a white man's world." It added:

> The ills of the ghetto, the difficulties of life there, the Negro's burning sense of grievance, are seldom conveyed. Slights and indignities are part of the Negro's daily life, and many of them come from what he now calls "the white press" — a press that repeatedly, if unconsciously, reflects the biases, the paternalism, the indifference of white America. This may be understandable, but it is not excusable in an institution that has the mission to inform and educate the whole of our society.

More forceful even than the report of the Kerner Commission was a statement by Stokely Carmichael, then chairman of the Student Nonviolent Coordinating Committee, who maintained that contrary to the folklore of social responsibility, the journalists who worked for the white press had little concern for representing the interests of blacks:

> Our experience with the national press has been that where they have managed to escape a meretricious special interest in "Git Whitey" sensationalism and race-warmongering, individual reporters and commentators have been conditioned by the enveloping racism of the society to the point where they are incapable even of objective observation and reporting of racial *incidents*, much less the analysis of *ideas*. But this limitation of vision and perceptions is an inevitable consequence of the dictatorship of definition, interpretation, and consciousness, along with the censorship of history that the society has inflicted upon the Negro — and itself.

If Carmichael was correct, then the "society" to which the press felt itself responsible was at best the society of whites, or that society which defines and interprets history. Certainly, in dealing with racial issues, the press failed to carry out its AWA model: it served neither as adversary of racist practices, nor as watchdog of government abuses, nor as setter of an agenda of public concern about racial matters. Instead, the press served the interests of the social order that had for hundreds of years practiced racism, either in the form of slavery or in the kinds of prejudices perpetuated by white society and its institutions.

Foes of the civil rights movement, on the other hand, accused the press of stirring up trouble with its reports on racial issues; to write such stories was to those persons a violation of social responsibility. In similar vein, the press comes under attack from all sides for its reporting on all controversial matters. So ingrained in public consciousness has the doctrine of social responsibility become that it is invoked across the country — and throughout the world — wherever one encounters discussions about the press.

THE PERIMETERS OF ACCEPTABLE DISSENT

It is not to be forgotten that the press is charged with the obligation to behave responsibly in all social, economic, and political systems. Capitalist analysts, such as the authors of the *Four Theories*, accuse the Marxist press of irresponsible behavior. Socialist theorists condemn the capitalist press as irresponsible. In the advancing world, the charge of irresponsibility is directed against both capitalist and socialist mass media. In short, everyone accuses the other guy of the wickedness of irresponsibility and exhorts his press to live up to the virtue of responsibility. The adjective social is not always employed, but it is clear that the benefits of a responsible press are to accrue to the people, to the public, to society. Almost never are these troublesome terms defined. It is well to keep in mind that under the censorship program in Brazil, responsibility is demanded of the press as it is in the repressive regimes in Chile and Burma, in South Africa and South Yemen; as it is under the guided journalism model in Indonesia; as it was under Gandhi in India and under Velasco in Peru; as it is demanded in the Soviet Union and in France, Britain, and the United States. The image is inevitably that of the press serving the needs of society. Lenin's three goals for the press are cast in the image of social responsibility just as are the five goals of the Hutchins Commission.

Yet it is also true that no authority wants its press to practice just any kind of social responsibility; what is wanted is the kind of social responsibility that suits a particular conception of the social order. Put another way, the Soviet rulers would in no way accept as virtuous the American model of social responsibility. Nor would the U.S. government accept the Soviet idea of social responsibility. In the same way, the leaders of many arriving nation-states reject both the Soviet and the American models. Inside each system, it is only those news media that are prepared to live in comfortable symbiosis with the leadership that are permitted to flourish. It is important for leaders in all nation-states to see to it that their press behaves in an acceptable fashion. The most painless method for ensuring this result is manipulation, the gentle direction of publishers, editors, and reporters into the promotion of the status quo. If manipulation fails, the wielders of power find themselves compelled to resort to less genteel practices, to rigid rules and regulations; to censorship; or, if necessary, to repression, prison sentences, torture, or death. Each of these practices is carried out in the name of protecting society and ensuring that the press behaves responsibly in reporting to society. The press in all instances is an agent of political and economic power.

Sociologist Max Weber recognized the agency role of the press early in the twentieth century. He argued that "so-called public opinion" in a modern democratic state was for the most part stage-managed by political leaders and the press; the press, he said, was lured by the politically powerful into manipulating the masses to accept the social order in good cheer. The notion of freedom of the press, Weber wrote, is a convenient vehicle for charismatic leadership. Believing this, Weber nonetheless pursued a career as a political journalist, imagining that he might somehow break the rules and exert an independent influence over the course of events. In this, Weber was behaving like many journalists and writers before and since, among them Karl Marx and Walter Lippmann!

Even more than Weber, Ferdinand Tönnies, another influential German sociologist, recognized the vulnerability of the press to manipulation. Writing before the advent of television and the highly sophisticated technical equipment of the modern mass media, Tönnies said that in the press, "judgments and opinion are wrapped up like grocers' goods and offered for consumption in their objective reality." Newspapers, he said, provide "the quickest production, multiplication, and distribution of facts and thoughts, just as the hotel kitchen provides food and drink in every conceivable form and quantity." Thus, Tönnies wrote:

> The press is the real instrument of public opinion, a weapon and tool in the hands of those who know how to use it and have to use it; it possesses universal power as the dreaded critic of events and changes in social conditions. It is comparable and, in some respects, superior to the material power which the states possess through their armies, their treasuries, and their bureaucratic civil service.

In Tönnies's analysis, public opinion was the expression not of the masses but of the elite of the social order; hence the press, when it gave voice to public opinion, was in reality expressing the viewpoint of the elite. No government would be likely to object to that kind of public opinion. After all, it would be socially irresponsible not to deliver such reports.

Those journalists who refused to be manipulated, who were determined to be independent of authority, who were, in short, revolutionary thinkers and writers followed the time-honored tradition of going underground. Many names have been applied to a revolutionary press of this nature. In modern times, we have heard of the new journalism, of the underground press, the alternative press, the advocacy press, and the investigative press. There are significant differences among these groups and not all are revolutionary, but all share the belief that a press can indeed be revolutionary and free to the extent that it raises challenges to the politically and economically powerful who normally control the press. The duty of a development journalist, according to India's Aggarwala, is similar to the duty the revolutionary journalists have identified for themselves: to examine public figures and issues critically and to call attention to the differences between the claims of government officials and the execution of their programs. Interestingly, revolutionary journalists, unlike those who operate in the mainstream of their trade, disclaim any kind of professional status and reject a symbiotic role for themselves. It is they, the revolutionary journalists say, who constitute the truly socially responsible press.

It was in the United States that the new journalism and the other modern forms of revolutionary press originated, reaching their zenith in the years of social upheaval in the 1960s. To those in power, it seemed necessary to neutralize these journalists, to prevent them from exercising their potential to influence the public or to effect the kinds of changes not desired by the leadership. It was for this reason that Nixon, Agnew, and others appealed to the patriotic public to help trim the sails of the runaway press. Even though they failed to produce new legal controls, they succeeded in raising serious doubts about the credibility of the press, especially those elements that were critical of the powerful. And although television networks and the most influential newspapers condemned the assault on their freedom of movement, many newspapers and television stations across the country reported themselves in agreement; some elements of the press had grown, they said, too powerful and needed to exercise greater social responsibility — meaning, of course, to assent to the status quo. Even political foes of Nixon and Agnew rallied to their side. Daniel Patrick Moynihan, a Harvard professor who had served as a diplomat under Nixon and who later became a Democratic U.S. senator from New York, complained of what he called a "culture of disparagement" in the U.S. press, in which the media acted as adversary and threatened the future of democratic institutions. Journalists, he said, referring not to the revolutionary press but to the mainstream reporters in Washington, were not engaging in serious inquiry but were guilty of "an almost reckless hostility to power."

The impact of the underground periodicals that sprang up across the United States in the 1960s was significant. The editors and journalists blithely disregarded profit and demonstrated contempt for those in power. In romantic vein they embarked on a quest for Truth. As one of their leaders, Ray Mungo, put it: "*Facts* are less important than truth and the two are far from equivalent. . .for cold facts are nearly always boring and may even distort the truth, but Truth is the highest achievement of human expression." Most mainstream journalists ridiculed such claims, accusing Mungo and his fellows of themselves distorting the truth in order to pursue their political objectives. The real path to truth, in their view, was through the time-honored tradition of dispassionate observation and objective reporting. The new journalists rejected objectivity altogether; truth, according to Tom Wolfe, Norman Mailer, and the others, could be discovered only if the writer, the journalist, were subjectively involved in his research. While the principles advocated by the revolutionary journalists were being publicly disavowed by the traditional press, some of their practices were being taken over. The layout and design of the mainstream press became splashier and easier to read, following the patterns of the underground press. Attacks on the powerful increased; emboldened columnists and editorial writers stepped up their criticism of the political leadership and its programs. In brief, the underground press was co-opted by the defenders of the status quo and its practices were adopted by the mainstream press, although in severely modified form.

The underground press disappeared and was shortly replaced by the investigative journalists. Whereas the motto of underground editors and reporters was the quest for truth, the objective of investigative journalists was to unearth evidence of wickedness in high places and to publish such scathing indictments that the evil perpetrators would be brought to justice, either in the courtroom or — as it was often said — in the court of public opinion. The quest was no longer for truth but for victory over evil. The "adversary culture" of which Moynihan had spoken had arrived. Anthony Smith wrote that the Western journalist, in Europe as well as in the United States, came to see his role "as a kind of institutionalized permanent opposition, always looking critically askance at the doings of those who hold official positions of power." The investigative journalists claim that their drumbeat of opposition is being pounded for the benefit of society; they are therefore the true upholders of the doctrine of social responsibility. On the other hand, critics of the investigators, especially those in the more visible medium of television, hold that they are by their very nature biased and hence are not using their power responsibly when they sap the ability of their leaders to govern effectively. Walter Annenberg, a veteran publisher and diplomat, put it this way: "The difference is that the President has power with responsibility; the press has power without responsibility."

Social responsibility, then, is a doctrine invoked by all parties to disputes about the relationship between the news media and other institutions. The joker is the assumption that the press is free and exercises independent power. The point to be remembered is that the maintenance of this fiction is in the interests of the wielders of true power, for it is only then that they are able to manipulate the press and direct it towards their own ends. For example, the investigative work of The Washington Post in exposing the abuses of the Nixon administration in the Watergate and related affairs assisted in maintaining the social and political order; leaks from the Federal Bureau of Investigation, not from any group of dissidents, supplied the *Post* with the information it needed to continue its investigation. It was the Nixon administration itself that fed the press hints and clues in the examination of the activities of Muskie and McGovern. When a revolutionary press goes too far, its activities are restricted; when it doesn't, it satisfies the desires of those who wield power. In the United States, the investigative press has been co-opted into doing the work of the wielders of power, in the name of social responsibility.

It is on this point in particular that the analysis of the Four Theorists is faulty. In their study, they held that the doctrine of social responsibility operates in the interests of "society," by which they meant the entire population of the country. We have seen how the coverage of racial issues failed to work for the benefit of black Americans. At the same time, it is clear that the reportage of political and economic events and trends works in the interests of the powerful, not of the powerless. Challenges are raised to individuals who stray from the norm, presidents among them, so much so that the press enjoys the reputation of being a kind of loyal opposition to power. Yet that opposition extends only so far, not beyond the perimeters of acceptable dissent, aside from a handful of periodicals that circulate to small audiences, usually unprofitably. Individuals may be attacked freely by the mainstream press, but not institutions. These are to be defended. It is ironical that in this activity the press is dutifully carrying out one of the five roles assigned to it by the Hutchins Commission: to present and clarify the goals and values of the society. The doctrine of social responsibility, in fact, excludes those goals and values that lie beyond the ideological perimeters established by the social order. The limits of investigative journalism are precisely those perimeters. The advice of India's Neville Jayaweera is admirable:

> The last thing media people can do is to come alive to the historical processes in which they are inextricably caught up and adapt their styles and priorities within them. Theirs has always been and will continue to be only a supportive role — supportive of values and systems that are not theirs to prescribe. Those values and systems are fashioned by economic and social forces much larger and more fundamental than themselves. The media ego must learn to diminish gracefully.

Of one trait journalists have rarely been accused: that of humility. If they are ever to develop a clear understanding of what they do, and how what they do fits into the social order around them, it will be necessary for them to surrender their arrogance — or, as Jayaweera says, to diminish it gracefully — and to remove the motes from their eyes.

UNESCO General Conference. (*UNESCO/Dominique Roger, photographer*)

Nine

UNESCO: A New International Information Order

THE QUARREL OVER "FREE FLOW OF INFORMATION"

With the breakup of the old colonial empires and the growth of interest in information as a tool of development in new nations, theoretical and philosophical questions about the nature of a mass press and flow of information became more and more emotionally charged and assumed an increasingly political coloration. While information obviously figures in every arena in which human beings are found, it has been inside the cultural arm of the United Nations that the politics of news has been exposed in its most dramatic manifestation; it would not be a gross exaggeration to assert that the politics of news has exploded inside UNESCO.

When the United Nations was created in 1944 and 1945, it was anticipated by the founders that the critical political issues facing the nations of the world would be hotly debated inside the Security Council and the General Assembly. It was anticipated that the allied international agencies, especially UNESCO, would win widespread — if not universal — support as they sought to build a pattern of global cooperation in attempting to resolve the challenges facing all of mankind. That the issues involving information, especially the flow of news, have divided the membership, often in bitter and acrimonious debate, in no way demonstrates deep divisions inside UNESCO as a whole, although sometimes emotionally worked-up bureaucrats and journalists have seemed to think so. News issues occupy less than 5 percent of the attention of UNESCO, whose main activities are concerned with scientific, literary, artistic, and educational matters. UNESCO officials tend to dismay, and sometimes to anger, over what they correctly believe to be misrepresentation in the press, especially in the United States, about the mission and activities of UNESCO.

Proposals for a "new international information order" surfaced in the 1970s, following more than a decade of discussions on increasing free flow of information around the world and as part of a campaign by Less-Developed Countries (LDCs) to redistribute the world's wealth under the banner of a "new economic order." The flow of information had been recognized as a significant topic for the United Nations from its inception. Members of the international organization without notable exception have endorsed and promoted the philosophy of a free press, following in a direct line from the First Amendment to the U.S. Constitution. Of all the statements of principle by the UN, the most sweeping is contained in the Universal Declaration of Human Rights adopted on December 10, 1948, asserting the rights of each individual in the world to *know*, to *impart*, and to *discuss*. Each of these is an element in a doctrine of free expression, but each is also capable of being interpreted in many ways, and lamentably also of being distorted consciously or unconsciously. The heart of the declaration's goals are contained in Article 19, which says: "Everybody has the right to freedom of opinion and expression; this right includes freedom to hold opinions without interference, and to seek, receive and impart information and ideas through any media and regardless of frontiers."

Throughout the 1960s and 1970s and into the 1980s, UNESCO has sought ways to implement the goal set forth in Article 19; many hundreds of conferences have been held, bringing together scholars, journalists, government officials, and media authorities. At its biennial meetings, UNESCO has adopted many resolutions, virtually all of them with the objective, stated or implied, of raising the levels of information in all parts of the world, not only in the expectation of increasing knowledge and understanding, but also of assisting thereby in preventing war and expanding the rights of individuals, groups, and nations.

Despite the steady increase in the number of news outlets around the world and the steady rise in the rates of literacy, the communication of news is not today a salient factor in the lives of most inhabitants of the planet. UNESCO has set a minimum standard of "adequate communications," but much of the world is nowhere near its target. In 1961, UNESCO proposed that for each one hundred inhabitants of a country, the minimum standard be at least ten copies of daily newspapers, five radio receivers, and two television sets. It has been estimated that to reach the minimum goal of ten copies of daily newspapers for each one hundred persons would take Asia at least until 1992 and Africa until 2035.

Obviously, then, as we see in Tables 9.1, 9.2, and 9.3, despite the gains in the number of mass-media outlets in the new nation-states, the industrialized countries of North America and Europe continue to monopolize the field. For example, in 1979, the total consumption of newsprint in the world amounted to 25,190,000 metric tons; of that total nearly half — 11,370,000 metric tons — was consumed in the United States and Canada. Consumption in Europe, exclusive of the Soviet Union, was 6,070,000 metric tons. Of the total world consumption, North America and Europe accounted for 69 percent. Despite increasing literacy in other parts of the world, the share of newsprint consumption in the capitalist world has fallen only slightly. Twenty years earlier, in 1959, North America and Europe accounted for 72 percent of the total world consumption.

The following tables approximate reality but cannot be taken as absolute. They are based on figures reported to UNESCO by the member governments and illustrate a comparison over a twenty-year period. Comparisons are frustrated not only by the different statistical methods used in various countries but also by the fact that in some years, certain countries do not report at all. For instance, in 1979, newspaper circulation figures are missing for Argentina, Brazil, Peru, and Uruguay, thus upsetting the data for Latin America. China is not counted in the South Asian data on circulation per 1,000. Nevertheless, the statistics taken as a whole illustrate the nature of the imbalance and point to the gap between existing figures and UNESCO goals.

UNESCO itself is an intergovernmental organization, that is to say, it is powerless to act on its own. Like all other international bodies associated with the United Nations, including the UN itself, UNESCO provides a platform for discussion and recommendations. It may take certain actions, but only if those actions are approved by the nations which make up the UNESCO membership. One of the chief sources of misunderstanding that has dogged the efforts of UNESCO staffers has been the barbs directed at the organization for proposals and recommendations made by experts who have participated in the conferences and meetings conducted under the auspices of UNESCO. Such are, of course, not UNESCO policies.

The genesis of the UNESCO discussions came — like the onset of so many ideological issues — from concrete events, primarily the Second World War and the power struggle between the United States and the Soviet Union that followed it, the so-called cold war. The sharpest kind of criticism of Nazi Germany came from newspaper editors and other U.S. ideologues who asserted that Hitler and his Fascist regime might never have been able to rise to power if they had not seized the German press and other communications facilities and put them to use as instruments of propaganda. The argument offered not only by journalists but by the U.S.

Table 9.1 Daily Newspapers

| | Number of Newspapers | | Estimated Circulation | | Circulation per | |
	1959	1979	(in millions)		1,000 Inhabitants	
Africa	220	129	2.9	4.3	12	15
North America	1,865	2,012	63	71	200	213
Latin America	714	758	14	54	69	71
East Asia	280	222	40.1	73	282	319
South Asia	1,300	2,812	10	24.7	12	44
Europe	2,020	2,439	106	122.9	252	318
Oceania	100	111	5	6	311	190
USSR	500	1,782	34	16	162	251
Totals	6,999	10,265	275	371.9	122	164

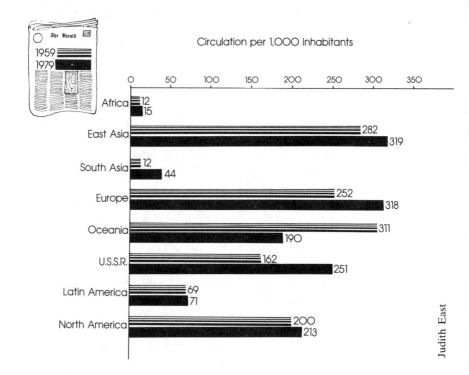

government as well was that only a society that has access to a "free flow of information" can be free. In the years that followed the victory over Germany, the free-flow issue became a central aspect of the cold war.

There was little new in these discussions. The subject of freedom of expression was at the heart of the troubles of Socrates and Galileo, of Milton and Voltaire. It was an issue of great importance, as we have seen, to the Founding Fathers of the United States and in the drafting of the First

Table 9.2 Radio Receivers

	Total receivers (in millions)		Receivers per 1,000 inhabitants	
	1959	1979	1959	1979
Africa	4	29	18	80
North America	177	506	903	1,437*
Latin America	18	47	89	259
East Asia	16	90	113	326
South Asia	8	38	46	167
Europe	91	172	216	352
Oceania	3	36	186	384
USSR	41	126	194	473
Totals	358	1,044	159	448

* North America includes the United States, Canada, and Mexico. For receivers per 1,000, the U.S. figure for 1959 was 948, for 1979 it was 2,040. Comparable figures for Canada were 431 and 1,104, for Mexico 94 and 288.

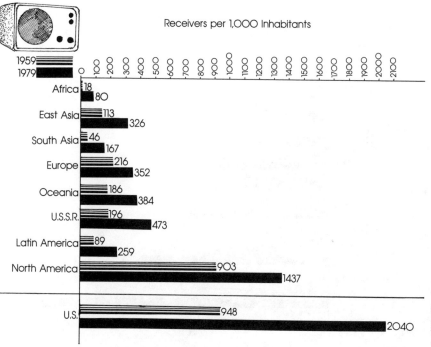

Receivers per 1,000 Inhabitants

Judith East

Amendment. Now, however, these discussions were cast in the context of nation-states. The free flow of information was, as the U.S. State Department asserted, "an integral part of our foreign policy."

The new nation-states of Asia and Africa, convinced that free flow of information had been denied them by their colonial masters, were to find

Table 9.3   Television Receivers

	Total receivers (in millions)		Receivers per 1,000 inhabitants	
	1959	1979	1959	1979
Africa	.04	6.4	0.2	14
North America	56.2	157	287	403*
Latin America	18	26	89	92
East Asia	18	37	113	133
South Asia	7.5	142	9	84
Europe	91	127	216	252
Oceania	3	7	186	225
USSR	40.8	80	194	303
Totals	234.5	582.4	39	213

* North America includes the United States, Canada, and Mexico. For receivers per 1,000, the U.S. figure for 1959 was 294, for 1979 it was 635. Comparable figures for Canada were 205 and 466, for Mexico 14 and 108.

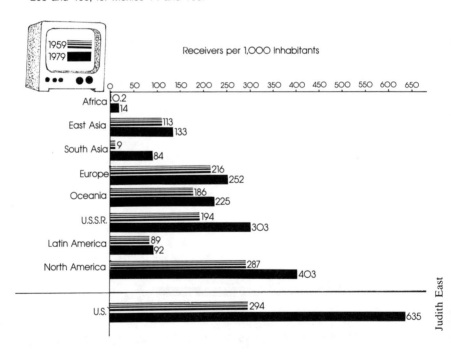

in the arguments for free flow of information by the United States and their former colonial overlords, Britain and France, a vehicle to use against those same countries. It is doubtful that the new nation-states needed the coaching, but it was provided for them nonetheless. As early as 1944, before the Second World War had ended, the directors of the American Society of Newspaper Editors issued a statement endorsing government policies that would remove all barriers, political, legal, or economic, to the free flow of information. In 1945, while the war was still going on, an ASNE delegation, joining with representatives of the two major U.S. news agencies, the Associated Press and United Press, traveled to twenty-two countries in U.S. military planes to carry tidings of the free-flow doctrine. A conference of Western Hemisphere leaders in the spring of 1945 endorsed the free-flow doctrine, and when UNESCO was created, its constitution, largely composed by U.S. representatives, called for the promotion of "the unrestricted pursuit of objective truth, and...the free exchange of ideas and knowledge." As new nation-states were created in the 1950s and early 1960s, they too enthusiastically endorsed the free-flow doctrine, but by it they meant something quite different from what was meant by the United States and her allies.

The difference from the outset was essentially economic. There can be little doubt of the honesty and good intentions of most of those who have engaged in the dispute about free flow over the years. But they have often perceived the world in such different ways, so locked into their own ideological stance, that they have been quite intractable, incapable, it has seemed, of comprehending the other person's point of view. While all parties believed in the intrinsic value of free exchange of information, free flow to the United States and her capitalist allies meant continued domination of the channels of communications, while to the advancing world it meant an end to the domination over information by the industrialized nations. Free flow is, like democracy and the people's right to know, a term so emotionally charged that it has lost its value in international dialogue. Once again, we can see how differences in labeling frustrate efforts at international accord and damage the opportunities for harmonious resolution of international issues. Indeed, one of the motives underlying the writing of this book is a desire to narrow the semantic differences and provide a framework for fruitful discussion.

At the first session of the General Conference of UNESCO in 1946, the U.S. delegation proposed that UNESCO join with other international bodies to examine and to report on obstacles to "the free flow of information and ideas." This proposal was clearly advanced in the expectation of isolating the Soviet Union, which made no pretense of the fact that it exercised control over the dissemination of information inside its borders. Two years later, at the United Nations Conference on Freedom of Information, the head of the U.S. delegation made it plain that Americans expected the new nation-states to join in condemning the Soviet Union and others "whose ideology drives them toward the destruction of freedom." When American ideas prevailed at that meeting, U.S. officials proclaimed the result a victory for the ideal of free expression, although some West Europeans saw the issue more in economic than in moral terms. They pointed to the fact that free flow had distinct commercial advantages for

U.S. information media in their efforts to market their wares in the advancing world and in Western Europe as well. Blinded by the folklore of the press, U.S. journalists failed to note the inextricable linkage of free expression and free exploitation of markets.

By the middle of the 1960s, the main arena for discussion about the press and the information media had become concentrated inside UNESCO, but no longer could the United States (with or without its European allies) control the direction of the discussions. So drastically had the mathematics changed with the appearance of an increasing number of new nation-states in Asia and Africa that all the international agencies, including the UN General Assembly, had come under the control of the advancing world. As before, military and economic power rested with the United States and its allies, but those countries were no longer able to direct the course of international bodies. It became necessary for the United States to exercise its veto power in the UN Security Council and to turn to diplomatic persuasion in an effort to impose its will on the advancing world in UNESCO and elsewhere.

Throughout most of the 1960s, discussions of the free flow of information at UNESCO tended to be unfocused, to a large extent because of the behavior of the Soviet Union and her allies. To the Kremlin, the opposition raised in the advancing world to the activities of the capitalist news media offered an opportunity for political advantage. In the early years of the United Nations, the psychological position of the Soviet Union had been damaged by the widespread support proclaimed in the advancing world for the free-press policies espoused by the United States. Now there was a chance for the Soviet Union to recapture some of that lost ground by joining with the advancing world to condemn the U.S. position on free flow as being hypocritical, as being a mechanism to practice cultural imperialism and to win lucrative markets for the products of U.S. corporations.

It was at the 16th General Conference of UNESCO in 1970 that the advancing-world demand for "a more balanced flow of information" was first heard at a UNESCO conference. Meetings of experts occupied much of the next two years, and at the general conference in 1972, UNESCO delegates heard much about the behavior of the news media in the richer half of the world as seeking to dominate world public opinion and as "a source of moral and cultural pollution." The issue of free flow had now become the most dramatic question on the floor at the biennial conferences of UNESCO. In the United States, the issue was seen as but another chapter in the ideological struggle between the United States and the Soviet Union, for the Russians were viewed as instigating the complaints by the advancing world.

Meetings and conferences followed in swift succession. Heads of state of the nonaligned countries gathered in Algiers in 1973 called for action among nations of the advancing world to free themselves of dependence on the industrialized world, both for manufactured goods and for news and information. Both were legacies of the colonial past they said; to replace those legacies, they demanded new structures. The charge of cultural imperialism was broadcast around the globe.

At the same time, delegates to UNESCO from the advancing world also spoke out against the use of the mass media as instruments of propaganda. At the 16th General Conference in 1970, the delegates affirmed "the inadmissibility of using information media for propaganda on behalf of war, racialism, and hatred among nations." Some speakers urged UNESCO to set up a code of conduct whereby the media would be encouraged to promote accord among nations rather than discord. No such resolution was passed, but UNESCO did create a panel of consultants that, a year later, proposed a massive research program on national, multinational, and international levels. It was at the 18th General Conference in 1974, following the meeting in Algiers of the nonaligned countries, that the dispute over "obstacles to the free flow of information" turned bitter.

Delegates, mainly from Marxist and advancing-world countries, argued that the only way in which "unbiased and objective reporting" could be guaranteed was under clearly defined codes created by national governments. Delegates from the capitalist countries countered by asserting that free flow could be achieved only if governments imposed no restraints. Some delegates argued that the main obstacles were not governments at all, but lack of basic materials such as paper. Others saw the imbalance resulting from the fact that the industrialized lands, primarily the United States, could send many correspondents abroad, whereas the advancing world could not afford to do so.

There then began a movement to attempt to create a new international news agency, or "pool," backed by UNESCO to challenge the power of the capitalist news agencies. Nonaligned nations gave unanimous approval to the plan at a conference of heads of state in Colombo, Sri Lanka, in August 1976. It was at that meeting in Colombo that the term "new world information order" achieved wide circulation. The term had been given expression for the first time earlier that year at a Symposium of Non-Aligned Countries on Communications held in Tunis. The chief Tunisian delegate, Mustapha Masmoudi, appears to have been the prime mover for this order; he continued to promote it in speeches and at regional and international conferences.

At Colombo, the idea of an international information order was linked intimately with a proposal by advancing-world leaders at the United Nations for a new world *economic* order. The connection between the two proposals is decisive. To right the imbalance in the flow of information, it was considered necessary that there also be a restructuring of the economies of the world.

In any case, the idea of an international news pool was approved by delegates to the 19th General Conference of UNESCO at Nairobi, Kenya, in November 1976. The United States and its allies went along reluctantly with the proposal, which was advanced by Masmoudi on behalf of the nonaligned countries. Neither the United States nor its allies saw merit in a "more balanced and diversified exchange of news," especially after Masmoudi had argued that international news agencies (meaning primarily the two U.S. giants, The Associated Press and United Press International) were presenting a distorted picture of the advancing world, concentrating on "negative aspects" of the poorer countries.

Support in the capitalist world for the Tunisian resolution resulted from two factors: a desire to avoid the anger and bitterness that had characterized the Paris conference in 1974; and an effort to prevent the endorsement of a stronger assault on the capitalist position on free flow that had been prepared by the Soviet Union, gleefully seeking to deepen the rift between the capitalist and advancing countries. The Russian draft resolution would not merely have condemned the news agencies for presenting distorted pictures of the new nation-states but would also have held their governments responsible. "States are responsible," the draft resolution declared, "for the activities in the international sphere of all mass media under their jurisdiction." Delegates from the United States and Western Europe sought to buy time by inducing the conference not to vote on the Soviet resolution but instead to create a commission to study the draft and report back with recommendations. A Soviet delegate denounced the United States for "blocking the will of the majority" but nevertheless did not insist on a formal vote on the Soviet proposal at the 1976 conference. The issue had at last attracted worldwide attention. The governments of the United States and Western Europe, as well as editors and reporters from the capitalist countries, began to pay close attention.

Perhaps the most significant action taken at Nairobi was the approval of a resolution calling on the director general of UNESCO, Amadou-Mahtar M'Bow of Senegal, to review all the problems of communications in contemporary society as seen against the backdrop of technological progress and the developments in international relations. M'Bow appointed a sixteen-member commission, which he pronounced to be a "brains trust" but which among the UNESCO delegates was often referred to as "the sixteen wise men" — even though one of its members was a woman. That commission, chaired by Seán MacBride, an Irish statesman and journalist who had won both the Nobel Peace Prize and the Lenin Peace Prize, included delegates from the United States and the Soviet Union as well as Tunisia's Masmoudi and other experts from market, Marxist, and advancing-world nations. The report of the MacBride Commission, which was presented to the 1980 General Conference in Belgrade, is the most important single document on the press in recent years.

By the time the 1978 General Conference convened in Paris, the press issue had become, for the first time, an important international issue, at least as far as the news media were concerned. Journalists had found in the UNESCO discussions a topic worth reporting. Characteristically, the issue was presented in conflictual terms, with the Soviet proposal portrayed in the capitalist media as a threat to democratic freedom and in the Marxist press as a challenge to capitalist exploitation. The U.S. government and the news media of the United States and its European partners approached the meeting with trepidation. For instance, Lord McGregor, a British sociology professor who had served for three years as chairman of a royal commission on the press, told a convention of Japanese editors that the Soviet draft before UNESCO was "a monstrous declaration" and argued that UNESCO was following the wrong course in moving towards international declarations on the news media. The press deficiencies in the advancing world, he said, could best be remedied in practical ways, by setting up radio stations and newspaper plants and by providing on-the-spot training. That approach — technical assistance and outright grants — was at the heart of the response by the capitalist countries to the challenges raised at UNESCO. Much of what appeared in the U.S. press was harshly critical of UNESCO and its program; even the moderate *Christian Science Monitor*, while acknowledging "manifest shortcomings...in international newsgathering," proclaimed as its solution technical assistance, training, and "practical efforts to raise the status of journalists as independent professionals."

Many U.S. news organizations lodged formal protests with the UNESCO secretariat, complaining about the Soviet proposal. The executive director of the American Newspaper Publishers Association issued a public appeal to the delegates to defeat the Soviet proposal on the ground that it threatened to undermine the rest of the work of UNESCO. *The Seattle Times* headlined a long story on the discussions at Paris: "UNESCO Declaration Threatens World Press Freedom." From its position, the Soviet Union, whose draft resolution was before the delegates, argued that only the power of national governments could enforce "a democratic role for the press."

Faced with intransigent positions on all sides of the issue, Director General M'Bow achieved a remarkable compromise, in which the Soviet draft was never brought to a vote and a final declaration on the press was approved by acclamation of all the delegates present. The Soviet draft was replaced by an eleven-point resolution that *The Manchester Guardian* could proclaim as a "world charter for a free press." Some delegates from the advancing world celebrated the approval by delegates of the 144 countries present as formal adoption of "a new international information order." The declaration did not, in fact, do anything of the sort. Like similar credos ratified by international bodies, it contained language sufficiently vague that it was capable of being interpreted as each nation saw fit. Roger Cans, writing in *Le Monde* on November 24, two days after the delegates had voted, observed that M'Bow had succeeded in presenting a multicolored harlequin's cloak in which each country could find something it approved in one paragraph while carefully ignoring what was in the following paragraph. Acclamation provided a mechanism whereby all delegates could vote without having to be counted. Only the delegates of Switzerland and China publicly distanced themselves from the resolution, the Swiss on the plausible ground that it was "an attempt to reconcile the irreconcilable that pleases no one," while the Chinese complained that in rejecting war, the declaration failed to distinguish between just wars, which the Chinese supported, and unjust wars, which they opposed.

On the subject of free flow, the resolution was straightforward. It demanded "a free flow and a wider and better-balanced dissemination of information." But it did not define free flow, and thus in reality the issue remained unresolved. The declaration called without equivocation for a better balance in the flow of information; what was needed was "a new equilibrium and greater reciprocity in the flow of information." Among other things, the resolution also: (1) called on the news media to contribute to the preservation of peace and to further human rights, as well as to aid in eliminating prejudice and misunderstandings between individuals and nations; (2) insisted on free access to information for both journalists and the general public to provide an opportunity for all points of view to be heard; (3) insisted that the news media be "responsive to concerns of peoples and individuals," thus promoting participation of the public "in the elaboration of information"; and (4) urged nation-states, "with due respect for constitutional provisions," to guarantee freedom of information.

The members of the U.S. delegation were delighted with the outcome. They described the declaration as "a triumph for the spirit of international cooperation, goodwill, and common sense." Such a statement was actually descriptive of the U.S. pleasure that the Soviet draft, which in one form or another had been before UNESCO for eight years, had not been approved. As Jim Browning wrote in *The Christian Science Monitor*, the United States and its allies "triumphed in their efforts to protect freedom of the press from what they viewed as a Soviet-inspired attack at UNESCO." The price of that triumph, he added, was agreement by the United States to provide funds and assistance estimated at several hundred millions of dollars for improving communications in the advancing world. In assessing the U.S. accomplishment, he expressed conventional wisdom in the capitalist countries — that they had managed to undo "the de facto alliance" between the Soviet Union and nation-states in the advancing world. Such an assessment implied a political naiveté in the advancing world that was at once inaccurate and condescending. Nevertheless, as

Browning pointed out, diplomats for the United States and its allies privately scoffed at the governments of the advancing world as being themselves largely authoritarian and ineffective, and not truly interested in a free flow of information. This assessment was not lost on the representatives of the new nation-states.

THE NEWS AGENCIES AND "CULTURAL IMPERIALISM"

Central to the discussion of imbalance in the flow of information are perceptions about the news agencies, which unquestionably distribute the greatest share of news on what is taking place in the advancing world. The news agencies in turn cannot be examined in their international manifestation without placing the issue in an economic context. Indeed, the pressure for an international information order came only after the advancing nation-states had proposed a new international economic order, under which there would be a major redistribution of wealth.

Statistical evidence gathered by the United Nations and its allied agencies had confirmed the second- — or even lower- — class status of the new nations. By 1964, the new nation-states had decided to organize themselves into a single pressure group aimed at reshaping the face of international trade and production. As their instrument of pressure they created the Group of 77 at the 1964 meeting of UNCTAD, the United Nations Conference on Trade and Development. A decade later, this pressure group, now swollen to 120 members but still retaining the name of the Group of 77 (or simply G-77), was demanding a new international economic order that would work to correct the imbalances in economic power that were the heritage of colonialism. Noting that the Less-Developed Countries, the LDCs, accounted for only 7 percent of the world's industrial production, they established a target of 25 percent by the end of the twentieth century. The demand for a new international economic order was made at a special session of the United Nations in the spring of 1974, and in the regular fall session, the UN membership formally adopted the Charter of the Economic Rights and Duties of States. The charter did not include all the demands embodied in the proposed new international economic order, but in many instances it came very close. Above all, the LDCs wanted a system of trade preferences that would give exports from the advancing world a competitive advantage over the products of the industrialized nations. In addition, they insisted that the industrialized nations provide through loans, grants, and the transfer of technology the kinds of resources the LDCs needed in order to compete effectively in the international market. The Group of 77 had less success in winning support for basic commodity agreements and for global mechanisms to regulate the actions within their own borders of transnational corporations. Especially, they wanted to insure that the transfer of resources from the industrialized nations to the new nation-states would be accomplished through international, multilateral agreements, rather than by direct assistance from one country to another. The United States, in particular, resisted the institution of a multilateral assistance program. Disagreement on this issue has been a major sticking point not only in the debates over new economic arrangements but over the proposed new international information order as well.

It is imperative that these moves by the advancing world, for correcting the global imbalance in economic power and in control over information, be seen as part of the same struggle. They are inseparable. In the center of the discussions are the news agencies, which are viewed by many in the advancing world as of enormous significance in maintaining and increasing the power imbalance in the arenas of *both* economics and information. As it is often said in this context, "Information is power." The news agencies are seen as the primary instruments of propaganda, presenting false pictures of the new nation-states, thus discouraging investment and aid, and ultimately keeping the advancing world in a state of subservience, if not slavery. This is a powerful indictment and requires close examination.

The charge of "media imperialism" that served as the banner of the critics of the news agencies has a sound historical basis. The news agencies that were established in the nineteenth century by Charles Havas in France, Paul Julius Reuter in England, and Bernhard Wolff in Germany were frankly commercial instruments, just as were the provincial correspondents who reported on the activities at the forum in ancient Rome. Journalists for Havas, Reuter, and Wolff fanned out through the colonial world to fill the demand for information about what was going on in regions that offered the promise of healthy financial rewards to enterprising businessmen. The interest of the European governments was substantial, and in order to prevent cutthroat competition, Britain, France, and Germany carved up the world into spheres of influence under the 1869 Agency Alliance Treaty, with Reuters being assigned the nations in the British empire as well those in the Far East; Havas the Spanish, French, Italian, and Portuguese empires; and Wolff the holdings of Austria, Germany, Scandinavia, and Russia. It was as a result of this agreement that Havas ultimately assumed a dominant role throughout Latin America.

Running about as emissaries of "the civilized world," the intrepid correspondents of these agencies and their fellows who worked for the great imperial newspapers, chief among them the *Times* of London, found a limitless source of magnificent drama to report. There were wars and pitched battles, exotic religions and strange customs, jungles and mountains, savages and heathens, disease and revolution. The mass audiences that emerged in the nineteenth century ate up these reports with relish and fed the desire for more and more spectacular and sensational news reports. The colonial British and French received most of their news from the home country through the telegraphic reports of Reuters and Havas, and so did the indigenous population. No force of socialization in the colonies was more powerful than the news agencies. Their impact on the perceptions of native citizens about the outside world remains a major influence today and is indeed one of the factors in the complaints lodged against media imperialism.

It is a source of consummate irony that the most widely publicized challenge to media imperialism directed against the European news agencies was lodged by none other than what has now become the very symbol of media imperialism, The Associated Press. The United States was a minor power in 1869 when the Agency Alliance Treaty was signed, and in 1893 the AP agreed to join the European cartel, thus receiving the right to distribute the dispatches of Reuters, Havas, and Wolff in the United States. It was not, however, permitted to operate its own news service outside the confines of the United States. By 1912, it was seeking to spread into what North Americans already considered to be in the U.S. sphere of influence, the countries of Latin America. Havas, which held a kind of monopoly in Latin America, refused, even though a number of newspapers in South America actively campaigned for the AP news report. Recalling the situation years later, the longtime general manager of the AP, Kent Cooper, wrote:

> The fact that Havas, a small, government-subsidized French news agency, could prevent the great Associated Press from sending news to South America was bad enough, but that The Associated Press could not present the news of my country to all the rest of the world shocked me. I resented the fact that The Associated Press submitted to such degrading news repression.

By the time the debates were taking place within UNESCO, it was the AP that was presenting its version of the news throughout the advancing world and the fledgling news agencies of those countries that were unable to afford the money needed to present their news about their countries to the rest of the world. The European cartel was broken in 1934, the result of the inexhaustible efforts of Cooper, who acted with the open assistance of the U.S. government. At that time, Cooper's campaign was directed primarily against Reuters:

> So Reuters decided what news was to be sent from America. It told the world about the Indians on the war path in the West, lynchings in the South and bizarre crimes in the North. The charge for decades was that nothing creditable to America ever was sent.

The words Cooper spoke in criticism of Reuters sounded astonishingly similar to the words spoken in the advancing world about the AP half a century later. To Cooper, Reuters was the instrument whose news reports "undertook to weld Britain's dependencies exclusively to the mother country." And in even more flamboyant vein, he added: "Reuters has done more for England in that respect than either England's great navy, which ruled the seas, or its shipping, which then led in carrying on the commerce of the world." Those who spoke of media imperialism in the 1970s relied on similar language to condemn the news reports of the AP. It is necessary, of course, to point out that the AP was never an open instrument of U.S. imperialism. In fact, the agency proclaimed itself from its early years as an objective news-gathering and reporting service that, as it was widely said, "called them as it saw them." Such was, and remains, the folklore that envelops The Associated Press. Yet its journalists were as socialized into the U.S. belief system as thoroughly as were the journalists for Reuters and Havas in the nineteenth century. And, as Anthony Smith has observed, journalists tend to follow the flag.

The rapid growth of the U.S. news agencies that followed Cooper's successful challenge propelled them into the forefront of the business of news. By the time the colonial world was breaking up in the 1950s, The Associated Press and United Press International (a merger of Scripps Howard's UP and Hearst's INS) had joined Reuters and Agence France Presse, the successor to Havas, as the dominant forces in international news. The stereotypes that evoked the pictures of the outside world that filled the brains of men and women everywhere were the stereotypes transmitted around the globe by the Big Four among the capitalist news agencies. It was the news dispatches filed by the agency correspondents that were the most visible bits of information about the outside world reaching the literate leaders of the advancing world. And they did not like what they read. To them, the pictures were not only inaccurate but condescending as well; they had been drawn by an arrogant band of men afflicted with the narrow horizons of the ethnocentric and who, wittingly or unwittingly, carried out the bidding of their wealthy, greedy masters. It cannot be surprising that the number-one target of the press reformers in the advancing world were the Big Four capitalist news agencies. To these four there sometimes was added TASS, but its circulation in the advancing world was limited, and it was far less visible. The history of the news agencies was also well known to the advancing-world leaders. Their role as agent of the imperialists of the nineteenth century was never far from the consciousness of the advancing-world press theorists.

In the beginning of the UNESCO discussions, the reaction of the capitalist community of journalists was simply hostile. Their perception of UNESCO-sponsored meetings was that they were being orchestrated from the Kremlin and represented but one more attempt on the part of the

Soviet Union to win friends among the new nation-states and to weaken the power of the capitalist nations in the advancing world. Organizations of editors and publishers condemned not only attacks on a free press but UNESCO itself. IAPA, the Inter American Press Association, published a statement in 1976 asserting that press freedom was being challenged in Latin America not merely by restrictive measures by some governments but also by threats from "a world organization where authoritarian governments consistently outvote Western democracies."

(The word Western in that statement is interesting. It appears to refer to certain capitalist countries, but certainly not only to Western nations. Japan is included; so is Australia, and sometimes even South Africa. Pro-Western countries of Latin America are included, but not others that oppose the United States and her allies. The semantic jungle is impenetrable. We have chosen to identify these countries as capitalist, or industrialized, or as those with market economies. In a certain poetic sense, they might be identified as the "information societies.")

Other organizations joined IAPA in its criticism, among them the International Press Institute (IPI) and Freedom House, a self-selected group of journalism authorities who monitor threats to "press freedom." Newspapers, as we have seen, also condemned UNESCO and often defended the news agencies as disinterested, objective reporters of the events taking place in the advancing world.

By the 20th General Conference in 1978, however, a shift had taken place. The inadequacies of the Big Four news agencies were being more generally observed and accepted. It appeared that the capitalist world was beginning to pursue a time-honored practice among the news media. Just as traditional newspapers had co-opted the underground press in the United States in the 1960s, the news industry was now acknowledging the validity of the central theme of the attacks on the news agencies. Yes, it was being said, the news agencies had been deficient in their reporting of the events in the new nation-states. There had been too many stories of wars and revolutions, pestilence and famine, earthquakes and murders. It was imperative, it was being said, that the journalists who toiled for the news agencies devote more time and space to slowly evolving trends and to the realities behind the appearances, even to "development news." Moreover, journalists, it was said, ought to be writing and broadcasting more than they had been doing about the daily lives of the unknown millions who resided in the advancing world. Yes, there were weaknesses, it was said, but there were also strengths. For the news agency journalists were risking their lives to learn the truth and to report that truth to the readers and viewers who were waiting eagerly for their reports. These journalists were professionals, and what better form of assistance could these journalists provide than to help train the young reporters of the advancing world in the techniques of sound journalism? Technology and training — these were the answers to the challenges raised at UNESCO.

As for the charge of media imperialism led by the troops of the news agencies, that was rejected. And to a substantial degree, as Oliver Boyd-Barrett chronicled, the emphasis on media imperialism that dominated the discussions in the 1970s seemed to retreat in the 1980s. But in no way has the importance of the news agencies as sources of the pictures in our heads been downgraded. It is well, now that some of the heat has gone out of the controversy over news agencies, to examine the question carefully.

The parties to the dispute over the news agencies have never agreed on the exact nature of their differences. On the one hand, the dispute is an economic one, related to the part that the news agencies play in opening up markets for manufactured goods. On this point, there is little agreement. To their capitalist defenders, news agencies are instruments of information, not economic expansion. They seek to ferret out the facts and to present those facts to readers and viewers in such a manner as to interest and educate them, following the traditional folklore of the press. To their opponents, the information function of the news agencies is a smoke screen to mask their real function, which is to popularize in the advancing world the life-style in the capitalist world and thus to awaken the desire to buy and to consume the products of that capitalist world; in short, they are the vanguard of the advertisers. For the most part, the agency defenders have paid little attention to this side of the dispute.

On another level, the dispute is ideological. The critics of the agencies accuse them of biased reporting. The pictures they portray are false pictures, the result of rigidity in the belief systems of the journalists themselves, who are seen as so stuffed full of adoration for everything new and modern that they are unable to recognize the worth of the traditional, the products of an alien social order. Part of this capitalist ideology, it is argued by many who condemn the news agencies, is openly racist. What is white is good and modern; what is black (or brown or yellow) is poor and outdated. It is often seen also as rooted in Christianity, so much so that the worth of other religious convictions, especially those of Islam, is not acknowledged. Apologists for the news agencies deny these allegations, arguing on the other hand that the lodestar of the agency journalists is one of truth and objectivity. Little progress has been made in resolving these ideological differences, even though they are not discussed with such volatility as in the past.

On yet another level, the dispute is professional, that is to say, over the definition of news. To critics in the advancing world, news-agency obsession with the dramatic and the conflictual gives the news reported a character so distorted that it bears little relationship to reality. The sensationalism that marked the reports of Reuters and Havas in the nineteenth century remains the hallmark of journalism of the late twentieth century about events in Africa and Asia, and even Latin America. The slow-unfolding patterns of life in the advancing world are largely ignored in the emphasis on action and conflict and on spot news. The important developments, it is said, are in trends, not in spot news. The processes of development are ignored. To this charge, the journalists of the industrialized world tend to plead guilty. But they argue that in quest of the dramatic and conflictual, they are not acting out of prejudice against the advancing world. Rather, they say, they are following the market and giving the readers what they want. Moreover, the emphasis on the dramatic and conflictual marks reporting in their own countries quite as much as it does reporting from the advancing world.

It can be seen that even where the views of the attackers and the defenders of the news agencies appear to coincide, the gap between them remains substantial. And while each side to the dispute perceives itself to be quite realistic in its assessment, that realism is based on the peculiar *Weltanschauung* of the holders of the opinion. This is not to say that the journalists of the advancing world pay no attention to drama and conflict. In fact, their eye for the dramatic is quite as keen as that of any American or West European. The difference lies in the fact that the attention of advancing-world journalists is not focused on the dramatic and conflictual as intensely and eternally as are the eyes of their brethren in the industrialized countries. Nor is it to say that in the United States and Western Europe one can find no journalists interested in trends and slow development. But far fewer of those analytical journalists can be found among the news agencies than among the quality newspapers. And while no one knows the exact percentage of world news distributed by the news agencies, it is clear that most of the information we receive through the news media about the world at large comes from the news agencies, especially the Big Four. While the large newspapers, news magazines, and television and radio networks base some journalists in foreign countries, their numbers are insignificant in comparison with the number of reporters stationed abroad by the news agencies.

A recent UNESCO compilation lists 559 correspondents abroad for The Associated Press, 578 for UPI, 171 for AFP (with 1,200 stringers), and 350 for Reuters (with 800 stringers). Neither the AP nor UPI lists the number of its stringers, but they too reach into the thousands. A stringer is a part-time employee who sells articles on a space rate; many stringers are nationals of the countries about which they report, but they are trained in the style and news values of their own organization. On the whole, the content of articles written by stringers and by correspondents is indistinguishable. Moreover, the correspondent usually is in a position to revise the raw material in the stringer's files. Estimates of the numbers of words distributed are high: for the AP, 17 million words a day; for the UPI, 11 million; for AFP, 3,350,000; and for Reuters, 1,500,000. Subscribers and clients range up to a high of 12,000 newspapers for Reuters. The raw figures tell us a lot, but even they cannot measure the pervasiveness of the pictures of the world that are distributed by the agencies. For among their subscribers are every major newspaper as well as all the radio and television networks, the other news agencies (including especially those agencies that are struggling to compete in their own countries), and nearly every government on earth. In addition, the Big Four agencies supply hundreds of photographs each day; photographs are selected on the same basis as are news stories, with emphasis on the dramatic and the conflictual. Of all the news media, it is to be remembered, the news agencies have the greatest investment in the status quo.

In acknowledging the imbalance in the flow of news, Roger Tatarian, former vice-president of UPI, commented that agency reportage has tended simplistically to emphasize conflicts between the United States and the Soviet Union in global settings that have few cold-war ramifications. Moreover, Tatarian said, "there is an acknowledged tendency among Western media...to devote the greatest attention to the Third World in times of disaster, crisis, and confrontation." It was in 1978 that Tatarian made this observation, at a meeting in Cairo. But then he was no longer with UPI; during his tenure as an executive of the news agency, he was not saying the same thing. In fact, it is rare that a newsman recognizes the implications of his definitions of news while he is on the job. The discovery usually comes later. Even in that declaration, however, Tatarian made the point that the news agencies are equally concerned with disaster, crisis, and confrontation when these occur in the industrialized world. This is true, but it makes little difference to the advancing-world critics of the news agencies how distorted reports inside the industrialized world may be.

Of all the discomfort generated in the advancing world by the omnipresence of the news agencies, none is more painful than the fact that most of the news the countries of the advancing world receive about events in other advancing-world nations comes from those same Big Four news agencies. This situation is partly historical but results primarily from the fact that few news agencies in the new nation-states possess either the financial resources or the technological organization (the operative word here is infrastructure) needed to send out their own correspondents to other countries and then to receive from them news reports for publication. As a result, the usual practice is for national news agencies throughout the advancing world to sign contracts with one or more of the Big Four agencies and simply redistribute the news reports of the AP or Reuters over their own national facilities. A news item from Chad would be reported by Agence France Presse; distributed to Senegal, Upper Volta, and Cameroon; and then appear in the newspapers in those countries. National news agencies exist now in about 120 countries; only about 40 still have no national agency. But few among these national agencies report foreign news directly. The Middle East News Agency in Egypt sends direct reports from eleven other Arab countries and several European countries, but its news report is limited. News agencies in most Asian countries do assign staffers abroad. China, Japan, and India operate thriving news agencies of their own, but the activities of those journalists are limited, and the main staple of their news diet remains the output of the capitalist news agencies. In Latin America, only twelve of the twenty-five countries have any kind of news agencies, and only Chile and Mexico operate even modest foreign bureaus.

In this situation, Third World critics of imbalance in the flow of news often turn to the remarks of the AP's Kent Cooper, who complained about the news monopoly enjoyed by Reuters with these prophetic words: "Americans want to look at the world through their own eyes, not through the British eyes." As India's D. R. Mankekar, who served as the first coordinating head of the pool of nonaligned news agencies, put it: "All that nonaligned countries are asking for is that they too want to look at the world through their own eyes instead of through the eyes of the Western news media."

The pool of nonaligned news agencies marks one of two major efforts on the part of critics of the Big Four to correct the imbalance they perceive. The pool was launched in January 1975. A decade earlier, in 1964, the Inter Press Service (IPS) was established. Although neither of these agencies commands much attention (or respect) in the industrialized world, they have been growing in both quality and prestige in the advancing world. In fact, movements to develop thriving regional news agencies have been gaining strength in the Caribbean, in Africa, in Asia, and in the Middle East. In all cases, the rationale for these agencies has been rooted in the desire to crack the monopolistic position of the Big Four. Each of the new agencies is portrayed as serving the cause of the new international information order.

The pool is not really a news agency, at least not in the sense that the Big Four are agencies. It has no budget, no board of directors, not even a headquarters. Transmissions are paid for by the sender of the news report. In the beginning, all the pool's transmissions were delivered over the facilities of Tanjug, the Yugoslav news agency, but the system was modified to permit transmission by other national agencies, chief among them those of Tunisia, Morocco, Iran, India, and Cuba. The original membership of twenty-six has increased to fifty; the members are satisfied the pool is here to stay and that it will increase in both size and quality. Meeting in Jakarta in 1978, the members agreed that they had already proved that the pool was not "a caprice of the moment," but that it served the long-term needs of the nonaligned movement for an alternative source of news about the happenings in the advancing world.

Critics have attacked the news-agency pool as being little more than a propaganda instrument for the governments of the advancing world, which may send out press releases over the pool network. Others, especially in the industrialized world, have argued that the quality of the writing is so turgid that few newspapers or broadcasters are using the material dispatched.

Certainly, the kind of news disseminated differs markedly from the kind of news sent out over the wires of the Big Four. There is little interest in spot news developments; much attention is paid to news of economic development, social change, trade, and commerce. Moreover, the articles tend to be longer than the concise, punchy reports of the Big Four. Newspapers in the United States and the other industrialized countries consider the output of the pool "non-news." The issue is one of definition. The pool countries maintain that much of what is reported by the Big Four is not news but sensationalism or come-ons for the economic benefit of the capitalist nations. While the pool has expanded, there is little evidence it is replacing the Big Four as a source of news for newspapers and broadcasters of the advancing world. In travels in different parts of the advancing world and in conversations with practicing journalists from those countries, we have found little enthusiasm for the kind of product being turned out by the pool countries, but this set of attitudes may merely reflect the power of the press folklore of the industrialized world.

In any case, the press of the capitalist countries seems to react with uncontained glee to evidence, purported or otherwise, to the effect that the news practices of the pool countries and of the advancing world in general are dull and uninteresting. One incident is enough to illustrate the point. In the fall of 1981, Ben Mkapa, a former editor of *The Daily News* in Dar-es-Salaam and at that time Tanzania's minister of information, spoke at the opening ceremonies for the new national school of journalism. In that address, he urged the students to make their reportage first of all factual and secondly interesting. Poor newspapers, he said, were inaccurate and dull. In due course, a report of Mkapa's address made its way to the newsrooms of West Germany, for on July 15, 1982, prominent display was given to it in *The Frankfurter Allgemeine Zeitung* (FAZ). By then, however, Mkapa was quoted as saying, "With only a few exceptions, the newspapers of Africa are deadly dull, so boring they drive the audience to tune in the BBC." The FAZ writer, Ernst-Otto Maetzke, used Mkapa's speech as a springboard to attack not only the quality of the African and socialist press but the new world information order as well. Acknowledging that there was something to be said for improvement in the press, Maetzke argued, however, that the only ones who would benefit from new information rules were authoritarian regimes of the socialist and advancing-world countries. Those rules would result, he wrote, in "a threatening boredom" that would enable repressive governments to maintain their monopoly over information. "The people in the developing countries," he said, "would scarcely notice."

In the advancing world, the only national news agency that mounts a serious challenge to the supremacy of the Big Four is TASS, the Soviet news agency. On the whole, however, the Russians have been unsuccessful in their challenge. Advancing-world editors read through the TASS dispatches, of course, often as a kind of check on the reports of the AP or AFP, but rarely are those reports printed without revision. Often they are ignored altogether. As Ulli Mwambutukulu, managing editor of *The Daily News* in Dar-es-Salaam, observed: "When a TASS report crosses my desk and I read something about American imperialism, I throw it on the floor." The U.S. news agencies, he said, are more factual: "The propaganda is there, all right, but you have to discover it." Mwambutukulu, echoing the sentiments of many African editors, said he wished fervently that the United States and the Soviet Union would quit attacking each other in their news agencies. "If they fight, we'll be the ones to be hurt," he observed.

The Inter Press Service (IPS), in operation a decade longer than the pool, has achieved considerable success, especially in Latin America, its chief base of operations for most of its existence. In the late 1970s, it began to extend itself actively into Asia and Africa, and forged links with thirty advancing-world national agencies. By the 1980s, IPS had become the sixth largest world agency, exceeded in scope only by the Big Four transnationals and TASS. It was established as a cooperative of Latin American journalists eager for social reform but soon abandoned its political activism in favor of what its director general, Italy's Roberto Savio, calls "alternative journalism." Its approach is horizontal rather than vertical; in other words, it rejects the concept of the transnationals and TASS that news properly flows from top to bottom, that is, from journalist to reader. Instead, Savio proposes "a horizontal process — the exchange of information between individuals, between social groups, and between nations."

In this effort, IPS has taken significant strides. Researcher Al Hester, who has made a thorough study of the content of IPS reports, concludes that IPS "is in actuality a truly alternative type of press agency, basically serving Third World countries and with content mainly about or affecting the Third World." More than three-fifths of the content of the IPS stories studied were grouped under economics and business (27 percent), foreign relations (20 percent), and domestic government politics (14 percent). Hester found almost no coverage of disasters, sports, or celebrities.

There is something of the missionary in Savio, who describes himself as a utopian who dreams of a democratic world free of hunger and scarcity; some of his experiences in striving for an alternative agency structure have been disturbing to him. For one thing, he has found that the conventional definitions of news have been so deeply ingrained in journalists all over the world that it is difficult to induce them, even those who write for IPS, to, switch from the emphasis on what he calls "spot news, that is, information which if it is to succeed in the market must have impact." That means it must be exceptional and it must attract attention. "As we say in the jargon," Savio told an international meeting in The Netherlands in the summer of 1982, "it must be 'sexy.'" For there to be a genuine new information order, in Savio's view, correction of imbalance in the flow of news is not enough. Nor will improvements in the infrastructure bring a new order. For such an order to come about, most importantly there must be change in the *content* of newspapers and broadcasting outlets. And for the content to change, the gatekeepers — that is, the editors who decide what to publish and what to slap on the dead hook — must be prepared to change their definition of news. The conventional criteria, Savio said, have little to do with the special problems of the advancing world nor with "the basic questions which concern mankind today, such as hunger, population, resources, environment, social structures, or culture."

In this Savio is quite correct.

THE REPORT OF THE MACBRIDE COMMISSION

Without doubt, the most important document that has emerged in the years of debating about the press at UNESCO and at other international forums has been the report of the MacBride Commission, which made public its findings and recommendations during the 21st General Conference of UNESCO at Belgrade in October 1980. Its report appeared in book form under the title *Many Voices, One World: Towards a New More Just and More Efficient World Information and Communication Order*. Of the sixteen members of the commission, eight, including Tunisia's Masmoudi, represented the advancing world. The other nations outside the industrial world were Chile, Colombia, Egypt, India, Indonesia, Nigeria, and Zaire. Marxist representatives included Sergei Losev of the Soviet Union, director general of TASS, and Bogdan Osolnik of Yugoslavia. MacBride was one of six representatives from capitalist countries; included in their number was Elie Abel, a former staffer for *The New York Times* and a well-known journalism scholar. Most members had journalism connections. Hubert Beuve-Méry of France was a founder of *Le Monde* and president of a French journalism society. Betty Zimmerman of Canada was director of Radio Canada International. Michio Nagai of Japan was an editorial writer for *Asahi Shimbun* and former Japanese minister of education. Johannes Pieter Pronk was a politician and economist in The Netherlands.

Perhaps most remarkable and encouraging of all was the fact that this disparate group of individuals, coming from a multitude of backgrounds, social and economic systems, and ideological roots, was able to agree on a single document aimed at "a new more just and more efficient world information and communication order." To be sure, there was not total agreement. The 312 pages of the MacBride Commission report contained many footnotes in which particular members took issue with statements in the text. For the most part, however, these differences were predictable and dealt with matters of degree. However, some differences were fundamental. Losev objected, for instance, to a commission recommendation that "censorship or arbitrary control of information should be abolished." As far as the TASS executive was concerned, "The whole problem of censorship or arbitrary control of information is within the national legislation of each country and is to be solved within the national, legal framework taking in due course the national interests of each country." In other words, for the Soviet Union, international declarations to the effect that the flow of information should be free and balanced were all to the good, so long as they did not impinge on the right of the USSR to protect its own national interests. At another point, Losev objected to a call for "free access to news sources [which] necessarily involves access to unofficial, as well as official sources of information, that is, access to the entire spectrum of opinion within any country." To provide access to private Soviet citizens for foreign correspondents was anathema to Losev. At still another point, Losev took objection to a commission declaration of "the right to communicate." Such a right, Losev wrote, "is not an internationally accepted right on either national or international level." To the Soviet official, the right to communicate, if it existed at all, was secondary to the national interests of member states. The other delegates may have had similar ideas, but if so they did not voice them.

Abel's chief objections seemed to arise over the issues of commercialism and advertising. At one point, he spoke up in opposition to a commission recommendation that acknowledged the need of the media for revenues but called for studying ways to "reduce the negative effects that the influence of the market and commercial considerations have in the organization and content of national and international communication flows." Abel argued that the commission had provided no evidence to show that market and commercial considerations necessarily exerted a negative effect on the flow of communication. He added:

> On the contrary, the Commission has praised elsewhere in this report courageous investigative journalism of the sort that can be sustained only by independent media whose survival depends upon their acceptance in the marketplace, rather than the favors of political leaders. The Commission also is aware that market mechanisms play an increasingly important role today even in so-called planned economies.

Abel also spoke out in criticism of a call for legal measures that would limit media concentration and monopolies, reduce the impact of advertising on editorial policy, and circumscribe the actions of transnationals. In an apparent reference to press policies of the Soviet Union and allied countries, Abel asserted that discussions of media concentration and monopolies were not relevant in countries where no press competition was even permitted: "It is a travesty to speak of measures against concentration and monopolization in countries where the media are themselves established as state monopolies." Abel agreed that it was proper to engage in careful study of the influence of advertisers on editorial policy where such influence could be shown to exist, "but a sweeping demand that such influence be reduced, without pausing to examine or attempting to measure that influence in particular circumstances, is a symptom of ideological prejudice." At another point, Abel objected to a commission declaration that there existed a "near monopoly of the industrialized countries" over scientific and technical information, industrial and commercial data, satellite transmissions, and so on, and that much of this information was "guarded by governments, large research centers or national and transnational corporations which, for various reasons, may restrict its release and dissemination." Abel said no evidence had been placed before the commission "in support of this doubtful proposition." The U.S. objections to commission findings and recommendations tended to concentrate in support of the market economic system and in defense of unlimited free expression for journalists in opposition to the Soviet model of government control of information.

Canada's Zimmerman, the only commission member with a primarily television background, took issue with some sweeping criticisms of television. The commission, in a quite moderate assessment of the global assaults on the quality of television programming, acknowledged that it was "useless to cry out" against the excesses of entertainment offered in the marketplace but expressed the hope that information would not be permitted to degenerate into becoming "a simple commodity" for the dissemination of mass culture and consumer goods. The commission said it rejected as exaggerated global assertions by some that television was anticultural. Still, it said the system did lead to programs that appeal to the widest possible audience and that "all too often lack content of the highest quality." Zimmerman, in a reference to the content of the Canadian Broadcasting System, called the generalization too sweeping: "Much programming done in the field of public broadcasting, even in competitive situations, is specifically planned for appeal to special interest, 'minority' audiences, as part of the service provided by such broadcasting organizations."

Zimmerman also chided the commission for a proposal that the "power" of the media be used for constructive purposes. In a particularly interesting section, the commission called attention to studies that show a correlation between what appears in the mass media, especially television, and public attitudes about those topics. The press, the commission said, is a powerful socializing agent along with the church, the family, associations, and schools. Some media reports about environmental pollution have stirred productive change, the commission wrote, but others — in certain unnamed countries — have been accused of creating a climate of fear and thus leading to government repression. The commission raised this question:

> If the media thus have the power to spread fear, why should they not exercise this same power in order to free men from distrust and fear and to assert their unshakable opposition to all forms of war and violence, and to all recourse to force in international relations?

This is a question of great significance, one that is at the heart of the differences in the perception of the role of the news media in the three press ideologies. Zimmerman's response was noteworthy:

> The Report is accusing the media of exerting too much power, while at the same time advocating the exertion of power for other (valuable) purposes. In both cases, however, the situation is being viewed from the standpoint of "using" the media, which is an unacceptable concept.

The question of media power is central in all discussions of the role of the media. It is instructive to note how often ideology and folklore interfere with understanding the realities of the power of the press. To Canada's Zimmerman, using the media is an unacceptable concept. Yet history demonstrates that the press, dating back to its origin, has always been used, and that individuals and groups in power have always sought to manipulate the press into serving their particular causes. That the news media are powerful instruments cannot be doubted; what is in dispute is *how* that power is exercised, and *who* does the exercising.

To call attention to some of the specific areas in which the sixteen members of the MacBride Commission took exception to one another is not to point to fundamental disagreement inside the commission. Rather, it is to place stress on the remarkable accomplishment of Seán MacBride and his fellow commission members in producing their report. Of course, several compromises were reached, and humankind is far from putting into practice many — if any — of the commission's eighty-two recommendations. Yet there does exist now a basic document with which authorities from all parts of the world are in essential accord. And in that document, in a section to which no objections were raised, the commission members specifically linked the proposed new information order to the calls for a new world economic order.

Reporting of the issues involved in the new economic order has, the commission said, contained "many misrepresentations." Later, the reporting of the findings and recommendations of the MacBride Commission were themselves to be misrepresented in the press. News reports about the UNESCO meetings contained — as the commission had said reports of the new economic order contained — "too much rhetoric on one side, too many prejudices on the other, too many blunt assertions and simplistic interpretations." The commission reduced to a single paragraph the "fundamental arguments" for a new information order:

> The disparity between North and South is not a mere matter of time-lag. Thus, it cannot be expected that the developing countries will "catch up" through being given financial and technical assistance by the developed. In reality, the disparities are becoming greater and more serious. This points to needs which go beyond the need for assistance: the elimination of unjust and oppressive structures, the revision of the present division of labor, the building of a new international economic order. Communication reflects the disparities which characterize the entire international scene, and therefore stands in need of equally far-reaching changes.

Clearly, efforts to respond to the findings of the MacBride Commission by resorting to infusions of money and technical aid are inadequate. More is demanded. The commission's recommendations on what that "more" ought to consist of can be grouped in three clusters:

First, that it must be recognized that communications is a personal right, belonging democratically to all individuals, not only journalists and governments, not only those who exercise political and economic power.

Second, that the imbalance in the flow of news and information around the world must be remedied.

Third, that the content of the news must be revised so as to help achieve human rights for all people and to reduce violence and the threat of war.

Although Soviet commission member Losev questioned the idea of an all-encompassing "right to communicate," he did not quarrel with the critical assertion by the commission that in a new world order, communication could not be permitted to travel in only one direction. On this point, the commission cited with enthusiasm a comment by Luis Ramiro Beltrán, a Mexican researcher, that it was necessary to build "a new concept of communication — a humanized, nonelitist, democratic, and nonmercantile model." What often passed as communication, Beltrán said, was "little more than a dominating monologue." For communication to take place, a dialogue was necessary between communicator and his or her audience. Beltrán's message was similar to that of Roberto Savio and the Inter Press Service in calling for a horizontal rather than a vertical pattern of communication. The commission said it recognized that the implications of this proposal were utopian but argued that a new relationship between journalist and audience was conceivable "if greater prominence is given to the idea of citizen involvement. The aim was to create more democratic relationships by integrating the citizen into the decision-making processes of public affairs." In a nice bit of phrase making, the commission suggested a change in the distribution of roles, "in which the media give and the public takes."

The second cluster of proposals by the MacBride Commission are also concerned with the direction of information, but in this situation the concern is over the passage of news and other intelligence from one part of the world to another. This is the "free flow" issue which was introduced into the United Nations by the United States at its inception, but which has returned now to haunt the Americans. The commission stated, simply and correctly, that recognition of imbalances in the flow of information was no longer a controversial issue. The imbalance was recognized in the market and Marxist nations, as well as in the advancing world. The flow of information was seen as proceeding from North to South, that is to say, from the industrial world to the advancing world. In this situation, the commission cited statements by political and journalism authorities in all parts of the world confirming awareness of and concern about the imbalance. Among those cited was Abel himself, who said that thoughtful journalists and students of communications "acknowledge that the present patterns of information flow, running heavily in one direction, must be altered for the benefit of all nations, developed and developing alike." The commission made the point that blame for the imbalance cannot be laid only at the doorsteps of the industrialized nations. In the new nation-states, the commission found examples of repression of information on the part of elites so that the masses were not brought into the information process. In his opening remarks to the commission, MacBride stressed his belief that the entire world had to share the blame for the imbalance in the flow of information, not merely the press monopolies of the industrialized world. The problem, he said, was that information all too often seemed to flow only from top to bottom. Still, the commission concluded that the primary factor in the imbalance was an economic one. The flow-of-information issue could not be resolved without also bringing about massive changes in the political and economic structures of the world. "Seen broadly," the commission said,

> the one-way flow in communication is basically a reflection of the world's dominant political and economic structures which tend to maintain or reinforce the dependence of poorer countries on the richer.

Jean d'Arcy of France, a prominent press theorist, put it this way:

> Over 50 years' experience of the mass media — press, film, radio, television — have conditioned us, both at the national and international levels, to a single

kind of information flow, which we have come to accept as normal and indeed as the only possible kind: a vertical, one-way flow from the top downwards of non-diversified anonymous messages, produced by a few and addressed to all. This is not communication.

It was not only an imbalance in news about which the commission complained. It was also an imbalance in the flow of all kinds of information, especially through instruments of advanced technology. To the members of the commission, transnationals were exerting a positive influence in extending "facilities for cultural development," but they were also having the negative effect of promoting "alien attitudes across cultural frontiers," thus practicing cultural imperialism through their control of "communication infrastructures, news circulation, cultural products, educational software, books, films, equipment, and training." The effect, according to the commission, was "to impose uniformity of taste, style, and content."

The third cluster of recommendations dealt with the content of the pages of newspapers and the reports on radio and television. After a sober, dispassionate examination of differences in the definitions of news in different parts of the world, the commission concluded that distortion occurs primarily when "inaccuracies replace authentic facts; or when a slanted interpretation is woven into the news report, for example through the use of pejorative adjectives and stereotypes." Sifting through the definitions, the commission held that differences in what makes news are not as great as they first appear, and that most journalists tend to agree that "good news is as worthy and interesting as bad news, provided it is authentic and significant." Expanding this perspective, the commission held that the role of the communicator included not only "objective reporting of 'hard' news," but also commentaries and analysis that might "play a vital role in the worldwide struggle to promote human progress." In this context, the commission cited with favor some critical observations made in 1979 by Zbigniew Brzezinski, then foreign policy adviser to President Carter, about the "philosophy of news" in the United States, which he said fails to present information in a systematic, thoughtful manner. The emphasis is on whatever is new, on disparate facts that are not related to one another, that are not interconnected: "It's very difficult to convey this kind of perspective in the context of an approach to reality which in America focuses very much on hard individual facts and is less interested in broad historical sweep."

News, in short, the commission held, must be redefined: the proper role of the journalist is activist, not disinterested bystander. The mass media, the commission said, have the power to help strengthen peace, international security, and cooperation and to lessen international tensions. The press has a duty "to mobilize public opinion in favor of disarmament and of ending the arms race." In the last three of its eighty-two recommendations, the commission declared that new communications policies around the world should center on "the contribution of the mass media to strengthening peace and international understanding, to the promotion of human rights, and to countering racialism, apartheid, and incitement to war." Moreover, "a new world information and communication order requires and must become the instrument for peaceful cooperation among nations."

In overdramatizing disagreements between the market and Marxist nations, the commission said, the press was raising tensions around the world and not lessening them. In a passage poetic in its scope, the commission asserted:

> The dangers of war are heightened by intolerance, national chauvinism, and a failure to understand varying points of view. This should never be forgotten by those who have responsibilities in the media. Above all national and political interests, there is the supreme interest of all humanity in peace.

THE DECLARATION OF TALLOIRES

It had taken three or four years of discussions, debates, speeches, and acrimony to forge the report of the MacBride Commission. And it was a remarkable accomplishment. In many ways, its findings and recommendations were vague and capable of various interpretations, but this was the price forced on the sixteen members if they were to reach agreement. That they were willing to pay that price is testimonial to their interest in international harmony. Whatever the political differences that divided the commission members, whatever their fears of losing political or economic ground to other nations or economic forces, these differences and fears were overcome in the final document. Few publications on the subject of the press have been as carefully thought out, as profound in scope and insight. When the twenty-first General Conference of UNESCO ended in October 1980, the delegates were congratulating themselves on the Mac-Bride Commission report and on the fact that they had worked their way through a UNESCO general conference with greater accord than discord. And yet, despite all this, the report and indeed the character of the general conference itself received a bad press in the United States. This was so even though the members of the U.S. delegation were themselves quite pleased with the outcome. They had won in their efforts to prevent UNESCO from adopting any international code of ethics or resolution that would require licensing of journalists. The commission had recommended in clear and unmistakable language the belief that journalists should have free access to all news sources. Moreover, the delegates had given unanimous approval to the establishment of a new agency to be known as

IPDC, the International Program for the Development of Communication, an agency that the United States had itself proposed in order to emphasize assistance grants and the financing of training of advancing-world journalists as a mechanism for righting the global imbalance.

What went wrong? Why did the U.S. press report critically on the proceedings of the general conference while it was in progress and then condemn UNESCO with such overt hostility at the end of the meeting? In most of the rest of the world, the reports were not unfriendly. The Soviet Union expressed modest disagreement with some of the recommendations but generally applauded the result. In the advancing world, most responses were enthusiastic, and among the capitalist nations allied with the United States, the press tended to report the conference with approval. In New York, the National News Council, itself concerned about the course of events at the UNESCO conference, was nonetheless disturbed by complaints that the U.S. press had reported the conference in a biased and distorted manner. So the News Council directed its staff to make a thorough study of the coverage of the UNESCO conference by the U.S. press.

The findings of the News Council study are revealing. With near unanimity, the American press reported and commented on the proceedings at UNESCO with unmasked antagonism, concentrating on the element of fear, fear that foreign authoritarians and bureaucrats were seeking to damage — if not destroy — freedom of the press as it had been experienced in the United States for more than two centuries. The News Council study showed that the single article most widely used in the American press was an AP report on October 21 that appeared in different versions in morning and afternoon papers. In the afternoon-paper article, the lead paragraph ran: "Communist and Third World nations used their majority in UNESCO to pass resolutions aimed at getting more control over international news reporting." The headlines prompted by that article included one in *The Independent-Record* of Helena, Montana, that read: "UNESCO Votes to Muzzle Press." So intense was the concentration on the discussion of news at the conference that not a single article appeared in any of the newspapers studied by the National News Council on any topic of discussion at UNESCO other than news policies. The approval of IPDC went "almost unreported." Even one of the U.S. delegates to UNESCO, William Harley, portrayed the American press coverage as "astigmatic"; and Leonard Sussman, executive director of Freedom House, which has actively opposed the campaign for a new information order, found the U.S. reporting unbalanced. Sussman, in his own survey of U.S. press accounts, found 60 percent of them unfavorable, 5 percent favorable, and 12 percent balanced.

A. H. Raskin, a former assistant editor of the editorial page of *The New York Times*, who reported the News Council findings, blamed the selection process for the unbalanced reporting. By finding newsworthy only those stories that seemed to fulfill the fears expressed so unanimously on the editorial pages of the U.S. press, the journalists systematically excluded opposing viewpoints. This procedure, Raskin wrote, was "inconsistent with the spirit of detachment that is invariably set forth as the touchstone of sound news judgment." His article quoted Stan Swinton, then head of world services for The Associated Press, as acknowledging that the many other activities at UNESCO were not reported but explaining this fact on the ground that none of the other UNESCO activities was newsworthy. Indeed, Swinton said, were it not for the controversy over the new international information order, "nobody from the press would be there at all. It's like a safe landing at an airport."

The irony is noteworthy. It was that very question of news judgment that underlay much of the MacBride Commission report and much of the discussion of the new international information order. It was the search for spot news, for the dramatic and the conflictual, that marked the U.S. press coverage of the UNESCO proceedings, just as it marked press coverage of other issues in the United States, and indeed throughout the capitalist world. Among the dangers of the existing information order, the MacBride Commission reported, was precisely this concentration on the immediate and the dramatic. What was overlooked and ignored were the great political, economic, and social issues.

News reports and commentary in the French press were generally similar to those in the U.S. news media, although the French wrote a good deal more about the establishment of the IPDC, and a number of French newspapers, mainly those on the political left, did react favorably to UNESCO. One of the most revealing elements in the French press coverage dealt with a statement by Director General M'Bow at a news conference. "Every intergovernmental organization," M'Bow said, "is a political organization par excellence, for political authorities participate in its proceedings." A not especially remarkable observation; after all, it is unthinkable to imagine that those who represent their governments in international bodies are not expected to reflect the views of the political leaders who sent them there in the first place. M'Bow's statement nonetheless served as a springboard in the French press for a series of comments that UNESCO was "too politicized" and concerned itself too much with ideological matters. Two dispatches by Agence France Presse quoted M'Bow as saying merely that "every intergovernmental organization is a political organization par excellence," dropping the remainder of the sentence in which he qualified and explained his point clearly.

The fear of "politicization" was evident in the French news reports, as it was in the press accounts in the United States. As noted earlier, one of the most important elements that separates press ideologies from one another is the matter of politicization. To the advancing world as to the

Marxist nations, the role played by the press is decidedly political. Among capitalist nations, the role assigned to the press is not political. The news media are expected, as Raskin wrote, to operate "in the spirit of detachment." A question that remains to be addressed is whether or not there are ways to reconcile this fundamental difference.

The MacBride Commission report was not formally voted upon at the 21st General Conference. It is probably a good thing it was not. Any call for a formal vote would no doubt have produced a great deal of rhetoric from all sides, and the findings and recommendations of the commission would have been lost in airy verbiage. Instead, the delegates voted to circulate the report to their governments, to journalists, scholars, and the general public, and then to take the recommendations into consideration at the next general conference in 1983, at which time a new five-year press plan (1984–1989) was to be considered. In addition, the delegates called once again for safeguarding "freedom of opinion, expression, and information," and for further development of communications capabilities for all countries. And, without saying so in the most unequivocal of language, the delegates approved a new order under this resolution: "The General Conference expresses the wish that UNESCO demonstrate its willingness in its short and medium-term activities to contribute to the delineation, broadening, and application of the concept of a new world information order." The most significant of all the resolutions adopted at the general conference was that which established the IPDC.

Within four months of the closing of the general conference, the global discussion of information policy was embroiled once again in a burning conflict, as bitter as any of those that had preceded it. The quarrel this time was over codes of ethics and the protection of journalists. A conference was arranged for February 1981 at the Paris headquarters of UNESCO, and a political science professor at the University of Paris, Pierre Gaborit, was invited to present some of his ideas for discussion. The plan Gaborit offered was entirely unacceptable to the United States and to many of its friends among capitalist nations. As it turned out, the dispute itself was much ado about very little, but it served as a launching platform for soaring flights of oratory and even for threats by the U.S. Congress to withdraw from UNESCO.

The UNESCO secretariat organizes many meetings and mini-conferences whose objective is to permit experts to air their points of view. When the topic under discussion is the press, UNESCO officials often turn to formal organizations of journalists for advice on whom to invite to present viewpoints. Among those organizations, two are especially visible in Europe, where UNESCO is headquartered. One is the International Organization of Journalists, the IOJ, which is located in Prague and whose perspective is frankly Marxist. The other is the International Federation of Journalists, the IFJ, whose headquarters is located in Brussels and whose ideology is essentially capitalist. It is difficult to piece together the precise sequence of steps, but it appears that UNESCO asked the two organizations to recommend experts to lead discussions at the February meeting. Gaborit's name was provided by the IOJ. Either the IFJ chose not to respond or else it did not receive an invitation; this point is in dispute. In any case, in due course Gaborit was invited, and letters of invitation also went out in routine fashion to news organizations and interested experts. Few of those organizations apparently paid attention to the invitations, a customary practice, since Gaborit was not a prominent, hence not an especially newsworthy, person.

However, at some point a few days before the conference, some journalists reported that a UNESCO meeting was about to take place at which a plan would be introduced to license journalists and insure that they complied with the "generally accepted" ethics of their profession. Gaborit's proposal, in these reports, was being elevated into a UNESCO plan. Moreover, it was said, the meeting was being held in secret and journalists representing the industrialized countries of the capitalist world had not been invited. *The New York Times* reported that "Westerners" were angered because UNESCO was moving ahead with plans to license journalists, even though, it said, the MacBride Commission had decided against any such idea.

The commission had indeed explored the question of the licensing of journalists as part of a plan to provide protection for reporters who otherwise might be placed under life-threatening risks. It decided against any such plan, however, over the vigorous objection of MacBride, who argued that it was more important to safeguard the lives of journalists than to adhere to the abstract principle that journalists deserved no special "privileges or favors" in their work situations. The United States and other countries had argued that any move to protect journalists would require some sort of licensing arrangement. MacBride said he simply could not understand the U.S. intransigence on this point at a time that journalists were suffering the highest death rate of any group of civilians. The commission rejected formal codes of ethics despite extensive support among the advancing countries, on the ground that no agreement on any such code was possible. The commission did say, however, that an international code was desirable if one could be worked out, recommending that it be voluntary and self-enforced. The Hutchins Commission would have saluted the idea, but Canada's Zimmerman protested that professional journalists themselves opposed any kind of formal codes, even if they were voluntary. In the face of this division, the commission sought to follow a cautious middle course.

The reports about the meeting featuring Gaborit's plan generated a great deal of interest. When UNESCO officials heard rumors that they were preparing a closed meeting and had not invited all journalists to attend, they reacted with some anger, asserting that invitations had been duly sent out but ignored. When the meeting finally took place, it was well attended, as journalists and officials of journalism organizations flocked to Paris to listen to Gaborit and to deliver themselves of speeches opposing any licensing plans. UNESCO aides, led by Director General M'Bow, insisted that any proposals for licensing journalists were those of Gaborit and did not reflect the views of UNESCO. The denials of M'Bow and his associates apparently did not satisfy the complainants. A UPI report spoke of "UNESCO's touchiness" and maintained that Third World delegates, who were portrayed as trying to sneak through a plan on the quiet, were angered because of the presence of "the Western groups who gate-crashed." Frank Campbell, information minister of Guyana, replied that what was needed was not a series of arguments but rather discussions on how to resolve differences of opinion. "UNESCO," he observed, "is merely the facilitator, not some kind of bogeyman trying to rob people of their freedom." On the other hand, Leonard H. Marks, secretary-treasurer of the World Press Freedom Committee and a former director of the U.S. Information Agency, said he would be opposed to any new information order if that meant "government or UNESCO control over the media, reporters' access, their freedom to cover what they want to cover, and censorship of their stories."

UNESCO officials said they had no such intentions, but no sooner had the meeting ended than press organizations, including Marks's World Press Freedom Committee, began organizing yet another conference, one that ultimately took place at a French resort town in May and that produced what came to be known as the Talloires Declaration on Press Freedom. The gathering at Talloires was assuredly one of the most distinguished assemblages ever of journalism organizations, scholars, and officials interested in the press. About sixty organizations were represented, including the Big Four news agencies. The leadership of the group was composed of representatives from the United States, but there were also authorities from most countries of Western Europe and some from Africa, Asia, and Latin America. UNESCO officials were invited to attend. M'Bow himself spoke to the participants; his address itself was moderate in tone, but when he was subjected to questioning by the journalists, he reacted with anger. Although the Declaration of Talloires was essentially affirmative in tone, hostility between the press theorists of the capitalist world and those of the advancing world was in no way assuaged.

Questioners complained to M'Bow that UNESCO was favoring government controls over the press, that it operated in secret, and that it was being manipulated by the Soviet Union. The director general's angry response was that none of those charges was true and that the press was delivering a distorted image of UNESCO. A news account of the Talloires meeting in *The International Herald Tribune* said M'Bow's statements and the hostile reaction on the part of some participants to a remark by Harley urging that ideology be kept out of the IPDC, the new assistance agency, led to a declaration even more hardened than was originally planned. *The New York Times* applauded the declaration as "the first time Western and other free newspapers and broadcasting networks took a united stand against the campaign by Soviet bloc and Third World countries to give UNESCO the authority to regulate the flow of news and information." A news report filed by the information arm of the U.S. State Department said the declaration "was seen as a major move against the establishment of a so-called 'New World Information Order,' involving arbitrary restrictions on the media, which is under consideration in UNESCO."

The line certainly appeared to be drawn by the Declaration of Talloires. And yet, ironically, there was little in the declaration that differed in spirit from the report and recommendations published by the MacBride Commission. The declaration supported "the free flow of information and ideas," opposed any "international code of ethics," and rejected any plan to license journalists or to provide any formal system for protecting journalists. None of these recommendations is inconsistent with the MacBride report, although they were, of course, in opposition to Gaborit's proposal. But his proposal was his own, not the recommendation of UNESCO. Indeed, both the MacBride Commission report and the Talloires declaration endorsed the Universal Declaration of Human Rights and the UNESCO constitution.

The essential differences were once again economic. The Talloires declaration specifically endorsed advertising as both a service to consumers and as provider of financial support for "a strong and self-supporting press." No press can be independent, the declaration asserted, "without financial independence." Moreover, the declaration said, the sensible approach to correcting the imbalance in the world of information was through "practical solutions," specifically "improving technological progress, increasing professional interchanges and equipment transfers, reducing communication tariffs, producing cheaper newsprint, and eliminating other barriers to the development of news media capabilities." The split between the have nations of the capitalist world and the have-nots of the advancing world was manifest in the division over the importance of advertising. To the advancing world, as evidenced in the MacBride report, advertising represents a threat to the free flow of information; to the industrialized nations, advertising provides the underpinning for an independent press free of government controls.

THE PERILOUS PUSH FOR INTERNATIONAL COOPERATION

One of the arguments underlying this book is that the press has never operated as an independent actor, that it has never been free from the direction of power, whether that power be of governments or of economic forces. The division between the capitalist and advancing-world countries turns out, on close examination, to be ephemeral. Each side loudly proclaims its mission as it marches under the ideological banner of a free flow of information; yet in neither case is the declared mission of the press what it seems. Skimmed milk, as W. S. Gilbert observed wisely, masquerades as cream.

In any case, the Talloires declaration turned out to be enormously popular with the press and with representatives of the U.S. government. For its part, as was to be expected, the Soviet Union condemned the declaration; Yuri Kornilov, a TASS analyst, portrayed the declaration as a fraud and accused the capitalist news media of waging "psychological war against sovereign states" under the guise of supporting free flow of information. The advancing world and UNESCO officials expressed less concern over the declaration itself than over the attacks on UNESCO that marked the Talloires meeting. Herve Bourges of France, at that time press spokesman for M'Bow, and author of a book entitled *Decoloniser L'information*, complained that certain elements of the U.S., British, and French press had turned their "war machine" against UNESCO. M'Bow, who in his speech at Talloires had said he welcomed the dialogue, was no longer as sure that he did.

Editorials in U.S. newspapers vigorously applauded the Declaration of Talloires. So did the outpourings of columns by such writers as Carl Rowan and John Roche. *Stars and Stripes* headlined the Roche column: "UNESCO Tries to Muzzle the Press." U.S. officials joined in criticizing the activities at UNESCO, although their comments were more reasoned and less inflammatory than some of the headlines. A speech by Sarah Goddard Power, a former aide to President Carter, in which she discussed in quiet tones issues involved in what she called a communications revolution, was reported by *Press Woman* under the headline: "Freedom of World Press in Danger."

The pace of criticism of UNESCO increased throughout the spring and summer of 1981. At a conference in Madrid held by the International Federation of Newspaper Publishers (FIEJ), an association of newspaper owners from twenty-five countries led by the United States, a resolution was adopted endorsing the Declaration of Talloires and urging UNESCO to "abandon attempts at regulating news content and formulating rules for the press." At the same time, the FIEJ called on the advancing world to find practical solutions to its problems, chiefly through accepting direct assistance and programs to train journalists. Following the approach at Talloires, the publishers expressed concern over international efforts to put the interests of governments above those of individuals. In a comment that might have been written by John Stuart Mill, the publishers expressed their belief that "the state exists for the individual." It said that "the ultimate definition of a press does not lie in actions of government or international bodies, but in the professionalism, vigor, and courage of individual newspapermen, freely accepting their duties and serving the community, and thereby the individual, by free and open reporting."

In an article in *The Wall Street Journal* in June, Leonard Sussman, executive director of Freedom House, applauded the Talloires declaration as representing "a free-press counterattack" to actions taken at UNESCO meetings where "free-press advocates have taken beatings in the last six years." He warned that the IPDC, the new agency for providing assistance to advancing-world countries, was "shorthand for institutionalized trouble," since it might be used to channel funds only to countries with repressive press policies. His summary of advancing-world press policies showed that censorship, either before or after publication, was practiced in 57 percent of African countries, 53 percent of Asian lands, and 38 percent of Latin American nations; that preventive detention of journalists was practiced in 51 percent of African nations, 89 percent of Asian, and 38 percent of Latin American nations. Moreover, he said, those countries with controlled presses held a majority of votes in UNESCO and on the thirty-five member council of IPDC. If those countries persisted in pursuing a campaign to "harass the free press," Sussman wrote, then the United States, with or without its allies, should consider withdrawing financial support from UNESCO.

In July, Elliot Abrams, assistant secretary of state for international organization affairs, spoke up against UNESCO meetings, such as the one at which Gaborit's plan was discussed, as an "assault on the very free press values which UNESCO is mandated to defend." But he opposed any effort to withdraw from UNESCO, arguing it was preferable to remain in the organization and "provide aggressive leadership" in defending the free flow of ideas. The United States would retain its UNESCO membership "as long as there is any hope of returning UNESCO to its mandated responsibility." The issue, Abrams said, was not so much the future of press freedom but the future of UNESCO. His position was set forth in a statement July 9 to subcommittees of the House Foreign Affairs Committee, which by then had taken an active interest in the discussions about UNESCO. By October, both the House and Senate had approved a bill that threatened the viability of UNESCO.

The UNESCO measure was tacked onto the regular appropriations bill for the State Department, a bill that was approved by the House and Senate in 1981, but in different forms. It took until August 1982 before the two chambers could agree on final passage, although the language of the UNESCO provision was not in dispute. President Reagan signed the measure into law on August 24, 1982. In the Senate, where the measure originated, Senators Dan Quayle of Indiana, a Republican, and Daniel Patrick Moynihan of New York, a Democrat, joined forces to sponsor an amendment that declared it the sense of Congress to oppose efforts by UNESCO "to attempt to regulate news content" and attempts by some members of UNESCO "to control access to and dissemination of news." Moreover, the amendment expressed the will of Congress that no U.S. contributions to UNESCO be used for any projects that would license journalists, impose mandatory codes of ethics, or restrict "the free flow of information." The amendment was adopted unanimously.

When the measure reached the floor of the House on September 17, 1981, Representative Robin L. Beard, a Tennessee Republican, moved to strengthen the language of the amendment. According to Beard, the possibility that UNESCO would adopt a plan to regulate the behavior of journalists had now grown "to dangerous levels." It was therefore essential that the United States threaten to cut off all its contributions to UNESCO — a figure of about $12 million — if the organization should implement any plan to license journalists or in any way restrict the free flow of information or impose a mandatory code of ethics. Beard read into the record a letter from President Reagan supporting his proposal and endorsing the Declaration of Talloires. The declaration was itself read into the record by Representative Millicent Fenwick, Republican of New Jersey. A dozen House members rose to join Beard and Fenwick in a series of ringing speeches endorsing the American concept of a free press, the First Amendment, and even speeches by Thomas Jefferson.

The power of the folklore of the press was evident in the speeches. Representative Ralph Regula, Ohio Republican, asserted that "an open press and an open flow of information...is fundamental to our nation." The importance of the Beard amendment, he said, cannot be overstated. Other congressmen spoke in a similar vein. Many among them openly condemned UNESCO. Representative Edward J. Derwinski, Illinois Republican, declared that UNESCO's goal was "muzzling of the press." Representative Clarence E. Miller, Ohio Republican, spoke out against "increasing efforts of UN bodies to control information." He expressed concern about the new information order, which he said was the "result of Soviet initiatives...to bring developing nations and totalitarian nations into an alliance to control...information the way it is controlled in their own countries." To Representative Jerry Lewis, California Republican, it was necessary to move against "those in world bodies such as the UN who would undermine free speech." Representative Gerald B. Solomon, New York Republican, applauding the U.S. press as a watchdog "checking abuses and rooting out corruption," asserted that there was nothing Communist leaders fear more than a free press:

> So it is really no surprise that the Soviet puppets and the various dictators around the world are trying to snuff out what press freedoms still exist in their countries. What is a surprise — a shock really — is that the United States

might be put in the position of tacitly approving this suppression. To think that UNESCO — an arm of the United Nations — would ever consider some sort of journalistic licensing. It is outrageous.

Only one House member, Representative Mervyn M. Dymally, California Democrat, spoke against the Beard amendment. He pointed out that UNESCO had taken no action to censor the press or license journalists and that he saw no need to respond "hysterically to what we perceive as censorship." Such a measure, he said, would be similar to voting to deny the American media free space and telephones in the Capitol in order to force them to be "responsible and objective in their reporting." Despite Dymally's intervention, 372 House members voted for the Beard amendment and only 19 opposed it.

Fenwick, supporting a second amendment calling on President Reagan to direct a far-ranging study of UNESCO's activities, argued that it was preferable to remain a UNESCO member and fight to safeguard the principles of a free press, but that the United States must be ready if the effort fails to "exercise more drastic options at a later date." Portraying the issue as a clash between the press ideology of the capitalist countries and that of the Marxist nations, she asserted:

> The Soviet Union and many other countries in the world believe that the press exists as an instrument — a tool — of the State: that its duty is to promote the power and stability of the State. They do not believe, as we do, and our First Amendment proves it, that the press exists for the people.

The distance between the market and the Marxist perceptions of the role of the press is supremely clear in Fenwick's remarks. To her, and indeed to the overwhelming majority of the members of the House (and of the Senate and of the capitalist journalistic community), the Marxist press is an instrument — or tool, as she put it — of the State, or of the Communist party. At the same time, to the majority of the members of the Supreme Soviet, the Communist party, and the Russian journalistic community, the market press is an instrument, a tool, of the capitalists. In the face of this diametrical division, the task of anyone who seeks some kind of accord on the role of the press internationally turns out to be Herculean. In fact, neither the United States nor the Soviet Union has shown any willingness to accommodate to any international agreements on the press except where those agreements are presented in terms so vague and general that they can be interpreted as any nation sees fit.

The amendment offered by Fenwick and Representative Bob Shamansky, Ohio Democrat, was approved by voice vote in the House, adopted by the Senate, and together with the Beard amendment enacted into law. Whether UNESCO has the power to enforce codes of ethics or licensing arrangements is another matter. The United States has vigorously opposed acceptance as binding in law of any recommendation, agreement, or convention adopted by any agency of the United Nations. So, in fact, have the Soviet Union and most of the allies of both the United States and the Soviet Union, with the notable exception of France, which is given historically to proposing and adopting sweeping moral declarations of principle. For the most part, it has been only the advancing-world countries that have sought to rewrite international law to require that regulations adopted by intergovernmental bodies be made binding on all nations. In any case, neither the United Nations nor any of its subagencies has the capacity to enforce its rules or regulations. Hence, the discussions in the House were political in nature, as well as symbolic. To Americans, symbolic actions have a long and honored tradition, dating back to the Boston Tea Party. Refusal to participate in the 1980 Olympic Games was in this tradition, as have been various embargoes. As with all these symbolic acts, the desire was both to hoist a red flag and to serve a warning. Members of the House were of the opinion that the threat to cut off funding for UNESCO would persuade the member nations to avoid taking any action that might be disapproved by the United States.

In November 1982, UNESCO delegates approved a six-year plan to cover all fourteen areas under their jurisdiction; at the 22nd General Conference in the fall of 1983 the organization adopted a $374 million budget to implement those plans for the following two years. As usual, it was the world information order that attracted the attention of the news media. In the United States and Western Europe, educational, cultural, and scientific issues achieved scarcely any mention at all. The tone of the debate over the information order was gentle, although once again advancing countries asked that something be done to curb the power of the Big Four news agencies and urged that technology be put to use to aid the new nation-states and not to subject them to Western domination. The United States and her allies continued to insist on the principle of free flow of information and to express the suspicion that the new information order was aimed at restricting freedom of movement by news media and transnationals. The Soviet Union accused the capitalist nations of hypocrisy. In other words, nothing new took place; in fact, the mood was one of accommodation, even among U.S. delegates. Nonetheless, a month after the end of the conference, the Reagan Administration in Washington announced its intention to withdraw from UNESCO at the close of 1984, primarily, it said, because of a perceived tendency on the part of UNESCO to "extraneously politicize" issues before it and to demonstrate hostility to free market and free press concepts. The future of UNESCO was uncertain in 1984.

Congressional debate took place after the first meeting of the IPDC Council, which convened in Paris in June 1981. The council met again in

Mexico in January 1982 and in Paris in December 1982; it planned to meet regularly through the 1980s, despite the fact that its fund-raising efforts were hampered by political differences. To limit IPDC funds is to reduce its capacity to provide the kind of assistance that might enable the advancing world to catch up with the industrialized nations and remedy the imbalance in communications. The chief concern voiced by the United States (and some of its allies) was that IPDC would operate not as a purely dispassionate mechanism for assistance but would serve rather as an ideological, or politicized, battleground. In fact, the United States made it clear it preferred IPDC to operate separately from UNESCO. The American effort to bring about this kind of arrangement failed inside the MacBride Commission. Over opposition of the members from the United States, France, and Canada, the commission approved as the seventy-eighth of its eighty-two recommendations the creation of IPDC "within the framework of UNESCO." Its purpose was to mobilize support within the industrialized world for direct financial assistance to be provided mainly on a multilateral basis for developing and strengthening communications infrastructures; for improvement of information-delivery systems among news agencies, press, cinema, radio, and television; for professional training of journalists and communications planners; and for the transfer of technology, in terms of the instruments of the press as well as satellites and data banks.

At the General Conference in 1980, the central issue was whether or not the money given to the IPDC either by governments or private interests should go into one large collection pot or whether the assistance was to be earmarked to be used only for specific purposes decreed by the donor. The United States wanted to make sure that the money that it provided went only to help countries whose press the United States considered to be free. As Clifford H. Block, director of research and development for the Agency for International Development (AID), put it, it was "simply unacceptable" for his government to fund any IPDC project that might be ideologically contentious. Any effort to promote a project of this kind would threaten U.S. support for the IPDC concept. Block saw bilateral funding as the way out of the impasse: "U.S. funds can go to those projects that are fully consistent with its views, as a nation, of the central importance of freedom of information to a society."

At the second IPDC Council meeting in Acapulco, a compromise was reached whereby the organization would exclude no source of finance. While this language was not endorsed by some advancing-world countries, it did at least provide the vehicle to get IPDC moving and to avoid any possible walkout by the United States. Following the adoption of the compromise, the United States offered for the first time to make a contribution — $100,000 supplied through AID in the form of expert services in various areas of communications development.

When the delegates departed from Acapulco, they seemed on the whole to be pleased with the spirit of cooperation, although they deplored the limited funds so far available to IPDC. Block saw the meeting as marking "a welcome reduction" in ideological posturing. He found the delegates businesslike in their approach to the issues but did express some concern over the introduction by a delegate from Mexico of the concept of social participation, a reminder of the Velasco experiment in Peru, which would certainly be what Block characterized as "ideologically contentious."

Block was not alone in seeing a lessening of tension in the discussions and a general willingness to cooperate among the delegates. Officials of UNESCO evaluated the meeting in the same spirit and expressed the hope that a stronger sense of international cooperation might arise through the activities of IPDC. Nevertheless, enactment of the Beard amendment came seven months after the Acapulco meeting, and some advancing-world delegates had not abandoned their efforts to organize IPDC as a multilateral program. Only if the program were multilateral, in their view, would IPDC be truly an international program and not a means for industrialized countries to maintain imperial power by tying ideological strings to aid money. Kaarle Nordenstreng of Finland, a leading international journalism scholar, found nothing surprising in the reluctance of the United States and some of its allies to contribute to a multilateral assistance program: "Why should they pay for music that does not follow their tune?"

On this point, Leonard Sussman of Freedom House is clear. He has proposed that the United States and its partners in the *Information Group* (IG), an informal union of capitalist countries supporting "free press" concepts, state openly and publicly that they will provide communication technology assistance only to Third World countries "that accept as a fundamental commitment the expansion of the free flow of information worldwide." At the same time, José Mayobré Machado of Venezuela, at that time a member of his country's delegation to UNESCO, rejected "paternalistic advice" from industrialized countries. Gifts of money or technological assistance were not enough either, he said: "We do not want to become the repository, at a very high price at that, of all the technology you have discarded as obsolete." Moreover, he said, advancing-world countries did not want to be classified as either communist or capitalist: "What we do want above all is an honest, intelligent, mutually respectful cooperation on an equal and equitable basis."

At Acapulco, the thirty-five-member IPDC Council considered hundreds of projects. Those that claimed the widest support and attracted the heaviest funding were regional news agencies and regional broadcasting organizations, facilities that, if adequately funded and staffed, might one day rival the Big Four and TASS. The actual pledges were limited, but it was a start. The delegates approved $100,000 for a Pan-African News Agency: $56,000 for an Arab Project for Communication Planning and Exchange; $80,000 for an Asia-Pacific News Network; $45,000 for a Caribbean regional project for broadcasting, training, and program exchange; and $70,000 for a Latin American Special Information Services Agency. Total funding approved was a modest $910,000, but IPDC also announced pledges of $3.4 million.

At the Paris meeting in December 1982, the total of grants rose to $1,900,000; this figure was but a small portion of the requests submitted. Requests totaled $8,200,000, itself a modest sum. For example, Bangladesh sought $180,000 to finance a 30-kilowatt transmitter to beam radio programs to otherwise newsless rural citizens; IPDC authorized $15,000. New funding of $749,000 was authorized at Paris, primarily, as before, for regional news agencies. The Pan-African News Agency, for instance, was awarded an additional $100,000. The other agencies received comparable amounts. For the first time, IPDC funding was approved for purely national projects, such as that of Bangladesh. The total number of projects funded rose to thirty-eight, fifteen of them national in scope. Additional sums of money were pledged into the IPDC Special Account, which is an umbrella for contributions from private sources and for bilateral assistance, the latter often involving political strings. The total pledged to the Special Fund reached some $8 million. The United States, clearly now prepared to "stay the course" in UNESCO, upped its contribution to $450,000, the $350,000 in new money to be allocated by IPDC itself under a special formula that permitted the United States some direct control. Delegate William G. Harley characterized the new U.S. contribution as showing "continued confidence in the IPDC, inspired by its operation to date and as a sincere attest of its belief in the potential of the IPDC idea."

What the future will hold for IPDC and UNESCO is far from clear. M'Bow, while acknowledging the enormity of the task faced by the intergovernmental bodies, expressed optimism — if action could be achieved on two levels: to enable the poorest of nations and peoples "to hear the rest of the world and to make their voices more clearly heard by others," and "to enable society to have perfect control over the instruments of its own progress." At almost the same time, a group of six prominent U.S. experts on foreign affairs was asking whether the United States should consider operating through "alternative institutions or mechanisms" rather than UNESCO. These authorities, who included former Secretaries of State Dean Rusk, Cyrus Vance, and Edmund Muskie, said they preferred to remain in UNESCO and argue the U.S. case there, but that if those efforts failed, the United States ought to consider withholding funds from UNESCO or withdrawing from it altogether.

While the issue is usually portrayed in terms of ideology or political philosophy, at its root the quarrel is economic.

The press as piper.

Press Content and Financing:
Paying the Piper

THE BOUNDARIES OF JOURNALISTIC AUTONOMY

Among the most remarkable aspects of the folklore of the press is the absence of references to money. The mythology casts the press as Athena, sprung full-born from the brow of the people. The Four Theorists mention the financing of the press only in passing and ignore the question of profit. In the report of the Hutchins Commission and the British Royal Commission, money takes the form of an ominous cloud, threatening to divert the press from the duty assigned it by the people, who are perhaps the representatives of Zeus. Even more startling is the cavalier treatment accorded by working journalists to the influence of money on their livelihood. To be sure, they are concerned about their own incomes and expense accounts, and they are cognizant of the costs of publishing and broadcasting. Yet little attention is given to the connection between those details of financing and the news product they deliver. It is as if the journalist, whose daily life is dedicated to close observation, blinds his senses to the realities of his calling. The advertiser is often held in contempt; he and his kind are not welcome in the newsroom, and the reporter or his editor would cheerfully go to prison rather than allow his news judgment to be influenced by the crass commercial world of the advertiser. He is willing — more than willing — to let it go at that. Beyond the surface of reality he is not prepared to go. Or, rather, beyond the surface of reality he does not permit himself to go — for in the shadows beyond, he fears, lies the verity that would surely explode the comforting folklore of the independence of the press.

Such, at least, is the pattern of journalistic life in the United States and, in varying degree, throughout the capitalist world. The financing of the press is a matter of no greater concern among socialist journalists than it is in the capitalist world. The part of Zeus is taken in the Soviet Union not by the people but by the Communist party, as the vanguard of the people. If pressures are brought on the Soviet journalist, they come not from the sellers of commercial notices but from party functionaries. In other words, the press mythology of both the United States and the Soviet Union (and their allies, as well) holds that it is from politicians that the pressure for conformity comes, not from the moneyed interests.

The reality, on the other hand, is that the content of the press is directly correlated with the interests of those who finance the press. The press is the piper, and the tune the piper plays is composed by those who pay the piper. This is so even though the identity of the paymaster is not always known; in fact, it is in the paymaster's interests to maintain the lowest sort of profile, for to do so contributes to the maintenance of the folklore. The relationship between the piper and his paymaster takes four different forms: official, commercial, interest, and informal. Rarely is the relationship a pure one; overlapping is quite common. So are exceptions. Still, the four basic patterns of relationships are clear enough. In the *official* pattern, the content of the newspaper, magazine, or broadcasting outlet is determined by rules, regulations, and decrees. Some news media may be themselves state enterprises, some may be directed through government regulations, and some may be controlled under a network of licensing arrangements. No nation is free of official controls; the variations come in the degree of autonomy that is permitted. In the *commercial* pattern, the content reflects the views of advertisers and their commercial allies, who are usually found among the owners and publishers. Even under planned economies, some commercial influences can be detected, although these are exerted only indirectly. In the *interest* pattern, the content of the medium echoes the concerns of the financing enterprise, a political party perhaps or a religious organization or any other body pursuing specific ends. In the *informal* pattern, media content mirrors the goals of relatives, friends, or acquaintances, who supply money directly or who exercise their influence to ensure that the tunes of the piper are heard.

To force the press into a classification system that is national in nature is to commit a grievous error. Freedom House and other organizations that rate the press of one country free and another controlled are simplifying patterns that are themselves highly complex. To be sure, we can set forth plausible arguments that the press has a greater degree of autonomy in, say, the United States than it does in the Soviet Union, or Indonesia, or Brazil. But in this situation, it must be recognized, we are talking about purely political autonomy. We are not taking into consideration questions of economic autonomy, or of cultural autonomy, for that matter. Moreover, such a rating system establishes the fiction that the press of any country is a monolith. The newspapers and magazines within the borders of a nation are not identical. The degree of political autonomy differs from one publication to another. For example, from the content of the *Literary Gazette* in Moscow we can infer a level of political autonomy higher than that of *Izvestia*. At the same time, from the content of the *Nation* we can infer a higher level of political autonomy — at least in terms of permitting criticism of the political order — than that of *U.S. News and World Report*. The mistake is to equate levels of political autonomy with freedom.

No newspaper, magazine, or broadcasting outlet exceeds the boundaries of autonomy acceptable to the paymasters. Those boundaries, it must be remembered, are not carved in stone. They are very flexible indeed, and in every place on earth the boundaries have changed over time. Measuring sticks that seek to classify the dynamic are inevitably flawed, as are those that affix national labels to the measuring sticks. The imperfect best we can do is to deal in degrees. For example, we can say with some confidence that the political system in a country derives from the economic power structure, and that the press of that country will therefore at any given time by and large reflect the ends of those who manage the economy. Those ends may be openly stated or they may be concealed. When the ends are openly stated, the press is likely to be subjected to a large measure of official control. Where they are concealed, the press is likely to be directed either through commercial channels or through informal arrangements. In all cases, interest groups, those that support the objectives of power and the dissidents who oppose those ends, use the press for their own different purposes.

In the Soviet Union, the identity of the paymaster is supremely clear. It is the Communist party that makes the ultimate decisions about how money is spent. In the U.S.S.R., there is no doubt in anyone's mind that newspapers, magazines, and broadcasting outlets are required to operate within the boundaries fixed by the Party. Journalism students in the Soviet orbit are instructed to present information "objectively" that will work to the end of benefiting society. To present contrary information is to serve reactionary interests and is thus unacceptable. In this case, the goals of the paymaster are carried out by the piper, whose tunes are played in the interests of his paymaster. While no attention is paid to the financing of the Soviet press in Marxist schools of journalism, it is taught that capitalist journalists serve the interests of their paymasters. The instruction holds that fairness and balance are mere pretenses and that objectivity is possible only under the banner of Marxism-Leninism.

Interestingly, statistical data on the financing of the Soviet press are difficult — if not impossible — to obtain. It is quite likely that no one knows the cost of conducting the Soviet press system. Take, for example, the case of *Pravda*, the official Party newspaper. The word may ring strangely in this context, but, according to Soviet authorities, *Pravda* operates at a profit. With a circulation of eleven million, the newspaper sells for three kopecks, or about five U.S. cents. Soviet officials say that newsprint for the six-page paper runs to less than one kopeck per issue. With a staff of only two hundred to be paid, subscriptions produce more revenue than it costs to publish the paper. According to Soviet estimates, any newspaper with a circulation in excess of ten thousand is a profit-making venture. In line with these estimates, Soviet officials say they must subsidize only the tiniest of papers. Radio and television are fully subsidized, inasmuch as they are operated by civil servants. Newspapers and magazines are not listed as state-run enterprises. What is missing from this curious financial accounting are all capital expenses. The cost of equipment is simply not counted; nor are the costs of the buildings housing the newspapers, nor the costs of maintenance of equipment and buildings. Even the costs of distribution are budgeted under other headings. By these standards, almost every newspaper on earth would be a profitable enterprise.

The Soviet accounting system is not designed especially for news-papers. Capital costs are simply not included in Soviet budget reckonings. The vertical system is highly compartmentalized; work units do not communicate with one another, only with authorities above. It is for this reason that so many buildings in the Soviet Union remain partially completed for long periods, sometimes several years. The builders of the walls may finish their job and go on to their next venture, leaving the tall cranes in place to await the completion of work by the masons and carpenters, who are under the direction of a different central authority. It is therefore difficult — if not impossible — to know just how much it costs to run a newspaper, or for that matter how much its costs to construct a building. Whatever the costs of producing newspapers, one can be certain that when they appear on the streets, their content is not displeasing to the managers of the papers or to their superiors in the Kremlin, who are footing the bill for the capital outlays under whatever budget heading they are hidden.

The Party is not the only paymaster in the Soviet Union, however. *Izvestia*, with a circulation equal to that of *Pravda*, is financed by the Council of Ministers. *Trud*, an influential paper published by the army, is financed by the military. The *Literary Gazette* is financed by cultural organizations. Throughout the Soviet Union, various interest groups are prominent as financiers of the pipers whose tunes are sung in the pages of the papers. In the tightly controlled society of the Soviet Union, the identity of the paymasters is not publicized; still, one can imagine that these paymasters are profiting personally from their positions, perhaps in terms of money, certainly in terms of power. To this extent, they are financing a kind of commercial venture. And informal arrangements clearly abound. For a long time, for instance, the son-in-law of Party Chairman Nikita Khrushchev held the position of chief editor of *Pravda*.

Thus, in one form or another, all the patterns of relationships between piper and paymaster exist in the Soviet Union. The same is true in the United States, although the emphases are different. While the most obvious relationship in the Soviet Union is official, in the United States it is the commercial pattern that is most evident. Exceptions are permitted — a modest dissident press has continued to persist, with limited resources and power — but the overriding concern of press paymasters in the United States is with profit, and the measure of profit is revenue from commercial notices. As in the Soviet Union, it is extraordinarily difficult to find out how much it costs to produce a newspaper. And it is quite impossible to determine the extent of profits, but some inferences can be drawn.

THE PROFITABILITY OF SELLING ACCESS

In the average U.S. newspaper, advertising occupies somewhat more than 60 percent of the space. Revenue from advertising has been increasing at a rate faster than the rise in the gross national product. By 1981, the newspaper industry's revenues from advertising had risen to nearly $17.5 billion, advancing 1,508 percent since the close of the Second World War. In that same period, the GNP advanced 1,403 percent. It is a widely accepted axiom that investment in the news media is a sound business venture. Even when profits decline, the newspapers or broadcasting outlets can be sold for financial gain to the rising number of combines and conglomerates that have been increasing their influence in the field. While profit is the goal of the industry, it is always represented as a means and not as an end. The phrase "a sound financial basis" often appears as a euphemism for profit, since it seems to connote a more altruistic purpose than the acquisition of money. The American Newspaper Publishers Association sums up the stance:

> Newspapers today, as always, play a vital, indispensable role in formulating the course of our future. Newspapers inform, they report on events, they prod, they investigate, they editorialize — all in a conscientious effort to keep the people informed of what is going on and to translate happenings into meaningful, understandable terms. Newspapers serve as a watchdog of government, as a beacon in a murky world, as a marketing voice for goods and services, as a source of entertainment, as a flagger of the important and the unpredictable — and as a source of the common knowledge that fashions common interests. To do that job, newspapers must remain strong and

independently free institutions — not only by exercising their right to express diverse views freely and openly, but also by maintaining a viable economic posture.

To maintain a viable economic posture, massive infusions of money from advertisers are mandatory. Thus, the vital interests of both publishers and advertisers lie in a healthy, profitable newspaper industry — as indeed they lie in a profitable television industry. No completely accurate figures are available, but it is clear that the rate of profitability of both television and newspapers is much higher than that of industry as a whole. Some analysts say it is more than twice as high. At a conservative estimate, before-tax profits are running at more than 20 percent a year for both newspapers and television. Daily newspapers total around 1,700 in the United States, compared to only 800 television stations. Yet the advertising revenues collected by television approach those of newspapers. In 1981, newspapers accounted for 28.4 percent of all advertising revenues, while television collected 20.6 percent. The three TV networks alone received 9 percent of all advertising revenues. The radio industry followed with 6.9 percent and magazines with 5.8. According to industry estimates, the cost of a commercial on television increased 230 percent between 1970 and 1982. In 1982, the TV networks ran no fewer than 220,000 commercials, and Proctor and Gamble, the heaviest advertiser, spent $577 million on TV in 1982. All told, the 15 largest customers of TV advertising purchased nearly $3 billion in commercial messages, 14 percent more than the amount spent the previous year. Total television advertising revenue came to $12.2 billion. Though high interest rates and declining sales brought on a profound business slump, 92 of the 100 leading companies in electronic communications showed increased revenue, four-fifths of them at a rate higher than the rise in the cost-of-living index. The interests of advertisers coincide with those of the owners of the print and the broadcast media. Whatever furthers the goals and values of the system that provides profit to both is good, and whatever puts that system at risk is bad. This same simple truth underlies the structure of the commercial mass media system and ideology.

As the content of the Soviet press reflects official goals and values, so does the content of the U.S. press reflect commercial goals and values. In neither case is censorship necessary. Only in the rarest of circumstances are challenges raised to basic goals and values. Three factors contribute to the absence of challenges. First, there is the educational system under which the journalists learn to adopt those goals and values as their own. Second, the hiring process weeds out nearly all those who might be likely to raise challenges. And third, those rebels who make it through the first two screening processes are pressured into conforming, either by their colleagues or by their own wish to rise up the ladder. Desirable assignments and promotions go to those who make the minimum of waves. A few independent thinkers survive this process and are tolerated as illustrations of "the true independence" of the media. Others give up the battle and move into different professions, as statistical evidence demonstrates.

Most journalists — in the United States, the Soviet Union, and everywhere else — are true believers. If they are the products of the schools of the capitalist or socialist systems, they tend to endorse and promote the goals and values they have learned. If they are from the advancing world, they are more likely to be dissidents, free thinkers, or perhaps learned supporters of either capitalist or socialist goals and values. Journalists from the advancing world continually experience conflicts between their cultural heritage and the modern educational systems they encounter. In their puzzlement, they are often more inclined to search than merely to accept. Moreover, peer pressures in the more fluid places of work in the advancing world are less persistent than in news offices in the industrialized world. In the newer nation-states, informal and interest patterns of relationships are more prevalent than official or commercial ones.

The revolutionary period in the advancing world was marked by discovery of the fact that groups committed to overthrowing the colonial powers had a most excellent tool at hand. The press, especially in Africa, was made to serve as a great rallying force for the revolutionaries. In this, the Africans were following the model of the United States, where the pages of the colonial press were used to promote first, opposition to British rules, and later, active support for rebellion. The African revolutionaries represented a particular interest group, and the financial resources they poured into their newspapers were meant to bring specific results: the end of colonial rule and their ascent to power. Once entrenched in power, they anticipated, much as did the Peruvian revolutionaries, that a press no longer under their direct control would still continue to support their goals and values. Once these leaders ceased to be the paymasters, however, the pipers no longer played the tunes they wanted or expected. The repression that followed was inevitable.

However, another avenue beyond repression was open to them. It was a far more fruitful road to travel than repression, since journalists everywhere react with hostility to censorship, threatening official directives, and direct pressures from commercial forces. The approach to which many of the leaders of the advancing world turned was the informal one, relying on a serpentine path that was difficult to trace but enormously effective. The device was that of the hidden subsidy. Such subsidies, as we have seen, have been common throughout the history of the press. In many cases, subsidies represented the difference between profit and loss for the owners of publications. The withdrawal of special low-cost mailing privileges to magazines in the United States in the 1970s forced so many closures and mergers that the face of the magazine industry was permanently altered. Printing subsidies still represent major sources of revenue in U.S. newspapers; those that are designated to publish official notices can be assured of guaranteed advertising revenue, revenue denied those without such designations. Usually, the nature of the subsidies has been masked, like the profit-and-loss statements of the owners of news-papers.

Public-disclosure laws in the capitalist countries have forced news-paper owners to use their imaginations to cloud their statements, lumping some of their profits into other categories such as reinvestment in new equipment or, increasingly, as newspapers have expanded into other financial activities, into diversified enterprises. The leading newspapers — *The New York Times, The Washington Post, Wall Street Journal* — and the television networks as well as press chains deal not only in newspapers and broadcasting outlets but in book and magazine publishing, record companies, recordings, cable television, satellites, computer hardware and software, even in auto rentals, toys, scenic attractions, and market analysis. At one time, CBS acquired and operated the New York Yankees.

Until the period after the Second World War, most newspaper enterprises were family-owned, and publishers steadfastly refused to provide any information about their profitability, holding that the public was not interested — even, it might be added, as they were demanding public disclosure of the financial activities of the government and other corporations. With the decline of competition and the growth of chain ownership, a number of newspapers went public and began offering shares on the stock exchanges. The figures are remarkable. They show that the work force employed in the newspaper industry, 432,000, is the highest among manufacturing industries in the United States. They show also that by 1981, the circulation of the newspapers owned by the six leading chains totaled 18 million, or 30 percent of the total daily circulation in the country. The Hutchins Commission expressed concern about the concen-tration of press ownership as early as 1947. By 1981, no fewer than 160 chains were active in the newspaper industry. All told, three of five daily newspapers were owned by conglomerates, four of five television stations, and more than a third of radio stations. Several among the chains had already entrenched themselves as leaders of the U.S. press. In 1981, the Gannett chain, the largest in the field, owned eighty-five daily newspapers, twenty-two weeklies, seven television stations, and thirteen radio prop-erties, as well as the Lou Harris polling organization, satellites, and motion-picture production units. In late 1982, Gannett launched its most ambitious project, a national daily newspaper called *USA Today*, whose front page was distributed by satellite transmission from Washington to fifteen printing plants across the country. In the year that ended September 30, 1981, Gannett's net earnings came to over $165 billion, an increase of nearly 14 percent over the previous year. The mere existence of chains and conglomerates does not necessarily mean a decline in diversity of opinion.

All along, the news media have tended to support the basic values of the political and economic system and reflected the ideology of the paymasters.

No one can know exactly how profitable newspapers are, and it is certainly true that the newspaper industry in the United States has been shrinking, at least in terms of competition in the great cities. But those newspapers that survive are doing very well indeed. E. F. Hutton, the market analyst, offers newspapers as one of the most lucrative investment opportunities available. To compare the newspaper industry with U.S. industry as a whole is instructive. In the five-year period 1977–1981, where industrial profitability is indexed at 100, the profitability of newspapers (after taxes) stands at 167. In 1981, the Dow Jones Company, which publishes *The Wall Street Journal*, earned a 29.1 percent net return on equity, highest in the industry. Gannett was next with 21.5 percent, and *The New York Times* third with 18.1 percent. The newspaper industry as a whole earned a net return on equity of 18.8 percent — at a time when the United States was experiencing a deep recession.

The chief reason that newspapers remain an excellent investment opportunity, according to E. F. Hutton, is because they sell access: "Advertisers buy access to potential purchasers of their products, providing newspapers with 70 to 80 percent of their revenues." At the same time, according to the market analyst, "readers pay for access to news, information, advertising, and entertainment arranged in a convenient, predictable, and cheap package." In the consumer capitalist society, no new purveyors of access have been arriving, Hutton reminds us, thus permitting advertising rates to rise steadily for both newspapers and broadcasters; they have rendered themselves even more attractive by becoming diversified communications complexes. After a careful study of the newspaper industry, Hutton offers a portrait of a typical U.S. newspaper with a circulation of 75,000. Its total revenues come to $19 million, and of that figure, $14.8 million, or 78 percent, derives from advertising. Only $4 million, or 21 percent, comes from circulation. The costs of the paper's news operations is only $2 million, or 11 percent of its total expenditures. Operating profits come to $4.5 million, or 24 percent of operating margin. It was assumed that this typical paper operated in a strong local economy and was well managed. It also had no local newspaper competition. The primary reason for the failure of those newspapers that have not ridden with the trend of profitability has rested in what Hutton describes as the growing sophistication of advertisers, who recognize it is not in their interests to print their commercial messages in two competing newspapers. In Washington, where the afternoon *Star* went out of business in 1981, it was selling more than 335,000 copies a day. Advertisers simply were not willing to underwrite the *Star* as well as the morning *Post* to gain access to the same pool of customers.

The direct relationship between advertising and the viability of newspapers that marks the press scene in the United States is not the usual pattern in the advancing world. There, the usual pattern of relationships between the piper and his paymaster is often informal; families and friends play an important part. Only those persons with substantial resources have been able to purchase controlling or total interest in newspapers, and those persons have inevitably had powerful friends or relatives in high positions in government. Even with initial capital, these owners have continued to need some form of subsidy to remain afloat, and they have naturally turned to their friends and relatives for help. The scenario frequently runs somewhat as follows:

The brother-in-law of Publisher A in a certain North African country held sway in the capital as finance minister. Since newsprint allotments were fixed by the finance ministry, the brother-in-law could count on regular shipments so long as his relative remained in power. Thus, it was no surprise that his newspaper served as an unofficial spokesman for the government and its financial interests. The content of his paper reflected the goals and values of the government. The position of power over information held by the government in this situation was unassailable. Not only was it able to ensure favorable news reports in the brother-in-law's paper, but it could bring other owners either into line or into bankruptcy by assigning or withholding shipments of newsprint. None of these transactions was reduced to writing, so there was no way to check up. It was possible that the head of government himself was not aware of the newsprint arrangements, and the finance minister, if he himself sought power, could use his control of newsprint as a device to help him gain public support for a bid to overthrow the head of government. Informal arrangements exist in all nations, always operating to the end of ensuring that the content of newspapers and broadcasting outlets does not stray far beyond the boundaries acceptable to those of the paymasters. This truth does not reflect on the integrity of the overwhelming majority of pipers; it needs to be clearly held in mind that the interests of the pipers and those of their paymasters are generally in harmony, so that pressure rarely needs to be applied.

Despite the high profitability of newspapers in the United States and among some of her allies, it is growing increasingly difficult in most places to operate newspapers without government subsidies. For a number of years, Sweden has provided direct government support to its press. In other capitalist countries, the support is less direct. In Africa, subventions are mandatory if a newspaper is to survive. In relatively prosperous Nigeria, it is estimated that it costs nearly twenty *kobo* (about fifty-five U.S. cents) to publish each copy of *The Daily Times* of Lagos, the country's most efficient newspaper. In order merely to break even, the paper requires a subsidy of nearly five *kobo* (fourteen cents) per copy. The other Nigerian papers need far greater subsidies, perhaps as much as two *naira* (a little over five dollars a copy). Press freedom exists officially in Nigeria, but as Segun Osoba, general manager of *The Sketch* in Ibadan, comments: "Once you ask for subventions, you are controlled." *The Sketch* was operating at the beginning of the 1980s without subsidies but was steadily losing money and had to go to interest groups for support. To provide sound information to Nigeria's millions, Osoba says, the country needs another forty newspapers, but "anyone would be crazy to start a paper today." One might amend that remark by adding, "unless one could be assured of adequate subsidies." For not only was the cost of salaries increasing, but the cost of raw materials, ink, and newsprint doubled in the decade of the 1970s.

THE UNEASY WORLD OF THE "INFORMATION SOCIETY"

The image of the press as piper is a perfectly natural one. It occurred to Johann Amos Komenský, a Moravian churchman and educator, as early as the first years of the seventeenth century, only a short time after newspapers made their appearance in Europe. Komenský, or Comenius as he called himself, was one of the most distinguished writers of his era, although his work has received only limited attention outside Eastern Europe and Western educational circles. In 1956, UNESCO, recognizing the internationalism in Comenius's vision, decided to publish a volume of excerpts of his work and commissioned Jean Piaget, the Swiss educator, to write a preface for the book. Complete translations of Comenius's writings are rare. His *Labyrinth of the World*, for instance, is best known in English in a translation by Count Lützow, published in London in 1901. The *Labyrinth* appeared in 1623 when Comenius, a thirty-one-year-old schoolmaster and Protestant pastor, had been dismissed from office and sent into exile by Counter-Reformation Roman Catholic forces. Despairing, Comenius cast his eyes at all forms of occupation and found them wanting. The *Labyrinth* bears some resemblance to Bunyan's *Pilgrim's Progress*, and indeed Comenius sends his Pilgrim into the world to study workers and their behavior. Chapter 22 finds the Pilgrim in the company of journalists. Count Lützow, recognizing how primitive was the state of journalism at the time, used the word newsmen, but Hudec, dean of the journalism school at the University of Prague, speaks of the workers as journalists. Hudec employs the English word piper as translation of Comenius's term; Count Lützow seemed unsettled as to whether the key word should be piper or whistler, but the effect is the same.

In whatever case, the Pilgrim finds the journalists in the marketplace of a city and notices them busying themselves with "strange whistles," which they pipe into the ears of bystanders. When the piping is pleasing, the audience rejoices, and when it is doleful, they are sad. The whistles played by the pipers are purchased from individuals Comenius identifies simply as vendors; he does not tell us anything about the nature of the vendors, but from our vantage point, three and a half centuries later, we can identify them as paymasters. Comenius is intrigued by the fact that those who hear the piper can be exulted by the sound or plunged into terrible grief, as "men allowed themselves to be deceived by every gust of wind." The seventeenth-century Czech writer perceives with rare pre-science an important fact of life in the universe of the press. To be a journalist is risky business. From all sides, the Pilgrim observes, the journalists find accusations falling on their shoulder, especially from those who have not listened carefully to what was being piped around them. "I see here...that it was not safe for all to use these whistles. For as these sounds appeared different to different ears, disputes and scuffles arose," the Pilgrim concludes, and the victims of these scuffles are most likely to be the journalists themselves. Many writers, Shakespeare among them, have called attention to the danger that lies in being the bearer of unwelcome news. It is a situation that distressed MacBride as well.

The tolerance of the paymaster for behavior he considers unsuitable is inevitably limited, as was that of Sir Sampson Legend, who introduced the piper-paying metaphor into the English language in Congreve's *Love for Love*. Sir Sampson announces that as a father he possesses both authority and arbitrary power, and that he will cut off his son without money in retaliation for his lack of subservience to his wishes and his offensive behavior. "I warrant you," he says, "if he dance'd till Doomsday, he thought I was to pay the Piper." That, in 1695, was the promise of an early paymaster. The threat of punishment for offenses has not been modified over the past three hundred years. Such is the case despite the fact that the faces of both piper and paymaster have changed drastically in that time frame. Few pipers work for a single paymaster any longer. Among journalists, the employer today is likely to be a syndicate or a conglomerate.

The word revolution is an overworked word, so much so that it may well have lost useful meaning. In any case, it rarely carries the image of anything so soul-wrenching and bloody as the French upheaval in the dying days of the eighteenth century or anything so shattering as the Russian uprising of 1917. Few current uses of the word would be permissible under T. S. Eliot's definition of a revolution as to murder and to create. In seeking to find a name for the scientific and technological breakthroughs associated with the development and impact of computer technology, writers have discovered a plethora of revolutions. Among the "key innovation technologies" of modern society are such phenomena as microelectronics, computer graphics, speech synthesis and voice recogni-tion, data-base management, data encryption, satellite television, artificial intelligence, and other ramifications of the computer revolution, which is sometimes characterized as the telecommunications revolution or the informatics revolution. We have arrived in the realm of the information society.

It is tempting to poke fun at the excesses of enthusiasm or despair with which these developments are viewed; certainly, the prophets of heaven and hell have multiplied in number with the increase of computers and microminiaturization devices. The significant questions for us here relate to the impact of modern technology on the press, on how the news media are to be financed as the pace of computerization continues, and on how the content and form of the media may change. No one can doubt that the form of the news media is already changing; newspapers may now be delivered to homes electronically. Britain has pioneered a "teletext" system under which the audience may select what it wishes to read by punching a series of buttons on their home computers. Other systems for delivering both news and advertising are being developed, for use not only in industrialized countries but in the advancing world as well. The costs of developing and marketing these systems are immense, so much so that only the wealthiest and most powerful international combines are capable of competing. J. N. Pelton, one of the top officials of INTELSAT, the International Telecommunications Satellite Organization, predicts that U.S. firms alone will invest well over a trillion dollars within the next ten or fifteen years in computer and telecommunications technologies and equipment. Britain, France, West Germany, Japan, and the Soviet Union will be pouring in additional trillions. Few among these firms operate entirely within national boundaries any longer. There has arisen a new paymaster whose power is increasing in the field of information — the transnational corporation. Only governments with wholly planned economies, such as the Soviet Union, seek to compete with the transnationals.

Our perception of transnationals inevitably colors our attitudes about their impact on the content of news and the transmission of news and advertising around the world. To some, the transnationals are cold, inhuman instruments for maximizing profits; to others, they are agencies for promoting international accord by cutting through national pride and prejudice. Both roles are possible for the transnationals. How they will affect humankind is still to be determined. That they are present and will grow in power and influence is certain. Already, a multitude of international organizations has emerged to study and to modify — if not to regulate — their power and influence.

The one overriding reality of the rapid growth of computer and miniaturization technology has been the emergence of an information industry. Among the leaders in that industry are those corporations that produce both the hardware and the software of news, among them American Telephone and Telegraph Company, International Business Machines, Xerox, Rockwell International, Westinghouse, Zenith, Radio

Corporation of America, and the Columbia Broadcasting System, all associated both financially and ideologically with the great broadcasting, newspaper, and wire service industries of the United States. In short, in the "information society," the power and influence of those who pay the bills for the news media industry has been markedly enhanced. The economic stake of the paymasters is markedly increasing also. Among the complaints of the advancing world has been that the dominant news media — the news agencies, the television networks, and the handful of newspapers that make up the international press, chief among them *The New York Times* and *The Wall Street Journal* — have not only practiced cultural imperialism but have also increased the flow of distortion and prejudice through the international news system. The advancing nations argue further that the aim of these practices has been to provide additional markets for the products of the information transnationals and their fellow producers, and thus to increase their profits at the expense of the advancing world. The journalists, in this image, have been portrayed as willing or unwilling tools in carrying out these objectives.

The German sociologist Ferdinand Tönnies appears to have been somewhat clairvoyant in foreseeing the growth of an international information society. Writing in 1922, he argued in effect that he who controls the press controls the world — or at the very least controls public opinion around the world. Like a number of U.S. sociologists of his era, Tönnies feared that where newspapers were wholly in the hands of capitalists, the public's interests would largely be ignored. In more optimistic vein, however, he predicted that the press would ultimately emerge as a liberalizing force. This was so, he wrote, because the press is so international in character that "its ultimate aim [is] to abolish the multiplicity of states and substitute for it a single world market." Tönnies's world market was to be ruled by "thinkers, scholars and writers and could dispense with means of coercion other than those of a psychological nature." The press might well be the instrument to lead the world away from a tightly knit xenophobic set of communities and towards a global society without boundaries. Power in such a social order would be global, rather than parochial or merely national. To Tönnies, the press was an instrument of public opinion, and public opinion was a kind of faith, religious in character and generally intolerant of anyone else's moral precepts. Only a press that was financed by circulation alone, that was free of advertising and not in the control of paymasters of any kind, could be expected to be free of propaganda and psychological pressures. Transnational control of the press would, in this view, be something for the entire world to fear.

News media account for only a small portion of the information disseminated around the world. Data bases — the jargon term for the information stored in the memory banks of computers — provide an unlimited volume of intelligence on any subject imaginable. The data bases may contain stored historical accounts or mathematical formulas; they may contain industrial secrets or personnel records of men and women; they may contain census information or military secrets. And computers are capable of passing this information to each other in optical twinklings. This information may be kept secret, it may be shared with colleagues, or it may be presented to the public directly. Rarely do transnationals share information with the news media, but they are very much concerned about what is written in newspapers and magazines and what is broadcast on radio and television. For the directors and financial backers of the transnationals are well aware of the fact that the only forces with the potential to limit their freedom of operation are national governments. The leaders of those governments pay heed to the news media. Hence, management of the content of the news media is a matter of vital interest both to the transnationals and to national governments. International organizations and agencies play an important part in this pattern of relationships as well, since even though international organizations possess no troops, they are in a position to generate a great deal of publicity and thus to influence both the transnationals and the national governments.

In this game of jockeying for position, the press is pivotal. Management of the ideological content of the news media becomes more important as the financial stakes increase and the numbers of paymasters shrink. Conglomerates and group owners are replacing single owners and families as the owners of the news media, even as transnational corporations wrest financial power from the families and partners who once controlled the wealth of capitalist countries. Maintenance of the status quo and of a peaceful social order has always been important for the owners of the press and for the commercial enterprises whose advertising financed those owners. For the faceless managers of the transnationals, maintenance of the social order is even more critical. Their interests can no longer tolerate strife between capitalist countries; their patterns of competition are with each other and not with the financial interests of like-believing nations. It is no longer in the interests of General Motors and Toyota to compete with one another; their concern is with the survival of a viable automobile industry. As Tönnies foresaw, the demands of a global market require an international press that preaches the kind of social order in which transnationals may flourish.

The press of the capitalist world itself is growing ever more international in character. Press groups already include in their chains newspapers in different countries. The great news agencies have already become global entities with subsidiary units in many parts of the world. Television no longer operates within single countries; simulcasts in a multitude of languages are increasing steadily. It can be seen that in a world of shrinking power and growing concentration, the interests of advertisers, press owners, and individual journalists are growing closer to those of one another. The links between the news media and the telecommunications and information industries are evident to all. Students of the press in both the advancing and the capitalist worlds who fear the power of concentrated technological and industrial power regularly call attention to these links and demand some measure of international regulation. The discussions inside UNESCO must be viewed in this light as well; it is not only cultural imperialism that is feared, but also mind control and the kind of psychological pressures for conformity envisaged by Tönnies two generations ago and by present-day scholars such as Herbert Schiller, Jeremy Tunstall, Cees Hamelink, and Kaarle Nordenstreng.

Schiller worries over the fact that technological advances now make it possible for direct transmission, via satellites, of U.S. television programs; thus, he says, there is good reason for there to be "traumatic anxiety in international communication-cultural circles." For, he says, the United States has incurred the animosity of the rest of the world "as the foremost source of global communications pollution." Criticism of this kind has dominated international discussions of communications and information for a score of years. The most vitriolic language uttered at UNESCO and other international forums has been directed at U.S. television programming.

The concern of the communications transnationals that such criticism may lead to the enactment of laws limiting their freedom of mobility is real and urgent. As early as 1972, the president of CBS was speaking out in impassioned language against proposals of UNESCO and other international bodies for the adoption of international agreements to authorize satellite transmissions across borders. In an article entitled "Will They Stop Our Satellites?", Frank Stanton wrote that to require such agreements was to violate the U.S. Constitution and to interfere with "the basic principle of free movement of ideas." In recent years, the interest of transnationals has no longer been merely with transmission of entertainment programs, but increasingly with transmissions between computers. As Business International said to its clients in a 1982 publication: "At stake is the flow of vital personnel information, financial reporting, technical specification changes, and other data that is centrally stored and constantly updated via computer hookups. Interruption of such information could be extremely damaging."

That transnational research and promotion company said that some governments putting up barriers against "the free and timely flow of data" were doing so out of genuine concern for safeguarding privacy, but that in other advancing countries, some leaders were "bent on protecting nascent, sensitive local industry in the computer hardware and software fields," obviously an unacceptable form of behavior for the transnationals. The move to regulate the flow of data in certain countries is obviously a major threat to the profitability of the transnationals.

Anthony Smith suggests that the efforts to control transborder data flow are likely to fail because of the logistical difficulties. In fact, he says, it may very well be that the nation as we know it is itself doomed, at least those without the technological know-how to maintain autonomy over the flow of information across their borders. Censorship becomes impossible if information can be freely sent from computer to computer across borders. As Smith observes: "There is no longer such a thing as national autonomy without control over data flow and informatics." What is at stake, Smith observes perceptively, is nationhood itself.

On the other hand, some U.S. officials express fear that pressure for a new international information order will lead instead to a nationalization of information. Industrial groups have been organized in the United States to exert pressure to prevent any restrictions on the flow of data. One leading official, B. C. Burgess, director of telecommunications regulatory policy for the Bank of America, said: "It's simple. If we can't move information, we go out of business." Nevertheless, some countries, led by Sweden in 1973, have adopted comprehensive laws designed to protect the flow of data. West Germany, France, Denmark, and Austria followed with similar laws, and many others are pending. In Europe, the fear has often been expressed that U.S.-based transnationals could, unless data flow is restricted, impose severe controls on their foreign subsidiaries. Louis Joinet, secretary general of the French commission on data processing and liberties, made the point succinctly: "Information is power, and economic information is economic power." An article in *The Wall Street Journal* in late summer 1981 presented a thorough view of the efforts by the transnationals to counter the growing concern around the world about the power of U.S.-based companies to control the flow of data; the article demonstrates the range of critical and challenging commentaries the press may present in a pluralist society. Despite the fact that the *Journal* is owned by the Dow Jones Company, a transnational in its own right, much of the material in the article is sharply critical of what it identifies as the U.S. giants. But "both sides" are carefully presented, and the orthodox view that free exchange of information represents ideological virtue emerges also, especially in the reports of hostility to proposals for imposing taxes on information in the same manner as they are applied to tangible imports and exports. The presentation of "both sides" is not likely to upset the social order, for orthodoxy is always assured a powerful voice.

The enigma in the international flow of information involves informatics, a term that emerged in 1974 when the United Nations General Assembly established the Intergovernmental Bureau for Informatics with headquarters in Rome. In less than a decade, IBI became one of the most active and potentially important of international organizations. IBI identifies informatics as being to the computer what astronomy is to the telescope. It is, in short, the discipline that deals with all aspects of the capture and processing of information, including both computer hardware and software; its objective is to create efficient mechanisms for the management of information. In the role it casts for itself, IBI is frankly on the side of the advancing countries, seeking ways to help them to modernize and to induce the industrialized world to correct the imbalance between it and the advancing world in terms of the capacity to use information. In fact, IBI actively campaigns for "worldwide action to introduce informatics into underdeveloped countries." If this kind of sharing does not take place, the result, IBI says, will be chaos. IBI is by no means satisfied with the modest efforts by the industrialized world to provide technical and financial assistance, as in the IPDC.

While the leaders of the IPDC Council proclaim their ideological purity and have agreed to avoid ideological discussions, IBI officials mince no words. They see the world in crisis and hold that international peace and harmony are threatened unless major strides are taken to reduce the inequality in the world. IBI has organized well-attended international conferences on information strategies and policies (called SPIN) and has demanded international controls to protect the advancing world against unauthorized transmission of data across its frontiers. More conferences are planned for the second half of the 1980s, a decade that IBI has characterized as the crucial one in narrowing the informatics gap between the industrialized and advancing worlds.

Not only the advancing countries have seen urgency in the field of informatics; the Scandinavian countries, Japan, and France have been especially outspoken in this campaign. The French have opened a world center that its founder, journalist Jean-Jacques Servan-Schreiber, says would work to place informatics at "the service of human resource development." Japan has announced plans to open a second such center. The date of the opening of the center by French President François Mitterand is significant. The month of November 1981 marked the one-hundredth anniversary of the International Electricity Exhibition in Paris, an occasion that provided a major impetus for the development of electricity in the twentieth century. Mitterand told a distinguished gathering of scientists and other experts that humankind faced this choice: to develop informatics as "nothing but another attack on individuals, the source of insecurity and of unemployment, of inequality and oppression," or as a mechanism to "transform the very nature of work, create jobs, foster decentralization, [and] the democratization of our institutions." Culturally, informatics could lead either to a monstrous alienation of mankind or to a new universality, to enslaving or to liberating men and women. He described the stakes as high:

> Those nations who are best able, within the context of their history and in the spirit of their institutions, to bring about this synthesis of culture and science,

will thus have the best chance of overcoming the difficulties of the present day and age. Consequently, it is essential for every nation to become a hub of development and of the social usage of these new techniques. This will not come about without will or without action — by chance, as it were. The laws of the market will not suffice to achieve this evolution in a harmonious way. To achieve this, it will be necessary to think, to organize and to foresee the necessary changes.

Responding to Mitterand, Kristen Nygaard, director of the Oslo Information Institute, expressed a sobering fear of the development of informatics up to then. "Thousands of millions," he said, "are being swallowed up in the world by aims which are those of big private enterprises and of them alone." Nygaard said he hoped that the establishment of the center in Paris would contribute to placing the new science of informatics "at the disposal of individual happiness." Seymour Papert, professor of the Department of Informatics at the Massachusetts Institute of Technology, applauded the establishment of the center and expressed the hope that it could become "the cradle of a new development based upon man's individual fulfillments, the cradle of social growth."

Those who spoke at the opening of the center in Paris, including communications scholars such as Schiller, are mainly concerned with the information that emanates from data bases and not with the news that passes through the conventional channels of the press. Often from a Marxist viewpoint, they deplore the control of telecommunications technology by the transnationals, the most powerful of which have their headquarters in the United States. They fear the marketing skills of the transnationals as well and point to the vast profits available to the transnationals able to sell their computer hardware to advancing countries. Through control of replacement parts and the software needed for operation of the machines, the transnationals have the capability of assuring that the technical gear is used only in pursuit of their ideological goals, chiefly the maintenance of the capitalist system and the largest possible volume of laissez faire outside the direction of government, national, regional, or international. To the extent that they ignore the content of the news media, these experts are failing to recognize the key role played by news, which is the crucial connecting medium in the survival of the capitalist social and economic order. At the same time, those students of mass culture who concentrate their research on the influence of the trivial fare disseminated by television programmers are equally overlooking the importance of the news reported by the broadcast and print media. Certainly, programs such as "Dallas" and "Three's Company" provide an exotic if erroneous portrait of U.S. society and are likely to stimulate unrealistic material aspirations, but they are on the whole less meaningful in spreading U.S. goals and values than is the content of the news broadcasts of the television networks that are transmitted around the world by the news-film distribution giants, Visnews and UPITN.

There is much that is persuasive in the argument of those who defend the growth of telecommunications transnationals that their interests are closer to those of humankind everywhere than were those of national and nationalistic companies, many of which profited from the production and sale of weapons. Indeed, wars and international violence are anathema to them. Their profits can be maximized only in a state of international harmony, where the chief values of individuals are consumption and the good life. However, the area of cooperation is limited largely to those societies that are already heavily industrialized and share the goals and values of the transnationals. Development of computer systems and telecommunications technology is of no less importance in the Marxist world than in capitalist society. In some areas of telemetry, the Soviet Union may rank as the world leader; certainly, Soviet work in space technology is illustrative of the value and importance placed by Marxist leaders on achieving at least parity with the capitalist world in the information society. Thus, the thrust of discussions in international settings is tending more and more to link the interests of the Marxist and market nation-states in a contest against those of the advancing world, in the shortcut terminology of North vs. South.

THE CHOICE: GOSSIP OR ANALYSIS

It is not the purpose of this book to predict the future. It is, rather, to call attention to the past and the present and to raise questions about the future. The subject is news, how news is perceived in all parts of the world. We suggest that the content of the news reflects the ideology of those who finance the press and argue that this relationship will continue, no matter what form or forms the news media may take in the next century. This is not meant to be a prediction; rather, it is a statement about the nature of news.

In this connection, it is well to keep in mind that reporters and editors have never ceased to buck the system. Dissent is permitted and, in some circumstances, even encouraged, just so long as it does not go beyond the perimeters of acceptable ideology. In the capitalist world in particular, dissent and social protest have long been acceptable behavior — provided, again, that no one goes too far, so as to threaten what is perceived to be in the vital interests of the paymasters. It is even acceptable for one organ of the press to attack another as a puppet of power. In France, for instance, *Le Monde* has for years accused *Le Figaro* and other rightist newspapers of serving as mouthpieces for industry and commerce. In West Germany, the *Frankfurter Rundschau* deposes in the same manner about *Die Welt*. And of course, the compliment is returned. In Britain and the United States and even in the Soviet Union, criticism in the press is regularly directed against corruption, mistakes in judgment, heartlessness, and inefficiency. Reporters for the major dailies and the television networks seek out these deficiencies in public and private behavior as a matter of course. Nothing gratifies the individual journalist more than a successful challenge to power, even as Don Quixote rejoiced in tilting at windmills. There is built into journalism the *possibility* of inducing change and of helping to create a world that is more just and more peaceful; it is this possibility that has fired and continues to fire the imagination of journalists everywhere on earth. Political and especially economic reality, however, severely circumscribes these possibilities. And to make sure of a substantial measure of satisfaction among journalists, it is almost always necessary for power to permit a limited volume of success to its critics. There is evidence that achievement of these successes is growing less likely, for in much of the press the volume of news about major public issues and substantive public questions is lessening.

What has been occurring slowly, so slowly that it has attracted little attention, is that the press, especially in the capitalist and Marxist nation-states, has been losing its character as an instrument of substantive information. The decline of competition in the newspaper industry has been widely noted and universally deplored. In fewer than 5 percent of U.S. cities are there daily newspapers in direct competition with one another. Television stations add another dimension to the competition, but competition in terms of news reporting between newspapers and television is more illusory than real. Few individuals acquire television sets for the purpose of watching reports of the news, and many individuals buy newspapers primarily for reasons other than to read the news. The quickest and cheapest instrument for learning the news remains the radio. Home computers may soon replace the radio in this role, but they are not likely for a long time to come — if ever — to perform the same function as newspapers and television news reports.

What are those functions? Why do people watch television? Why do they read newspapers? Many studies have been conducted on this question. They demonstrate, not surprisingly, that people expend time, money, and energy in order to satisfy their own desires, or needs. And news clearly represents only a small portion of those needs. If not, the content of newspapers and television programming would be far more heavily devoted to news than it is. The greatest share of the content is, of course, advertising. Beyond that, the words and pictures of newspapers and television address themselves to a wide variety of information, not much of it news as it is usually conceived. On television, there are "programs," fictive, of course; watching television is rather like reading an illustrated novel. In newspapers, the fare is more diverse: comic strips; sports pages; recipes; columns on gardening, health, and bridge, among other things;

advice to the lovelorn and to the stamp collector; stock market citations and the Dow-Jones Index. None of this is news as far as the news industry is concerned. All of this material is more than acceptable to the paymasters, since it tends to sell apples and leave the apple cart right side up.

As the audience for television has increased and as individual ownership of newspapers has declined, the content of newspapers and of magazines has shifted. Readers have been given more information about "people" and about "celebrities" than about events of great political, economic, or social significance. As a substitute for news, the press has been increasing its reportage of gossip. And gossip is no more likely to upset apple carts than are commercial notices about undergarments or horoscope columns.

In the past in Western Europe, newspapers tended to serve as open party organs or at least as apologists for particular political movements, but this pattern has been changing. Newspapers, especially those outside the capital cities, have been turning their attention increasingly to problems of local and regional interest, and as a result have been attracting more advertising as well as readership. The greatest circulations in Europe by far are enjoyed by the boulevard press, such as West Germany's *Bild Zeitung*, the flagship publication of the Springer press empire. Like its fellow papers in Britain, France, Italy, and elsewhere, it makes no pretense of reporting news. Instead, these papers, like *The National Enquirer* in the United States, publish large doses of reports about the private lives of celebrities and about exotic crimes. That little of what appears in these periodicals is accurate seems not to disturb the readers. Indeed, it is stretching the word to its outer limits to describe these publications as newspapers. The traditional press has noticed that the number of such publications is increasing and that their circulations remain high. Significantly, the traditional press has been copying their success story.

Just as the traditional press co-opted the underground press movement in the United States, it is seeking to co-opt the boulevard press. Characteristically, the Luce publications jumped on the boulevard bandwagon early and achieved success, both in terms of advertising and circulation, in its magazine *People*. Newspapers, among them even *The New York Times*, began publishing special sections on celebrities. Gossip, which had always been a factor in the news, has now become perhaps its most valuable staple. This development is particularly cheering to those in power, who fear the possibility of disaffection among their pipers in the press. News media that devote large amounts of their precious space to gossip and trivia are less likely to pursue challenges to power than those with large newsholes.

There is another side to these developments. Confronted, through the rise of radio and television, with the recognition that they no longer have the capability to present information most quickly, newspapers in the

United States have undertaken a role somewhat different from the one they had traditionally played. They began to produce longer stories, concerning themselves less with being first, less with timeliness, and began more in-depth treatment of complex issues. In short, they began to set aside their long-held admiration for the code of objectivity and to produce analytical and interpretive reports, often at considerable length. In this, they were following a practice long pursued by the leading European newspapers; moreover, they were responding to complaints issued by the underground press and the new journalists. Such an approach represented the precise opposite to that taken by the boulevard press and posed a substantial threat to power. The bitter attacks on the press by the Nixon administration and other admirers of the status quo have continued without cease. This development can be explained to a large degree by the shift in emphasis on the part of certain newspapers, and by the television networks, having learned that an occasional exposé or hard-hitting documentary can produce a high level of interest among the powerful.

Still, this kind of reporting represents but a small portion of the content of even those newspapers and broadcasting outlets that engage in analytical journalism. And the smaller, provincial press, both print and broadcast, is content to rake in the profits without spreading the muck. Censorship is not required. Self-censorship is adequate to do the job. And, as we have seen, hiring practices as well as pressures from colleagues and ambition join together in ensuring that the bulk of the U.S. news media pushes the apple cart along its appointed highway.

In an anthologized article on the future of the press in a computerized world, Jon Udell sees little danger of the death of the traditional newspaper. In fact, he foresees advertisers turning to newspapers with even greater enthusiasm as technological developments permit the daily paper to become "a more sophisticated and widely used advertising medium." By splitting their printing runs, they may reach different commercial targets for different advertisers, thus increasing the efficiency of the commercial messages. Many additional innovations are possible and are already being used, enhancing the economic viability of newspapers. The newspaper of the future, Udell says, will be able to deliver more news more quickly. Of this there is no doubt. What is uncertain is what kind of news will be delivered more quickly. It might be profound analytical articles. Or it might be gossip about celebrities. Or it might be advertising. Among a group surveyed by the American Newspaper Publishers Association in 1980, two-thirds said they wanted more newspaper advertising. "Ads of interest" ranked second among a list of thirty-four kinds of newspaper information possible.

The scholars and industry leaders who participated in a symposium on telecommunications in the year 2000 held at Rutgers University in 1981 agreed that it was unlikely the "old media" would wither and die. Rather, they concluded, the media were presented with an opportunity to change directions in such a way as "to benefit the world information need and not the world information power." To move in this direction would require a change in emphasis on profits and a dedication to cooperate with those struggling to achieve information equality. Kenneth Edwards completed a thorough examination of the growth of electronic news-delivery systems with an equally sober assessment:

> There is no question that teletext will become international, with multilanguage transmission over much of Western Europe. Some of its enthusiasts believe it offers new opportunities for international cooperation through vastly improved communication. They see it as a medium promoting understanding and peace.

Such, of course, was the vision of the report of the MacBride Commission. This vision is also a basic element in the press ideology of the advancing world. Perhaps it could also be detected in the ideologies of the market and Marxist worlds if one's eyes were but strong enough to see it. Sadly, only Supereyes, with his X-ray sight, can penetrate the dark, menacing clouds that obscure the vision. In those clouds lurk conflict and confrontation, and not far off in the distance one can hear the ominous thunder of martial music. The music salutes the quest either for the maximization of profit or for the bearing of witness to historical destiny. And it is those who lead the parades who are the paymasters of the press. While Lenin's answer may have been exposed as inadequate and threatening, his question remains — to trouble us as it did the world at the turn of the twentieth century: What is to be done?

PART 4

The symphony of the press. (*Mary Miller*)

Eleven

The Symphony of the Press: A Classification System

The roles assigned to the press can be compared to the movements of a global symphony, with their many themes, melodies, and variations. One perhaps surprising truth that emerges from an examination of the news media in all societies and all countries is that their similarities are often as great as their differences. In a quite real sense, we can speak of the news media of the world as a single unit, as a symphony is a single unit but one composed of a variety of themes and melodies. A symphony does not have to be harmonious. In fact, it can be anything but — filled with dissonance and discordant notes. We might be tempted to speak not of a symphony of the press but of a cacophony of the press. Still, with all the dissonance and discord, there is a fundamental unity. Like a Wagnerian opera, a leitmotiv runs through the structures and the ideologies of the news media of the world. The unifying element is agreement on the role of the media as educator.

In this symphony of the press, we can identify three movements, each containing a basic theme, but also numerous variations on that basic theme. A number of possible names can be given to these movements, and since the names given to things inevitably shape our perceptions of them, it is crucial that we approach the names with a great deal of caution. We might, for instance, simply give them numerical identity — as first, second, and third. There is some comfort and familiarity in the numerical identification. After all, the three movements do parallel the political designations of First, Second, and Third Worlds. Or, we might use economic identifications, substituting market for First, Marxist for Second, and developing for Third. Or we might apply geographical names, Western, Eastern, and Southern. Our difficulties clearly increase if we attempt to impose value-laden terms on any of the three movements. Words such as democratic or libertarian or communist or authoritarian hinder understanding. Even socialist is a troublesome term; after all, it has been used to stand for the monstrous regime of the Third Reich. So, in fact, is revolutionary, a term that can be used to stand for what is good or what is evil. In the classification scheme outlined in these pages, I have chosen to use somewhat modified economic identifications by substituting advancing for developing. This terminology is used in the full realization that it possesses the fragility of all nomenclature. One may, however, compensate for this fragility by recognizing the richness of the many melody variations in each movement. It needs to be kept in mind also that although the names of the movements reflect economic philosophies, the themes do not by any means limit themselves to matters of economics. Each movement embraces all the realities of the environments in which the press exists, historical, political, social, cultural, and — importantly — psychological. With all these qualifications in mind, let us identify the movements of the symphony of the press as market, Marxist, and advancing.

In each of the three movements, the press is assigned a central role in the social order: to educate the people so that they can carry out their own individual roles in society. But the ends of education are far from identical in the three movements. In the market movement, the education of the people is designed to help them vote wisely, so that the social order will be safeguarded. In the United States, there is some uneasiness over describing the press as a source of education; the preferred word is information. But this seems to be mere quibbling, since information is of little use unless it increases the level of education of the audience. Aside from the United States, the capitalist countries seem little inclined to draw distinctions between information and education. U.S. hostility to an educational function is probably the result of unwillingness to be associated with anything that might smell of propaganda, for it is the Soviet union that is said to be using the press for the purposes of propaganda.

Indeed, in the Marxist movement, the press is frankly given the role of instrument of propaganda. Again, there is an element of quibbling over words here, for the theme of the chief Marxist melody is that the education of the people is to help them behave wisely, so that the social order will be safeguarded. The three roles Lenin assigned to the press are in essence all educative, just as Marx's image of the press was as an instrument that went beyond the Prussian censors to educate the people to an awareness of reality.

Of the three movements, the third is the most open and direct about the press as an instrument of education. The model of the press throughout the advancing world is as an instrument both to help safeguard the social order and to educate the people to change that social order, where necessary. In fact, it is at this point that the third movement brings a decisive change in the pace of the symphony. For while education in the first and second movements has an essentially static character, that is, of preserving a form of the status quo, in the third movement its character is dynamic, dedicated to change. Nevertheless, the motif of the press as an instrument of education unifies the symphony. The least sophisticated of observers can recognize this fundamental unity, although this recognition is all too often concealed from those blinded by ideological rigidity. Thus, an American editor can dismiss the Soviet news media as propaganda arms of the Communist party; or a Soviet editor can dismiss the America media as tools of Wall Street; and both can dismiss the advancing press as childlike, tribal, and xenophic. For their part, advancing-world editors can scoff at the Soviet and the American press as devices of colonial exploiters. The level of global understanding world certainly be raised if editors everywhere acknowledged the similarities in the press everywhere.

Interestingly, recognition of the similarities is far more likely among journalists who spend time with one another than among those reporters, editors, and scholars who theorize about the press from afar. Journalists who fraternize with their colleagues often develop a sense of camaraderie that transcends social, political, and national differences. Among journalists, foreign correspondents represent but a small percentage, and many who answer to the name of foreign correspondent are themselves itinerants, who flit back and forth from place to place and spend much of their time at their home base. Thus, the opportunity for developing strong cross-national social contacts is limited. When those contacts are developed, however, journalists discover the similarity in their thinking and a remarkable agreement that the best journalism occurs when the reporter is not burdened by restrictions, political, economic, or otherwise. As for those who pontificate from afar or even from an isolated nearness, it is not surprising that they fail to detect the similarities in both theory and practice. Discussions at international gatherings are bedeviled by this failure. Editors give voice to the most sweeping of condemnations of journalists from other countries, condemning them as propagandists or puppets or profiteers without ever having so much as chased down a news story in the places under attack. Delegates to international gatherings of journalists or educators issue impassioned pronunciamentos about one another without ever having so much as read a newspaper or a book published in the other's country. How absurd to identify such meetings as seeking agreements. Instead, they merely strengthen ideological purity and increase discord.

Chapters 5, 6, and 7 attempted to provide the background for the classification system offered in the present chapter. It is hoped that the character of the system will be clarified by likening it to a symphony. A symphony is, one must remember, a unit composed of segments; these movements are nevertheless part of the same unity. Inside the movements, variations on themes are sometimes striking. In the market movement, for instance, there are important structural variations. Radio and television in the United States are organized in a fashion quite different from the broadcasting industries of Western Europe and Japan. In the United States, financing of broadcasting is accomplished almost entirely by advertising, whereas in the other capitalist countries, advertising plays only a limited role in the financing of radio and television. Tax revenues and public funding provide the resources for broadcasting in Western Europe and Japan. Important differences occur in the broadcasting content of capitalist countries, but the root similarity remains. All these countries — some to a greater, some to a lesser degree — practice capitalism. In some countries, more industries are state-owned than in others, but modern capitalism has adapted to acceptance of a measure of state ownership. What unites all capitalist countries, whatever the level of socialist enterprises permitted, is their belief systems and a common hostility to a Marxist social order. The first movement of the symphony encompasses variations in the level of this hostility as well. While certain capitalist countries have gone so far as to adapt to certain aspects of Marxism, their belief systems remain intact. The press remains an instrument to safeguard the social order. Although the ideological boundaries beyond which the press may not go are not identical among the capitalist countries, or even inside an individual country at different time periods, the boundaries exist. In the end, the paymasters see to it that those boundaries are not violated.

Each of the three movements of the press symphony is filled with a variety of melodies, and they sometimes clash. There is no shortage of discord in any of the movements. No one has yet studied in exhaustive detail the differences in the views of the newspaper reader or television viewer in the different parts of Europe about the role of the press. The French reader will likely differ in important detail from the Dutch reader; the Belgian TV viewer will likely differ from the viewer in Norway. Still, all these readers and viewers approach the topic from a common perspective, one that is rooted in a common belief system. So, discord notwithstanding, the broad sweep of the first movement of the symphony is heard throughout the industrialized capitalist world, in Japan as in Denmark and Canada. The same kind of broad sweep can be detected in each of the other two movements as well.

Throughout Eastern Europe, Marxist nations, led by Yugoslavia, have sought different roads to socialism. The latitude for criticism of the social order varies from place to place, and from time to time. In the advancing world, the variations in the movements are many, some approaching the leitmotiv of the market movement, others that of the Marxist movement. Some insist on tight central control of the press; others permit considerable scope for individual decisions about what is news. These variations are rich indeed, presenting a texture as far-ranging as a symphony by Mahler. And yet the fundamental unity remains. It is that unity that can encourage us to hope for a reconciliation that could be of service to all of us, whichever movement of the symphony we may be hearing.

Although the differences among the movements of the press symphony can be seen most easily by assigning them national characteristics, it is well to keep in mind that these differences are not peculiarly national. These differences exist inside countries as well as between them. Believers in the Marxist folklore can be found in Kenya and the United States, in Venezuela and Japan. Believers in the market folklore can be found in Indonesia and Poland, in China and Cuba. Believers in the advancing-world ideology can be found in Germany and the Soviet Union, in Canada and Hungary. Still, while presenting the three movements in national terms may well be somewhat of a distortion, such imagery offers a convenient passage to comprehension of the reality of the universe of the press.

Let us examine first the perceptions of the purposes of journalism in the three movements. Why does journalism exist? What is its mission? The chart on page 284 illustrates the similarities and the differences in these perceptions.

It is quite apparent that everywhere, under whatever political, economic, or social system, the mission of the press is seen to be the pursuit of truth under the banner of social responsibility. Moreover, this pursuit is to be undertaken by means of informing, or of educating, the people who consume the news media. On these fundamentals, agreement is universal. Yet these terms are defined in different ways in different places, and among different people in the same places. Examination of the chart also points to the crucial differences among the three models. In the Marxist and the advancing world, one of the purposes assigned to the press is political. In the market countries, the reverse is true; among the missions of the press is to be above politics, to present information impartially, without taking sides. On this point, however, the defenders of the market melody are deceiving themselves. There is no way in which the press can be above politics.

As Aristotle observed long ago, a human being is by his nature a political animal. He exists in society. To live outside the social order is to be less than a human being. By virtue of his humanity alone, a journalist is a political creature. Moreover, in carrying out his trade, a journalist attains a political rank far above that of most other men and women. Everything

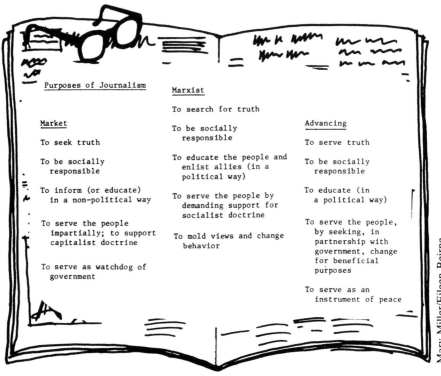

Purposes of Journalism

Market

To seek truth

To be socially responsible

To inform (or educate) in a non-political way

To serve the people impartially; to support capitalist doctrine

To serve as watchdog of government

Marxist

To search for truth

To be socially responsible

To educate the people and enlist allies (in a political way)

To serve the people by demanding support for socialist doctrine

To mold views and change behavior

Advancing

To serve truth

To be socially responsible

To educate (in a political way)

To serve the people, by seeking, in partnership with government, change for beneficial purposes

To serve as an instrument of peace

Mary Miller/Eileen Beirne

he writes is related to the social and political order that he inhabits. To take sides for a certain political point of view is to be clearly political. To take no side is also to be political, for if one does not oppose the status quo, one is giving it his tacit support. There can be no impartiality about what exists. Either you are for it and are a political supporter, or you are against it and a political antagonist. And to take no position is also to support that which exists. The folklore of the press in capitalist countries, especially in the United States, overlooks this fundamental truth. Only one who imagines that the journalist can be free of this essential element of his humanness can condemn the activities of UNESCO on the ground that they are politicized.

When they pause to consider the nature of mankind, journalists may recognize the political quality of the work they perform. But far too few journalists take time off from their busy schedules of reporting and editing the news to undertake this kind of consideration. The dogmas inherent in folklore inevitably limit our capacity for independent analysis. So it is with the dogmas in the folklore of the press in the market nations, especially the United States. Thus, many otherwise reasonable individuals, inside and outside the world of journalism, are able to state with utter conviction that reporters and editors are above politics, that they are impartial observers and chroniclers. Those who observe the press scene in the United States from other vantage points, in the Marxist and advancing worlds, are able to see more clearly and can recognize that the debate over politicization of the press is, in fact, a non-debate. The press is, simply, a political institution.

Part of the problem is definitional. In the United States, when it is said that the press is above politics, what is often meant is that the press is above *partisan* politics. In this imagery, the press does assume a kind of political character: It is supposed to serve an AWA role, as adversary, watchdog, agenda-setter. But this political character is said to be nonpartisan, neither Democratic nor Republican, neither liberal nor conservative, neither pro-civil rights nor anti-civil rights. In short, the kind of political role seen for the press in the U.S. construction is that of objective fact-finder and dispassionate channel of information.

It is true that the typical American journalist perceives this to be his highest calling: to get the facts and to lay out the facts for the reader, who may or may not act on those facts, as he or she sees fit. It is not recognized that in this quest the journalist is anything but nonpartisan. Objectivity is a mechanism for ensuring the status quo, an instrument to guarantee the preservation of institutions and of the social order. It permits criticism of individuals but not of the system, political, economic, or social. The state of impartiality is, in fact, defensive of the system. That in this model the press retains the *potential* to challenge the social order is the element that poses a threat to those who exercise power. Inasmuch as the press fails to live up to its potential, it is carrying out the political role that is desired of it by those in power. To the extent that the press endorses the idea that it is above politics, it is serving the needs of power.

Among the Marxist perceptions of the purposes of the press is that the news media lend their unswerving support to the doctrines of Marxism-Leninism. To fail in this support is to fail to serve the people; if the failure is severe enough, it can be called treasonable, a betrayal of the people. Lenin's charge to the press goes unchallenged in the Marxist nations. The purpose of the press is seen as to operate as a collective organizer — to mold attitudes and to alter behavior. There is not much give in this position. Such dogmas do not lend themselves to compromise. Disputes between Marxist press theorists and those of other systems are not likely to be resolved unless some ways can be found to convince Marxists that modifications of Lenin's stricture can be accomplished without subverting the social order itself. However difficult the resolution may be, it will be achieved more easily by awareness of the actual nature of the problem.

In all three movements of the symphony, the press is assigned the purpose of serving the people. This service is described in different terms. To those who believe in the virtue of the market system of economics, the news media are meant to support that system; to those who believe in Marxism-Leninism, the media are meant to support socialist doctrine. In the market image, the press is seen as operating outside the control of government, as a watchdog, or even a kind of adversary of the government. In the Marxist image, the press is the creature of the government (or the Party), endorsing its actions and seeking to persuade its readers and viewers to the same kind of endorsement. Among the advancing nations, however, the image is different: It is of news media that serve as partners of government, of (as in the words of Bode Oyewolo) twin agents of socioeconomic progress. Neither the market nor the Marxist theorists perceive the purpose of the press in these terms. In the market model, the press reports *about* change; it is not an agent *of* change. And in the Marxist model, the press supports change when that is the desire of the people, as reflected in the Communist party and in the government; it is not itself an agent of change. Of course, it needs to be kept in mind that we are talking here about *perceptions* of the purpose of the press. As with all institutions, the practice is quite different from the theory.

The three movements of the symphony of the press are systemic, that is to say, they combine all the elements that make up the realities described here as market, Marxist, and advancing. These elements include not only the political structure and environments and the economic forces and the paymasters of the press, but also the other ingredients of life, both public and private. Here we refer to the aesthetic components of the human experience: to literature, architecture, painting, sculpture, theater; to the scientific components; and to all the social institutions, the churches, the schools, the universities. The ideology of a sociopolitical system is made up of all these ingredients, inseparable from one another except as units of operational description. Inasmuch as the press is part of this unity, we cannot withdraw it from the system for independent examination unless it is with acceptance of the fact that our aim is to understand the role of the press inside the unity. We are halting the motion of the system, suspending it in space, so that we can understand the components of the system. Thus, it is to be kept in mind that the three-movement taxonomy outlined here is itself fictional, a suspension in space of that which is always in motion. It is a static representation of the dynamic and hence itself illusory. Still, insofar as it contributes to understanding of the system as a whole, it serves a distinctly useful end. With this reality in mind, let us look at the following table of the articles of faith about the press inside the three movements of the symphony.

Articles of faith are by definition irrational, that is to say, they are not arrived at by reason. They are often held with the passion of true believers. An article of faith is not subject to critical analysis. One believes or one does not believe. One is of the faith or one is an outsider, an infidel. Much of the acrimony that has marked international discussions of the press,

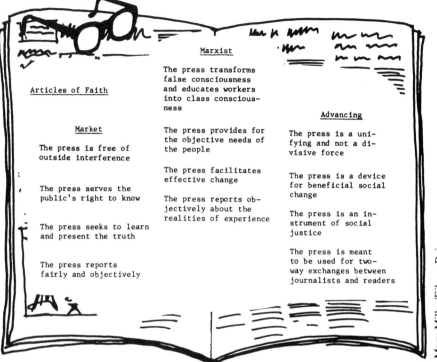

Articles of Faith

Market

The press is free of
outside interference

The press serves the
public's right to know

The press seeks to learn
and present the truth

The press reports
fairly and objectively

Marxist

The press transforms
false consciousness
and educates workers
into class conscious-
ness

The press provides for
the objective needs of
the people

The press facilitates
effective change

The press reports ob-
jectively about the
realities of experience

Advancing

The press is a uni-
fying and not a di-
visive force

The press is a device
for beneficial social
change

The press is an in-
strument of social
justice

The press is meant
to be used for two-
way exchanges between
journalists and readers

Mary Miller/Eileen Beirne

whether at UNESCO or elsewhere, has grown out of conflicting articles of faith, and indeed out of charges and accusations by true believers and apostates, by those who adhere passionately to their articles of faith and those who counter that such beliefs are spurious. For example, journalists and press theorists from industrialized capitalist countries argue with inflexible fervor that their press is free of outside interference, that no government body or advertising agency tells the press what to write or how to construct its news reports. To this, journalists and press theorists of Marxist and advancing societies reply: "Nonsense. It just isn't so." In such a collision of words, there is no compromise.

At the same time, Marxist journalists and press theorists argue that their newspapers are educational instruments that, in keeping with the arguments of Marx and Lenin, help rid their readers of false consciousness of what is going on in the world. These newspapers serve the true interests of their readers by pointing to the deceits and hypocrisies of capitalist or advancing-world officials who mislead the people and subvert the true interests of the working class. To this, the journalists and press theorists of the market and advancing lands reply: "Nonsense. It just isn't so. The Marxist press is presenting mere propaganda and not serving the true interests of its readers." Once again, compromise seems unlikely.

When advancing-world journalists and press theorists argue that their news media are forces that serve the interests of their readers by avoiding the kind of divisive reporting characteristic of the news media in market and Marxist societies, the response in both capitalist and socialist countries is once again: "Nonsense. It just isn't so. Your reports are very much divisive. You attack your neighbor quite as fiercely as we attack each other." The difficulty of accommodating opposing articles of faith ought never to be minimized.

There is no article of faith in the symphony of the press that is not subject to violent attack. Outside the market countries, for example, one is not likely to find many who agree that the news media of the capitalist countries seek to learn the truth and present that truth to their readers. It is far more likely that the capitalist media will be criticized for concealing the truth from their readers as they work mainly to turn profits for their owners. The Marxist article of faith that the press facilitates effective change is rejected outside the Marxist sphere; there, it is argued that the only kind of change the Marxist press is interested in is change that will work to help the rulers to maintain their sway over the people and not to help the people for whose benefit the press is supposed to be working. And advancing-world ideologues who see the press as an instrument of social justice are ridiculed in other parts of the world by those who point to diatribes of hate that have appeared in advancing-world newspapers. Any claim of objectivity in the press in one movement of the symphony is mocked in the other two.

Among the articles of faith, none is more intriguing than the belief in the advancing world that the press is meant to be used for two-way exchanges, not as devices for the one-way flow of information, from the top down, from the journalist to the reader. Proper journalism, according to this article of faith, is participatory. The readers and viewers are meant not to be mere vacuum cleaners, sweeping up the information pushed at them by the journalists. Instead, they are meant to participate in deciding what news is sent out into the general flow of information. The flow of news, in this image, is horizontal, not vertical. This article of faith is absent from the market and the Marxist movements of the symphony. In fact, the subject of participatory journalism is a difficult one for both market and Marxist theorists, since they do not wish to be seen as journalistic elitists. They do not perceive themselves as journalistic elitists. It is an article of faith in the market movement that the news media serve the public's right to know. It is their raison d'être. Without serving the public, in the United States they would not be able to assert their special status under the First Amendment. Their constitutional freedom is predicated on the concept of service to the public. Yet they maintain, as we have seen, the right to be sole judges of what constitutes news. By so defining the news, they isolate themselves from their readers, who are left, in a sense, to take it or leave it.

In the market model, the news media remain subject to the same laws of the market as all other institutions. The marketplace offers the consumer a choice: He may buy or he may not. He may purchase the newspaper or he may not; he may watch the TV news show or he may turn it off. In this sense, he votes with his dollars. If he approves of what is in the press, he will pay the bill; if he doesn't, he will refuse to pay. In market imagery, the reader and the viewer are the actual paymasters, not the owners of the newspaper or broadcasting outlet. Such, however, is not the reality of the press world in market economies. The essence of Adam Smith's invisible hand is that it arranges for the powerful to limit their selfish desires if they are to be successful in marketing their products: They must serve the interests of the people or suffer the financial consequences. Smith envisioned a social order that was devoted to virtue, not vice; he did not foresee the rise of monopolies and oligopolies, of transnational corporations. He did not imagine the growth of great press empires and information conglomerates. Against such entrenched financial power, the individual reader or viewer voting with his few dollars has little or no clout. The public's right to know is a euphemism for the right of the press to tell the public what *it* wants the public to know.

Journalists — including the owners of the news media as well as their reporters and editors — are for the most part true believers in the doctrine of the public's right to know. To the extent that we can characterize this fraternity and sorority as a monolith, we can say that the serious American press as a whole is convinced that what it is doing, it is doing in the interests of the public, the public that has a right to know what is going on in the public life in order to carry out its duties as citizens, thereby fulfilling the democratic assumption. This conviction is self-delusion, but it is a cardinal article of faith of the market movement.

The Marxist articles of faith assert the belief that the news media in Marxist society serve the needs and the interests of the masses. To assure that the masses participate in the process, major emphasis is placed on letters to the editor as a mechanism for interaction. In the United States, the interaction is seen chiefly in terms of the marketplace. If the reader reacts negatively to the content of his newspaper, he will cease to buy it, and the newspaper will be forced to modify its behavior in order to survive in the marketplace. In both the Soviet Union and the United States, then, the image of the press is that of an instrument that responds to the wants and needs of the reader. It is in this sense that readers participate in the formulation of news. Despite this imagery, it is clear that in both the United States and the Soviet Union, the movement of news is vertical — from the journalist, who decides what is "news," to the reader, who is for the most part simply a receiver of news.

In the advancing world, efforts have been undertaken to bring about a more horizontal pattern. Among the leaders of this movement has been

Roland Schreyer, a Swiss researcher who for more than a decade has devoted his career to attempting to generate in the rural reaches of Africa a "rural press" to serve the real needs of the readers by operating not in the traditional way, as an agent of power, but rather as what Schreyer calls "an instrument of dialogue." Working inside the framework of UNESCO, Schreyer has traveled extensively in Africa and has often worked on the scene in an effort to assist unlettered Africans in expanding their awareness of the world and in learning what it is that they need to know to create a better life for themselves. "The readers are not interested in political debates," Schreyer says, "but in subjects such as culture and marketing of their products, education, improvement of sanitary conditions, etc."

In Schreyer's view, the newspaper is the most useful device to achieve genuine dialogue that is available to humankind: "With the newspaper is born dialogue, the possibility of reply." Schreyer began his work in 1972 in Africa in the remote, landlocked country of Mali, whose skimpy population of 7 million is extended across 465,000 square miles and whose chief city, Bamako, is peopled by only 450,000 persons. Working with officials of the Mali Ministry of Information, Schreyer established a monthly newspaper, *Kibaru*, printed in the Bambara language. Its aims at the outset were to supply general information to the public and to further rural development. Over the years, *Kibaru* has broadened its scope and now not only provides news of current events but also aims at raising living standards and increasing civic consciousness. None among the staff, which includes an editor-in-chief, two subeditors, and a newswriter, is a formally trained journalist, but each goes through a brief training period, from instructors themselves only modestly trained. *Kibaru* began as a four-page mimeographed publication and has expanded over a ten-year period into a printed, offset publication of eight to ten pages. Circulation has risen from 5,000 to 12,500, and the paper attracts an ever-widening string of letters and other communications from readers.

From the outset, the effort in Mali was to involve the readership, to convince them that *Kibaru* was their paper and not a government propaganda device. To reinforce this conviction, Schreyer and his colleagues introduced the concepts of a council of editors and of a network of what Schreyer identified as "rural communicators." The council consists of experts in different subject areas who meet regularly to discuss what the readers of *Kibaru* need and ought to know. This information is then passed along to the editors, who in turn track down the information suggested and produce news items. In this way, the definition of news is supplied not only by the journalists but by the readers as well. In fact, the network of rural communicators, none of whom are staffers but all of whom qualify as stringers, write most of the items in the paper.

Schreyer has insisted, over the opposition of a number of officials, that the newspapers be sold for a price and not distributed free. "It is only then," Schreyer says, "that the reader can actually feel that the newspaper is his. We tell them: 'This is your newspaper. You can write us and provide a dialogue, but for us to continue the paper, you must pay. You must be the owner." In the context of this book, such a practice converts the reader from a mere consumer to the status of paymaster.

Since the Mali experiment was begun, rural press systems have been established in sixteen African countries. Schreyer and his colleagues have also begun to develop rural press outlets in Asia and Latin America. Circulation of the papers, most of them monthlies but some of them weeklies, varies from a bare 500 to the thriving agricultural newspaper *Terre et Progrès* of the Ivory Coast, with a circulation of 60,000. While Schreyer sees a good beginning in Mali and several other countries, he acknowledges that successes have been outnumbered by failures. He and his colleagues urge greater investment in a rural press by national and international bodies, by journalism research institutes, and by reporters and editors themselves. Pay scales for the reporters and editors are meager, and available research at journalism schools is channeled primarily into urban news centers. Moreover, some governments have sought to convert their rural press into instruments of propaganda to boost the images of the national leaders. Still, Schreyer is convinced the rural press offers an opportunity to develop the kind of dialogue between journalist and reader that can elevate human understanding. And he points to the heavy volume of letters from readers of the rural press, who find through them a sense of participation in their own future.

Not all advancing-world ideologues are as enthusiastic about the rural press as Schreyer. They call attention to the fact that the kind of participatory journalism possible in remote rural areas is not feasible in industrialized society, nor even in the large cities of Africa. However, development theorists have come up with a modification of the rural press concept that shows distinct promise. It is a concept that has sometimes been identified as "community journalism." In this concept, the citizen has direct access to the pages of the news media and participates in editorial decision making. Like the rural press concept, it is seeking to carve out a new role for the press, one in which it serves not as the agent of paymasters or of political power, but as the agent of the consumer, of the interested and articulate citizen.

As difficult an achievement it is, the idea is worth exploring as widely as possible. Ideally, the news media would serve as instruments *of* the community, rather than as instruments for disseminating information *to* or *for* the community. In this way, the press could help give the citizen a sense of participation in working out his own fate. One of the characteristics of modern society has been the sense of isolation of the citizen from his community. The existence of a malaise that accompanies this sense of powerlessness has been widely recognized. People do not feel that they are the captains of their fate. In the United States, for example, participation in elections has been declining for a generation. More and more people seem convinced that their votes do not count and, by indirection, that they do not count for much either. Under the appropriate circumstances, the news media could provide them with a sense of participation, of importance, and of counting. Under the present circumstances, few persons seem to believe they have personal access to the pages of their newspapers or to the broadcasts of their radio and television stations. A community journalism structure would offer them that opportunity. A powerless citizenry might sit dispiritedly by as its world drifted into nuclear holocaust. A positive citizenry that felt it counted would be tempted to intervene. A participatory press could give it that opportunity.

To the argument that community access and participation will not be permitted by those in power, it can be answered that no serious effort has yet been made, and the answer cannot be known until the question is raised. It is certainly not likely that the news media and their paymasters, locked in their symbiotic embrace, will easily yield their monopolistic control over the definition of news; for them, the stakes in terms of power and prestige are too great. To them, press freedom means their right to judge what is and what is not news. To surrender this right to the participating citizen is to change the nature of the institution and to invite, at the very least, anarchy. In this environment, market and Marxist ideologues are in perfect agreement, as are many theorists of the advancing world.

And yet, change does not have to be total to be productive. A greater degree of public participation in the definition of news is entirely possible, and even modest beginnings of shifts in power relationships carry with them the seeds of progress. Several such programs have been attempted, in industrialized market countries as well as in the newer nations. One of the more interesting among them was undertaken in Finland. In that country, television producers made an attempt to select the subject matter of some of their news and current-events programs on the basis of relevance to the audience, rather than on the usual basis of drama and conflict. Producers of one such program, "Tietolaari," invited its audience to write in suggestions about how to resolve local problems. A film unit was then dispatched to the area to work with the people there to report their situation. The resulting documentary was aired, followed by a live question-and-answer period between the inhabitants and decision-makers with the power to remedy some of the problems. This series was only an experiment and is not practiced on a widespread basis, but it demonstrates that citizen participation in defining the news is more than an idle dream. The Finnish experiment was not unique. A number of broadcasters and newspapers have produced documentaries drawn from human needs, but they have rarely permitted their audiences to assume any means of control over the product. The approach comes close to Schreyer's goal of dialogue through the mass media.

In this form of community journalism, Frances Berrigan says, the members of the community have access to the media — "for information, education, entertainment, when they want access." The goal is the goal expressed by all press ideologies: The mass media are meant to serve as instruments of education. The difference lies in who decides what is to be taught. Julius Nyerere, the president of Tanzania, has provided a thoughtful definition of education. Its purpose, he says,

> is the liberation of Man from the restraints and limitations of ignorance and dependency. Education has to increase men's physical and mental freedom — to increase their control over themselves, their own lives, and the environment in which they live. The ideas imparted by education, or released in the mind through education, should therefore be liberating ideas; the skills acquired by education should be liberating skills. Nothing else can properly be called education.

Few will be inclined to quarrel with the lofty goals set forth by Nyerere. The selfsame goals listed for education might be enunciated also for the press: Its purpose too might be to help liberate humankind from ignorance and dependency, to help men and women to increase their control over their lives and their environment.

It is ironic and will be noticed by all students of Tanzania that neither the education system nor the press system of Tanzania practices what Nyerere preaches. The ideal remains distant from the reach of man; the considerations of practical politics and practical economics inevitably take precedence in the real world over the needs of the individual. It is thus utopian and probably counterproductive, since it runs against the nature of man, to expect the mass media to become communal property working for the needs of each individual.

What is possible, however, is a greater measure of access to the mass media by the individual citizen. Here too it is utopian and wildly impractical to imagine that the mass media can ever provide access to all persons. One of the weaknesses in Schreyer's vision is that it holds that the individual *wants* access to the pages of the newspaper. Most men and women everywhere on earth seem prepared to be mere consumers of news, even as they are quiescent absorbers of education in the schools. Few persons are interested in participating, but even those who care little about participating themselves argue for the principle of participation.

The gatekeeper role of the mass media is what is at issue here. In all ideologies of the press, the decisions about what constitutes news are made by the journalists themselves. We have seen, however, that journalists are subject to manipulation by the wielders of power about what constitutes news. In the symbiotic relationship between journalists and the sources of their news, the odd one out is the reading and viewing public. Steps in the direction of increasing the level of citizen participation in the definition of news, using some elements of Schreyer's participation program and some of the ideas of community journalism, would surely make of the press a stronger instrument of education than it has ever been before.

There is a third way to classify the melodies in the three movements of the symphony of the press: the positions on freedom of the press. The following table is illustrative:

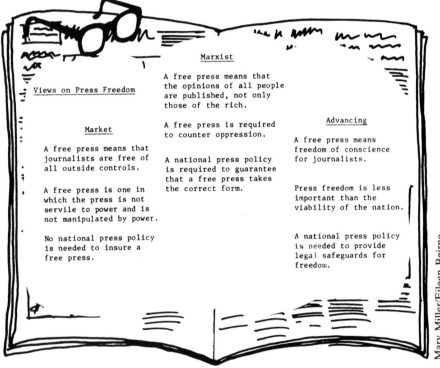

Views on Press Freedom

Market

A free press means that journalists are free of all outside controls.

A free press is one in which the press is not servile to power and is not manipulated by power.

No national press policy is needed to insure a free press.

Marxist

A free press means that the opinions of all people are published, not only those of the rich.

A free press is required to counter oppression.

A national press policy is required to guarantee that a free press takes the correct form.

Advancing

A free press means freedom of conscience for journalists.

Press freedom is less important than the viability of the nation.

A national press policy is needed to provide legal safeguards for freedom.

Mary Miller/Eileen Beirne

In every social order, free expression is glorified. No nation publicly opposes the ideal of free expression. And few segments of society, national, domestic, or cross-national, argue against laws or regulations that promote the general idea that anyone has the right to say what he wants or to write what he wants, provided such expression does not cause injury to anyone. In all social orders, important restrictions are placed on the right of free expression. In the United States, for example, it is considered unlawful to shout "fire" in a crowded theater. In the Soviet Union, it is illegal to voice public criticism of elected officials. In India, it is against the law to endorse racism. Indeed, in all countries, freedom of expression does not include the right to call for the overthrow of the government by force and violence. The key problem here, as with most philosophical questions, is one of definition.

In capitalist countries, emphasis is placed on freedom of *information*. What ought to be guaranteed, it is held, is the right to send out whatever information one wishes to send. The theory is that the receiver of the information will be able to make wise decisions on the basis of that information. Such a belief is at the heart of what is identified as the democratic assumption. On closer inspection, it can be seen that the theory as stated is incomplete. For the receiver of the information to make decisions, he needs more than just the information provided by the press. He also needs the intelligence and the background knowledge required to place that information in a context that will facilitate his decision making. Without intelligence and education — without literacy, for that matter — the information will be of no utility to him. In the United States and other market social orders, it is assumed that the freedom to express oneself in print is part of a broad sociopolitical and economic system that makes provision for public education and public health facilities. Without schools and hospitals, free expression is largely irrelevant.

On the whole, the systems under which the Marxist and advancing press operate also include devotion to public education and public health. In many — perhaps most — of the countries of the advancing world and in a substantial number of Marxist nations, inadequate financial resources mean also inadequate schools and medical facilities. To the underprivileged people of those countries, freedom of expression may well appear to be a luxury of far less significance than the availability of schools and hospitals. Not surprisingly in those social orders, there is far less devotion to abstract principles of free expression than among the United States and her allies. And while in all parts of the world the free flow of information is recognized as a universal goal, outside the capitalist world, it is of itself not usually considered a matter of urgency.

Moreover, as we have seen, it is doubted in both Marxist and advancing societies that the press of the United States and her allies is actually free of outside controls. Inevitably, as the MacBride Commission argues, the content of the press in the capitalist world is influenced — if not directed — by the commercial forces, spearheaded by advertising agencies and transnational corporations.

The assertion by Lenin that in the capitalist world a free press means only freedom for the rich is accepted as fundamental truth in all Marxist nations, in most advancing countries, and among many dissident individuals and groups in the capitalist world. In the nineteenth century, Marx issued impassioned defenses of a press system of total freedom. And before the Bolsheviks had solidified their power in the Soviet Union, Lenin also strongly supported the idea of total press freedom. In fact, both Marx and Lenin argued that if oppression was to be overcome, it was necessary for a free press to lead the battle as a crucial element in the advance guard of the working class. In the capitalist and advancing societies, those statements by Marx and Lenin are largely ignored. Critics of today's Marxist press point instead to the practices of the Soviet press; they argue, correctly, that the media in Marxist countries are not free.

In the advancing world, there is by no means universal agreement on the meaning of freedom of the press or even on exactly what is desirable press behavior. Inasmuch as many of these societies are not yet completely formed or institutionalized, it is not surprising that there should be no precise agreement on these points. In fact, it is a healthy thing that agreement is not universal, for openness of mind is often barred by the institutions and folklore that have become formalized and encrusted in tradition. For much of the advancing world, a free press is not much concerned with freedom of mere information. It is more important, as Marroquín Rojas observed in discussing attitudes in Latin America, that the individual be assured freedom of conscience than that he be flooded with information.

Why has so much of the debate about the role of the press revolved around that word information? Discussions of the role of the press would surely have been of greater profit to all if addressed more to questions of the *kind* of information that is being demanded. Outpourings of words about football games, bank robberies, film stars, fires, fashions, exotic sexual practices, and auto design seem on reflection to be of little significance to discussions of anything so lofty as freedom and morality. Nor do the pages of advertising in newspapers and magazines, or the commercial announcements on radio and television. It is doubtful that the guarantees of a free press included in the First Amendment or in the constitutions of most nations, Marxist, advancing, and capitalist, are meant to assure such news stories or advertising messages that could be circulated in broadsheets devoted solely to commercial notices. It is no doubt the presence of the encrusted folklore of the press that leads to the largely irrelevant discussions of press freedom at international gatherings and in newsrooms around the world.

To the struggling, insecure nations of the advancing world, abstract principles of press freedom are less important than the viability of their nations. This stance is often condemned among journalists and press theorists in the capitalist world. According to the folklore of the press in the United States, a free press brings to light the "truth" wherever it finds it, regardless of the consequences of such exposure. Thus, the withholding of "news" in the advancing world in the name of saving the state from collapse is usually perceived as a transparent defense for keeping the truth from being known. What those critical journalists overlook, however, is their own willingness to withhold information that they (and their sources) perceive to be threats to the security of their own state. Lost in the folklore of the watchdog, they fail to recognize the symbiotic nature of the relationship of the press to government in their own society, while they have no difficulty observing the same phenomenon in another social order.

It is largely to assure that the press plays an institutional role subservient to the legitimate interests of the state that every country in the advancing world endorses the idea of national and international press policies. The Inca Plan in Peru was one such national press policy. National programs, different in content but similar in structure, have been developed all over the advancing world as, unsurprisingly, they have appeared among Marxist nations. Most capitalist countries have looked with suspicion on the construction of formal press policies, and many have openly opposed any formal policies. Still, it is a fact that all countries have adopted press policies. The difference is that the market nations have called them by other names. Press councils; associations of publishers, editors, journalists, broadcasters, and photographers; and journalism educators all concern themselves with proper behavior for the press, and hence with policy. But to these individuals and groups, they are discussing practices and not policy. To them, policy is something directed by government and hence political. Operating in a belief system that is suspicious of politics and finds direct political intervention in press behavior repugnant, these individuals and groups respond with horror and loathing to proposals that political bodies assume leading roles in dealing with the press. We have seen many illustrations of this loathing in these pages.

On the other hand, press theorists of both the Marxist and advancing social orders see political intervention as natural and potentially beneficial. Marxist and advancing-world press theorists part company, however, on what kind of government intervention is desirable. The result is a kind of journalistic anarchy. With little agreement on what *is*, there is none on what *ought* to be.

Each side is ever ready to hold forth on abstract principles of journalism, relying on the folklore of its particular social order. Consequently, few journalists or press theorists anywhere have come forward to grapple with concrete problems in the field of journalism. In writing of ethics in general, Sissela Bok has suggested that hard ethical choices are avoided in most fields: "Why tackle such choice when there are so many abstract questions of meaning and definition, of classification and structure, which remain to challenge the imagination?" It is hoped that the classification system presented here will serve to remove some of those abstract questions from the field of journalism and clear the way for concrete applications, such as the Inca Plan, however one may judge its wisdom.

In summary of the truths that have emerged from this study of the role of the press, and from the classification system embodied in the metaphor of the symphony of the press, we offer here seven laws of journalism on which reasonable people might agree. Hopefully, in doing so, we may put in place a floor to serve as a foundation for the development of concrete ways for the press to cease serving as a force to divide humankind and to begin serving as a force to help resolve the terrible challenges we face in the closing years of the twentieth century.

THE SEVEN LAWS OF JOURNALISM

1. In all press systems, the news media are agents of those who exercise political and economic power. Newspapers, magazines, and broadcasting outlets thus are not independent actors, although they have the potential to exercise independent power.

2. The content of the news media always reflects the interests of those who finance the press.

3. All press systems are based on belief in free expression, although free expression is defined in different ways.

4. All press systems endorse the doctrine of social responsibility, proclaim that they serve the needs and interests of the people, and state their willingness to provide access to the people.

5. In each of the three press models, the press of the other models is perceived to be deviant.

6. Schools of journalism transmit ideologies and value systems of the society in which they exist and inevitably assist those in power to maintain their control of the news media.

7. Press practices always differ from theory.

The contemporary world has sometimes been called the Nuclear Age and sometimes the Age of the Information Explosion. These terms refer to the same thing — a world that has been transformed by science and technology, a world of promise and hope, but also a world of great peril in which there exists a real threat of its extermination. The mushroom clouds carry the seeds of both knowledge and death. The men and women of the press — the merchants of news — are crucial figures in this transformed social order, for it is they who paint the pictures of the world on which decisive human actions are based. To fail to understand this basic but grim truth is to fail to understand the role of the press in the affairs of humankind. The last notes of the symphony of the press are yet to be played.

Three possibilities are available. The press can render it easier for humankind to destroy itself, to the accompaniment of drums and crashing cymbals, in a kind of Wagnerian explosion. Or it can assist in the creation of a global harmony, to a satisfying resolution that resembles those of

Vivaldi. Or, finally, it can serve out its days as an uninvolved outsider, subject to the shifting winds of the moment, as a kind of brainless robot awaiting but not participating in its fate. The immodest hope that lies behind this book is that the press will turn away from its historic role as blind chronicler of conflict and search out a different role, that of conflict resolver. Harmony and global survival rest on the peaceful resolution of conflicts.

The classification system presented here provides little comfort. There is more conflict than resolution. The good guys are on "our" side, whoever "we" may be. The bad guys are on the "other" side, whoever "they" may be. The history of the press demonstrates that newspapers and the more modern variations of the press have tended to serve the selfish interests of the paymasters, while at the same time perpetuating the image of a press operating in the service of the consumers of the news. To expect that the news media will make a dramatic U-turn and scoff at the wishes of the paymasters is to engage in the wildest kind of utopian fantasies.

Students of conflict tend to agree that most disputes among individuals as well as among nations involve questions of identity, security, and recognition. The needs of each person and of each nation require a feeling of being safe from irrational aggression and a sense of personal or national dignity. If their needs are not met, according to John Burton, the deprived individual or nation will resort to behavior that is described by those in power as deviant. In this situation, "we," or those who live by the codes or norms of the prevailing ideology, are the Good Guys, and "they," or those who engage in "deviant" behavior, are the Bad Guys. To understand how people behave and how people think outside the accepted and comfortable ideological system in which they live is imperative for those journalists who would truly inform, or educate, or assist in the resolution of problems. Access to the news media must be given to the Bad Guys as well as the Good Guys if there is to be genuine understanding. The code of objectivity may not be discarded at the water's edge.

Burton speaks of the valuable role in the resolution of conflict that may be played by "third parties," to whom he assigns the role of articulating precisely and dispassionately the issues involved in the conflict and, more importantly, of assuring that the opposing sides become involved not in "confrontation, competition, bargaining or power," but rather as solvers of problems.

What stronger role could the press play?

In accepting the Nobel Prize for literature in 1957, Albert Camus, novelist, essayist, and journalist, said this: "The nobility of our calling will always be rooted in two commitments difficult to observe: refusal to lie about what we know, and resistance to oppression." He might have added for the journalist a third commitment: to write and edit in such a way as to help resolve the problems of humankind and not to exacerbate them.

Appendix

THE ABSURDITY OF "SOCIAL RESPONSIBILITY"

The term social responsibility is of obscure origin, but it seems to be associated with the philosophy of utilitarianism, which attained a wide following in England and the United States in the nineteenth century, deriving many of its ideas from the writings of Jeremy Bentham and John Stuart Mill. The latter, hero of liberals and democratic thinkers for a century and a half, introduced a moral factor into Bentham's principle that virtue consists in whatever brings the greatest pleasure to the greatest number. Bentham, laying out a moral principle that is widely endorsed in most non-Marxist societies, held that good is determined by its consequences: When an action produces well-being among the public — e.g., reduces the level of poverty — it is good. Mill's important addition to Bentham's equation was his insistence that not only must the consequences be good, but the motive of the actor must be good as well. If not, good may result from evil intentions. Although neither Bentham nor Mill was asserting an original idea (the Greeks had wrestled with similar conceptions two millennia earlier), what they said seemed amazingly applicable to the Anglo-Saxon world of the mid-nineteenth century. It was the incorporation of Mill's concept of moral utilitarianism with the image of the supreme virtue of the General Will enunciated by Jean-Jacques Rousseau that provided the philosophical foundation for the modern doctrine of social responsibility. To Rousseau, who like Mill opposed arbitrary power, the voice of the people was supreme, and that voice was heard in the mystical expression of what he called the General Will.

The most significant political contribution of Bentham and the utilitarians was the enactment of the Poor Law in Britain in 1834. Passage of that law followed years of campaigning by Bentham and the Whig politicians who were advocating social reform. It was the first assumption by the national government of responsibility for caring for the poor, a practice up to that time entrusted to the Church and local relief agencies. Moreover, the Poor Law was a perfect illustration of the execution of the doctrine of social responsibility. In short order, the term was being used throughout the Anglo-Saxon world, in the United States by the Abolitionists and the supporters of prison reform and compulsory education, as well as those who demanded laws against the sale of alcoholic beverages. In 1857, a British-born expatriate to the United States, John Bartholomew Gough, electrified temperance workers and foes of poverty and slavery with a lecture at Exeter Hall in London that he entitled, "Social Responsibilities." Gough's message, which was so well received that he was invited to deliver the same tidings for a score of years thereafter, was that each of us is indeed his brother's keeper and is responsible for seeking out the poor and the downtrodden and offering him our help.

Gough's message was of one's *individual* responsibility to society, and this was the essence of Mill's message, but Mill also went beyond a call for assistance by individuals and assigned responsibility to institutions, not the least of which was the press. An unbending advocate of free expression and open discussion, Mill waxed dramatic in speaking of the potential for good in the press. To censure the press, he said, is to revive

> ignorance and imbecility, against which it is the only safeguard. Conceive the horrors of an oriental despotism — from this and worse we are protected only by the press. Carry next the imagination, not to any living example of prosperity and good government, but to the furthest limit of happiness which is compatible with human nature; and behold that which may in time be attained, if the restrictions under which the press still groans, merely for the security of the holders of mischievous power, be removed. Such are the blessings of a free press.

By the time the term social responsibility was employed by the Hutchins Commission, it was becoming commonplace in the United States and Britain. The number of books dealing with the concept is increasing every year. The greatest number are appearing in connection with business practices, especially in marketing, and in the world of science. The U.S. National Education Association published a slim book in 1963 urging the public and the government to make adequate financial provisions so that schools and colleges might continue to teach young people to concern themselves with the country's problems: "The continued health of the American society — perhaps its very survival — demands a high and rising awareness of social responsibility on the part of the people." The literature of business and science as well as journalism demands that these institutions practice their social responsibilities. A journal called *Social Responsibility* appeared in 1975.

And yet the painful reality is that the term social responsibility is a term devoid of meaning. Put another way, it is a term whose content is so vague that almost any meaning can be placed upon it. As such it too serves the ultimate end of social control in ways that would have horrified Mill and Rousseau. Perhaps this is the reason one cannot find the term social responsibility in the *Oxford English Dictionary* or in the *Dictionary of the History of Ideas*. Several pages in the *OED* are devoted to other compounds with "social," as are many references in *Notes and Queries for Readers and Writers, Collectors and Librarians*. Indeed, an exhaustive compendium of the ideas of Mill published in *Notes and Queries* contains page after page of compounds with "social," but not social responsibility. One finds, on the other hand, valuable references to social *morality* and social *obligation*.

Nevertheless, even though the term is meaningless and operates as a mechanism of social control, it has considerable value for the working journalist. *First*, it gives the journalist the positive feeling that he or she is making a contribution to society, and that he or she is working in the public interest, carrying out a public service, in the image of the BBC. *Second*, it allows him to avoid uncertainty about his purpose; as Freud and others have pointed out, feelings of uncertainty and ambiguity are difficult and painful to sustain. *Third*, it enables the journalist to ignore the economic realities of his or her trade. He can choose to report the conflictual because it is socially responsible to do so, not because in so doing he is pandering to the baser interests of his readers, in gossip as well as in sex and violence. *Fourth*, it heads off the threat of government intervention, a threat of primary concern to the Hutchins Commission.

What if the journalist recognized the masquerade of social responsibility? Would this recognition shatter his self-image? Would it reduce him to cynicism or to blatantly seeking the greatest amount of money, prestige, and power by openly yielding to the basest tastes? Would he quit his job and seek other work? All of these things have indeed occurred. Many U.S. journalists abandon their jobs for other employment, in advertising and public relations, as civil servants, as attorneys, as politicians, as teachers and professors. A remarkable 1971 study demonstrated that the average age of the working American journalist is three years lower than that of others in professional-type careers, an indication that many newsmen and women grow disillusioned with their work and seek their rewards elsewhere. In this way, some of the most thoughtful and potentially productive journalists make their way out of the trade. It is likely that they have discovered the spuriousness of the doctrine of social responsibility. Unquestionably, awareness of how difficult it is to meet the needs of his or her audience will be accompanied by the pain that grieves all human beings who recognize their impotence in effecting social change. Yet there remains for the individual journalist the possibility of performing important services for the public — and, more significantly, the possibility of uniting institutionally with his or her colleagues to help change the course of human history.

Our problem in dealing with the term social responsibility is similar to the problem we face with the term freedom. Neither can be defined in a universal way. Each depends entirely on our ethical system, on our set of values. We cannot be responsible for our actions unless we are free. Since the journalist is not free, he cannot be responsible, at least in any institutional sense. He may, on the other hand, be a free *individual*. Certainly he has free choice. He may choose to carry out the orders given by his publisher or he may not. He is free to continue to work or to quit. He is free to choose to go to prison, if that is the punishment. And since he possesses these kinds of individual freedom, he acts out of his own individual sense of duty. The English philosopher T. H. Green makes a useful distinction between obligation and duty. Obligation, Green says, may be enforced by law; duty may not. Thus, in a situation in which the journalist is obliged to report only information that is acceptable to his publisher or his government, he is fulfilling his responsibility (i.e., obligation) by following orders. On the other hand, if the journalist refuses to report only this kind of information because he finds it morally repugnant to do so, he is equally fulfilling his responsibility (i.e., duty). Responsibility can be defined either as obligation or duty. It has never been possible to separate legal (obligatory) responsibility from moral duty, and discussions of the ethics of journalism are eternally muddied by the confusion generated by this semantic puzzle. When *social* responsibility is invoked, it is usually in terms of morals or, in Green's phrasing, duty. The question remains: To whom is one socially responsible, and for what? Assuming that at least in theory one is responsible for the presentation of reasonably accurate information on a variety of subjects, to whom is this responsibility owed? It could not be to oneself, for then the word "social" would be irrelevant. If it is to a publisher or government, we would be talking principally of one's obligation, or legal responsibilities, either through a private contract with an employer or through the implied citizenship contract by which one is affiliated with one's government. It seems that the charge is for the responsibility to be owed to "society." And thus it is related to the duty described by Gough in his famous temperance lecture, or the duty to Rousseau's General Will or to the greatest number, as invoked by Bentham and Mill.

Yet "society" turns out itself to be an absurd concept. It is at best an indefinable abstraction. Consider its relationship to the concept of "state," a term introduced by political theorists in the nineteenth century, and ever since a source of massive confusion, not only in terminology but also in relation to thought. Sometimes "state" has been used to refer to government, sometimes to nation, sometimes to society. All three, government, nation, and society, are vague words. A renowned student of political philosophy has observed that although vague, these words are by no means interchangeable. In fact, society seems to incorporate both government and nation. To Green, when one speaks of the function of society, one is using a meaningless combination of words.

Still, since journalists have something in mind when they speak of society, it is likely that they are referring to the society they know, that is, the men and women of the upper middle class, literate, articulate, interested in public affairs, those who are well educated and affluent. Michael Novak suggests that because of this affiliation, the working man hates the news media and is jealous of the social benefits that accrue to those who practice the trade. History does indeed indicate that, for the most part, journalists have interpreted their societal responsibility as to their own kind. The coverage of racial minorities in the United States sustains this analysis. Thus, the doctrine of social responsibility reaffirms the existing social order while at the same time providing the cloak of moral rectitude for those who claim to follow the doctrine. As Hobhouse pointed out, any institution that says it serves society may lay claim to a moral dignity and authority it otherwise cannot justify. This is not to say that the institution of the press lacks moral dignity; it is rather to point out that the doctrine of social responsibility offers its practitioners the opportunity to lay claim to moral dignity whether or not it affirms the status quo or whether or not it operates in the interests of all people.

However, social responsibility can be adapted to refer to the duty to work for the benefit not of a social elite but of those who often suffer at the hands of that social elite. For the advancing world, the only kind of social responsibility that counts is directed to the benefit of the underclass, especially in the liberated colonies. In similar vein, Louis Finkelstein, chancellor of the Jewish Theological Seminary in New York, has proposed in his *Social Responsibility in an Age of Revolution* that the doctrine of social responsibility be directed toward "all those who are lacking essential needs and a sense of self-worth." He adds:

> The disprivileged of this country and of the world need self-respect; they need to believe in themselves. If we cannot help all men everywhere to recapture their sense of human dignity and individual worth, our failure may have consequences impossible to predict.

To set one's bearings on this course, Finkelstein says, is the responsibility of the privileged. Surely, the privileged includes the men and women who engage in the practice of journalism. In the advancing world, it is taken as a matter of fact that the responsibility of the journalist is precisely to work to help people develop a sense of human dignity and individual worth. To this end, advancing-world journalists have proposed a new world information order.

That order is frankly political, in that it follows a policy for journalists enunciated by Mahatma Gandhi in his role as editor of an English-language newspaper, *Young India*, when in 1919 he began his campaign for Indian independence. The policy of *Young India*, he wrote in its first issue, was not only to draw attention to "injustices to individuals," but also to devote its attention to constructive "'Satyagraha,'. . .civil resistance where resistance becomes a duty to remove a persistent and degrading injustice." Not everyone will agree on what constitutes such an injustice, but journalists who overlook "a persistent and degrading injustice" in pursuit of an ephemeral role free of politics are hardly carrying out a role that can be praised as moral or responsible.

Bibliography

This bibliography is presented as a series of essays, not only setting forth the principal sources I have relied upon, but also indicating my assessment of their strengths and weaknesses. In this way, the interested reader will be able to recognize clearly the thrust of my prejudices. I have elected not to rely on the traditional pattern of footnotes, but rather to direct attention only to the major sources and to indicate page references only in particularly significant situations. The interested scholar is invited to address the author for further citations, either at the School of Journalism, Indiana University, Bloomington, Indiana 47405, or at Longman Inc., the publisher of this book.

CHAPTER 1

Among the writings on the origin of the press, I find most satisfactory the work of Karl Bücher, a German scholar of political economy who wrote several articles on the press between 1901 and 1926. None of his later historical and analytical writing surpassed that in his first entry into the field, a chapter entitled "The Genesis of Journalism," which appeared as pp. 215–243 in his book translated into English as *Industrial Revolution* in 1901 (New York: Henry Holt). The translation by S. Morley Wickett was drawn from Bücher's *Die Entstehung der Volkswirtschaft: Vorträge und Aufsätze* (Tübingen: Laupp'sche, 1893). Those interested in pursuing Bücher's work are referred to "Die Presse" in *Handbuch der Politik* (Berlin: Paul Laband, 1914) and "Ursprung der Begriff der Zeitung" ("The Origin and Idea of the Newspaper") in *Gesammelte Aufsätze zur Zeitungskunde* (Tübingen:

Laupp'sche, 1926). The Bücher citations in this chapter are drawn from the 1901 study. Hanno Hardt provides an interesting chapter on Bücher in *Social Theories of the Press: Early German and American Perspectives* (Beverly Hills: Sage, 1979). See chapter 4, "The Linkage of Society," pp. 99–131.

In general, historians of the press have tended to pay little attention to the ancients, to the press in the Middle Ages or even during the Renaissance and Reformation. This deficiency is evident in Marxist press history as well as in the histories written in capitalist countries. German historians seem to have been more thorough in this area than their colleagues in Britain, France, and the United States. In this context, see especially Otto Groth, *Die Zeitung*, 4 vols. (Berlin, 1928–30). See also Max Bestler, *Das Absinken der parteipolitischen Führungsfähigkeit deutscher Tageszeitungen in der Jahren 1919–1932* (dissertation, Friedrich-Wilhelm University, Berlin, 1942); and Emil Dovifat, "Die Presse am Ende der Weimarer Republik" (*Das Parlament*, vol. IV, no. 38, September 15, 1954). All contain excellent short accounts of German press history.

It is impossible to state authoritatively the identity of the first newspaper. Differences exist, for one thing, in the definition of newspaper. It does seem evident, though, that the first regularly published newspaper in Europe appeared in the early years of the seventeenth century. On page 3, I have identified the first newspaper as being published in Belgium in 1605. This identification derives from the Czech journalism scholar Vladimir Hudec in *Journalism: Substance, Social Functions, Development* (Prague: IOJ, 1978). Other authorities say the first paper appeared in Bremen or Cologne, Germany, while others give the location as Sweden. Indeed, Hans Muenster, in *Geschichte der deutschen Presse: in Ihren Grundzeugen* (Leipzig: Bibliographisches Institute, 1941), p. 21, says the first printed handbill containing news reports appeared in Germany as early as 1482.

An interesting account of the *Cato Letters* and of the lives of the men who wrote them can be found in Frederick Seaton Siebert, *Freedom of the Press in England from 1476 to 1776* (Urbana: University of Illinois Press, 1965), pp. 333–345. Additional valuable material is contained in Leonard M. Levy, ed., *Freedom of the Press from Zenger to Jefferson* (Indianapolis: Bobbs-Merrill, 1966), pp. 10–11.

For an examination of the role of Frederick the Great in press history, see among other sources the works of Dovifat and Groth, and my article "Chronicle of a Democratic Press in Germany Before the Hitler Takeover" (*Journalism Quarterly*, vol. 53, no. 2, Summer 1975), pp. 229–238. A fuller account of German press history is included in my dissertation, "The Papen Putsch: A Contribution to Understanding Why Opinion Leaders Failed to Rally Support for the Rape of Prussia" (Seattle: University of Washington, 1971). See also Erich Eyck, *Bismarck and the German Empire*, 3rd ed. (London: Allen and Unwin, 1968). For a study of the French press at the time of the Revolution, see especially Henri Avenel, *Histoire de la press française* (Paris: Flammarion, 1900).

The Weekly News, printed by Nathaniel Butter in 1622, was the first publication to be issued from a printing press and published regularly in England. See James Grant, *The Newspaper Press: Its Origin — Progress — and Present Position* (London: Tinsley Bros., 1871), p. 24; and Alexander Andrews, *History of British Journalism* (London: Bentley, 1959), p. 18. The *Oxford English Dictionary* (vol. 7, p. 120) lists the first published reference to the word newspaper in the *Western*

Gazette in the year 1670. The popular interpretation that used the points of the compass to indicate the origin of news is illustrated in a poem that appeared in *Wits and Recreation* in 1640:

> When doth come, if any would discuss
> The letter of the word, resolve it thus:
> Newes is conveyed by letter word or mouth,
> And comes to us from north, east, west, or south.

The story is told by Andrews, p. 18. News was probably derived from *nova, nouvelles, das neue,* or *nieuws.* In any case, the association was from the beginning with the idea of what was new.

The citations from David Hume (pp. 3, 4) can be found in *A Treatise of Human Nature,* abridged and brilliantly analyzed by Isaiah Berlin in *The Age of Enlightenment* (New York: George Braziller, 1957). See pp. 162–260, especially "Of Knowledge," pp. 180–190. Harold Lasswell's catalog of three communication activities (p. 5) appears in "The Structure and Function of Communication in Society," reprinted in Bernard Berelson and Morris Janowitz, *Reader in Public Opinion and Communication,* 2nd ed. (New York: Free Press), p. 179. Milton's *Areopagitica* is reproduced in a number of places. A convenient reprint appears in *The Portable Milton* (New York: Viking Press, 1949). An interesting and instructive analysis of Milton's essay appears in Clifford Christians, "Liberty Within the Bounds of Virtue," in A. van der Meiden, ed. *Ethics in Mass Communication* (Utrecht: State University of Utrecht Press), pp. 16–41.

CHAPTER 2

There are many accounts of the history and significance of the First Amendment. I find especially congenial the brief sketch and analysis by Marvin L. Summers, *Free Speech and Political Protest* (Lexington, Mass.: Heath, 1969), notably pp. 29–85. All the standard journalism histories discuss the history of the First Amendment, as of course do all general histories of the United States and numerous articles and monographs. I am indebted in substantial degree to Arthur Bestor, under whom I studied constitutional history at the University of Washington, for revealing insights about the issues involved in discussions of free expression. Bestor's mimeographed notes are invaluable.

For early U.S. press history, there is no better work than Clyde A. Duniway, *The Development of the Press in Massachusetts* (New York: Longman, Green, 1906). Duniway's bibliography is indispensable for all scholars. Also useful in tracing the development of perceptions of the role of the press in early U.S. history are the writings of Jefferson and Madison. The interpretation in Leonard W. Levy, *Legacy of Suppression* (Harvard University Press, 1960), is interesting: Levy provides a counterview to the usual adoring stance taken towards Jefferson by liberal scholars. Levy's analysis is refreshing, although certainly overstated. He has subsequently backed away from some of his most extreme revisionist assertions. In any case, in my view, Madison is even more unwavering in his support of an absolutely free press than is Jefferson. As for Jefferson, I am not prepared to follow Levy, or Fawn Brodie, *Thomas Jefferson: An Intimate History* (New York: Norton,

1974), or other Jefferson detractors. Even though he reacted with anger and hostility to the press that was attacking him unmercifully, especially during the days of the trial of Aaron Burr, Jefferson clung tenaciously to his reverence for free expression. See especially Dumas Malone's biography, *Jefferson the President: First Term 1801–1805*, vol. 4 (Boston: Little, Brown), pp. 206–235.

It is always refreshing to reread the *Virginia Resolution*. The Resolution and Madison's notes on its creation have been reproduced in a number of places. For the original, see *Letters and Other Writings of James Madison, Fourth President of the United States, in Four Volumes, published by Order of Congress* (New York: R. Washington, 1884), vol. IV. Some of the most noteworthy letters of Jefferson are included in the excellent reader by John Somerville and Ronald Santoni, *Social and Political Philosophy* (Garden City, N.Y.: Doubleday, 1963). Madison's *Notes of the Debates in the Federal Convention of 1787* (New York: Norton, 1966) are required reading for anyone interested in the development of the Constitution. See also Winton U. Solberg, ed. *The Federal Convention and the Formation of the American States* (New York: Liberal Arts Press, 1958). Opposing views of the significance of the American Revolution are conveniently available in Clinton L. Rossiter, *Conservatism in America: The Thankless Persuasion* (New York: Knopf, 1955); and Merrill Jensen, *The Founding of a Nation: History of the American Revolution 1763–1776* (New York: Oxford University Press, 1968). Rossiter sees the rebellion as essentially a conservative movement, and Jensen sees it as genuinely revolutionary. Reality, I suspect, lies somewhere between Rossiter and Jensen, probably closer to Rossiter's vision, at least as far as most of the "revolutionaries" were concerned.

Benjamin Franklin certainly qualifies as a conservative revolutionary. The words of Franklin quoted here can be found in many collections of his writings. The classic work, of course, is *The Selected Works of Benjamin Franklin, Including His Autobiography* (Boston: Phillips, Sampson, 1856). Rossiter has described Franklin's "Apology for Printers" as "an accurate representation of the principles of a free press which governed popular thinking in eighteenth-century America." Levy (*Freedom of the Press from Zenger to Jefferson*, p. 3) observes correctly that the Apology "hardly represented a definition of a philosophy of a free press." For an interesting discussion of Franklin and his role as a journalist, see J. H. Plumb, "Ravaged by Common Sense," *New York Review of Books*, April 19, 1973.

The roles of Franklin and his older brother James are reviewed, in the context of a passionate dedication to free expression, by Isaiah Thomas in his influential *The History of Printing in America with a Biography of Printers and an Account of Newspapers* (New York: Weathervane Books, 1970). There is a curious lack of reliable historical data on the life and practices of James Franklin, although all standard journalism histories cover the activities of *The New England Courant*. The most thorough study with which I am acquainted is contained in the unpublished dissertation of my student Carolyn Garrett Cline, "The Hell-Fire Club: A Study of the Men Who Founded *The New England Courant* and the Inoculation Dispute They Fathered" (Indiana University, 1976).

The Emery text — Edwin Emery and Michael Emery, *The Press and America: An Interpretive History of the Mass Media*, 4th ed. (Englewood Cliffs, N. J.: Prentice-Hall, 1978) — is the most widely used text in journalism history courses in the United States. In its interpretation of the growth of U.S. journalism, it follows the tradition of progressive historiography that dominated the field in the days of the growth of journalism as an academic discipline. The forerunners of Emery, all cast in the same progressive mold, are must reading for the journalism scholar, but they inevitably paint a distorted picture, owing among other factors to the one-sided view of U.S. history that dominated the thinking of the writers. Moreover, these histories are, as I have suggested elsewhere, "mediocentric," that is, exaggerated in their view of the importance and significance of newspapers in the overall growth of the United States. See my "Mediocentricity or ...?" (*Mass Comm Review*, Winter 1978).

The standard journalism histories that preceded Emery include: Frederic Hudson, *Journalism in the United States from 1690 to 1872* (New York: Harper, 1891); Willard G. Bleyer, *Main Currents in the History of Journalism* (Boston: Houghton Mifflin, 1927); and Frank Luther Mott, *American Journalism: A History of Newspapers in the United States Through 250 Years, 1690–1940* (New York: Macmillan, 1941).

The most complete account in English of the controversy over the press in France in the early years of the nineteenth century is contained in Daniel L. Rader, *The Journalist in the July Revolution in France; The Role of the Political Press in the Overthrow of the Bourbon Restoration, 1827–1830* (The Hague: Nijhoff, 1973). David H. Pinkney provides a needed modification in "The Media and the Monarchy in France, 1827–1830" *(Reviews in European History*, vol. I, March, 1975), pp. 519–525. Other useful works on French press history during that time period include Irene Collins, *The Government and the Newspaper Press in France, 1814–1881* (London: Oxford University Press, 1959); Charles Ledré, *La Presse à l'assaut de la monarchie, 1815–1848* (Paris: Armand Colin), 1960; and Frederick B. Artz, *France Under the Bourbon Restoration 1814–1830* (New York: Russell and Russell, 1931). The entire text of the fascinating 1827 debate in the Chamber of Deputies is included in *Le Moniteur*, the government newspaper. The intriguing exchange of correspondence among Jefferson, John Norvell, Lafayette, Madison, and Nicholas Trist can be found in the collected *Works* of Jefferson and Madison; and in the Trist papers, some of which are in the library of the University of North Carolina and some in the Virginia Historical Society Collections.

The useful study conducted in Ann Arbor and Tallahassee (p. 20) was by James W. Prothro and Charles M. Quigg. See their "Fundamental Principles of Democracy: Bases of Agreement and Disagreement" (*Journal of Politics*, vol. XX, May 1960).

CHAPTER 3

The age of the penny press is well covered in all standard journalism texts. In addition, many historical accounts are available of the growth and development of the individual newspapers of the era. For instance, one can consult with profit Frank M. O'Brien, *Story of the Sun* (New York: Doran, 1928); Isaac C. Pray, *Memoirs of James Gordon Bennett and His Times* (New York: Stringer and Townsend, 1955); Henry Luther Stoddard, *Horace Greeley: Printer, Editor, Crusader* (New York: Putnam, 1946); and Glyndon G. Van Deusen, *Horace Greeley: Nineteenth Century Crusader* (University of Pennsylvania Press, 1953). In addition to Myron Berger's *The Story of The New York Times, 1851–1951* (New York: Simon & Schuster, 1951), of considerable value in examining *The New York Times* and other early newspapers is Gay Talese's *The Kingdom and the Power* (Cleveland: World, 1966).

There is no shortage of studies of the newspapers and the men who controlled them in the early years of the nineteenth century. However, the historian must regard them carefully, since many — in fact, most — of the authors are biased recorders. I find the most valuable of the many general works on the press of this era to be Alfred McClung Lee's *The Daily Newspaper in America* (New York: Macmillan, 1937). Lee is especially insightful in his examination of the financial basis of these newspapers and in correcting some of the excessive adulation that marks the work of Hudson, Bleyer, Mott, and Emery.

The reader will note that in my discussion of this era, I have chosen to concentrate on the press of New York City. Of course, cheap newspapers existed across the country, and, to a limited degree, they followed courses somewhat different from that of the New York press. But the differences are of degree, not of kind. Moreover, the New York press has been studied more carefully than the others, and source material is more plentiful. In terms of their influence on newspaper development in the country, the New York papers were, of course, the most important.

Standard journalism history, as observed in the bibliographic notes of chapter 2, is rooted in the progressive, or Whig, tradition, following the lead of Parrington, Turner, and Beard. Journalism of the penny press era is cast in the mold of "the age of the common man," as popularized by early-nineteenth-century historians such as George Bancroft, and later by Edwin Emery. The popular work by Arthur Schlesinger, Jr., *The Age of Jackson* (Boston: Little Brown, 1945), idealized Andrew Jackson and his colleagues, no longer portraying them as coonskin Democrats but rather as the leaders of a radical movement among urban workers and artisans. However, the image of the heroic journalist fighting for the cause of the little man remained consistent with the Schlesinger image. Later historians — among them Richard B. Morris, "Andrew Jackson, Strikebreaker" (*American Historical Review* vol. 55, no. 1, October 1949, pp. 54–58); and Richard Hofstadter, *The American Political Tradition and the Men Who Made It* (New York: Knopf, 1948) — challenged this traditional view. The best-known revision of Schlesinger's imagery was provided by Lee Benson, *The Concept of Jacksonian Democracy: New York, A Test Case* (Princeton University Press, 1961); Benson challenged the idea of urban input into Jackson's policies and substituted "the age of egalitarianism," a concept as weak as that of "the age of the common man". Historians continue to disagree over the meaning of what took place in the age of Jackson, but it is clear this period was critical in the growth of American journalism. Perhaps each generation must revise the meaning of the Jacksonian age; it is my position that neither Schlesinger nor Benson is to be endorsed and that Jackson is to be viewed as a remarkably astute politician who was an early exponent of image building, especially in the manipulation of the press.

Herbert Gutman's perceptive comments on the persistence of progressive history theory (p. 46) are contained in "What Happened to History?" (*Nation*, Nov. 21, 1981).

No full-scale study of Amos Kendall has yet appeared, but his *Autobiography*, edited by William Stickney (Boston: Lee and Shepard, 1872), is useful. Additional insights into Kendall and his behavior, especially as the leader of Jackson's kitchen cabinet, is provided by Lynn L. Marshall, "The Authorship of Jackson's Bank Veto Message" (*Mississippi Valley Historical Review* vol. 50, no. 3, December 1963, pp. 466–477). I am indebted also for original research into the career of Kendall by my graduate student Corban Goble. Like many others, I have been impressed by the analysis of Jacksonian America and of the press in that era by Alexis de Tocqueville in his *Democracy in America*. An excellent edition, edited and abridged by Richard D. Heffner, is available as a Mentor paperback from New American Library. See especially the section entitled "Liberty of the Press in the United States," pp. 91–95. According to de Tocqueville (p. 94): "The journalists of the United States are generally in a very humble position, with a scanty education and a vulgar turn of mind." A scarcely accurate portrait, but one the contemporary journalist might ponder with profit.

On the subject of John Winthrop and the contribution of the Puritans to American thought and tradition, I have followed Perry Miller, *The New England Mind: The Seventeenth Century: From Colony to Province* (Harvard University Press, 1954); and Edmund S. Morgan, *The Puritan Dilemma: The Story of John Winthrop* (Boston: Little, Brown, 1958). On the Mexican War, I have relied heavily on Frederick Merk, *Manifest Destiny and Mission in American History* (New York: Knopf, 1963). The role of the press in the Mexican War is well covered in Armin Rappaport, *The War with Mexico: Why Did It Happen?* in the Berkeley Series in American History (Chicago: Rand-McNally, 1963).

In the extensive literature on Hearst and Pulitzer, I have found W. A. Swanberg's biographies — *Citizen Hearst* (New York: Scribner's, 1964) and *Pulitzer* (New York: Scribner's, 1967) — entertaining but not entirely reliable. The early work on Pulitzer, *Joseph Pulitzer: His Life and Letters*, by Don Carlos Seitz (New York: Simon and Schuster, 1924), is interesting. An especially strong account, not only of the man but of his newspaper, is provided by George Juergens in *Joseph Pulitzer and the New York World* (Princeton University Press, 1966). Sidney Kobre's *The Yellow Press and Gilded Age Journalism* (Florida State University Press, 1964), gives a breezy account of the Hearst-Pulitzer circulation war, but the account in Lee's *The Daily Newspaper in America* is more accurate.

Hearst's boast that it was he who caused the Spanish-American War was popularized in James Creelman, *On The Great Highway* (Boston: Lothrop, 1901), a highly unreliable account by a Hearst colleague. Hearst himself is quoted on his own exploits in Edward Coblentz, ed., *William Randolph Hearst: A Portrait in His Own Words* (New York: Simon & Schuster, 1952). For a different contemporary perspective on Pulitzer and Hearst, see the intriguing *When Dana Was the Sun* by Charles J. Rosebault (Westport, Conn.: Greenwood, 1970).

For Avery Craven and the Civil War press (p. 43), see his *Civil War in the Making, 1815–1860* (Louisiana State University Press, 1919), pp. 89–115. The literature on the Civil War press, both in the North and the South, is extensive and often instructive.

Dickens is at his malicious best in his characterization of the U.S. press during his visit to the United States. See the final chapter of his *American Notes for General Circulation* (Baltimore: Penguin Books, 1972). Dickens wrote (p. 287): "The foul growth of America has a...tangled root...it strikes its fibres deep in its licentious press.... While the newspaper press of America is in, or near, its present abject state, high moral improvement in that country is hopeless."

CHAPTER 4

Although advertising is a subject that is universally recognized as of decisive importance in the lives of the press, it has been infrequently examined by critical historians. The definitive study of the role of advertising in the direction and shape of the news media has yet to be written. In my research, I found no study of the rise of advertising in the press superior to that of Alfred McClung Lee in *The Newspaper in America*. I am indebted to Lee for his painstaking research and for the inferences he has drawn from his work, much of it quantitative. I am also indebted to the diligent research in the field by a student of mine, Paul Hagner. A quick and entertaining overview can be found in "How Advertising Agencies Started in the U.S.: A Brief History" (*Advertising Age*, December 7, 1964). Other useful general works are: Leslie McLure, *Newspaper Advertising and Promotion* (New York: Macmillan, 1950); John V. Lund, *Newspaper Advertising* (Garden City, N.Y.: Prentice-Hall, 1947); Frank Presbrey, *The History and Development of Advertising* (Garden City, N.Y.: Doubleday, 1929); and James Playsted Wood, *The Story of Advertising* (New York: Ronald Press, 1958). The impressive, heavily emotional analysis by Will Irwin, the muckraker, is useful as well, provided one is cautious with regard to Irwin's conclusions. In any case, I have always enjoyed the fifteen articles on the growth of the press Irwin wrote for *Collier's* in 1911. I find myself in fundamental agreement with Irwin's basic argument about the influence and power of the financial interests that dominated the press of the nineteenth and early twentieth centuries, the period under scrutiny by Irwin. The lengthy citation from Irwin (pp. 64–65) can be found in *Collier's* XI. The entire series has been reprinted by the Iowa State University Press and published as *The American Newspaper*, 1969. The citations from *The Publick Advisor* (p. 61), the *New York Morning Courier* (p. 62), *The New York Herald* (p. 63), and *The New York Tribune* (p. 68) can be found in Lee.

The importance of the muckrakers in American and general press history can be assessed only in the context of the historical era in which they were prominent, the Age of the Progressives. The historical literature on the Progressives is extensive, and, like the assessment of the revolutionary and Jacksonian eras, the analysis has often been contradictory. Early historians occupied themselves primarily with the study of important individual muckrakers. Later historians, however, shifted their emphasis from the individuals to the social forces let loose in the era, to questions of social control, of the growth of institutions, of the influence of bureaucracies, and of power issues generally. Standard journalism histories, pursuing great-man theories and the Whig interpretation of events, have held that the muckrakers profoundly influenced the course of events and set a pattern of interpreting the power of journalists that persists to the present. I find these analyses faulty and certainly contributory to the present-day folklore of the press. Among the stronger general histories of the muckrakers, see Arthur and Lila Weinberg, *The Muckrakers* (New York: Capricorn, 1964), a book that reprints liberally from the original writings; and Harold Wilson, *McClure's Magazine and the Muckrakers* (Princeton University Press, 1970). The autobiographies of the principal muckrakers make fascinating reading. I am particularly impressed by Ray Stannard Baker's *American Chronicle: The Autobiography of Ray Stannard Baker* (New York: Scribner's, 1945). The best-known self-examination, of course, is

Lincoln Steffens, *The Autobiography of Lincoln Steffens* (New York: Harcourt Brace, 1931). See also Ida Tarbell, *All in a Day's Work* (New York: Macmillan, 1939). Robert Bannister's biography *Ray Stannard Baker: The Mind and Thought of a Progressive* (Yale University Press, 1966), offers some interesting insights. Baker's poem, "The Lonely Rider," is reprinted in Bannister, p. 78. Bannister notes that the date of the poem is uncertain and that Baker gives the time merely as "while in Arizona." Baker spent a brief time in the Southwest and in California before undertaking his career as a muckraker. Presumably, it was while there that he internalized the image of the cowboy as the symbol not only for his poem but also for his lone fighter article. For Baker's own account of how the lone fighter image originated, see his *American Chronicle*, pp. 123–133. History and human beings are perverse; it is sadly ironical that Baker, the lonely fighter, in his later years joined the "crowd" as a blatant press apologist for Woodrow Wilson.

Other biographies are valuable, especially Justin Kaplan's *Lincoln Steffens: A Biography* (New York: Simon and Schuster, 1974). In fact, for a portrait of the world of the press from the last third of the nineteenth century to the middle of the twentieth century, one would have to search long and hard to find an equal to Kaplan's book. It is concise and insightful in a variety of areas. See also Mary E. Tomkins, *Ida M. Tarbell* (New York: Twayne, 1974). Theodore Greene, *America's Heroes: The Changing Models of Success in American Magazines* (New York: Oxford University Press, 1970), examines the world of the lonely hero in a discussion of the muckraker era (see pp. 59–165). For yet another valuable contribution to an understanding of the era, see Ronald Steel, *Walter Lippmann and the American Century* (Boston: Little Brown, 1980). Much has been written about William Allen White, nearly all of it laudatory. His own *Autobiography* (New York: Macmillan, 1946), is an indispensable source.

The literature on Theodore Roosevelt is also exhaustive. Of special interest to the student of news management is Gabriel Kolko, *Railroads and Regulation, 1877–1916* (Princeton University Press, 1968). See also Kolko's *The Triumph of Conservatism: A Reinterpretation of American History, 1900–1916* (New York: Free Press, 1963); and James Morton Blum, *The Republican Roosevelt* (Harvard University Press, 1954). Of monumental importance to the student of news management in the muckraking period is George Juergens, *News from the White House: The Presidential-Press Relationship in the Progressive Era* (University of Chicago Press, 1981).

The most thorough study of news management in an earlier era is provided in Culver Smith's excellent *The Press, Patronage and Politics* (University of Georgia Press, 1977). I am indebted to Smith for the account (pp. 68–71) of the use of patronage to influence the content of the early press.

Among the most useful studies of the Progressive Era is Russell Nye's *Midwestern Progressive Politics: A Historical Study of Its Origins and Development, 1870–1950* (Michigan State University Press, 1951), a book that argues powerfully that the reforms of the New Deal, studied in chapter 6, derive in a linear fashion from those of the Progressives. Like Schlesinger on Jackson, Nye was motivated in substantial degree by the overriding liberal endorsement prevalent at the time of the accomplishments of the second Roosevelt. A modifying element was introduced by, among others, Richard Hofstadter in *The Age of Reform: Bryan to F.D.R.* (New York: Knopf, 1956); and Robert H. Wiebe in *The Search for Order:*

1877–1920 (New York: Hill and Wang, 1967). Hofstadter, Wiebe, and their colleagues lay stress not on the individual greats but on the importance of social forces and the quest for power among the Progressive reformers. Indeed, contemporary scholarship tends to see the Progressive reforms less as assaults on big business than as the manipulation of reform by the great corporations, and as the beginning of the modern corporate state. This view is well expressed by Alfred D. Chandler, Jr., in his *Strategy and Structure: Chapters in the History of Industrial Enterprise* (MIT Press, 1962). See also Ray Ginger, *Age of Excess: The United States from 1877 to 1914* (New York: Macmillan, 1965), for an analysis of the Progressive Era as a period of industrial tension characterized by harsh oppression of the working class and an imperialistic struggle for markets abroad. Certainly, Lenin's analysis of imperialism (chapter 5) is rooted in such an understanding of the age of the muckrakers. The citation from Lasswell (p. 78) is from *Psychopathology and Politics* (New York: Viking Press, 1930).

Sources for the material on Bismarck and the reptile press are identified in the bibliographic essay on chapter 2. The story of *The New York Times*'s investigation is, of course, recounted in the histories of the *Times*, including those of Berger and Talese, already cited. Other interesting accounts can be found in Sydney Mandelbaum, *Boss Tweed's New York* (New York: Wiley, 1965); and Alexander Callow, *The Tweed Ring* (New York: Oxford University Press, 1966). I am especially indebted to my graduate student Emily Nottingham for her work in researching the Tweed story thoroughly.

CHAPTER 5

Editions of the published work of Marx and commentaries on those works are so numerous that it is folly to attempt to list more than a few titles. Yet on the specific issues of Marx the journalist or even of Marx's views on the press, there is almost nothing. It is difficult to understand the failure of Marxist scholars to undertake a study of this subject; perhaps it is because most of what Marx had to say about the press was in his earlier years, and Marxist scholars have tended to the belief — erroneous, in my view — that Marx utterly disavowed his earlier writings and thought. The best work in English on Marx's earlier writings appears in Lloyd D. Easton and Kurt H. Guddat, ed. and trans., *Writings of the Young Marx on Philosophy and Society* (Garden City, N.Y.: Doubleday, 1967). Examples of Marx's early writings as a journalist are, of course, available in editions of his works, but I have not been able to find many of these in English-language renditions. In fact, even in the German-language originals, the greatest attention is paid to Marx's longer and later works. Fruitful opportunities are available for researchers, in whatever language, in specific issues raised by Marx the journalist. The case of the Moselle Valley peasants is illustrative.

Marx's journalistic output in English for Greeley and Dana has been collected and reprinted in Henry M. Christian's useful compilation, *The American Journalism of Marx and Engels: A Selection* (New York: New American Library, 1966). Trevor Pateman's *Language, Truth and Politics* (Nottingham: Russell Press, 1975) is valuable for its analysis of the way Marx used words for his political objectives. Pateman is a bit too doctrinaire for my taste, but the book is nonetheless interesting. Also of interest in this connection is S. S. Prawer, *Karl Marx and World Literature* (London: Oxford University Press, 1976). I am especially indebted to Patrick Daley and John Solosky for their detailed examination of the role played by language in Marx's views on consciousness. Their paper, "Marxism and Communication," was presented to the Qualitative Studies Division of the Association for Education in Journalism convention in Seattle, 1978.

Erich Fromm's analysis in his *Marx's Concept of Man* (New York: Frederick Ungar, 1961), is especially appealing to me. Fromm's attempt to place Marx's life in a continuum·of growth and to reject a decisive division between the earlier and later Marx is persuasive. I am also happier with his classification of Marx as a humanist *throughout* his life than I am with the traditional view of Marx as swinging into a fully developed revolutionary. Isaiah Berlin's splendid biography *Karl Marx: His Life and Environment* (New York: Oxford University Press, 1963) also stresses Marx's continued dedication to a humanistic world view.

The four-volume series published as *Issues in Marxist Philosophy* contains a valuable compendium of views about Marx's philosophy on a wide range of topics. I recommend these volumes without hesitation. They are edited by John Mepham and David-Hillel Ruben and published by Humanities Press (Atlantic Highlands, N J.). I am especially indebted to the essays in volume 2, *Materialism*, published in 1979, and volume 4, *Social and Political Philosophy*, published in 1981. See the articles in volume 4 by Andrew Collier and Timothy O'Hargan. No analysis of Marx's thought is complete without a close study of Karl Korsch, *Marxism and Philosophy*, a collection of four essays written between 1922 and 1930. A translation into English was published in 1970 by Monthly Review Press. See also John Lachs, *Marxist Philosophy, A Bibliography* (London: Oxford University Press, 1968).

Other secondary works on Marx that I found useful are: Philip Corrigan, Harvie Ramsay, and Derek Sayer, *Socialist Construction and Marxist Theory: Bolshevism and Its Critics* (New York: Monthly Review Press, 1978); Roger Garaudt, *Karl Marx: The Evolution of His Thought*, a translation from the French (New York: Frederick Ungar, 1961); and Robert Kilroy-Silk, *Socialism Since Marx:* (Penguin Harmondsworth Books, 1972). Of course, the patient researcher must devote considerable attention to reading Marx himself. For a useful compilation in English, see his *Revolution and Counter-Revolution*, edited by his daughter, Eleanor Marx Aveling (New York: Capricorn Books, 1961).

Fromm's book includes a translation of Marx's *Economic and Philosophical Manuscripts*; the Easton-Guddat compilation includes the important *Theses on Feuerbach*, in which Marx insisted it was the duty of philosophers, historians, and all communicators, journalists included, to concern themselves not merely with interpreting the world but with changing it as well (pp. 96–98). The Marxist historian Staughton Lynd argues that the task for historians is never to "be content with measuring the dimensions of our prisons instead of chipping away, however inadequately against the bars": "Historical Past and Existential Present," in Theodore Roszak, ed. *The Dissenting Academy* (New York: Pantheon Books, 1967), p. 107. To David Hackett Fischer, a delightfully witty historiographer, in his *Historians' Fallacies: Toward a Logic of Historical Thought* (New York: Harper Torchbooks, 1970), Lynd and Marx before him were guilty of what Fischer calls the pragmatic fallacy, in which the historian selects only facts useful to his own purposes in his analysis. Fisher (pp. 82–87) rejects the idea of history as prescriptive. The essence of the difference between Marxist and non-Marxist (or capitalist) theory lies in the difference between Lynd and Fischer.

Lenin is the best source of his own views on the press, and on this subject he is prolific. An indispensable compilation of Lenin's views is included in a volume entitled *Lenin About the Press*, published in English by the International Organization of Journalists (Prague, 1972). Nearly all the citations from Lenin here are taken from this book. The best concise analysis of Lenin's thoughts about the press is contained in Vladimir Hudec, *Journalism: Substance, Social Functions, Development*, previously cited. Hudec, professor of journalism at the University in Prague, has, of course, written extensively in Czech. His most recent work is *Uvod do teorie zurnalistiky* (Prague: Novinar, 1982).

The material about Marxist-Leninist views on the press included here is drawn not only from published literature but also from interviews with Marxist journalists and journalism professors, in the Soviet Union and Eastern and Western Europe as well as in the United States. A visit to the Moscow State University and its school of journalism in 1979 permitted me to observe journalism education at first hand. I also had the opportunity to discuss Marxist-Leninist press theory with the dean of the school, Yassen Zassurskiy. Conversations with a variety of U.S. journalists based in Moscow provided other point of views. During the six years I spent as a journalist in Europe, I held many conversations with reporters and editors from Eastern Europe and, moreover, was able to watch them at work. It was especially useful to spend an evening with Svetlana Starodomskaya and other Soviet television journalists (p. 107) in 1980.

The study by Ellen Propper Mickiewicz, *Media and the Russian Public* (New York: Praeger, 1981), is the first examination of public opinion surveys about the mass media in the Soviet Union. Further studies will be valuable in clarifying and expanding the viewpoints expressed in this book. Most discussions of the Soviet press in English are either avowedly political or unwittingly so, and of questionable validity because of their hostility to the Marxist system. See, for example, Paul Lendvai's *The Bureaucracy of Truth: How Communist Governments Manage the News* (London: Burnett, 1981). The Rand Corporation began in 1980 a study aimed at testing the hypothesis that the news media in Marxist countries are used as instruments for debate on policy. Its first study on Poland was summarized in Rand Report R-2627, December 1980. In 1982 the Rand Corporation published *The Media and Intra-Elite Communication in the USSR*, by Lilita Dzirkals, Thane Gustafsan, and A. Ross Johnson. For an interesting study of the role of the press in a specific policy issue in Eastern Europe, see Owen V. Johnson, "The Media and Nuclear Policy in Czechoslovakia," *Soviet Studies*, in press. See also Theodore E. Kruglak, "The Role and Evolution of Press Agencies in the Socialist Countries," in Bondan Harasymiw, ed., *Education and the Mass Media in the Soviet Union and Eastern Europe* (New York: Praeger, 1976).

Two standard sources on the Soviet press in English are James Markham, *Voices of the Red Giants* (Iowa State University Press, 1967); and Mark Hopkins, "Lenin, Stalin, Khrushchev: Three Concepts of the Press" (*Journalism Quarterly*, vol. 43, no. 4, Autumn, 1965), pp. 523–531. The stance taken in these works resembles the philosophical and historical posture adopted by Wilbur Schramm in his influential analysis "The Soviet Communist Theory," in the book he authored with Fred S. Siebert and Theodore Peterson, *Four Theories of the Press: The Authoritarian, Libertarian, Social Responsibility and Soviet Communist Concepts of What the Press Should Be and Do* (University of Illinois Press, 1956). All the citations from Schramm in my chapter 5 are drawn from his chapter in that book, pp. 105–146. It and the other three chapters in the book are must reading.

De Tocqueville's remarkable bit of prognostication (p. 85) appears in the Signet edition of *Democracy in America*, previously cited, p. 142.

On the general subject of the import of ideology in the world of journalism, no statement is more direct, more succinct, and more accurate than that of George Gerbner in "Ideological Perspectives and Political Traction in News Reporting" (*Journalism Quarterly*, vol. 41, no. 4, Autumn, 1964), pp. 495–508: "There is no fundamentally non-ideological, apolitical, non-partisan news gathering and reporting system" (p. 508). See also Stuart Hall, "Culture, the Media and the 'Ideological Effect,'" in James Curran, Michael Gurevitch, and Janet Woolacott, *Mass Communication and Society* (London: Edward Arnold, 1977), pp. 315–338. Hall speaks (p. 346) of a systematic tendency in the news media "to reproduce the ideological field of a society in such a way as to reproduce, also, its structure of domination."

CHAPTER 6

Most major U.S. universities include sections on journalism education in their official histories. In a number of cases, specific books and monographs have been written on the origin and growth of journalism schools and departments. Most, of course, emphasize the local and stress the significance of their own institution. In the early years of journalism education, several general works were written, the most prominent among them being De Forest O'Dell, *The History of Journalism Education in the United States* (Columbia University Press, 1935). Also of general interest is Albert A. Sutton, *Education for Journalism in the United States From Its Beginning to 1940* (Northwestern University Press, 1945).

Pulitzer himself made a major contribution to the literature in his article "The College of Journalism" (*North American Review*, vol. 178, May 1904). In that article, Pulitzer described his rationale for creating the school at Columbia University. A more detailed study is to be found in Richard Terrill Baker, *A History of the Graduate School of Journalism* (Columbia University Press, 1954). The story of the journalism schools at Missouri and Wisconsin are related in Sara Lockwood Williams, *Twenty Years of Education for Journalism: A Complete History of the School of Journalism of the University of Missouri* (Columbia, Mo.: Stephens, 1930); and Merle Curti and Vernon Carstenen, *The University of Wisconsin*, 3 vols. (University of Wisconsin, 1949). The second volume of the latter work discusses Bleyer and the school of journalism. Additional material on Bleyer and Williams can be found in Frank Luther Mott, *Time Enough: Essays in Autobiography* (University of North Carolina Press, 1962); and in Donald K. Ross, "Willard G. Bleyer and Journalism Education" (*Journalism Quarterly*, vol. 34, 1957). I am especially indebted to an unpublished 1982 monograph by Janice R. Wood of the Greenville (S.C.) *News* entitled "The Foundation Years of American Journalism Education." On current political jockeying about journalism schools, see Eric Nadler, "'Righting' The Audience" (*Columbia Journalism Review*, November/December, 1982), pp. 8–9.

My discussion of journalism education abroad is derived in large measure from observation. I have traveled extensively about the world and have visited many universities in which journalism courses are taught. I have also interviewed professors, journalism students, and practicing journalists in various countries. For a number of years, Indiana University organized a special program for visiting foreign journalists, and I spent many pleasant hours discussing journalism education with them. I have also taught journalism courses to students in a variety of places, including Berlin, where I had the opportunity to learn much while meeting students at an international school for training journalists from advancing-world countries. A particular foreign experience is instructive. I was asked at one time to help organize a course in practical journalism at a university in West Germany, where a program of education for journalists was well established. The course envisioned by the faculty included a single assignment: to prepare during the semester one important article or series of articles. By contrast, a U.S. university would require during a semester, among other things, at least a dozen important pieces of journalism. Foreign journalists and students regularly have expressed astonishment and envy over the opportunity enjoyed by U.S. journalism students to conceive, write, edit, and produce their own daily newspapers.

The standard examination of Luce and the growth of *Time* magazine is the two-volume authorized work by Robert T. Elson, *Time Inc.: The Intimate History of a Publishing Enterprise 1923–1960* (New York: Atheneum, 1968 and 1973). More readable and entertaining is W. A. Swanberg, *Luce and His Empire* (New York: Scribner's, 1972).

The outpouring of literature on the subject of objectivity in the field of journalism is exhaustive. Far too much has already been written, in my opinion, and I would greet with gratification a moratorium on literature on objectivity. All journalism texts apparently find it *de rigueur* to preach the cause of objectivity in newswriting, editing, photography, and design, even though in many cases it is now said that "pure" objectivity is a phantom to be pursued but never captured. Students reading this are nonetheless inspired to thirst after the chimera of objectivity. No one was a more thoroughgoing proselytizer in the cause of journalistic objectivity than Kent Cooper, who served as general manager of The Associated Press during the quarter-century in which that news agency rose to the position of preeminence among newsgatherers on the planet. I worked as a reporter and editor for The Associated Press during the last years of Cooper's life and during the tenure of the most powerful individual to succeed him, Wes Gallagher. That both of these men were dedicated to their craft is something to which I can attest personally. It is also true that both men were ideologues, utterly unable to perceive a chink in their dogmatic armor. It was in an address in New York City in 1945 that Cooper introduced into the tradition of journalism the idea that the public had "a right to know." Such a right does not exist in law, although it can be (and often is) argued that the journalist is morally obligated to fulfill that right.

The rise of the AP is chronicled in Cooper's *Kent Cooper and The Associated Press* (New York: Random House, 1959); and his *Barriers Down* (New York: Farrar and Rinehart, 1942). The authorized history is by Oliver Gramling, a colleague of Cooper, in *AP: The Story of News* (New York: Scribner's, 1938). A somewhat more disinterested account can be found in Victor Rosewater, *History of Cooperative News-Gathering in the United States* (New York: Appleton, 1930). For an insider's account of the growth of the chief AP rival, see Joe Alex Morris, *Deadline Every Minute: The Story of the United Press* (Garden City, N.Y.: Doubleday, 1957). The assertion that objectivity is the Holy Grail of journalism was made by Wes Gallagher in an unpublished speech, "Ego Journalism versus Integrity," with which he dedicated the Kent Cooper room at the library at Indiana University, May 16, 1971.

Not all journalism scholars have endorsed the concept of objectivity. A classic reinterpretation of journalistic folklore and dogma appears in Warren Breed's pioneering "Social Control in the Newsroom: A Functional Analysis" *(Social Forces*, vol. 33, 1955), pp. 326–335. Breed pointed to the importance of socialization factors not only in influencing the behavior of reporters and editors but also their definitions of news. Earlier, Dexter Manning White had coined the word gatekeeper to clarify the process under which "news" is selected. The editor stands at the gate and permits only that which he considers to be newsworthy passage through it and into the newspapers. White's article "The 'Gatekeeper': A Case Study on the Selection of News" (*Journalism Quarterly*, vol. 27, no. 4, Fall 1950) points out that it is not careful, logical analysis that determines what is news but a series of conventional responses by editors. The point is splendidly developed with regard to newspapers by Leon V. Sigal, *Reporters and Officials* (Lexington, Mass.: Heath, 1973); and with regard to television by Edward Jay Epstein, *News from Nowhere* (New York: Random House, 1973).

J. K. Hvistendahl, in "The Reporter as Activist: A Fourth Revolution in Journalism" (*Quill*, February 1970), condemns the code of objectivity as invalid. Dennis Chase, in "The Aphilosophy of Journalism" (*Quill*, September 1971), argues persuasively that U.S. journalists have not developed a philosophical underpinning for their craft and have relied willy-nilly on a kind of instinct theory that operates within the framework of a pragmatic tradition in deciding what is news. Herbert Gans has pursued these ideas systematically in his excellent *Deciding What's News* (New York: Free Press/Vintage 1980). My earlier observations on objectivity can be found in "What Is News?" (*Mass Comm Review*, Winter 1978). I have not found a clearer, more tough-minded analysis of the role the concept of objectivity plays in the psychological life of the journalist than Gaye Tuchman's (p. 128) "Objectivity as Strategic Ritual: An Examination of Newsmen's Notions of Objectivity" (*American Journal of Sociology*, vol. 5, no. 4, January, 1972), pp. 660–679.

The earliest discussion of the conventions of journalism and their importance I have found is in Walter Lippmann's *Public Opinion* (New York: Macmillan, 1922). See also the interesting re-creation and analysis in Ronald Steel, cited in chapter 4, especially pp. 171–185. Douglass Cater, in *The Fourth Branch of Government* (Boston: Houghton Mifflin, 1963), offers a contrary view. Bernard Cohen's excellent analysis of the diplomatic press corps, *The Press and Foreign Policy* (Princeton University Press, 1970), indicates by implication, if not directly, how a quest for objectivity plays into the hands of manipulators of the press. Dan Schiller, *Objectivity and the News: The Public and the Rise of Commercial Journalism* (University of Pennsylvania Press, 1981), offers a Marxist analysis that suggests objectivity was used by early journalists as an excuse for burying stories that might have antagonized commercial forces.

The citations from I. William Hill and Derek Daniels (p. 134) appeared in the *Bulletin of the American Society of Newspaper Editors* in January 1970 (Hill's "Some Subjective Jottings on Objectivity") and in February 1970 (Daniels's "Separating Fact, Emotion, by Edict or Example?").

Of all the recent examinations of objectivity in the news media, the most ambitious and one of the most intriguing is Michael Schudson's *Discovering the News* (New York: Basic Books, 1978). Schudson defines objectivity (p. 8) and goes on to argue (pp. 121–159) that it became an ideology in the 1930s as a reaction against the skepticism that he says characterized U.S. society during the Great Depression. Schudson's book provides many important insights, especially in placing the concept of objectivity in historical perspective. The concept itself has indeed changed over time. Still, Schudson is weak on history generally and tends to force past activities into patterns that fit his model. For instance, he sees the penny press (p. 60) as expressing and building the culture of a democratic society. Expressing yes, but building no. Throughout the Western world, novelists and pamphleteers were already concentrating on the lives of ordinary people, a reaction to the impersonal world of the Industrial Revolution. The romantic movement was already in high gear.

The ideological perimeters of the press are well analyzed in Haluk Sahin's "Broadcasting Autonomy in Turkey 1961–1971," dissertation (Indiana University, 1974), pp. 31–75. See especially chapter 3, "Areas of Autonomy and Areas of Control"; Sahin argues that the autonomy in broadcasting (and by indirection in the press in general) is circumscribed not only by economic and political considerations but also by the limits of the prevailing belief system. See also John H. Boyer, "How Editors View Objectivity" (*Journalism Quarterly*, vol. 58, no. 1, Spring 1981), in which he holds that standard views of objectivity (presenting "both sides," being free of editorial comment, etc.) are vague and offer little help to inquiring editors. Paul H. Weaver, "The Politics of a News Story," in Harry M. Clor, ed., *The Mass Media and Modern Democracy* (Chicago: Rand McNally, 1974), demonstrates effectively how an article that clings most carefully to the maxims of objectivity in fact merely reinforces already held biases and prejudices of the reader.

There is a growing literature on the special qualities of television news, both among academicians and in the popular journals. Nothing approaching a definitive work has yet been written. The mix of essays in *Television: A Selection of Readings from TV Guide Magazine*, edited by Barry G. Cole (New York: The Free Press, 1970), covers a wide range of opinion about critical aspects of television news. Cole edited a successor volume, *Television Today: A Close-up View: Readings from TV Guide* (New York, Oxford University Press, 1981); the section on TV news is most useful. Current articles in *TV Guide* are must reading for students of television news, although they are inevitably brief and superficial; still, virtually all the important questions are raised in those articles. The most valuable general history of broadcast news is the three-volume work by Erik Barnouw, *A Tower in Babel, The Golden Web*, and *The Image Empire* (New York: Oxford University Press, 1966, 1968, and 1970). See also Barnouw's *Tube of Plenty: The Evolution of American Television*, a one-volume Galaxy paperback (Oxford University Press,

1975). Other general histories include Sidney M. Head, *Broadcasting in America: A Survey of Television and Radio*, 3rd ed. (Boston: Houghton Mifflin, 1976); Edward W. Chester, *Television and American Politics* (New York: Sheed and Ward, 1969); and Christopher H. Sterling and John M. Kittross, *Stay Tuned: A Concise History of American Broadcasting* (Belmont, Calif.: Wadsworth, 1978). The best short account of the growth of television is included in Peter M. Sandman, David M. Rubin, and David B. Sachsman, *Media: An Introductory Analysis of American Mass Communications*, 3rd ed. (Englewood Cliffs, N.J.: Prentice-Hall, 1982), pp. 299–344. The notes and bibliography are especially useful. A volume of articles edited by Gaye Tuchman, *The TV Establishment: Programming for Power and Profit* (Englewood Cliffs, N.J.: Spectrum, 1974), covers television news programming critically. For an up-to-date review of TV advertising costs (p. 136), see "Advertisers Growing Restless Over Rising Cost of TV Time" (*Wall Street Journal*, January 27, 1983).

The best examination of a specific court case involving license regulation and renewal by the Federal Communications Commission is included in the fascinating account of the WLBT-TV case, the first in which the FCC denied a license renewal to a television station because of unfairness in programming, in Charles W. Clift, *The WLBT-TV Case, 1964–1969: An Historical Analysis*, dissertation (Indiana University, 1976).

Anyone interested in pursuing problems that arise from ideological considerations in television is directed to *The Critique of Pure Tolerance*, a collection of essays by three leftist sociologist-historians, Robert Paul Wolff, Barrington Moore Jr., and Herbert Marcuse (Boston: Beacon Press, 1965). Marcuse is predictably polemical, arguing that the press is so completely right-wing that elements of it ought to be suppressed in order to give proper weight to leftist points of view. Moore's essay is interesting, but it is Wolff's thoughtful essay, "Beyond Tolerance," that I find of immense value in spreading enlightenment about the practices of the U.S. press. The press, like other majoritarian institutions, Wolff points out, permits only certain actors to arrive on the stage of public awareness and systematically excludes others — not deliberately, from an overtly political perspective, but blindly, operating on the basis of conventional definitions of news. The entire essay, pp. 3–52, merits careful reading.

CHAPTER 7

The derivation of Third World is to be found in *Encyclopedia of Sociology* (Guilford, Conn.: Dushkin Publishing, 1974), p. 295, in an article by Gail Omvedt. See also William Safire, *Safire's Political Dictionary*, rev. ed. (New York: Random House, 1978), pp. 723–724. The influential work by Frantz Fanon (1925–1961), *Les Damnés de la Terre*, was published in English as *The Wretched of the Earth* (New York: Grove Press, 1963).

There is a growing number of publications dealing with the rise and the importance of the news media of the new countries of Asia and Africa, of the older, less-developed press of Latin America, and certain other countries of Asia and Africa. Many national studies of these countries have also appeared, some of them devoted entirely to the press, others to patterns of "development." I can direct attention here to but a handful of these works. The careful reader will of course be able to detect my own biases.

One of the earlier studies was the influential collection of articles edited by Lucien Pye, entitled *Communication and Political Development* (Princeton University Press, 1964). Also noteworthy in Daniel Lerner's *Passing of Traditional Society* (New York: Macmillan, 1958), as indeed are Wilbur Schramm's *Mass Media and National Development* (Stanford University Press, 1964); Everett Rogers and L. Svenning, *Modernization Among Peasants: The Impact of Communication* (New York: Holt, Rinehart and Winston, 1969); Everett Rogers and Floyd Shoemaker, *Communication of Innovations* (New York: Macmillan, 1971); and George Gerbner, ed., *Mass Media Policies in Changing Cultures* (New York: Wiley, 1977).

The most thoughtful and significant study of the news media in the advancing world, in my view, is the book by Anthony Smith entitled *The Geopolitics of Information: How Western Culture Dominates the World* (New York: Oxford University Press, 1980). Smith, who has written extensively on this and other themes, undertakes in *Geopolitics* an examination of the critical importance of news agencies in the advancing world. A more detailed examination of this topic appears in chapter 9 of this book. The numerous pamphlets and articles prepared for and circulated by UNESCO are required reading in any study of the history and practices of the news media in different countries. In this chapter, I have relied heavily on *Communication Policies in Peru*, a volume written by Carlos Ortega and published by UNESCO in 1977. Ortega, of course, is a not disinterested reporter, for he was one of the chief designers of the Peruvian press policies under President Velasco. Ortega must be read with great care, but his report is indispensable for an understanding of the Peruvian experiment. For the most part, I find Ortega seeking to be as dispassionate as he can be in his account; that he does not always succeed should not be taken as proof that his reports are to be discounted.

The best single-volume discussion of what has come to be called "cultural imperialism" is Herbert Schiller's *Mass Communications and American Empire* (New York: A. M. Kelly, 1969). Schiller has written profusely on this subject, and the topic cannot be studied without careful attention to the body of Schiller's work. As a Marxist, he is, of course, sharply critical of what he considers the basically imperialistic role of the news media in clearing the way for marketing of capitalist goods in the advancing countries and as a special kind of propaganda agency of corporate society. Others have pursued the same line of reasoning.

A trio of articles in *Index on Censorship*, vol. 6, no. 5, Sept./Oct., 1977, casts considerable light on patterns of media development in the advancing world, all critical of the penetration of capitalist news media in the "Third World." See John A. Lent, "The Guiding Light," pp. 17–26; Phil Harris, "Behind the Smokescreen," pp. 27–34; and Graham Mitten, "Tanzania — A Case Study," pp. 35–46. For another, remarkably well-balanced, account of the mass media and other market institutions in the advancing world, see June Kronholz's lengthy article "Tanzania's Case Shows Foreign Aid's Pluses and Its Many Minuses," in the August 27, 1982, issue of *The Wall Street Journal*. An excellent, up-to-date account of the growth of "development journalism" is included in a study by my colleague Christine L. Ogan, "Development Journalism/Communication: The Status of the

Concept" (*Gazette*, vol. 29, 1982, pp. 3–13). William A. Hachten, in *The World News Prism: Changing Media, Clashing Ideologies* (Iowa State University Press, 1981), has made an interesting attempt to update the views of the Four Theories by adding a fifth "concept," altering the names in the original to Authoritarian, Western, Communist, and Revolutionary, and adding a fifth which he calls "Developmental" (pp. 60–77).

The most exhaustive examination of the press in Asia appears in a volume edited by John A. Lent, *The Asian Newspapers' Reluctant Revolution* (Iowa State University Press, 1971). The chapter by John Liu, pp. 43–52, is an excellent distillation of Liu's *Communications and National Integration in Communist China* (Berkeley: University of California Press, 1971), and is well worth reading, as is Liu's entire book should the reader be interested in pursuing Chinese press developments in detail. Another useful study of the Chinese press is Frederick T. C. Yu, *Mass Persuasion in Communist China* (New York: Praeger, 1964). I have relied heavily for material on the Indonesian press on Oey Hong Lee's *Indonesian Government and Press During Guided Democracy* (Zug, Switzerland: Inter Documentation, 1971). With regard to India and Nehru, I have found most useful passages in Donald Eugene Smith's *Nehru and Democracy: The Political Thought of an Asian Democrat* (Bombay: Orient Longman, 1958). More current is the 1977 UNESCO booklet *Communication Policies in India*. On the press in Japan, see UNESCO's *Communication Policies in Japan* by Hidetoshi Kato, 1978. The most up-to-date book on Japan is Young C. Kim, *Japanese Journalists and Their World* (University of Virginia Press, 1981). A number of yearbooks are available on the Japanese press, all of which would interest the specialized researcher.

I have relied heavily on Nora C. Quebral for examination of the press in the Philippines. See her "Development Journalism," in Juan F. Famias, ed., *Development Communication* (Laguna: University of Philippines at Los Baños, 1975); and her "Development Communication: Where Does It Stand Today?" in *Media Asia* (vol. 3, no. 4, 1975). A thoughtful study of the growth of the philosophy of a development press appears in Narinder K. Aggarwala's "What Is Development News?" (*Journal of Communication*, vol. 29, no. 2, 1979).

On the press in the Middle East, see especially William A. Rugh, *The Arab Press: News Media and the Political Process in the Arab World* (Syracuse University Press, 1979).

Of particular interest, in connection with the African press, are the great variety of newspapers and magazines published in English and French throughout the African continent. See also the booklets published by UNESCO on different African countries, among them *Communication Policies in Nigeria*, by Frank Okwu Ogboajah 1980. An excellent companion is the booklet on the press in Zaire.

The quotations from Nkrumah, Nyerere, and Mboya appear in two slim volumes. One is Nkrumah's *The African Journalism* Dar es Salaam: Tanzania Publishers, 1965. This is primarily a reproduction of a speech by Nkrumah in 1963, together with commentary. See also Frank Barton, *The Press in Africa* (Zurich: International Press Institute, 1969). Barton has written extensively on Africa for the IPI; many of his studies are readily available. The reference to the IPI training manual (p. 172) is drawn from an article by Barton cited in Peter Golding, "Media Professionalism," p. 301. Much of the material in the African section of this chapter is derived from personal experience, attendance at journalism conferences in Nigeria and Tanzania, and private conversations with journalists and journalism scholars.

Among the writings on the revolutionary press experiment in Peru, the most intriguing are included in unpublished works by Peruvian Juan Gargurevich and Chilean Raquel Salinas. Gargurevich is the author of several important works on the Latin American press, including *Introductión a la historia de los medios de comunicación en el Peru* (Lima: Editorial Horizonte, 1977). His writings have not yet appeared to any important degree in English, but that oversight may soon be corrected. The most important of Salinas's work is included in a paper, "Development Theories and Communication Models: A Critical Approach," presented at a conference of the International Association of Mass Communications Research (IAMCR), 1980.

Indeed, I am indebted to Salinas for the concept of the arrow as a symbol of certain communication scholars. Among her other works of interest is "Culture in the Process of Dependent Development: Theoretical Perspectives," in Kaarle Nordenstreng and Herbert I. Schiller, *National Sovereignty and International Communication* (Norwood, N.J.: Ablex, 1979). See also Rita Cruise O'Brien, *Media Professionalism: Dependence on Rich Country Models* (Sussex, England: Institute of Development Studies, 1976); and Peter Golding and Graham Murdock, "Theories of Communication and Theories of Society" (paper presented to IAMCR convention, Leicester, England, 1976).

I am also indebted to both Gargurevich and Salinas for responses to questions raised in letters. The UNESCO analysis by Juan Ortega, previously cited, is also of considerable value. It is to be noted that Gargurevich, Salinas, and Ortega all approach the Peruvian story sympathetically. As the reader will have recognized, I too view the experiment with sympathy, if also with a large dose of sadness over the way it was conducted. The account by Robert Pierce in his *Keeping the Flame: Media and Government in America* (New York: Hastings, 1979), pp. 119–145, provides a rather mixed account of the events in Peru. Pierce obviously is attempting to be as objective as he can, but he is more than once blinded by the folklore of Us vs. Them and fails to see behind the critical shadings. Still, Pierce is well worth reading. For a blatantly anti-Peruvian account, see the brief report by George Thomas Kurian in *World Press Encyclopedia*, vol. 2 (New York: Facts on File, 1982), pp. 735–739. A sometimes impressionistic but most useful analysis of the press of Peru, and indeed of all Latin America, is included in the intriguing book by journalist Georgie Ann Geyer, *The New Latins: Fateful Change in South and Central America* (Garden City, N.Y.: Doubleday, 1970). The crucial quotation from Marroquín Rojas appears on p. 57. On p. 261, she classifies Velasco's Peru as the "land of revolutionary colonels." Geyer today is considerably less than enthusiastic over the Velasco press experiment, holding that the naiveté of the revolutionaries contributed to a rebirth of tyranny in that country. For a Latin American overview, see Marvin Alisky, *Latin American Media: Guidance and Censorship* (Iowa State University Press, 1981).

My graduate student Gonzalo Soruco wrote a fascinating paper, "Press Development in Venezuela and the Lippmann Model," for the convention of the International Division of the Association for Education on Journalism (Boston, 1980). In it, Soruco traced the early history of the first Latin American press in

Venezuela. Other interesting studies on the Latin American press include: Erling H. Erlandson, "The Press in Mexico: Past, Present and Future" (*Journalism Quarterly*, vol. 41, 1964), pp. 232–36; Danton Jobim, "French and U.S. Influences Upon the Latin American Press" (*Journalism Quarterly*, vol. 31, 1954), pp. 61–66; and Mary A. Gardner, "Latin American Newspapers" (*Community College Journalism*, vol. 8, no. 4, Summer 1980), pp. 10–13. For an account of Brazilian censorship, see the chapter on Brazil in Pierce's *Keeping the Flame*, pp. 23–54. Among the other sources on the press in Latin America are individual journalists from a variety of countries, whom I have interviewed in different places. It is inappropriate to indicate their identities.

For a general history of Peru and of the place of the Velasco experiment in it, see Victor Alba, *Peru* (Boulder, Colo.: Westview, 1977). Alba believes that Peru's geography and social history have prevented it from developing a national consciousness. His chapter 10, "The Coup Within the Coup," about the Velasco years, provides an excellent overview. Otherwise, little can be found in English on the thrust of Peruvian history. For a standard historical account, see Martin C. Needler, *Latin American Politics in Perspective* (Princeton University Press, 1963).

On the socialization and training of journalists in the advancing world, the indispensable work is the study by Peter Golding, "Media Professionalism in the Third World: The Transfer of an Ideology," in James Curran, Michael Gurevitch, Janet Woollacott, eds. *Mass Communication in Society*, previously cited.

CHAPTER 8

The report of the Hutchins Commission was published in 1947 in a book entitled *A Free and Responsible Press*, subtitled *A General Report on Mass Communication: Newspapers, Radio, Motion Pictures, Magazines, and Books*. It appeared in two volumes, the first on newspapers, the second on the other media. Its collective author was the Commission on Freedom of the Press. In some libraries, its author is identified as Zechariah H. Chafee, Jr., one of the members of the commission and himself a prominent authority on free expression. His monumental work *Free Speech in the United States* appeared in a revised edition in 1964, published by the Harvard University Press. The commission report was published by Chicago University Press. The principal findings of the commission first appeared in print in *Fortune* magazine, as a supplement to the issue of April 1947.

There have been many commentaries on its contents, both in part and in whole. Certainly, the growing numbers of books, monographs, and articles on the ethics of journalism regularly hark back to the Hutchins Commission report and in general adopt its major conclusions as a kind of normative law for the mass media. The "theory" of social responsibility enunciated in the *Four Theories* is drawn from the recommendations of the Hutchins Commission. In various forms, those conclusions have also been applauded by creators of codes of conduct in other countries. The report of the MacBride Commission, discussed in chapter 9, also endorses most of the recommendations of the Hutchins Commission.

In the years immediately after the report of the Hutchins Commission, editors and journalism scholars found much in it with which to disagree. Some of those criticisms can be found in the *Fortune* article. Others appear in publications of the

American Society of Newspaper Editors and in *Journalism Quarterly*. The critical comments by Robert Desmond, "Of a Free and Responsible Press," appeared as an editorial in the June 1947 issue of that publication (vol. 24, no. 2, pp. 188–192). Forest's address at the ASNE convention on April 17, 1947, was reprinted in *Problems of Journalism*, p. 19. An interesting summary of the Hutchins Commission report, together with certain criticisms, appears in *Nieman Reports* (Autumn 1976), pp. 18–25, in an article written by Louis M. Lyons, the longtime curator of the Nieman Foundation. No better summary of the report and its findings is available anywhere. Among other things, Lyons criticizes the report for failing to provide for policing of rulings of the news councils that are recommended by the commission.

The National News Council is an excellent source for background material on its own operations. It was created in the spirit of the Hutchins Commission recommendation for a nongovernmental organization not only to protect the news media against unwarranted government interference but also to protect the public against excesses perpetrated by the news media. The council, however, has no enforcement powers. For an overview of council background and policy, see *A Free and Responsive Press: The Twentieth Century Fund Task Force Report for a National News Council*, by Alfred Balk (New York: Twentieth Century Fund, 1973). Among the many books and articles on news councils, one of the most valuable is *Backtalk: Press Councils in America*, by William L. Rivers, William B. Blankenburg, Kenneth Starck, and Earl Reeves (San Francisco: Canfield Press, 1972). The most thorough account of the history and growth of the British council is contained in H. Phillip Levy, *The Press Council: History, Procedure and Cause* (New York: St. Martin's, 1967). For a report on an intriguing British press council case, see my "'Moment of Truth' for the BBC" (*Columbia Journalism Review*, November/December, 1971). The UNESCO publication *Mass Media, Codes of Ethics and Councils* (Paris 1980), provides the most up-to-date account of news council developments around the world. Anthony Smith, in *The Geopolitics of Information*, casts considerable light on the growth of the Indian press council. The ombudsman idea is generally discussed in connection with the development of press councils. See, for instance, the account in *Media*, by Sandman, Rubin, and Sachsman, previously cited.

As with so many other issues dealt with in this book, the topic of the power of the press has attracted the attention of a vast number of writers, among them scholars in several fields, politicians, journalists, and often simply thoughtful members of the general public. Most writers seem to assign tremendous power to the mass media, especially television. Such independent power is difficult, indeed impossible, to document — and one of the major conclusions of this book is that although the potential for independent power exists, it seems not to be exercised. And perhaps it may never be exercised.

The citation from Robert Stein, *Media Power: Who Is Shaping the Picture of The World?* (Englewood Cliffs, N.J.: Prentice-Hall, 1970), appears on p. xii. For the citations from television journalists, see Marvin Barrett, ed. *Moment of Truth? The Fifth Alfred I. du Pont Columbia University School of Broadcast Journalism Lecture* (New York: Thomas Y. Crowell, 1975). A contrary view is expressed in the excellent analysis by H. A. Innis, *The Press: A Neglected Factor in the Economic History of the Twentieth Century* (London: Oxford University Press,

1949). Innis, a Canadian scholar who exerted a strong influence over Marshall McLuhan, sees the press as utterly without power of its own, as simply a puppet in the control of the very economic and political forces it purports to watch over.

The power issue has been associated in recent years with the concept of agenda setting. Its earlier full treatment came in the book by the pioneers in the field of this research, Donald L. Shaw and Maxwell E. McCombs, *The Emergence of American Political Issues: The Agenda-Setting Function of the Press* (St. Paul: West, 1977). That work drew on an insight by Bernard C. Cohen in his *The Press and Foreign Policy* (Princeton University Press, 1957). Cohen's excellent study, still the best in its field, examines the processes by which "news" emanates from the U.S. State Department and the journalists who report on diplomatic affairs from Washington and diplomatic posts abroad. It was Cohen who wrote that while the press might not tell people what to think, it did tell them what to think *about*. His careful examination of how this "agenda" was delivered to the press was given less attention by the agenda-setters in their early work than his perhaps offhand comment about telling people what to think about. A study of *political* agenda setting can be found in Roger W. Cobb and Charles D. Elder, *Participation in American Politics: The Dynamics of Agenda-Building* (Boston: Allyn and Bacon, 1972). With regard to election campaigns, see David H. Weaver, Doris A. Graber, Maxwell E. McCombs, and Chaim Eyal, *Media Agenda-Setting in a Presidential Election: Issues, Images, and Interest* (New York: Praeger, 1981). For a thorough, up-to-date account of the "state of the art" in agenda setting, see the essay by my colleague David H. Weaver, "Media Agenda-Setting and Media Manipulation," in *Mass Communication Review Yearbook*, vol. 3, edited by D. Charles Whitney (Beverly Hills: Sage, 1982).

Ben Bagdikian, in *The Information Machines: Their Impact on Men and the Media* (New York: Harper and Row, 1971), offers a different interpretation of agenda setting, holding that information and agendas are supplied to a large degree by authorities acting "to control information for the public good as they see it" (p. 8). The reader will have observed that this view accords with mine. It is likely that information is more tightly controlled in smaller communities than in great cities, to a considerable extent by editors themselves, who see their press serving as a cohesive force to protect against disruptive efforts. See Clarice N. Olien, George A. Donohue, and Phillip J. Tichenor, "The Community Editor's Power and Reporting of Conflict" (*Journalism Quarterly*, vol. 45, Spring 1968), pp. 243–252. Willard G. Bleyer, in *The Profession of Journalism* (Boston: Atlantic Monthly Press, 1981), pointed to the loyalty of the press to its community and its promotion of positive community values.

John C. Merrill discusses media power to a considerable degree in his influential *The Imperative of Freedom: A Philosophy of Journalistic Autonomy* (New York: Hastings, 1974). Merrill calls attention to a number of remarks long attributed to powerful statesmen, such as Napoleon, about the power of the press. Adolf Hitler in *Mein Kampf* assigned similar power to the press. There is certainly nothing new in the current discussions about press power, although the emphasis has shifted more to the power of television. Merrill's views on ethical topics and on social responsibility are treated fully in *Imperative*, but the reader can find the essential Merrill in the two chapters from that book that are included in the excellent collection of readings edited by Merrill and Rex Barney, *Ethics and the*

Press: Readings in Mass Media Morality (New York: Hastings, 1975), especially pp. 8–17 and pp. 117–131. A more recent version of Merrill's thought appears in a book he authored jointly with S. Jack Odell, titled *Philosophy and Journalism* (New York: Longman, 1983). Raymond Williams's theories of press responsibility and power appear in his book *Communications*, rev. ed. (London: Chatto and Windus, 1966). See especially pp. 123–132 and pp. 147–173.

In this connection, Walter Lippmann's *Liberty and the News* (New York: Harcourt Brace, 1920), may be read with profit, along with his *Public Opinion*, previously cited. The intriguing study conducted of reportage by *The New York Times* of the Bolshevik Revolution is by Charles Merz and Lippmann; it is entitled "A Test of the News" and appeared as a special supplement to the *New Republic* issue of August 4, 1920. William Hachten's norm for the socially responsible press (p. 189) is contained in his *The World News Prism: Changing Media, Clashing Ideologies* (Iowa State University Press, 1981), p. 66. This norm very much resembles the model assigned to itself by the BBC (see discussion in chapter 7). The Anthony Downs reference (p. 191) is to his excellent offbeat study *An Economic Theory of Democracy* (New York: Harper and Row, 1957).

How the power of the press relates to specific U.S. political developments is interestingly traced in David L. Paletz and Robert M. Entman. *Media Power Politics: A Timely, Provocative Look at How the Media Affect Public Opinion and Political Power in the United States* (New York: Free Press, 1981). The discussion of the press and how it "admits" groups to power is drawn largely from Robert Paul Wolff, "Beyond Tolerance," previously cited. For an intriguing personal report of the election campaign of 1972, see James M. Perry, *Us and Them: How the Press Covered the 1972 Election* (New York: Potter, 1973). The account by Theodore H. White, *The Making of the President 1972* (New York: Atheneum, 1973), provides substantial confirmation.

On the role of the press in the coverage of crime, see the interesting analysis in Hal E. Pepinsky, *Crime and Conflict*, Law in Society Series (New York: Academic Press, 1976).

Must reading for anyone interested in the role of the mass media in the reporting of news about blacks in the United States is the appropriate section in the report of the Kerner Commission. See *Report of the National Advisory Commission on Civil Disorders* (Washington, D. C., 1968), pp. 362–389. Stokely Carmichael's challenging discussion of the behavior of the white press appears in "Toward Black Liberation" (*The Massachusetts Review*, vol. 7, Autumn 1966), pp. 639–651. For an analysis of institutions in general as they relate to racial questions, see Louis L. Knowles and Kenneth Prewitt, eds., *Institutional Racism in the United States* (Englewood Cliffs, N. J.: Prentice-Hall, 1969). See also August Meier and Elliott Rudwick, eds., *Black Protest in the Sixties* (Chicago: Quadrangle, 1970). This book provides a good deal of interesting information on the press in its dealing with racial issues. For an up-to-date account of the progress of black journalists in mainsteam U.S. media, see Phyl Garland, "The Black Press: Down But Not Out" (*Columbia Journalism Review*, September/October, 1982), pp. 43–50. Her report is less than optimistic.

The history of the modern-day underground press in the United States, especially in the dramatic years between 1965 and 1969, is well told in Robert J. Glessing, *The Underground Press in America* (Indiana University Press, 1970). The citation from Ray Mungo is from his *Famous Long Ago: My Life and Hard Times with Liberation News Service* (Boston: Beacon Press, 1970), pp. 75–76. For a supporting view on the importance of an alternative press, including a high school underground, see, e.g., John Grell, "Why the Underground Press," in Diane Divoky, ed., *How Will You Be? Expressions of Student Outrage from the High School Press* (New York: Avon Books, 1969), pp. 145–148. The fervor for alternative presses that burned in the 1960s all but disappeared in the 1970s and 1980s.

Jerome A. Barron has been the principal challenger of the revered position of the press that it is the sole judge of to whom it grants access to its pages. However, his position has been rejected by the U.S. Supreme Court, in the case of *Miami Herald Publishing Co. v. Tornillo*, 418 U.S. 241, 94 S. Ct. 2831 (1974). The most complete argument advanced by Barron is contained in his *Freedom of the Press For Whom? The Right of Access to Mass Media* (Indiana University Press, 1973). The pros and cons of the access question as it relates to the government and press are discussed in a series of writings in the book edited by William L. Rivers and Michael J. Nyhan, *Aspen Notebook on Government and the Media* (New York: Praeger, 1977). See especially Douglass Cater, "Prologue: Toward a Public Philosophy on Government-Media Relations"; and Ithiel de Sola Pool, "Newsmen and Statesmen: Adversaries or Cronies?" The observations of Clifton Daniel of *The New York Times* on the access issue are presented in his article "Rights of Access and Reply," reprinted in Michael E. Emery and Ted Curtis Smythe, *Readings in Mass Communication: Concepts and Issues in the Mass Media*, 2nd ed. (Dubuque, Iowa: William C. Brown, 1974). Another interesting compilation is included in George Will, ed. (*Press, Politics and Popular Government*) (Washington: American Enterprise Institute for Public Policy Research, 1972). See especially the articles by Robert L. Bartley, "The Press: Adversary, Surrogate, Sovereign, or Both?" and by Irving Kristol, "Crisis for Journalism: The Missing Elite." Walter Annenberg's defense of the press (p. 204) is contained in his "The Fourth Branch of Government" (*TV Guide*, May 15, 1982). Annenberg drew his title from the well-known book by Cater, previously cited. The advice of Neville Jayaweera (p. 205) is cited in Anthony Smith's *The Geopolitics of Information*, previously cited, p. 154.

Several additional citations on the issue of the role of the media are worth noting. See, for instance, James Carey's "Mass Communication Research and Cultural Studies: An American View" in the Curran reader, previously cited, pp. 409–425. See also Bernard Rubin, *Questioning Media Ethics* (New York: Praeger, 1978). Rubin correctly points out that the press remains uncertain of the definition of its role. See also the master's thesis of Linda M. Baker, "Four Theories of the Press: A Reevaluation" (University of Washington, 1979). She challenges the classification system of the Four Theorists on the ground that it tends to ignore broadcasting technology, economics, and the rise of the Third World.

The literature on the relationship between President Nixon and the press is extensive and needs not be detailed here. The series of speeches by Vice-President Spiro Agnew criticizing the press are reproduced in *Collected Speeches of Spiro Agnew* (New York: Audubon Books, 1971). The article by Daniel P. Moynihan, "The Presidency and the Press," appeared in *Commentary* (vol. 51, March 1971), pp. 41–52. It was in this article that Moynihan, a Democrat and no political friend of Nixon and Agnew, accused the leading newspapers and television networks of being leading forces in a kind of "adversary culture," which he though at that time might undermine faith in U.S. institutions. As a member of the U.S. Senate later, Moynihan moved away from this position, but he continues to be quoted on the topic.

For a discussion of broadcasters and the fairness doctrine, see Henry Geller, *The Fairness Doctrine in Broadcasting: Problems and Suggested Courses of Action* (RAND R-1412-FF, December 1975).

The best source in English of accounts of the philosophical positions of the sociologists Max Weber and Ferdinand Tönnies is Hanno Hardt's *Social Theories of the Press: Early German and American Perspectives* (Beverly Hills, Calif.: Sage, 1979). See chapters 5 and 6, pp. 133–186. Weber's monograph, *"Politik als Beruf"* has been widely reprinted and is worth reading for an insight into Weber's theories of politics and information. I am especially fond of the ideas expressed by Tönnies. See the bibliographic references to Tönnies's writing in Hardt, p. 236. For a quick overview of Tönnies's thoughts on the press and public opinion, see "The Power and Value of Public Opinion," which is chapter 18 in *Ferdinand Tönnies on Sociology: Pure, Applied, and Empirical*, edited by Werner Cahnman and Rudolf Heberle (University of Chicago Press, 1971). The chapter originally appeared as "Macht und Wert der Oeffentlichen Meinung" in *Die Dioskuren, Jahrobuch fuer Geisteswissenschaften* (vol. 2, 1923), pp. 72–99.

CHAPTER 9

The majority of documents cited in chapter 9 are from publications of UNESCO. The interested reader is directed to the biennial reports of the proceedings of the General Conference of UNESCO. Of special interest are the proceedings of the 16th (1970), 17th (1972), 18th (1974), 19th (1976), 20th (1978), and 21st (1980) General Conferences. The 19th was held in Nairobi and the 21st in Belgrade. The others took place at UNESCO headquarters in Paris. These reports are must reading for anyone seeking an accurate account of the positions taken by various delegations and by official statements of UNESCO officials. Understanding of the issues involved is frustrated by the fact that so many individuals and groups, on all sides of the press issues involved, have based their positions on second-hand accounts and on interpretations that are often misreading of the motives of participants. In addition to the General Conferences, one would do well to study in detail other relevant UNESCO publications and the official reports of meetings and conferences on press issues held by other international and national organizations. One such meeting that requires close attention was the Symposium of Non-Aligned Countries on Communication that was held at Tunis in 1976.

The text of the 1978 "Charter" (pp. 217–218) is reported in the proceedings of the 20th General Conference. It was titled: "Declaration on Fundamental Principles Concerning the Contribution of the Mass Media to Strengthening Peace and International Understanding, the Promotion of Human Rights and to Countering Racialism, Apartheid and Incitement to War." A full-scale treatment of that declaration is included in Kaarle Nordenstreng, *The Mass Media Declaration of UNESCO* (Norwood, N.J.: Ablex, 1982). In that book, Nordenstreng, in association with Lauri Hannihainen, a Finnish expert on international law, argues that there is developing an international law on communications. U.S. legal authorities take a contrary view. See p. 209 in Nordenstreng and pp. 245–248.

Newspaper and magazine articles reporting on the activities of UNESCO at its general conferences and at other intergovernmental meetings can be found in the files of the newspapers themselves. Among the more interesting and representative articles are these cited ones: *New York Times*, November 29, 1944; *Editor and Publisher*, June 16, 1945; *Christian Science Monitor*, October 24, 1978 ("Keep World Press Free"), and November 24, 1978 ("West Averts Press Crimp, Agrees to Aid Third World"); *Seattle Times*, November 12, 1978 ("UNESCO Declaration Threatens World Press Freedom"); *Manchester Guardian*, December 3, 1978 ("World Charter for Free Press"); and *Le Monde*,November, 24, 1978 ("UN Consensus Fragile"). Citations from these articles appear on pp. 217–219.

Discussions of news agencies, their histories and development, have increased markedly in recent years. A good quick account can be found in Anthony Smith's *The Geopolitics of Information*, already cited. J. Oliver Boyd-Barrett casts doubt on the traditional allegation among advancing-world critics that the four major news agencies (AP, UPI, Reuters, and AFP) are practicing media imperialism. Boyd-Barrett holds that advancing-world governments are in a position to control the activities of those news agencies within their own borders. See "Western News Agencies and the 'Media Imperialism' Debate: What Kind of Data-Base?" (*Journal of International Affairs*, vol. 35, no. 2, Fall/Winter, 1981–82), pp. 247–260. That issue of the *Journal of International Affairs* is a treasure trove for students of the "free flow" issue; it is devoted entirely to the information-order issue and contains interesting articles by such diverse thinkers as UNESCO's Doudou Diene and the U.S. critic Leonard R. Sussman of Freedom House. The articles provide a reasonably clear statement of opposing points of view on the issue. The most thorough and up-to-date accounting of news agencies' activities is contained in the UNESCO document "The World of News Agencies," prepared for the MacBride Commission in 1980. It is document number 11 in the files of the commission, whose official title is the International Commission for the Study of Communication Problems. All the documents prepared for the commission have been published at UNESCO headquarters in Paris.

The report of the commission, *Many Voices, One World: Towards a New More Just and More Efficient World Information and Communication Order*, was published by Kogan Press (London, 1980). The many quotations and summaries from the report can be found on the following pages: 142–144, 148, 153, 157–158, 163, 172, 177, 179, 183, 200, 238; 244, 260, 263–264, 266, 270–271. The student of the flow-of-information issue is required, however, to read the entire book and many of the documents prepared for the commission by UNESCO staff members and by international researchers. The holdings in the library at UNESCO headquarters are substantial. In addition to relying on these printed documents, I also interviewed Seán MacBride, U.S. commission delegate Elie Abel, and dozens of employees of the UNESCO secretariat and national delegates to the UNESCO sessions. The reports published by the IPDC, the Intergovernment Programme for Development of Communication, all make for interesting and instructive reading. The first council meeting took place at Paris in June 1981; the second at Acapulco, Mexico, in January 1982; the third at Paris in December 1982.

Repeated assertions by UNESCO officials that the U.S. press had not reported the Belgrade General Conference accurately are noted in John Massee's article in *Editor and Publisher* (vol. 114, 1981), pp. 42–52. This article was titled "UNESCO Defends MacBride Report." The study authorized by the National News Council and led by A. H. Raskin was published in the *Journal of Communication* (vol. 31, no. 4, Autumn 1981) as "U.S. News Coverage of the Belgrade UNESCO Conference," pp. 164–174. That issue of the journal included a number of other articles supporting (or criticizing, in part) Raskin's findings. See especially Colleen Roach, "French Press Coverage of the Belgrade UNESCO Conference," pp. 175–187. That same issue reported also on the meeting that was held several months after the Belgrade meeting at Talloires in France. The Declaration of Talloires was reproduced on pp. 113–115. U.S. delegate William G. Harley reported on "The U.S. Stake in the IPDC," pp. 150–158, and law professor Howard C. Anawalt asked, "Is the MacBride Commission's Approach Compatible with the United States Constitution?" pp. 122–128. Anawalt said it is.

The Declaration of Talloires was also read into the record of the House debate on the Beard amendment (pp. 245–247). See the *Congressional Record*, H6348, September 17, 1981; and H7903, October 29, 1981.

The world press, and in this case the U.S. press in particular, wrote extensively of the meeting at Talloires. U.S. coverage was markedly friendly. Citations here are drawn in large part from editions of the *International Herald Tribune* and *The New York Times*, both of which provided extensive coverage (pp. 241–243). Carl Rowan's article in *The Washington Star*, May 24, 1981, was typical of most of the press accounts friendly to Talloires and hostile to MacBride and the commission. The headline on that article was: "A Misguided Effort to Shackle the World's Press." Sarah Goddard Power's article was reprinted in *Press Woman*, September 1981. Leonard R. Sussman's article, "Opposing Assaults on the World's Free Press," appeared in *The Wall Street Journal* on June 16, 1981. Elliot Abrams's statement to subcommittees of the House Foreign Affairs Committee, "Statement to Congressional Subcommittees on International Operations and Human Rights and on International Organizations," was delivered July 9, 1981. Another interesting attack on UNESCO policy can be found in Leonard J. Theberge, "UNESCO's 'New World Information Order': Colliding With First Amendment Values" *American Bar Association Journal*, June 1981. It is all too clear that the full weight of official opinion, government and private, was directed against UNESCO and its activities in the summer of 1981.

Responses to the work of the IPDC and the efforts of the United States and other industrial nations to upgrade the level of assistance to advancing-world nations are examined in some detail in the *Journal of Communications* (vol. 32, no. 3, Summer 1982) in three interesting articles: Kaarle Nordenstreng, "U.S. Policy and the Third World: A Critique," pp. 54–59; Clifford H. Block, "Promising Aid at Acapulco: A U.S. View," pp. 60–70; and Colleen Rauch, "Mexican and U.S. News Coverage of the IPDC at Acapulco," pp. 71–85. It is to be noted that Nordenstreng (p. 55) harks back to the Hutchins Commission report as the norm for appropriate press behavior. For preliminary reports on the IPDC meeting at Paris in December 1982, see *IPDC Newsletter* and "IPDC — Where the Money Went," in *IPI Report* (vol. 32, no. 2, February 1983), p. 4. The *Report* is the monthly bulletin of the International Press Institute. See also UNESCO preliminary report, March 1983. For an account of the November 1982 UNESCO meeting, see *The New York Times*, November 28, 1982.

The speech by José A. Mayobré Machado, "The New World Information and Communication Order: Common Approaches to a Mutual Problem," was delivered at a symposium at Southern Illinois University, Carbondale, Illinois, April 5, 1981. I have also had the opportunity to speak extensively with Mayobré at UNESCO headquarters at Paris.

The account of the Tanzanian press (pp. 228–229) is drawn from interviews in the United States and Tanzania with journalists directly involved. The article in the *Frankfurter Allgemeine Zeitung* appeared on the front page, July 15, 1982.

Among other useful works on the subjects addressed in chapter 9, see especially Jim Richstad and Michael H. Anderson, eds., *Crisis in International News: Policies and Practices* (New York: Columbia University Press, 1981). The article by Herbert I. Schiller, "Genesis of the Free Flow of Information Principles," pp. 162–183, is perhaps the best single work on the history and development of the free-flow concept. I have drawn extensively from the article. It appeared originally in *Instant Research on Peace and Violence*, a journal published in Tampere, Finland, 1975. Schiller's citations are excellent; the great majority are government documents. Another useful historical monograph is Roger Heacock, *UNESCO and the Media* (Geneva: Institut Universitaire des Hautes Etudes Internationales, 1977). Heacock examines U.S. and Latin American newspaper coverage of UNESCO activities in the information and communication areas during the years 1974–1976. I am indebted also to the master's thesis by my student Hemant Shah, "News Coverage of the New World Information Order: A Content Analysis of Five U.S. Elite Newspapers" (Purdue University, 1982), p. 484.

Some of the material on news agencies is drawn from the works of Kent Cooper, cited in chapter 6, and other general material on news agencies. A special issue of the *Journal of Communications* (vol. 28, no. 4, Autumn 1978) includes a series of excellent background articles on the news pool and the debate no news agencies for the nonaligned countries. See the articles by Jonathan F. Gunther, Pero Ivacic, Edward T. Pinch, Carolyn Marvin, and Herbert I. Schiller, pp. 142–193. The primary source for the material on Roberto Savio and the IPS is Savio himself, whom I interviewed in 1982, and a speech that he delivered at the annual general meeting of the Netherlands Organization for International Development Cooperation at The Hague, June 26, 1982. The speech was entitled, "Communication and Development in the 1980s." Also of considerable interest in understanding Savio and the IPS is an article by Peter Hall in the *Columbia Journalism Review* (January/February 1983), pp. 53–57, in which Savio is interviewed. In that article, Savio attributes the position of the United States on many global questions to inadequate news coverage by television and the regional press: "It is very dangerous that the country with the leading responsibility in the world is directed by a public opinion that has very little knowledge of international affairs" (p. 54). See also the article by Savio and his IPS colleague Phil Harris, "Inter Press Service: the NIIO in Practice," in *Media Development* (vol. 27, 1980), pp. 38–42. This journal is published by the World Association for Christian Communication, an organization that actively promotes a new world information order. The issue in which the article by Savio and Harris appears is filled with brief, informative examinations of international press issues by a number of liberal scholars. See among others Cees Hamelink, "The NIIO: The Recognition of Many Different Worlds," pp. 3–6; Breda Pavlic, "NIIO and National Communication Policies," pp. 7–9; and Ithiel de Sola Pool, "Technological Consequences of the NIIO," pp. 43–44. The article by Al Hester, "Inter Press Service: News From and About the World," is scheduled for publication.

In connection with the accusations directed against the Big Four news agencies that they do not provide a balanced report of news about the advancing world, one can read with profit Mort Rosenblum's *Coups and Earthquakes: Reporting the World for America* (New York: Harper and Row, 1979), in which he recounts some of his experiences as an AP reporter in Third World countries. His thesis is that life as a journalist in those places is an exciting one, and that the reporter delivers to his audience what it wants to read. Rosenblum later became editor of the *International Herald Tribune* in Paris and in that capacity regularly editorialized against the efforts at UNESCO to adopt a new world information order. As a former AP staffer myself, I can attest to the strong bias inside that organization in support of the free-press folklore in the United States. Recognition of the actual nature of the press, of its agency role, rarely comes to the journalist while on his or her daily assignments. It is likely to come, as it did to me, only later, when I was no longer busy meeting deadlines.

For an examination of coverage of international news in news-agency reports received by certain U.S. newspapers, see David H. Weaver and G. Cleveland Wilhoit, "Foreign News Coverage in Two U.S. Wire Services" (*Journal of Communication*, vol. 31, no. 3, Spring 1981), pp. 55–63. Their finding was that in the time period studied (1979) there were more foreign news stories from advancing-world countries than from the more developed countries in both AP and UPI reports. Of course, the bulk of those stories from the advancing world were about dramatic events, including the revolution in Iran; fighting in Vietnam, Uganda, and Nicaragua; and disputes in the Middle East — more "coups and earthquakes."

Advancing-world countries in some parts of the world have made progress in organizing news agencies on a regional basis that aspire to rival the Big Four (pp. 226–228). The most successful of these to date has been CANA, the Caribbean News Agency, which has been receiving money from the IPDC as well as from regional governments and private organizations, and which seeks to replace the Big Four, especially Reuters, as the chief source of news in the Caribbean. See Marlene Cuthbert, *The Caribbean News Agency: Third World Model* (Lexington, Ky.: *Journalism Monographs*, No. 71, 1981).

CHAPTER 10

Historically, press ownership has been reluctant to provide detailed information about its financial structure and profitability. As rising costs have pushed newspaper owners into chains and conglomerates and to sell their stock on the open market, figures on profits and losses have become more commonplace. The most reliable indicator of these figures appears to be E. F. Hutton, the brokerage firm that has been aggressive in investigating and reporting on the newspaper and broadcasting industry. Most of the statistical information in this chapter on the financial structure of U.S. newspapers is drawn from reports by E. F. Hutton and by the American Newspaper Publishers Association. The annual ANPA report, *Facts About Newspapers*, is a useful if incomplete source of fundamental information. *Facts* is identified as "A Statistical Summary of the Newspaper Business" and is published annually by ANPA's Newspaper Center, Washington, D.C. The figures here are from the 1982 report. A most interesting analysis is contained in the E. F. Hutton publication *Institutional Industry Review*, in an article in its February 12, 1982, edition by Patrick O'Donnell, entitled "The Business of Newspapers: An Essay for Investors." Additional E. F. Hutton material on newspaper profitability is included in a pamphlet, "Institutional Recommendations," appearing September 14, 1982. See also regular reports entitled, "FactSet Data Systems." Far and away the most thorough accounting of the financial status and profitability of radio and television appears in annual reviews by *Broadcasting*. I have relied in this chapter on the *Broadcasting* survey that appeared in the May 9, 1983, issue. *The Wall Street Journal* article of January 27, 1983, previously cited, updates that report. See also *The Wall Street Journal* March 31, 1983.

No standard work of journalism omits considerations of the economic realities of the U.S. mass media, but few examine the financial realities thoroughly or dispassionately. One widely read book, which on the whole reinforces the conventional view of a free commercial press, is Bruce M. Owen, *Economics and Freedom of Expression: Media Structure and the First Amendment* (Cambridge, Mass.: Ballinger, 1975). See also chapters 10 and 11 in Ben Bagdikian's *The Information Machines*, previously cited, for a thoughtful examination of — as Bagdikian puts it — "who pays for the news." An interesting brief account of the U.S. press in the economy is contained in an article by Arnold H. Ismach, "The Economic Connection: Mass Media Profits, Ownership and Performance," in Everette E. Dennis, Arnold H. Ismach, and Donald M. Gillmor, eds. *Enduring Issues in Mass Communication* (St. Paul: West, 1978), pp. 243–259.

Much of the information in this chapter on the financial structure of the news media in countries outside the United States is drawn from personal interviews and conversations, especially in the Soviet Union, Western Europe, Africa, and the Middle East. Greater attention seems to be paid by European scholars to the economic power of the mass media than by American researchers, aside from Marxists such as Herbert I. Schiller, whose work in this field is exhaustive if narrow in interpretation. See especially his *Mass Communications and American Empire* (New York: Augustus M. Kelley, 1969). The examination of the press in the Soviet economy is drawn from interviews with several Soviet officials, as well as U.S. and European diplomats and journalists in the Soviet Union. It is not appropriate to identify all these sources by name, nor, in fact, is it appropriate to identify sources in certain other countries. I am pleased to note, however, that the comment by Segun Osoba (p. 263) was made at a conference of journalists in Ibadan, Nigeria, in 1980.

The discussion of Comenius (Komenský) is drawn from the Count Lützow translation of *The Labyrinth of the World and the Paradise of the Heart* (London: Swan Sonnenschein, 1901); from the reference in Vladimir Hudec, *Journalism, Substance, Social Functions, Development*, previously cited; and from Comenius's *On Education* (New York: Teachers College Press, Columbia University, 1957). The latter appeared with an introduction by Jean Piaget, writing on behalf of

UNESCO, which was honoring Comenius as an international educator. Piaget observed (p. 22) that Comenius believed in a universal right to education on the basis of equality, for girls as well as boys, for poor as well as wealthy. Since Comenius believed, as Piaget wrote, that educators should "teach all things to all men and from all points of view" (p. 7), he qualifies as a kind of patron saint of this book. Comenius was born in 1592 and died in 1670; it was in his lifetime that a press first appeared in Europe. Already journalists (Comenius used the Czech word *novinář*, which is the common word for journalist today) were figures of interest. Comenius made use also of the word *pištal*, which today refers to a whistle. However, it is likely that in the seventeenth century it referred to a musical instrument. In any case, it is even today associated with the idea of piping or playing the fife. I am indebted to my colleague Owen Johnson for a close examination of the Czech words. William Congreve's *Love for Love*, in which the paying-the-piper image first appeared in English (act 2, scene 1), was originally performed in 1695. See his *Complete Plays*, ed. Herbert Davis (University of Chicago Press, 1967).

Examinations of the new phenomenon of teletext and of similar developments in the field of "electronic newspapers" are growing at a rapid rate. Among the best studies available are: Benjamin M. Compaine, *The Newspaper Industry in the 1980s: An Assessment of Economics and Technology* (White Plains, N.Y.: Knowledge Industry Publications, 1980); Anthony Smith, *Good-bye Gutenberg: The Newspaper Revolution of the 1980s* (New York: Oxford University Press, 1980); David H. Weaver, *Videotex Journalism: Teletext, Viewdata and the News* (Hillsdale, N.J.: Lawrence Erlbaum, 1983); and Rex Winsbury, *The Electronic Bookstall: Push-Button Publishing on Videotex* (London: International Institute of Communications, 1979). The book by INTELSAT's J. N. Pelton, *Global Talk* (Alphen aan den Rijn, Netherlands: Sijthoff and Nordhoff, 1981), p. 265, presents a sobering examination of the opportunities and the dangers inherent in technological development. Pelton expresses an urgent need, in the application of high-tech gear, for a "better understanding of the social and political dynamics of technological change," as well as answers to the question of how technology can help build a better world. The benefits and dangers of what he calls Global Talk are, he says, enormous. On the other side, he notes (p. 284): "Our greatest challenge for the twenty-first century will likely be survival. At the negative end of the scale, this means avoidance of catastrophic warfare and ecological disaster; on the positive end of the scale, this means developing institutions and processes that will help us build a better humane and livable version of the World of Global Talk." Hear, hear.

The potential dangers are uppermost in the mind of Herbert Schiller in· his "The Electronic Invaders," reprinted in Michael Emery and Ted Curtis Smythe, eds., *Readings in Mass Communication: Concepts and Issues in the Mass Media*, 4th ed. (Dubuque, Iowa: William C. Brown, 1980), pp. 435–439. Among other writers who deal with the potential negative impact of technological growth are Cees J. Hamelink, Kaarle Nordenstreng, Jeremy Tunstall, and Dan Schiller. The writings of these men are voluminous, and the interested reader is invited to pick and choose. See among other works Hamelink's *The Corporate Village: The Role of Transnational Corporations in International Communication* (Rome: IDOC International, 1977). See also Dan Schiller, *Telematics and Government* (Norwood, N.J.: Ablex, 1982).

Concern about the flow of data across national borders is one of increasing interest to IBI, the Intergovernmental Bureau for Informatics. Anyone interested in this field is referred to the various publications issued by IBI from its headquarters at Viale Civilta del Lavoro 12, Rome. The IBI magazine, *Agora*, and its *Newsletter*, both issued regularly, are valuable sources of information. The citation from Business International (p. 268) is drawn from a newsletter entitled "Transborder Data Flow," undated but circulated in 1982. The best all-inclusive single examination of the data-flow issue can be found in an article in *The Wall Street Journal* by David E. Sanger on August 26, 1981. It is headlined: "Multinationals Worry as Countries Regulate Data Crossing Borders." Anthony Smith's prediction that the passage of data across borders may mean the end of national sovereignty as we know it appears on p. 128 and 142 of his book *The Geopolitics of Information*, previously cited.

Additional predictions about the future of the communications and news media industries can be found in a series of articles reprinted in Michael Emery and Ted Curtis Smythe, *Readings in Mass Communication: Concepts and Issues in the mass Media*, 5th ed. (Dubuque, Iowa: William C. Brown, 1983), pp. 247–303. See especially Kenneth Edwards, "Delivering Information to the Home Electronically," pp. 268–286; and Jon G. Udell, "The Newspaper of the Next Decade," pp. 287–299. The listing of technologies (p. 264) is drawn from *Telecommunications in the Year 2000*, a task-force report on national and international telecommunications, prepared at the conclusion of a 1981 conference organized by Rutgers University International Communication Training and Research (PICTAR). The report of international issues was prepared by Christine Ogan of Indiana University. The delegates — from the academic and industrial worlds — urged all industrialized countries and all appropriate transnational organizations involved in communications activities to increase the level of their research and their contributions of both technology and money to assist advancing countries to develop their communications facilities, in keeping with the spirit of the World Communications Year of 1983. "Clearly," the report said in a memorable passage (p. 22), "a global society of economic, social and cultural interchange is dependent upon our modern satellite and terrestrial communications systems. In this respect, communications is perhaps as important as defense as a means to achieving and maintaining global peace."

CHAPTER 11

The material on Roland Schreyer and his activities for UNESCO are derived from interviews with Schreyer and the use of some of his personal notes, as well as the UNESCO publication "Rural Journalism in Africa," in the series *Reports and Papers on Mass Communication* (No. 88, 1981). Also of interest, particularly for the views of Frances Berrigan and Julius Nyerere, is No. 87 in the same series, "Communication in the Community."

Much has been written on socialization and social control. I am particularly attracted to the slim book by Robert Weissberg, *Political Learning, Political Choice, and Democratic Leadership* (Englewood Cliffs, N.J.: Prentice-Hall, 1974). In this connection, see also P. Jean Frazier and Cecelie Gaziano, *Robert Ezra Park's Theory of News, Public Opinion and Social Control*, No. 64 in the series *Journalism Monographs*, published by the Association for Education in Journalism (1979).

Like many others, I am particularly fond also of Sissela Bok's revealing little book *Lying*, previously cited. See the reference on p. 297. The reference to John Burton (p. 299) is to another writer to whose ideas I am much indebted. See his *Deviance, Terrorism and War: The Process of Solving Unsolved Social and Political Problems* (New York: St. Martin's Press, 1979).

APPENDIX

John Bartholomew Gough's temperance lecture is reprinted in *Famous Lectures*, volume 8 of the series *Modern Eloquence*, (London: Modern Eloquence Corporation), pp. 192–214. The lecture is titled "Social Responsibilities."

The passage on the press from John Stuart Mill is contained in G. L. Williams, ed. *John Stuart Mill on Politics and Society* (Hassock, England: The Harvester Press, 1975), p. 169. The essay in question, "Law of Libel and Liberty of the Press," originally appeared in *Westminster Review* (vol. 3, 1825).

The slim NEA volume appeared as *Social Responsibility in a Free Society*, published by the Educational Policies Commission, NEA, 1963.

The reader interested in the thought of the neo-Hegelian Thomas Hill Green is referred especially to his lecture on "Liberal Legislation and Freedom of Contract," in his *Works*, vol. 3, 3rd ed. (London: Longman, Green, 1891–1908). See also his *Lectures on the Principles of Political Obligation* (London: Longman, Green, 1917). See also the section on Green in George H. Sabine, *A History of Political Theory*, 3rd ed. (New York: Holt, Rinehart and Winston, 1961). See especially chapter 32, "Liberalism Modernized," pp. 701–754. See also Stuart Hampshire, *Thought and Action* (London: Chatto and Windus, 1960).

The volume edited by Louis Finkelstein is titled *Social Responsibility in an Age of Reason* (New York: Jewish Theological Seminary, 1971). In one essay, Philip Spoon's "Ethics and Business," pp. 153–175, the author is sharply critical of the press along with government and business for exhibiting "moral failure" in its treatment of the Apollo space vehicle accident in which Virgil Grissom died.

In recent years, journalism scholars and sociologists have turned their attention in increasing numbers to an attempt to chart the personalities and value systems of journalists in the United States. The first significant such effort was Leo C. Rosten's *The Washington Correspondents* (New York: Harcourt Brace, 1937). Bernard C. Cohen, in *The Press and Foreign Policy*, previously cited, made a similar attempt in 1957. William L. Rivers, in *The Opinionmakers* (Boston: Beacon Press, 1965), updated the characterization once again, as did Stephen Hess, *The Washington Reporters* (Washington, D. C.: Brookings, 1981). In thee studies, it needs to be pointed out, the primary — if not the entire — emphasis was on leading journalists in Washington. The most exhaustive study of the characteristics and values of journalists has been the work of John W. C. Johnstone, Edward J.

Slawski, and William W. Bowman, three University of Illinois sociologists, whose study *The News People: A Sociological Portrait of American Journalists and Their Work* was published by the University of Illinois Press in 1976. Among the most interesting observations made in the Johnstone study is that the average age of individuals practicing journalism in the United States is three years below that of other "professionals" in the work force, leading to the conclusion that a substantial number of men and women grow disillusioned in their inability to effect social change as reporters and editors and move into other activities, among them government, advertising, public relations, and teaching (pp. 258–259, 303). I can attest to this pattern of disillusion from conversations with many former journalists. It is to some extent true also of myself. As Rosten observed in the first study cited here, "Scratch a journalist and you find a reformer."

Gandhi's journalistic writings can be found in *The Collected Works of Mahatma Gandhi*, published in New Delhi by the Navajivan Trust. The passage cited on p. 305 appears on pp. 386–387 of volume 8, 1971. See also S. Natarajan, *The History of the Press in India* (New York: Asia Publishing House, 1962).

Name Index

Subject Index